Hugh Jackman

Contents

Articles

References

Article Licenses

Hugh Jackman

Hugh Jackman	
 Jackman at the *X-Men Origins: Wolverine* premiere in April 2009	
Born	Hugh Michael Jackman 12 October 1968 Sydney, New South Wales, Australia
Occupation	Actor
Years active	1994–present
Spouse	Deborra-Lee Furness (1996–present)

Hugh Michael Jackman (born 12 October 1968) is an Australian actor and producer who is involved in film, musical theatre and television.

Jackman has won international recognition for his roles in major films, notably as action/superhero, period and romance characters. He is well known from his role as Wolverine in the *X-Men* series, in addition to his leads in *Kate & Leopold*, *Van Helsing*, *The Prestige*, and *Australia*. Jackman is a singer, dancer, and actor in stage musicals, and won a Tony Award for his role in *The Boy from Oz*.

In November 2008, *Open Salon* named Hugh Jackman one of the sexiest men alive.[1] Later that same month, *People* magazine named Jackman "Sexiest Man Alive."[2]

A three-time host of the Tony Awards, winning an Emmy for one of these appearances, Jackman also hosted the 81st Academy Awards on 22 February 2009.[3]

Early life

Jackman was born in Sydney, New South Wales, the youngest of five children of English parents Chris Jackman and Grace Watson, and the second child to be born in Australia (he also has a younger half sister).[4] [5] His parents divorced when he was eight, and he remained with his accountant father and siblings, while his mother moved back to England.[6] As a child, Jackman liked the outdoors, spending a lot of time at the beach and on camping trips and vacations all over Australia. He wanted to see the world: "I used to spend nights looking at atlases. I decided I wanted to be a chef on a plane. Because I'd been on a plane and there was food on board, I presumed there was a chef. I thought that would be an ideal job."[7]

Jackman went to primary school at Pymble Public School and later attended the all-boys Knox Grammar School, where he starred in its production of *My Fair Lady* in 1985 and became the captain of the School in 1986.[8] Following graduation, he spent a gap year working at Uppingham School in England. On his return, he studied at the University of Technology, Sydney, graduating in 1991 with a BA in Communications.[9] After obtaining his BA, Jackman completed the one-year course "The Journey" at the Actors' Centre in Sydney.[4] About studying acting full-time, he stated, "It wasn't until I was 22 that I ever thought about my hobby being something I could make a living out of. As a boy, I'd always had an interest in theater. But the idea at my school was that drama and music were to round out the man. It wasn't what one did for a living. I got over that. I found the courage to stand up and say, 'I want to do it'."[7]

After completing "The Journey", he was offered a role on the popular soap opera *Neighbours* but turned it down[10] to attend the Western Australian Academy of Performing Arts of Edith Cowan University in Perth, Western Australia, from which he graduated in 1994.[11]

Career

Early stage, film, and television work

On the night of his final Academy graduation performance, Jackman got a phone call offering him a role on *Correlli*: "I was technically unemployed for thirteen seconds." *Correlli*, devised by Australian actress Denise Roberts, was a 10-part drama series on ABC, Jackman's first major professional job, and where he met his future wife Deborra-Lee Furness: "Meeting my wife was the greatest thing to come out of it."[7] The show lasted only one season.

After *Correlli* Jackman went on the stage in Melbourne. In 1996, Jackman played Gaston in the local Walt Disney production of *Beauty and the Beast*, and Joe Gillis in *Sunset Boulevard*. During his stage musical career in Melbourne, he starred in the 1998 Midsumma festival cabaret production *Summa Cabaret*. He also hosted Melbourne's Carols by Candlelight and Sydney's Carols in the Domain.

Jackman's early film work includes *Erskineville Kings* and *Paperback Hero* (1999), and his television work includes *Law of the Land, Halifax f.p., Blue Heelers,* and *Banjo Paterson's The Man from Snowy River*.

International stardom

Oklahoma!

Jackman became known outside of Australia in 1998, when he played the leading role of Curly in the Royal National Theatre's acclaimed stage production of *Oklahoma!*, in London's West End. The performance earned him an Olivier Award nomination for Best Actor in a Musical. Jackman said," I totally felt like it can't get any better than this. On some level that production will be one of the highlights of my career."[7] He also starred in the 1999 film version of the same stage musical, which has been screened in many countries.

X-Men

In 2000, Jackman was cast as Wolverine in Bryan Singer's *X-Men*, replacing Dougray Scott. His co-stars include Patrick Stewart, James Marsden, Famke Janssen, and Ian McKellen. According to a CBS interview in November 2006, Jackman's wife Deborra-Lee Furness told him not to take the role, a comment she later told him she was glad he ignored.

Wolverine was tough for Jackman to portray because he had few lines, but a lot of emotion to convey in them. To prepare, he watched Clint Eastwood in the Dirty Harry movies and Mel Gibson in Road Warrior. "Here were guys who had relatively little dialogue, like Wolverine had, but you knew and felt everything. I'm not normally one to copy, but I wanted to see how these guys achieved it."[7]

Jackman was adamant about doing his own stunts for the movie. "We worked a lot on the movement style of Wolverine, and I studied some martial arts. I watched a lot of Mike Tyson fights, especially his early fights. There's something about his style, the animal rage, that seemed right for Wolverine. I kept saying to the writers, 'Don't give me long, choreographed fights for the sake of it. Don't make the fights pretty."[7]

Jackman also had to get used to wearing Wolverine's claws. "Every day in my living room, I'd just walk around with those claws, to get used to them. I've got scars on one leg, punctures straight through the cheek, on my forehead. I'm a bit clumsy. I'm lucky I didn't tell them that when I auditioned."[7]

Jackman, at 6'2½ (1.89 m),[12] stands a foot taller than Wolverine, who is said in the original comic book to be 5' 3".[13] Hence, the filmmakers were frequently forced to shoot Jackman at unusual angles or only from the waist up to make him appear shorter than he actually is, and his co-stars wore platform soles. Jackman was also required to add a great deal of muscle for the role, and in preparing for the fourth film in the series, he bench-pressed over 300 pounds.[14] An instant star upon the film's release, Jackman later reprised his role in 2003's *X-Men 2*, 2006's *X-Men: The Last Stand*, and *X-Men Origins: Wolverine*, which was released May 1, 2009.

2001

Jackman starred as Leopold in the 2001 romantic comedy film *Kate & Leopold*, a role for which he received a Best Actor Golden Globe nomination. Jackman plays a Victorian English duke who accidentally time-travels to 21st-century Manhattan, where he meets Kate (Meg Ryan), a cynical advertising executive.

In 2001, Jackman also starred in the action/drama *Swordfish* with John Travolta and Halle Berry. This was the second time Jackman worked with Berry, and the two have worked together twice more in the X-Men movies.

He also hosted an episode of "Saturday Night Live" in 2001.[15]

Stage 2002–2009

In 2002, Jackman sang the role of Billy Bigelow in the musical *Carousel* in a special concert performance at Carnegie Hall with the Orchestra of St. Luke's.

In 2004, Jackman won the Tony Award and the Drama Desk Award for Outstanding Actor in a Musical for his 2003–2004 Broadway portrayal of Australian songwriter and performer Peter Allen in the hit musical *The Boy from Oz*, which he also performed in Australia in 2006.

In addition, Jackman hosted the Tony Awards in 2003, 2004, and 2005, garnering positive reviews. His hosting of the 2004 Tony Awards earned him an Emmy Award for Outstanding Individual Performer in a Variety, Musical or Comedy program.

Jackman co-starred with Daniel Craig on Broadway at the Schoenfeld Theatre in a limited engagement of the play *A Steady Rain*, opening in previews on 10 September 2009 and closing on 6 December 2009.[16]

Local advertising for the musical *The Boy from Oz* starring Jackman in New York City (2004)

Films 2003–2008

After 2003's *X2: X-Men United*, Jackman played the title role of monster killer Gabriel Van Helsing in the 2004 film *Van Helsing*. Jackman and the film were noted in Bruce A. McClelland's book "Slayers and Their Vampires: A Cultural History of Killing the Dead".

Jackman was one of the choices to play James Bond in 2006's *Casino Royale*, but eventually lost out to Daniel Craig.[17]

Jackman starred in the 2006 film *The Prestige*, directed by Christopher Nolan and co-starring Christian Bale, Michael Caine, and Scarlett Johansson. As Robert Angier, Jackman portrayed a magician who built up a rivalry with contemporary Alfred Borden in attempt to one-up each other in the art of deception. Jackman stated that his main reason for doing *The Prestige* was to work with the musician David Bowie, who played scientist Nikola Tesla.

Hugh Jackman and Ryan Reynolds (right) at the *X-Men Origins: Wolverine* premiere in Tempe, Arizona (2009)

Jackman portrayed three different characters in Darren Aronofsky's science-fiction film *The Fountain*: Tommy Creo, a neuroscientist, who's torn between his wife, Izzi (Rachel Weisz) who is dying of a brain tumor, and his work at trying to cure her; Captain Tomas Creo, a Spanish Conquistador in 1532 Seville; and a future astronaut, Tom, travelling to a golden nebula in an eco-spacecraft seeking to be reunited with Izzi. Jackman said *The Fountain* was his most difficult film thus far due to the physical and emotional demands of the part.

Jackman also starred in Woody Allen's 2006 film *Scoop* opposite Scarlett Johansson. He rounded out 2006 with two animated films: *Happy Feet*, directed by George Miller, in which he voiced the part of Memphis, an emperor penguin; and *Flushed Away*, where Jackman supplied the voice of a rat named Roddy who ends up being flushed down a family's toilet into the London sewer system. *Flushed Away* co-starred Kate Winslet and Ian McKellen (Jackman's fourth time working with him).

In 2007, Jackman produced and guest-starred in the television musical-dramedy series *Viva Laughlin*, which was canceled by CBS after two episodes.

Jackman's 2008 movies included *Deception* (which he starred in and produced), *Uncle Jonny*, and *Australia*.

Australia

In 2008, director Baz Luhrmann cast Jackman to replace Russell Crowe as the male lead in his much-publicized epic film, *Australia*, which co-starred Nicole Kidman. The movie was released in late November 2008 in Australia and the U.S.

Jackman played a tough, independent cattle drover, who reluctantly helps an English noblewoman in her quest to save both her philandering husband's Australian cattle station and the half-caste Aboriginal child she finds there.

Of the movie, Jackman said, "This is pretty much one of those roles that had me pinching myself all the way through the shoot. I got to shoot a big-budget, shamelessly old-fashioned romantic epic set against one of the most turbulent times in my native country's history, while, at the same time, celebrating that country's natural beauty, its people, its cultures.... I'll die a happy man knowing I've got this film on my CV."[18]

Future projects

- An action drama, *Drive*, starring Jackman, is currently in production.[19]
- Jackman also plans to play Billy Bigelow in a remake of *Carousel*, scheduled to be released in 2010.[20] [21]
- Jackman is being considered, along with Ewan McGregor, to reprise the role of Joe Gillis in a new film version of the Andrew Lloyd Webber musical *Sunset Boulevard*.[22]
- Jackman is working on creating a new comic book series, *Nowhere Man,* with U.S. publisher Virgin Comics and writer Marc Guggenheim, with hopes of adapting it to a film as well.[23]
- Jackman stars in an upcoming movie named *Unbound Captives*, where he will play alongside his past co-star Rachel Weisz and Robert Pattinson.[24]
- Jackman will star in *The Greatest American Showman*, a contemporary musical based on the life of P.T. Barnum. The female love interest part is being written with Anne Hathaway in mind.[25]
- *Real Steel* (2011), a DreamWorks science fiction film.[26] [27]
- Director Lee Daniels has confirmed Jackman has joined the cast of his upcoming film *Selma*, a film about Martin Luther King Jr. and Lyndon Baines Johnson and the civil rights marches.[28]
- Jackman will star in *Snow Flower and the Secret Fan*, originally scheduled to start filming February 2010.[29]

Production company

In 2005, Jackman joined with longtime assistant John Palermo to form a production company, Seed Productions, whose first project was *Viva Laughlin* in 2007. Jackman's wife Deborra-Lee Furness is also involved in the company, and Palermo had three rings made with a "unity" inscription for himself, Furness, and Jackman.[30] Jackman said, "I'm very lucky in the partners I work with in my life, Deb and John Palermo. It really works. We all have different strengths. I love it. It's very exciting."[31]

The Fox-based Seed label has grown in size to include execs Amanda Schweitzer, Kathryn Tamblyn, Allan Mandelbaum and Joe Marino, with Alana Free operating the Sydney-based production office whose goal is to mount modest-budget films to harness local talent in Jackman's home country.

Other interests

Charity work

As a philanthropist, Jackman is a longtime proponent of microcredit — the extension of very small loans to impoverished prospective entrepreneurs in undeveloped countries. He is a vocal supporter of Muhammad Yunus, microcredit pioneer and the 2006 Nobel Peace Prize winner.[32] [33] [34]

Jackman is a global advisor of the Global Poverty Project, for which he narrated a documentary;[35] and he and the project's founder Hugh Evans visited the UN for the cause in 2009.[36] Jackman hosted a preview of the Global Poverty Project Presentation in New York together with Donna Karran, Lisa Fox and his wife Debbora-lee .[37] He is also a World Vision ambassador and participated in the climate week NYC ceremony on September 21, 2009.[38] [39]

Jackman supports The Art of Elysium[40] and the MPTV Fund Foundation,[41] and he and his wife Deborra-Lee Furness are patrons of the Bone Marrow Institute in Australia.[42] Jackman also narrated the 2008 documentary about global warming, *The Burning Season*.[43]

Jackman also uses his Twitter account for charity. On April 14, 2009 Jackman posted on his Twitter page that he would donate $100,000 to one individual's favorite non profit organization.[44] On April 21, 2009 he revealed his decision to donate $50,000 to Charity:Water and $50,000 to Operation of Hope.[45] [46]

Hugh Jackman and Daniel Craig made a unique place for themselves in the history of Broadway Cares/Equity Fights AIDS fundraising 8 December 2009, when it was announced that they had raised $1,549,953 in the 21st annual Gypsy of the Year competition, from six weeks of curtain appeals at their hit Broadway drama, *A Steady Rain*.[47]

Sports and other activities

Jackman has shown keen interest in a variety of sports. In high school, he played rugby union and cricket, took part in high jumping and was on the swimming team.[48] He also enjoys basketball and kayaking.[49] He has also expressed an interest in football, committing his support to Norwich City FC.

Jackman is a longtime fan and supporter of the Manly Warringah Sea Eagles, a NRL club based in Sydney's north.[50] He sang the national anthem at the 1999 NRL Grand Final.[51] Hugh also revealed on Sky Sports Soccer AM that he was a Norwich City F.C Fan.[52]

Jackman can also play the piano,[53] does yoga every day,[54] and has been a member of the School of Practical Philosophy since 1992.[55]

Jackman aboard the amphibious assault ship USS Kearsarge in New York (2006)

Personal life

Jackman has two older brothers and two older sisters, as well as a half-sister from when his mother re-married.

Jackman married Deborra-Lee Furness on 11 April 1996. They met on *Correlli*, an Australian television series. Jackman personally designed an engagement ring for Furness, and their wedding rings bore the Sanskrit inscription "Om paramar mainamar," translated as "we dedicate our union to a greater source."[56] They currently divide their time between Sydney and New York City.[57]

Furness had two miscarriages,[58] following which she and Jackman adopted two children, Oscar Maximillian (born 15 May 2000) and Ava Eliot (born 10 July 2005).

Filmography

Year	Film	Role	Notes
1994	*Law of the Land*	Charles McCray	One episode
1995	*Correlli*	Kevin Jones	Main role
	Blue Heelers	Brady Jackson	One episode
1996	*The Man from Snowy River*	Duncan Jones	Five episodes
1999	*Erskineville Kings*	Wace	Film Critics Circle of Australia Award for Best Actor Nominated — Australian Film Institute Award for Best Actor
	Paperback Hero	Jack Willis	
2000	*X-Men*	Logan / Wolverine	Saturn Award
2001	*Kate & Leopold*	Leopold	Nominated — Golden Globe Award for Best Actor – Motion Picture Musical or Comedy
	Someone Like You	Eddie	
	Swordfish	Stanley Jobson	
2003	*X2*	Logan / Wolverine	Nominated — Empire Award for Best Actor
2004	*Van Helsing*	Gabriel Van Helsing	
	Van Helsing: The London Assignment	Gabriel Van Helsing	(voice)

2005	*Stories of Lost Souls*	Roger	segment "Standing Room Only"
2006	*Happy Feet*	Memphis	(voice)
	Flushed Away	Roddy	(voice)
	The Prestige	Robert Angier	Nominated — Australian Film Institute Award for Best Actor
	The Fountain	Tomas / Tommy / Tom Creo	Nominated — Satellite Award for Best Actor - Motion Picture Drama
	Scoop	Peter Lyman	
	X-Men: The Last Stand	Logan / Wolverine	
2007	*Viva Laughlin*	Nicky Fontana	TV series, also executive producer
2008	*Deception*	Wyatt Bose	Producer
	Uncle Jonny	Uncle Russell	Tropfest 2008 Finalist Film[59]
	Australia	The Drover	
	The Burning Season	Narrator	Documentary
2009	*X-Men Origins: Wolverine*	Logan / Wolverine	Producer
2011	*Real Steel*	Charlie Kenton	

Awards and nominations

Awards

- 1997 Variety Club Award for Best Actor in a Musical - *Sunset Boulevard*
- 1998 Mo Award for Best Actor in a Musical — *Sunset Boulevard*
- 1999 Australian Movie Convention, Australian Star of the Year
- 2000 Saturn Award for Best Actor - *X-Men*
- 2004 Drama Desk Award for Outstanding Actor in a Musical — *The Boy from Oz*
- 2004 Theatre World Award — *The Boy from Oz*
- 2004 Broadway Audience Award — *The Boy from Oz*
- 2004 Drama League Award for Distinguished Performance of the Year - *The Boy from Oz*
- 2004 Outer Critics Circle Award for Best Actor in a Musical - *The Boy from Oz*
- 2004 TDF-Astaire Award for Best Male Dancer in Theatre - *The Boy from Oz*
- 2004 Theater Fan's Choice Award for Best Leading Actor in a Musical - *The Boy from Oz*
- 2004 Tony Award for Best Leading Actor in a Musical — *The Boy from Oz*
- 2004 New York International Independent Film & Video Festival - Short Film Award for Best Actor - "Making the Grade"
- 2004 Australian Showbusiness Ambassador of the Year
- 2005 Emmy Award for Outstanding Individual Performance in a Variety or Music Program — 58th Annual Tony Awards Ceremonies
- 2006 ShoWest Award for Male Star of the Year
- 2006 Mo Award for Australian Performer of the Year
- 2008 WAAPA - Chancellor's Alumni Award for Excellence, UTS Towering Achievement Award
- 2008 Australian Dance Award for Outstanding Performance in a Stage Musical - *The Boy from Oz*
- 2008 Australian Film Institute Award Readers' Choice

Jackman's signature at Grauman's Chinese Theatre

- 2008 *People* Magazine's Sexiest Man Alive Award
- 2008 Australian GQ Man of the Year
- 2008 Teen Choice Award for Choice Actor in an Action Adventure *X-Men Origins: Wolverine*
- 2009 Jackman had his hand and footprint ceremony on the Hollywood Walk of Fame on April 21, 2009.[60]
- 2009 Best Performance By A Human Male at the 2009 Spike Video Game Awards as Wolverine in *X-Men Origins: Wolverine*
- 2010 People's Choice Award for Favorite Action Star — *X-Men Origins: Wolverine*

Nominations

- 1997 Mo Award for Best Actor in a Musical — *Beauty and the Beast*
- 1998 Olivier Award for Best Actor in a Musical — *Oklahoma!*
- 2001 Golden Globe for Best Actor in a Motion Picture Musical or Comedy - *Kate & Leopold*
- 2001 CFCA Award for Most Promising Actor
- 2006 Emmy Award for Outstanding Individual Performance in a Variety or Music Program — 59th Annual Tony Awards Ceremonies
- 2006 Green Room Award for Best Male Artist in a Leading Role — *The Boy from Oz*

Mentions in popular culture

- Jackman was chosen as *People* magazine's Sexiest Man Alive of 2008.[2]
- In the ABC comedy-drama *Scrubs*, one of the more prominent running gags is Dr. Cox's (John C. McGinley) seemingly irrational hatred of Jackman.
- In the 7th season of *Punk'd*, Jackman was led to believe that he had accidentally blown up director Brett Ratner's house.[61]
- On the Season 6, Episode 13 of *Will & Grace*, which aired on February 10, 2004, the character Jack McFarland (Sean Hayes), mentions he's going to see *The Boy From Oz*, because he can't wait to see Hugh Jackman.[62] He later discusses wanting to sue Jackman for stealing some of his dance moves.

References

[1] http://open.salon.com/blog/kaysong/2008/11/10/my_sexiest_men_living
[2] "Hugh Jackman: The Sexiest Man Alive" (http://www.people.com/people/article/0,,20241213,00.html). People.com. 2008-11-19. . Retrieved 2010-09-06.
[3] Gans, Andrew. "Tony Winner Jackman to Host Academy Awards," (http://www.playbill.com/news/article/124292.html) playbill.com, 12 December 2008
[4] " Hugh Jackman (http://www.imdb.com/title/tt0611206/)". *Inside the Actors Studio*. Bravo. 7 March 2004. No. 11, season 10.
[5] "MATINEE IDOL." (http://www.highbeam.com/doc/1G1-116102276.html) *The Independent*. 1 May 2004.
[6] "Hugh Jackman relishes performing - More news and other features - MSNBC.com" (http://www.msnbc.msn.com/id/4893079/). . Retrieved 2009-05-27.
[7] *Biography Today*. Detroit, Michigan: Omnigraphics. 2010. p. 86. ISBN 978-0-7808-1058-7.
[8] Scobie, Claire (2008-12-18). "Hugh Jackman: X Appeal" (http://www.telegraph.co.uk/culture/film/starsandstories/3833405/ Hugh-Jackman-X-appeal.html). London: Telegraph.co.uk. . Retrieved 2010-09-06.
[9] "Alumnus Hugh Jackman honoured at UTS 20-year celebration" (http://www.newsroom.uts.edu.au/news/detail.cfm?ItemId=11098). . Retrieved 2009-05-27.
[10] "*home and away*" (http://www.tiscali.co.uk/entertainment/film/biographies/hugh_jackman_biog/2.html). . Retrieved 2009-05-27.
[11] "Jackman back as boy from Waapa" (http://www.thewest.com.au/default.aspx?MenuID=77&ContentID=8095). . Retrieved 2009-05-27.
[12] "Hugh Jackman" (http://www.imdb.com/name/nm0413168/bio). *imdb.com*. . Retrieved 18 December 2008.
[13] Marvel Universe: Wolverine (James Howlett) (http://www.marvel.com/universe/Wolverine_(James_Howlett)) *Marvel.com*
[14] Fleming, Michael (December 2008). "*Playboy* Interview: Hugh Jackman". *Playboy*: 62.
[15] "saturday night live" (http://www.imdb.com/title/tt0694825/) imdb.com
[16] Gans, Andrew. "A Steady Rain, with Craig and Jackman, to Play Broadway's Schoenfeld" (http://www.playbill.com/news/article/ 130947-A_Steady_Rain_with_Craig_and_Jackman_to_Play_Broadway's_Schoenfeld) playbill.com, July 9, 2009

[17] "Call him Bland, James Bland - MSNBC" (http://www.msnbc.msn.com/id/9546090/). .

[18] "Big Down Under - HQ, Entertainment" (http://www.herald.ie/entertainment/hq/big-down-under-1570944.html). Herald.ie. 2008-12-11. . Retrieved 2010-09-06.

[19] http://www.imdb.com/title/tt0730504/

[20] "Hugh Jackman Will Host 81st Academy Awards" (http://www.broadwayworld.com/article/ Hugh_Jackman_Will_Host_81st_Academy_Awards_20081212). Broadwayworld.com. . Retrieved 2010-09-06.

[21] http://www.imdb.com/title/tt0837787/

[22] Hastings, Chris; Jones, Beth (2007-08-05). "Meryl Streep competes for Sunset Boulevard" (http://www.telegraph.co.uk/news/ worldnews/1559524/Meryl-Streep-competes-for-Sunset-Boulevard.html). The Daily Telegraph (London). . Retrieved 2010-05-04.

[23] Fleming, Michael (2008-03-24) "Jackman, Guggenheim go 'Nowhere'" (http://www.variety.com/article/VR1117982842. html?categoryid=13&cs=1). Variety. .

[24] Fleming, Michael (2009-05-13) "Trio bound to Stow's 'captives'" (http://www.variety.com/article/VR1118003529. html?categoryid=13&cs=1). Variety.com. . Retrieved 2010-09-06.

[25] Adam Bryant (4 August 2009). "Hugh Jackman Signs on for Circus Musical" (http://www.tvguide.com/News/ Hugh-Jackman-Signs-1008661.aspx). TVGuide.com. . Retrieved 2009-08-04.

[26] Graser, Marc; Siegel, Tatiana (2009-11-23). "Hugh Jackman to Star in "Real Steel"." (http://www.variety.com/article/VR1118011766. html?categoryid=1237&cs=1&ref=mv). Variety.com. . Retrieved 2010-09-06.

[27] Real Steel (http://www.imdb.com/title/tt0433035/) at the Internet Movie Database

[28] "Hugh Jackman To Topline Daniel's 'Selma'" (http://www.hollywood.com/news/Hugh_Jackman_To_Topline_Daniels_Selma/6830009). hollywood.com. . Retrieved May 11, 2010.

[29] "Hugh Jackman onboard 'Secret Fan' with Li Bingbing" (http://english.cri.cn/6666/2010/02/02/1261s547254.htm). English.cri.cn. 2010-02-02. . Retrieved 2010-09-06.

[30] "Movies Online" (http://www.moviesonline.ca/movienews_10478.html). Moviesonline.ca. . Retrieved 2010-09-06.

[31] "Movie News" (http://www.comingsoon.net/news/movienews.php?id=17540). Comingsoon.net. . Retrieved 2010-09-06.

[32] Hugh Jackman Congratulates Professor Yunus (http://www.youtube.com/watch?v=p0rMrUcM8Cc) (video)

[33] "Books That Made a Difference to Hugh Jackman." (http://www.oprah.com/article/omagazine/books/obc_omag_200711_books) Oprah.com

[34] "Hugh Jackman's Bookshelf: Banker to the Poor, by Muhammad Yunus." (http://www.oprah.com/article/omagazine/ omag_books_hjack_a/1) Oprah.com

[35] "Global Poverty Project narrated by Hugh Jackman" (http://www.looktothestars.org/video/ 84-global-poverty-project-narrated-by-hugh-jackman). Looktothestars.org. . Retrieved 2010-09-06.

[36] Hugh Jackman goes to UN (http://www.news.com.au/heraldsun/story/0,21985,25723171-5012974,00.html)

[37] "Hugh Evans, LIsa Fox, Deborra-Lee Furness - The Global Poverty Project Presents "1.4 Billion Reasons" - Photo" (http://www.life.com/ image/94457143). LIFE. 2009-12-14. . Retrieved 2010-09-06.

[38] Dennis Shanahan, Political editor in New York (2009-09-22). "Hugh Jackman steals lead role on climate" (http://www.theaustralian.news. com.au/story/0,25197,26108892-5013871,00.html). Theaustralian.news.com.au. . Retrieved 2010-09-06.

[39] "World Vision ambassador Hugh Jackman speaks on climate change" (http://www.worldvision.org/content.nsf/about/ 20090916-hugh-jackman). Worldvision.org. 2009-09-16. . Retrieved 2010-09-06.

[40] The Art of Elysium (http://theartofelysium.org)

[41] "MPTV Fund Foundation" (http://www.mptvfund.org/cm/about-us/Home.html). Mptvfund.org. . Retrieved 2010-09-06.

[42] "Bone Marrow Donor Institute" (http://www.bmdi.org.au). Bmdi.org.au. . Retrieved 2010-09-06.

[43] "The Burning Season" (http://www.theburningseasonmovie.com). Theburningseasonmovie.com. 2010-01-15. . Retrieved 2010-09-06.

[44] "Charity Tweet" (http://twitter.com/RealHughJackman/status/1519899038). Twitter.com. 2009-04-14. . Retrieved 2010-09-06.

[45] April 19, 2009 Pete Cashmore View Comments (2009-04-19). "Jackman Reveals Charity Donation" (http://mashable.com/2009/04/24/ twitter-on-the-radio-hugh-jackman-reveals-100k-charity-donation/Hugh). Mashable.com. . Retrieved 2010-09-06.

[46] "Operation of Hope" (http://www.operationofhope.org/). Operation of Hope. 2009-06-13. . Retrieved 2010-09-06.

[47] "Broadway Cares" (http://www.broadwaycares.org). Broadway Cares. 2010-02-09. . Retrieved 2010-09-06.

[48] "Inside the actors studio" (http://www.youtube.com/watch?v=PjxzcvrUohE). Youtube.com. . Retrieved 2010-09-06.

[49] "Sydney Morning Herald - Kayaking" (http://www.smh.com.au/news/people/jackman-in-training-for-boy-from-oz/2006/02/13/ 1139679526894.html). Smh.com.au. 2006-02-13. . Retrieved 2010-09-06.

[50] "ManlySeaEagles.com.au" (http://www.manlyseaeagles.com.au/news.asp?newsid=2155&Mth=7&Yr=2007). ManlySeaEagles.com.au. . Retrieved 2010-09-06.

[51] "Hugh Jackman Biography" (http://www.monstersandcritics.com/people/archive/peoplearchive.php/Hugh_Jackman/biography/). Monsters and Critics. . Retrieved 2010-09-06.

[52] "Sky Sports Interview" (http://www.skysports.com/socceram/media/video/0,21631,,00.html). Skysports.com. . Retrieved 2010-09-06.

[53] "Hugh Jackman takes up piano lessons" (http://www.starswelove.com/scriptsphp/news.php?newsid=3524). Starswelove.com. . Retrieved 2010-09-06.

[54] "People Magazine - yoga" (http://www.people.com/people/archive/article/0,,20134364,00.html). People.com. 2001-05-14. . Retrieved 2010-09-06.

[55] *School of Practical Philosophy* (http://www.jackmanslanding.com/news/news-articles/interviewmag.html)

[56] "Enough Rope with Andrew Denton" (http://www.abc.net.au/tv/enoughrope/transcripts/s1076056.htm). Abc.net.au. 2004-03-29. . Retrieved 2010-09-06.

[57] November 15, 2008 12:00AM (2008-11-15). "Jackman buys apartment in Manhattan" (http://www.news.com.au/entertainment/story/0,26278,24655015-5013560,00.html). News.com.au. . Retrieved 2010-09-06.

[58] "Furness on enough rope-adoption" (http://www.abc.net.au/tv/enoughrope/transcripts/s1076056.htm). Abc.net.au. 2004-03-29. . Retrieved 2010-09-06.

[59] "Uncle Jonny - ninemsn Video" (http://video.msn.com/video.aspx?mkt=en-AU&brand=ninemsn&vid=08f0e8cc-bf3b-4651-bf8a-6bae1a695b86). Video.msn.com. . Retrieved 2010-09-06.

[60] Mitchell, Peter (2009-04-22). "Hugh Jackman's prints recorded in cement" (http://www.news.com.au/heraldsun/story/0,21985,25368931-5012748,00.html). News.com.au. . Retrieved 2010-09-06.

[61] "Hugh Jackman gets seriously punk'd" (http://www.celebrific.com/x-men-hugh-jackman-gets-seriously-punkd-by-ashton-kutcher). Celebrific.com. . Retrieved 2010-09-06.

[62] http://www.imdb.com/title/tt0748812/plotsummary

External links

- Hugh Jackman (http://www.imdb.com/name/nm413168/) at the Internet Movie Database
- Hugh Jackman (http://www.ibdb.com/person.asp?ID=101172) at the Internet Broadway Database
- Hugh Jackman (http://www.people.com/people/hugh_jackman) at People.com
- Hugh Jackman interview (http://sci-fi-online.50megs.com/2006_Interviews/06-05-16_HughJackman.htm) at www.sci-fi-online.com (http://www.sci-fi-online.com)
- Video interview with Hugh Jackman (http://movies.go.com/feature?featureid=855390) on movies.com
- Hugh Jackman Photos (http://www.hunkparty.com/hugh-jackman/) on Hunk Party! (http://www.hunkparty.com)
- A Steady Rain On Broadway opening night blog (http://www.broadway.tv/broadway-features-reviews/a-steady-rain-rules-broadway) at broadway.tv (http://www.broadway.tv)
- Jackman, Hugh (http://nla.gov.au/nla.party-1446737) National Library of Australia, *Trove, People and Organisation* record for Hugh Jackman

Law of the Land

Law of the Land	
Format	Drama
Created by	Ro Hume Sue Masters
Starring	Lisa Hensley David Roberts Wyn Roberts Richard Moir Tamblyn Lord
Country of origin	Australia
No. of seasons	4
No. of episodes	52
Production	
Running time	50 min.
Broadcast	
Original channel	Nine Network
Original run	1993 – January 22, 1999

Law of the Land (1993–1999) was an Australian television drama series that screened on the Nine Network. The series was set in the fictional country town of Merringanee and centered on the unique way that locals dealt with and enforced the law.

The series was created by Ro Hume and Sue Masters and produced by Bruce Best, Matt Carroll, Richard Clendinnen and Terrie Vincent.

Cast

- Lisa Hensley - Kate Chalmers
- David Roberts - Peter Lawrence
- Wyn Roberts - Hamilton Chalmers
- Richard Moir - Sergeant Clive O'Connor
- David Walters - Sean O'Connor
- Angelo D'Angelo - Sergeant Marc Rosetti
- Debbie Byrne - Jean Jardine
- Tamblyn Lord - David Jardine
- Lindy Wallis - Trish Miles
- Shane Connor - Harry Miles
- Radha Mitchell - Alicia Miles
- Abbie Holmes - Audrey O'Connor
- Peter O'Brien - Andy Cochrane
- Frances O'Connor - Marissa Green
- Alexandra Fowler - Jacqui Rushcutter
- Fiona Spence - Magistrate Maggie Mulcahy
- Rebecca Frith - Alex Lentini

- Tessa Humphries - Hannah Scott
- Mike Bishop - Ray Richmond
- Michael O'Neill - Michael Delaney
- Sapidah Kian - Shirin Rasidi
- Bruce Hughes - Nick Rogers
- Karmen Raspovic - Heather Coleman

See also

- *Lex loci* - the Legal Latin phrase for conflicts of law
- List of Australian television series

External links

- *Law of the Land* [1] at the Internet Movie Database

References

[1] http://www.imdb.com/title/tt0106054/

Correlli

Correlli	
Format	Drama
Starring	Deborra-Lee Furness Hugh Jackman Neil Melville
Country of origin	Australia
No. of episodes	10
Production	
Running time	50 minutes
Broadcast	
Original channel	ABC TV
Original run	July 1, 1995 – September 1, 1995

For other uses see Corelli

Correlli was an Australian television series first broadcast by ABC TV in 1995. It starred Deborra-Lee Furness as prison psychologist Louisa Correlli. The series also featured her future husband Hugh Jackman in one of his earliest roles. The first episode entitled "The Rat Tamer" has been released on to DVD.

External links

- Australian Television Archive: Correlli [1]
- *Correlli* [2] at the Internet Movie Database
- *Correlli* [3] at TV.com

References

[1] http://www.australiantelevision.net/correlli/correlli.html
[2] http://www.imdb.com/title/tt0111927/
[3] http://www.tv.com/show/2780/summary.html

Blue Heelers

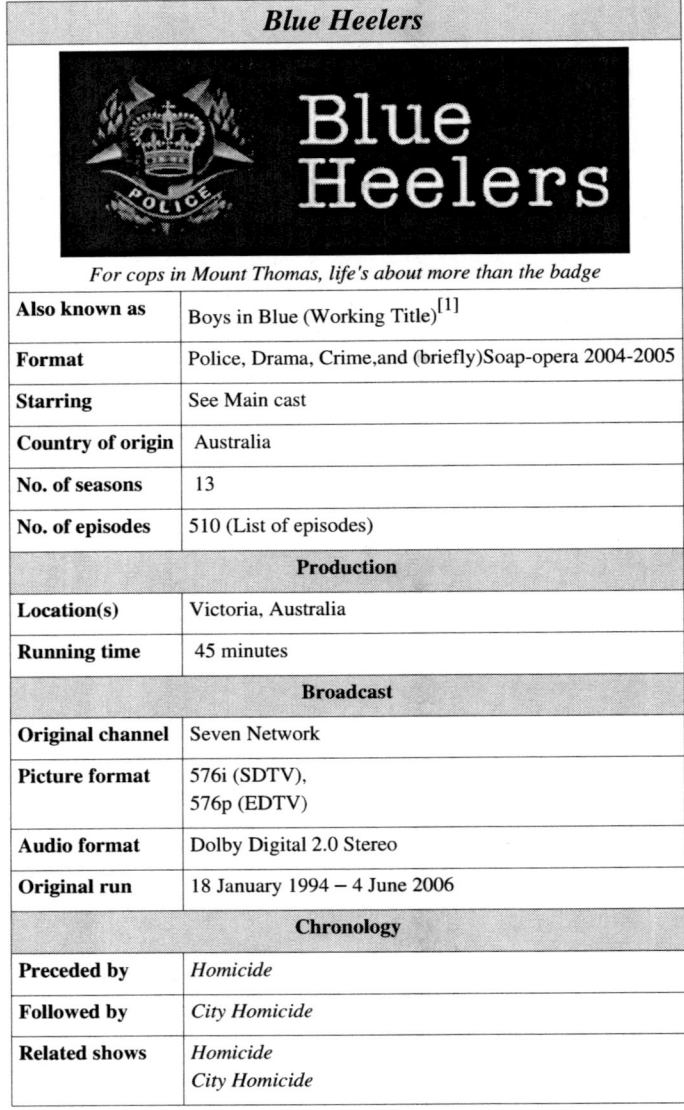

Blue Heelers	
For cops in Mount Thomas, life's about more than the badge	
Also known as	Boys in Blue (Working Title)[1]
Format	Police, Drama, Crime,and (briefly)Soap-opera 2004-2005
Starring	See Main cast
Country of origin	Australia
No. of seasons	13
No. of episodes	510 (List of episodes)
Production	
Location(s)	Victoria, Australia
Running time	45 minutes
Broadcast	
Original channel	Seven Network
Picture format	576i (SDTV), 576p (EDTV)
Audio format	Dolby Digital 2.0 Stereo
Original run	18 January 1994 – 4 June 2006
Chronology	
Preceded by	*Homicide*
Followed by	*City Homicide*
Related shows	*Homicide* *City Homicide*

Blue Heelers is an Australian police drama series which depicted the lives of police officers stationed at the fictional Mount Thomas police station in a small town in Victoria.

Overview

Blue Heelers was produced by Southern Star for the Seven Network. The series dealt with many controversial and "touchy" subjects. The series was also the first to examine the stressful world of young police officers who are invariably "thrown into the deep end where they are left to sink or swim".[2] During its 13-season run it won a total of 32 awards and was nominated for a further 50.[3] This included 25 Logie Awards, five of which were the Gold Logie, the most coveted television award in Australia.[4] Blue Heelers first aired on January 18, 1994 with the episode "A Woman's Place", and last aired on June 4, 2006 with its 510th episode "One Day More".

It was Australia's most popular television drama, drawing more than 2.5 million viewers every week at its peak.[4] It jointly (with *Homicide*) holds the Australian record for most episodes produced of a weekly prime time drama. It was also almost the longest-running series,[5] [6] however, *Homicide* lasted one calendar month longer and, due to five feature-length episodes, had more actual on-air time across the 510 episodes.

Blue Heelers also gained recognition worldwide, particularly in Britain, Ireland, New Zealand and Canada, where it had a strong following in syndication. Worldwide, *Blue Heelers* has been sold to 108 territories.[7]

Blue Heelers launched the careers of many Australian actors such as Lisa McCune, Grant Bowler, Ditch Davey, Rachel Gordon, Tasma Walton, Charlie Clausen and Jane Allsop. While many of these actors are still best known for their character on *Blue Heelers*, some have gone on to bigger roles. Many major actors of today also called Mount Thomas home, including Hugh Jackman, Charles 'Bud' Tingwell, Peter O'Brien and John Howard. *Blue Heelers* veterans actors John Wood and Julie Nihill remained with *Blue Heelers* during its entire 12 year run, portraying Senior Sergeant Tom Croydon and publican, Chris Riley respectively.

Plot

For more information on each season, see the individual season pages

The series primarily focused on the daily lives of Victorian police officers working at a police station in the semi-rural, fictional town of Mount Thomas. Each episode was presented from the perspective of the officers themselves, as opposed to the criminals and various individuals they dealt with. This was a specific technique creator Hal McElroy wanted to employ.[8]

Mount Thomas and police officers—commonly referred to as "Heelers"—were always active, sorting out the town's many problems. These problems ranged from trivial complaints such as land and fencing disputes, to more serious offenses, such as homicides and assaults. The small town was also faced with many other significant occurrences including bank robberies, escaped criminals, police shootings, kidnappings and the acts of many deluded criminals. Of these, one of the

P.J. Hasham, Tom Croydon and Maggie Doyle

more significant events included the bombing of the police station during the show's eleventh season. Whenever overwhelmed, the Heelers would call on the assistance of the police in the nearby, larger town of St. Davids, home of the resident police inspector, Russell Falcon-Price. An antagonist in the series, Falcon-Price often tried to terminate the employment of the Mount Thomas sergeant or to close the entire station.

Along with their police work, aspects of the Heeler's personal lives were regularly featured in the series. The most well-known of these plot arcs is the relationship between colleagues Maggie and PJ which ended in Maggie's death; one of the most watched moments on Australian television to this day. The environment of Mount Thomas Police station was like that of a big family where everybody usually got along. However, like all families, there were always disagreements. These were usually settled over a beer at the bar at the Imperial Hotel, where Chris Riley was always ready to listen.

Casting

Main cast

Blue Heelers original cast of 1994

Blue Heelers final cast of 2006

Actor/Actress	Character	Tenure	Position
John Wood	Thomas 'Tom' Croydon	1993-2006 Ep. 1 - 510	Sergeant, Senior Sergeant
Julie Nihill	Christine 'Chris' Riley	1993-2006 Ep. 1 - 510	Civilian (Publican)
Martin Sacks	Patrick Joseph 'P.J.' Hasham	1993-2005 Ep. 1 - 484	Detective Senior Constable, Senior Detective, Acting Sergeant
Lisa McCune	Margaret 'Maggie' Doyle	1993-2000 Ep. 1 - 256	Constable, Senior Constable, Acting Sergeant
William McInnes	Nicholas 'Nick' Schultz	1993-1998, Ep. 1 - 207 2004 *(guest)*, 2005 *(guest)*season 11 & season 12	Senior Constable, Acting Sergeant, Sergeant, Detective Sergeant
Grant Bowler	Wayne Patterson	1993-1996 Ep. 1 - 96	Constable
Ann Burbrook	Roz Patterson	1993-1994, Ep. 1 - 30 1996 *(guest)* season 3's episode 97	Civilian (Mount Thomas police station admin. officer)
Damian Walshe-Howling	Adam Cooper	1994-1998, Ep. 34 - 211 2006 *(guest)* season 13	Probationary Constable, Constable
Tasma Walton	Deirdre 'Dash' McKinley	1996-1999 Ep. 107 - 236 (guest) 1995 season 2	Probationary Constable, Constable
Paul Bishop	Benjamin 'Ben' Stewart	1998-2004 Ep. 198 - 451 1998 (guest) season 5 190-193	Detective Acting Sergeant, Senior Constable, Acting Sergeant, Sergeant
Jane Allsop	Joanna 'Jo' Parrish	1999-2004 Ep. 239 - 440 1997 (guest) season 4	Probationary Constable, Constable, Senior Constable

Rupert Reid	Jack Lawson	1999-2001 Ep. 212 - 313	Probationary Constable, Constable
Caroline Craig	Teresa 'Tess' Gallagher	2000-2003 Ep. 270 - 407	Detective Sergeant, Sergeant
Ditch Davey	Evan 'Jonesy' Jones	2001-2006 Ep. 316 - 510	Probationary Constable, Constable, Senior Constable, Detective Senior Constable
Simone McAullay	Susie Raynor	2003-2006 Ep. 409 - 510	Probationary Constable, Constable, Senior Constable, Acting Sergeant
Geoff Morrell	Mark Jacobs	2004-2005 Ep. 441 - 489	Sergeant
Rachel Gordon	Amy Fox	2004-2006 Ep. 441 - 510	Detective Senior Constable
Samantha Tolj	Kelly O'Rourke	2004-2006 Ep. 442 - 510 2002-2003. (guest)	Probationary Constable, Constable
Danny Raco	Giuseppe 'Joss' Peroni	2004-2006 Ep. 442 - 510	Probationary Constable, Constable
Charlie Clausen	Alexander 'Alex' Kirby	2005-2006 Ep. 461 - 510	Leading Senior Constable, Acting Sergeant "Sk"
Matthew Holmes	Matthew 'Matt' Graham	2005-2006 Ep. 490 - 510	Probationary Constable, Constable

Recurring/semi-regular cast

Each episode featured a range of guest cast members, and over the run of the series hundreds of actors featured in these roles.[9]

As well as the main (regular) cast members, a number of well-known Australian actors frequently appeared as either recurring or semi-regular characters. These included Terry Gill as Superintendent Clive Adamson,[10] Neil Pigot as Inspector Russel Falcon-Price,[11] Jeremy Kewley as Mt Thomas journalist Tony Timms,[11] Frankie J. Holden as Snr. Det. Jack Woodley,[12] Catherine Wilkin,[13] Debra Lawrance,[10] Emily Browning,[14] Josh Lawson, [15] along with Suzi Dougherty as Dr. Mel Carter, Peta Doodson as Inspector Monica Draper, Beth Buchanan as Susan Croydon, Michael Isaacs as Clancy Freeman, and the late Reg Evans as Keith Purvis.

Many other notable actors also had one-off or recurring guest roles in *Blue Heelers* including Shane Bourne,[16] Hugh Jackman,[17] Gerard Kennedy,[18] David Wenham,[19] Marcus Graham,[20] Peter O'Brien,[21] Gary Sweet,[22] Vince Colosimo,[23], Alan Cinis and Alan Dale.

Production

On average, 42 episodes of *Blue Heelers* were broadcast per year on Australian television, with each episode comprising fifty scenes. One episode was made every week. The scripts were written to a formula which allowed one day for rehearsal, two days on location and two days in the studio.[9] Episodes were shot eight to ten weeks ahead of their scheduled broadcast date[24] . There were 16 episodes in various stages of production at any one time (from the conception of new storylines to post-production). In addition, there were always seven complete episodes waiting to go to air.[9] Apart from the regular cast members, the show employed 4,300 guest actors annually, plus 30 extras every week. A total of 150 people were involved in some way with the show's production each week, including cast members, crew, wardrobe, publicists and writers.[9]

Conception and development

Blue Heelers creator/producer, Hal McElroy, conceived the idea of *Blue Heelers* when he heard that a eighteen-year-old friend was planning to become a police officer. Intrigued, McElroy his inquired as to why this young boy, fresh out of school, would want to become a police officer, as opposed to the many other opportunities he had open to him. McElroy soon discovered that, at the time, a staggering 60% of Australian police officers were under the age of 26.[25] This, coupled with McElroy's desire to create a country cop show, formed the basis of the programme. When this same young officer left the force only a year later due to the shooting death of his colleague, McElroy was even more intrigued to learn about the very fickle, yet rewarding job of policing the community.[8] McElroy continued his quest by asking ex-police officer Michael Winter to write down what it was like to be a city cop who transferred to a country town. These became the ideas that *Blue Heelers* was based around.[26] Michael Winter also conceived the name of the programme by recounting the common names for a country police officer: "tyre-biters"—referring to the fact that country cops are often involved in car chases—and "blue heelers"—referring to their blue uniforms and overall similar appearance and persona to a Blue Heeler dog, a protective and intuitive breed of Australian dog.[25] From the time that McElroy's idea was initially conceived, to the time the programme was ready to air, three years passed.

During *Blue Heelers* early development, two completely different pilots were shot: one depicting the story from the perspective of a police officer and the other from the perspective of a criminal. When these were presented to the Seven Network, the network committed to 13 episodes of the first pilot. The pilot went on to become the official first episode of *Blue Heelers*, telling the story of a new cop in town, Maggie Doyle, and her beginnings in Mount Thomas. McElroy chose to discard the second pilot realising it was a fatal mistake to be "with the criminals as they plotted the crime". He also conceived his rule that the producers of the show "couldn't have a camera in a room unless there was a copper there as well" (a rule shared by long-running UK Police drama *The Bill*). Hence, the basis of the show being from a police officer's perspective became a firm reality.[8]

McElroy tells his police advisor's opinion:

> He had been posted to Yass (in New South Wales) and he really loved it up there because the routine was so simple and straightforward-most often you knew the victim and sometimes you knew the culprit, and someone in charge would give them a clip behind the ear and say 'wash the police car' or 'sweep the yard' and 'don't ever do it again', rather than sending a juvenile to jail.

> I loved it, and I said 'Hey this is great'. But all the writers said, 'No it's boring, we want that gritty, inner-city police stuff. (We had Boys in Blue set up in Leichhardt in Sydney.) And I still remember the moment I was driving home up River Road and I thought, 'Then we can have two shows'. I said to this copper 'What are you called in the country? What is your nickname?' And he said they call highway patrol 'tyre biters' and coppers 'blue heelers'. And I thought 'That's the title!' So I rang [scriptwriter] Tony Morphett and said 'Let's do a show about young cops in the country. It's called Blue Heelers.

> —Hal McElroy, [8]

By creating the programme, McElroy and Morphett hoped to close the gap between to police and the public. They hoped to show the human side of the policing and that, like other citizens, police officers have feelings, regrets, aspirations and fears.[2] They also hoped that the show would act as a tribute to the courage of police officers, who risk their lives everyday, never knowing if they'd return home at the end of the day.[25]

Filming locations

Only about half of the footage for each episode was shot on location.[24] Most of the scenes, including scenes in the police station and pub, were filmed inside Stags Head hotel in Williamstown.[24] [27] Much of the filming on location was carried out in towns such as Williamstown,[27] and the more established parts of Werribee.[28] The scenes of the outside of the Mount Thomas police station were actually filmed at the old, disused Williamstown police station, which was then a private residence. Scenes at Mount Thomas High School were filmed at Williamstown High School. The town of Castlemaine was most often used as the backdrop for Mount Thomas, seen in almost every episode.[29] [30] Although the Blue Heelers' pilot was shot in Castlemaine, the cast and crew very rarely returned there to shoot further episodes;[24] the scenes in Castlemaine were usually just generic scenes where no "action" actually takes place. Chris Riley's fictional Imperial Hotel, for example, was actually the real Imperial Hotel in Castlemaine.[29] [30] Mount Thomas' fictional Commercial Hotel was filmed at the Willy Tavern in Williamstown.[27] The second Mount Thomas police station, adopted during the programme's reform of 2004, was filmed at Newport Railway workshops. The Mount Thomas Hospital was filmed at the Werribee Mercy Hospital.[31]

Reception

Described by critics before its launch as "*A Country Practice* meets *Cop Shop*",[26] and as "the contemporary cousin of British cop show, *Heartbeat*",[32] *Blue Heelers* was not anticipated by critics to become a hugely popular programme. However, it became a hit TV show soon after it began airing. During most of its broadcast, *Blue Heelers* was very popular in Australia, regularly attracting up to 2.5 million viewers,[4] and up to 3.5 million viewers at its peak.[33] Throughout the show's broadcast it continually drew a strong audience, regularly appearing among the top-rating prime time programmes on Australian television. Viewership of Blue Heelers never dropped below 1 million viewers.[7] The episodes "Gold" and "Fool's Gold" (episodes 140 and 141), which aired during the programme's fourth season, were two of the most popular *Blue Heelers* episodes. Each drew 2.5 million viewers, considered a huge achievement in 1997.[6]

Blue Heelers' executive producer, Gus Howard believed the show's popularity was due mainly to the quality of the cast.

> Much of the success of Blue Heelers has been attributed to one of the best ensemble casts of any drama on television, with most every cast member becoming a household name... The basic vocation for the show has always been about shedding a little light on the human condition, something Australian audiences have readily identified with. The show epitomises and represents the Australian ethos in a way that truly reflects Australian life.
>
> —Gus Howard, [7]

Much of the show's sixth season, as well as the first 10 episodes of its seventh season, were the most watched episodes of the series. These episodes focus of the death of Maggie Doyle (played by Lisa McCune). Maggie's being shot and left for dead during episode 255, "One More Day", was ranked by TV Week as the third most memorable moment of a drama series on Australian television.[34]

2004 Revamp: The Station Bombing

After low ratings in 2003 and 2004, the producers and executives of *Blue Heelers* realised that there were apparent problems which could potentially lead to the series's downfall. In 2004 *Blue Heelers* lost the top ratings spot to *McLeod's Daughters*.[35] During 2003 and 2004, Australian television drama was also at its "lowest point in a decade" and many popular shows were cancelled.[36] As the show remained basically unchanged from its debut, ten years ago, the production team decided that a revamp was in order.

Blue Heelers' revamp started with a new opening credits to make it feel more modern in the 21st century taking out the acoustic putting in an electric guitar which started in the beginning of season 11 and also a broadcast of a live episode which did not feature Ben Stewart played by(Paul Bishop) who didn't appear due to film commitments,titled "Reasonable Doubt", which the producers hoped would offer a short-term ratings rise and encourage more long-term viewers. Although an immediate success, the live episode did not bring about a sustained increase in ratings.[35] Producers also hoped that a shift in direction, a change of mood and setting, and the addition of four cast members would cement *Blue Heelers*' long-term future.[35] They also wanted the show to remain relevant and more accurately reflect today's modern world:[37]

> Mount Thomas was created in 1993 and the world has changed... It will now be more reflective of today's country towns, not the sleepy backwater it was. It wasn't an easy task but the creative team responded brilliantly and there's a real feeling of excitement again... The old girl can still dance. And dance to new tunes.
>
> —John Holmes, [38]

The main plot, setting and character changes started in July 2004, with the airing of the episode "End of Innocence". In this episode, the main storyline was the bombing of the Mount Thomas police station. The blast killed popular main character Snr. Const. Jo Parrish (Jane Allsop) and recurring cast member Clancy Freeman, and injured the show's main protagonist,[39] Senior Sergeant Croydon. After the bombing it was revealed that Croydon's wife, the Reverend Curtis, was missing. It was later revealed she had been brutally raped and murdered.[35] These events brought about sweeping changes to the mood of not only Croydon, but also the mood of the entire show. The Daily Telegraph television writer Marcus Casey commented, "Mount Thomas has become a darker, grittier place, the people and cops in it transformed by an invasion of evil".[38] Consequently, the story changed its focus from the old Mount Thomas police station to the new one that was used until the show's cancellation in 2006. The Seven Network feared that in the modern post-9/11 world, a show about country police was no longer what audiences wanted.[40] Storylines of the proceeding five episodes focused on the bombing of the station and the 4 new main characters: Rachel Gordon as Amy Fox, Geoff Morrell as Mark Jacobs, Samantha Tolj as Kelly O'Rourke and Danny Raco as Joss Peroni.[35] [38] Popular former cast member William McInnes also returned to the show, temporarily reprising his role as Nick Schultz. Producers hoped the new tone of the series, the new younger actors, and McInnes's role reprisal would lure back viewers who had stopped watching the programme.[38] This new style of programme that *Blue Heelers* was embracing was a sign of the show trying to keep up with other larger television shows, particularly the CSI franchise.[38]

The revamp of the series resulted in a 25% ratings increase, bringing the series's weekly viewership to 1.6 million people.[41] Critical response after the event was reassuring, and it appeared that critics were approving of the drastic moves by Seven and Southern Star:

> The recent shake-up at the old station has swept aside an unhealthy staleness that had settled on the place and there's some much-needed fresh energy provided by the new recruits, including Samantha Tolj as true-blue Aussie gal Kelly O'Rourke and Danny Raco as Italian stallion Joss Peroni.
>
> —Debi Enker, [42]

Cancellation

In the hope that viewing would increase, an 11-episode season in 2006 was commissioned by the Seven Network.[43] However, the ratings spike begun in 2004 was not sufficient for the Seven Network to commit to continuing to produce the show. In January 2006, Seven officially announced that they had cancelled *Blue Heelers*, but would air a final shortened season of 11 episodes in mid-2006.[44] At the time the show was still drawing 1.2 million viewers per week on average, down from the 3.5 million it was drawing at its peak.[45] The announcement was front-page news on nearly all of Australia's major newspapers including The Sydney Morning Herald, Sydney's Daily Telegraph, The Melbourne Herald Sun, The Melbourne Age and Brisbane's Courier Mail.[46] Two different endings were shot for the final episode, which finished filming on December 20, 2005. The first ending wrapped up all the show's storylines, while the second left the show open for another season; the first was version was used.[28]

For *Blue Heelers*' final season, it was moved from its primetime Wednesday-night timeslot, to a lower rating Saturday-night timeslot.[47] In the Saturday timeslot *Blue Heelers* competed with *The Bill*, a British police drama which had become quite popular in Australia.[39] This move was slammed by leading cast member, John Wood.[39] *Blue Heelers* cancellation may also be related to Seven's AFL broadcast, which saw Seven invest $780m for the 5 year broadcasting rights of the game.[6]

Episodes

Seasons generally ran in Australia from early February to late November. Each season generally consisted of 41 to 42 episodes. The eleventh season however, only consisted of 39 episodes, as the Seven Network had gained the rights to televise the 2004 Athens Olympic Games. In total, 510 episodes were aired: 509 hour-long standard episodes and one live episode. The live episode, titled "Reasonable Doubts", was filmed to celebrate *Blue Heelers* 10th year on the air.[48] To prepare, the cast was given six days to memorise their lines.[49]

The final episode of the 13th season aired as a 2-hour tribute. It opened with an introduction from John Wood and concluded with a compilation of *Blue Heelers* moments from over its 13-season run.[50]

Australian television quiz-show, *The Weakest Link*, hosted by Cornelia Frances, also aired a *Blue Heelers* special episode on August 9th, 2001. Cast members John Wood, Neil Pigot, Ditch Davey, Jeremy Kewley, Jane Allsop, Suzi Dougherty, Paul Bishop, Caroline Craig and Peta Doodson took part in this special event.[51] [52]

Season	Ep. #	Season Premiere	Season Finale
Season 1	45	18 January 1994	22 November 1994
Season 2	41	21 February 1995	21 November 1995
Season 3	41	12 February 1996	26 November 1996
Season 4	42	10 February 1997	25 November 1997
Season 5	41	24 February 1998	25 November 1998
Season 6	42	10 February 1999	24 November 1999
Season 7	41	9 February 2000	22 November 2000
Season 8	41	21 February 2001	28 November 2001
Season 9	41	13 February 2002	20 November 2002
Season 10	42	12 February 2003	26 November 2003
Season 11	39	4 February 2004	5 November 2004
Season 12	42	2 February 2005	26 November 2005
Season 13	11	1 April 2006	4 June 2006

Merchandise

The first full *Blue Heelers* novel, *Maggie's Story*, was written by Roger Dunn and released in 1997 by Coronet Books. In August 1998, a second novel, *Tom's Story*, written by Cassandra Carter was released by Bolinda Publishing.

Several episodes of *Blue Heelers*, including "In The Gun" and "Fair Crack of the Whip" were released on [VHS]] video cassette format in the later 1990s.

DVD releases

Further information: see the individual season pages

Seasons 1-12 of *Blue Heelers* have been released on DVD. The DVD release is only available in Australia and New Zealand. It is not known if the series will be released on DVD internationally.

In November 2005, Paramount Home Entertainment released the *Blue Heelers—The Complete First Season* box set in Australia in Region 4 DVD format. This was shortly followed by *Blue Heelers—The Complete Second Season: Part 1* and *Blue Heelers—The Complete Second Season: Part 2*, which were released together in December 2005. However, the "seasons", as defined by the DVD releases, are markedly different to the original seasons as they aired on television. It

Blue Heelers DVD release.

appears that the episodes are being released according to what year the episodes were "produced" in, as opposed to the year they aired. For example: *The Complete First Season* DVDs contain some episodes from season 1 (1994), while *The Complete Second Season* contains the remainder of season 1 (1994) episodes and some from season 2 (1995).

In January 2007, Paramount Home Entertainment announced that they would be releasing each already released season of *Blue Heelers* as one complete set, rather than in two parts as they had done prior. These new sets, rather than being box sets with special slipcase packaging, were now just both parts, packed in a standard DVD case, packaged together in plastic. Each of these DVD sets now consists of 10 or 11 discs, rather than 5 or 6 each. The new sets were released on 15 February 2007.[53]

In July 2009, Southern Star announced that seasons 10 - 13 would be released throughout 2010 and season 14 would be released in early 2011.

Blue Heelers Initial Season Release Dates for Australia (DVD)		
DVD Name	**Release Date**	**Episodes**
Complete First Season	2 November 2005[54]	Season 1 episodes 1 -> 17.
Complete Second Season	1 December 2005[55]	Season 1 episodes 18 -> 45, Season 2 episodes 46 -> 54.
Complete Third Season	16 February 2006[56]	Season 2 episodes 55 -> 86, Season 3 episodes 87 -> 96.
Complete Fourth Season	6 April 2006[57]	Season 3 episodes 97 -> 128, Season 4 episodes 129 -> 139.
Complete Fifth Season	6 June 2006[58]	Season 4 episodes 140 -> 170, Season 5 episodes 171 -> 181.
Complete Sixth Season	10 August 2006[59]	Season 5 episodes 182 -> 211, Season 6 episodes 212 -> 223.
Complete Seventh Season	31 July 2008[60]	Season 6 episodes 224 -> 253, Season 7 episodes 254 -> 265.
Complete Eighth Season	1 October 2008[61]	Season 7 episodes 266 -> 287, Season 8 episodes 288 -> 306.

Complete Ninth Season	5 November 2009[62]	Season 8 episodes 307 -> 335, Season 9 episodes 336 -> 348.
Complete Tenth Season	6 May 2010[63]	Season 9 episodes 349 -> 376, Season 10 episodes 377 -> 388.
Complete Eleventh Season	5 August 2010[64]	Season 10 episodes 389 -> 418, Season 11 episodes 419 -> 428.
Complete Twelfth Season	4 November 2010 [65]	Season 11 Episodes 429 -> 457.
Complete Thirteenth Season	Late 2010/Early 2011	TBA Episodes
Complete Fourteenth Season	Early 2011	TBA Episodes

Awards

In terms of awards, Blue Heelers is regarded as one of the most successful programmes on Australian television.[66] *Blue Heelers* has been the recipient of many awards, including 25 Logie Awards, five of which are the prestigious Gold Logie, 3 AFI Television Awards, 3 People's Choice Awards, and 1 AWGIE Awards.[67] [68] *Blue Heelers* was nominated for a further twelve Gold Logies. *Blue Heelers* has also won multiple Silver Logies, including numerous Most Popular Actor, Most Popular Actress and Most Popular Programme awards, as well as many Outstanding Awards. Many *Blue Heelers* cast members have also hosted the Logie Award ceremony. In the 2005 50 Years 50 Shows poll,*Blue Heelers* was voted 37th greatest show on Australian television and ranked within the top ten dramas.

Blue Heelers award summary[3]		
Award	**Wins**	**Nominations**
Gold Logie Awards[69]	5	3
Silver Logie Awards[70]	20	35
AFI Television Awards[71]	3	4
AWGIE Awards[72] [73]	1	1
People's Choice Awards[74] [75]	3	6
Australian Screen Editors' Awards[3]	0	1
TOTAL	**32**	**50**

Broadcasting

Blue Heelers had a strong following not only in Australia, but also worldwide; it has been sold to 108 territories[7] and is shown in over 70 countries.[76]

Australia

Blue Heelers originally aired on Tuesday nights at 7:30 pm on the Seven Network, thus it was limited to a PG content level restriction. When the series was hailed as a success it began the transition from this timeslot to the 8:30pm timeslot on the same day. After the move, writers could explore more diverse storylines, as the show was restricted to an M rating. The third and fourth season premiers aired on Monday nights during the 8:30 pm timeslot, but the show moved back to its original slot before the next episode. In its fifth season, *Blue Heelers* moved to the Wednesday night 8:30 pm timeslot, which it occupied for most of its run, until the end of its twelfth season. This move was made to make way for hospital drama *All Saints*.

Starting in 2004, the Seven Network aired *Blue Heelers* in their weekday "early days drama" slot at 2:00 pm. They aired all the episodes of Blue Heelers, starting from its first season. In this slot, *Blue Heelers* was a replacement for the broadcast of the early episodes of *Home and Away*. *Blue Heelers* concluded airing in this slot in 2007, with the broadcast of its final episode, and made way for the broadcast of early episodes of *All Saints*.

Blue Heelers has also screened on Foxtel The Hallmark Channel in Australia in various timeslots.

New Zealand

In New Zealand *Blue Heelers* screened on TV One in a popular timeslot. However, following the on-screen death of Maggie Doyle, ratings fell, and the show was moved to a 9:30 pm slot on Friday. Following that, the show moved to a late night Thursday slot where the rest of the episodes played out, with the show beginning anywhere between 11:30 pm and midnight. It aired its final episode on TV One on 20 March 2008.

Ireland

Irish broadcaster RTÉ originally began airing *Blue Heelers* on Friday afternoons at 4:30 pm. Episodes were only a few months behind the Australian broadcast. The series took a two year break in 2000, before re-commencing in a five-day-a-week timeslot at 10:30 am in early 2002. The show quickly caught up with the Australian broadcast; by 2004 the show was scaled back to the original one episode a week, and moved to a late night Thursday–early Friday morning timeslot, typically around 1:00 am. RTÉ commenced broadcasting the final season on 30 May 2008 in a late night Saturday–early Sunday morning timeslot. RTÉ screened the final episode on 30 November 2008. RTÉ began re-airing Blue Heelers weekly from episode one, commencing on 24 June 2009, usually around 4 am. RTÉ screened all episodes in their original unedited state. The drama proved very popular in Ireland and rated very well.

United States

Blue Heelers aired briefly in the United States of America in the early 2000s on the short-lived cable channel Trio (carried primarily by DirecTV). No episode after number 76 was ever shown in the United States, and when Trio changed their programming in 2004, *Blue Heelers* was dropped from the schedule.

Canada

Blue Heelers was broadcast on Showcase in Canada, last airing on 15 May 1998.[77]

Iran

Blue Heelers is broadcasting on IRIB. All episodes were dubbed in Persian.

Italy

In Italy *Blue Heelers* was broadcast on Italia 7 Gold (now called *7 Gold*), from the 1st to the 6th season. All episodes were dubbed in Italian.

United Kingdom

In the United Kingdom the series was broadcast on most stations on the ITV Network. Many companies tended to screen the show as hour-long episodes in the afternoon (occasionally with necessary edits to suit the time slot), however Central Television started with a late night 11:40 pm slot before following other regions with a typically 2:20 pm slot.

In Britain, Carlton Television often showed the episodes in two halves, as was common with other Australian soap operas in London. Several regions including Yorkshire Television and Tyne Tees Television chose not to import the show. When the ITV contractors reformatted as one company in 2002, regionally-run programmes such as *Blue Heelers* (which were at different points of the series in each region) disappeared from screens. No ITV region ever screened the series in full.

The show also aired on UK cable channel Carlton Select in the late 1990s, first screening the early episodes daily and then in a weekly slot Fridays at 8:00 pm as episodes became more recent. Episodes to the later part of the 1997 season were shown before the series was dropped.

Blue Heelers was also aired on Meridian Television and Channel Television, typically Mondays at 2:20 pm, but some episodes also aired in a morning slot during school holidays. On Westcountry Television *Blue Heelers* was broadcast beginning 3 January 1995 at 2:50 pm in half-episode format.

Scottish Television (STV) aired hour-long episodes, airing on Fridays, and then later on Tuesdays. STV dropped *Blue Heelers* after episode 10.

Ulster Television (UTV) began airing *Blue Heelers* in early 1995. The show initially screened 3 times a week, on Monday, Wednesday and Friday afternoons at 1:50 pm. They then moved it to the 2:20 pm slot later in the series. A few episodes also ran at 11:40 pm on Thursday nights, as they were considered unsuitable for daytime viewing. UTV cancelled *Blue Heelers* in 1998.

See also

- List of Australian television series
- Mount Thomas
- Victoria Police

References

[1] Editors. Blue Heelers: Release Dates (http://www.imdb.com/title/tt0108709/releaseinfo#akas), IMDb. Retrieved 4 May 2008.

[2] Hallett,Bryce "Bush coppers show mettle" (http://australiantelevision.net/bh/articles/bushcoppers.html), *The Australian*, 18 January 1994.

[3] Zuk, Tim. Blue Heelers Awards (http://australiantelevision.net/bh/awards.html), Australian Television Information Archive. Retrieved 8 June 2008.

[4] Idato, Michael. "Final Farewell" (http://australiantelevision.net/bh/articles/finalfarewell.html), Sydney Morning Herald, 29 May 2006.

[5] television.au AUSSIE COP SHOWS (http://www.televisionau.com/copshows.htm)

[6] "*Blue Heelers* axed, and AFL the main suspect (http://www.smh.com.au/news/tv--radio/blue-heelers-axed/2006/01/13/ 1137118960344.html), Sydney Morning Herald, 14 January 2004.

[7] Blue Heelers Final Episodes to Air in 2006 (http://www.southernstargroup.com/NewsDetails.aspx?niid=1523&d=0), Southern Star Group, 13 January 2006. Retrieved 4 June 2008.

[8] Government of the Commonwealth of Australia. Small screen, big picture, big future (http://archive.dcita.gov.au/2000/07/ artbeat_july_2000/small_screen_big_picture_huge_future), Department of Communications, Information Technology and the Arts, July 2000. Retrieved 17 May 2008.

[9] James, Carol. Heelers hit 150 (http://www.lisamccune.net/index2.php?option=com_content&do_pdf=1&id=213), TV Week, 5 July 1997. Retrieved from LisaMcCune.net (http://www.lisamccune.net/) on 13 August 2008.

[10] "Paranoia (Part 2)". *Blue Heelers*. 1995-07-25. No. 26, season 2.

[11] "Random Breath". *Blue Heelers*. 1997-06-03. No. 17, season 4.

[12] "A Fair Crack Of The Whip (Part 1)". *Blue Heelers*. 1996-04-30. No. 14, season 4.

[13] "The Lord Giveth". *Blue Heelers*. 2001-10-03. No. 32, season 8.

[14] "Small Potatoes". *Blue Heelers*. 2000-07-05. No. 22, season 7.

[15] "Burning Up". *Blue Heelers*. 2007-05-13. No. 7, season 13.

[16] "Unfinished Business". *Blue Heelers*. 2000-04-05. No. 9, season 7.

[17] "Just Deserts". *Blue Heelers*. 1995-10-03. No. 33, season 2.

[18] "The Discount Suit". *Blue Heelers*. 1995-11-07. No. 39, season 2.

[19] "Happy Families". *Blue Heelers*. 1996-04-09. No. 12, season 3.

[20] "Moonlighting". *Blue Heelers*. 2006-05-27. No. 9, season 13.

[21] "Lost". *Blue Heelers*. 2005-11-26. No. 41, season 12.

[22] "Chasing Smoke". *Blue Heelers*. 2005-03-02. No. 5, season 12.

[23] "Killing Time". *Blue Heelers*. 2006-04-13. No. 10, season 12.

[24] Blue Heelers in town (http://www.australiantelevision.net/bh/articles/castlemaine.html), Bendigo Advertiser, 8 April 2005. Retrieved 6 May 2008.

[25] Farmer, Monique. "Bush Bobbies" (http://australiantelevision.net/bh/articles/bushbobbies.html), *Sydney Morning Herald* 17 January 1994

[26] Schembri, Jim: "A Country Cop Show" (http://australiantelevision.net/bh/articles/countrycopshop.html), *The Age* 14 January 1994

[27] Webster, Di. Blue Appealers (http://www.australiantelevision.net/bh/articles/blueappealers.html), Who Weekly, 10 February 1997. Retrieved 3 May 2008.

[28] Webb, Caroline; Idato, Michael. "Axe falls on *Blue Heelers*" (http://www.theage.com.au/news/tv--radio/ axe-falls-on-blue-heelers-sevens-institution/2006/01/13/1137118970295.html), The Age, 14 January 2006. Retrieved 26 March 2008.

[29] Castlemaine, Australia (http://www.australiaeguide.com.au/castlemaine.php), Australia eguide. Retrieved 3 May 2008.

[30] Victorian Government. Famous television locations (http://www.acmi.net.au/tv50_tour.htm), Australian Centre for the Moving Image (http://www.acmi.net.au/). Retrieved 3 May 2008.

[31] Hobson's Bay City Council. Tourism & Places of Interest (http://www.hobsonsbay.vic.gov.au/Page/page.asp?Page_Id=128&h=0). Retrieved 4 May 2008.

[32] Reviewers. Blue Heelers review (http://www.law4u.com.au/lil/tv_blue_heelers.html), Law4u. Retrieved 12 June 2008

[33] Freeman, Jane. The top dogs of local TV drama (http://australiantelevision.net/bh/articles/topdogs.html), The Age, 17 April 1997. Retrieved 16 June 2008

[34] TV Week, 50 most memorable TV moments (http://tvweek.ninemsn.com.au/article.aspx?id=145967). Retrieved 8 September 2008.

[35] Miller, Kylie. Investing in Blue Heelers' future (http://australiantelevision.net/bh/articles/backwiththepack.html), The Age, 7 July 2004. Retrieved 12 July 2008.

[36] Warneke, Ross. The Publicity People Did It (http://australiantelevision.net/bh/articles/publicitypeople.html), The Age, 8 July 2008. Retrieved 12 June 2008.

[37] Fidgeon, Robert. Blue if Heelers axed (http://australiantelevision.net/bh/articles/blueifheelersaxed.html), The Herald Sun, 14 July 2004. Retrieved 12 June 2008.

[38] Casey, Marcus. The Force Is With Them (http://australiantelevision.net/bh/articles/forceiswiththem.html), The Daily Telegraph, 25 August 2005. Retrieved 12 June 2008.

[39] Dennehy, Luke. Blue Heeler sees red (http://www.australiantelevision.net/bh/articles/blueheelerseesred.html), The Herald Sun, 29 April 2006. Retrieved 26 March 2008.

[40] "Can John get Heelers out of the woods?" (http://australiantelevision.net/bh/articles/outofthewoods.html), The Daily Telegraph, 1 July 2004

[41] Fidegon, Robert. New Lease of Life for Blue Heelers (http://australiantelevision.net/bh/articles/newlease.html), The Herald Sun, 7 August 2008. Retrieved 12 June 2008.

[42] Enker, Debi. *Blue Heelers* review (http://australiantelevision.net/bh/articles/review.html), The Age, 24 February 2005. Retrieved 13 June 2008.

[43] Miller, Kylie. Heelers stay (http://www.australiantelevision.net/bh/articles/heelersstay.html), The Age, 29 September 2005. Retrieved 26 March 2008.

[44] Le Marquand, Sarah. Boot for Heelers (http://www.australiantelevision.net/bh/articles/bootforheelers.html), The Daily Telegraph, 14 January 2006. Retrieved 26 March 2008.

[45] Nicholson, Sarah. Every Dog Had Its Day (http://www.australiantelevision.net/bh/articles/everydog.html), 31 May 2006, The Courier-Mail. Retrieved 9 September 2008.

[46] "Blue Heelers" (1994) (http://www.imdb.com/title/tt0108709/trivia)

[47] *Blue Heelers* Returns For Final Season (http://www.australiantelevision.net/bh/articles/finalseason.html), Seven Network, 13 March 2006. Retrieved 26 March 2008.

[48] Witham, Katrina. Live and Laughing (http://australiantelevision.net/bh/articles/liveandlaughing.html), The Courier-Mail, 15 April 2004. Retrieved 9 June 2008.

[49] Miller, Kylie. Heelers Try New Trick (http://australiantelevision.net/bh/articles/heelerstrynewtrick.html), The Age, 15 April 2004. Retrieved 9 June 2008.

[50] Blundell, Graeme. Cop Out (http://www.australiantelevision.net/bh/articles/copout.html), The Australian, 3 June 2006. Retrieved 26 March 2008.

[51] Zuk, Tim. Blue Heelers season 8 (2001) episode guide (http://www.australiantelevision.net/bh/series8.html), Australian Television Information Archive (http://www.australiantelevision.net/). Retrieved 11 July 2008.

[52] "Blue Heelers Special". *The Weakest Link*. 2001-08-09.

[53] Editors. *Blue Heelers*: Season 1 DVD (http://chaos.com/product/blue_heelers_season_1_643915_147110.html). Chaos.com (http://chaos.com/). Retrieved 26 April 2008.

[54] Idato, Michael. *Blue Heelers* - Season 1 - DVD Review (http://www.smh.com.au/news/dvd-reviews/blue-heelers--season-1/2005/11/14/1131816846238.html), Sydney Morning Herald, 14 January 2007.

[55] Editors. *Blue Heelers*: Season 2, Part 1 DVD (http://chaos.com/product/blue_heelers_season_2_645722_147110.html). Chaos.com (http://chaos.com/). Retrieved 26 April 2008.

[56] Editors. *Blue Heelers*: Season 3, Part 1 DVD (http://chaos.com/product/blue_heelers_season_3_658406_147110.html). Chaos.com (http://chaos.com/). Retrieved 26 April 2008.

[57] Editors. *Blue Heelers*: Season 4, Part 1 DVD (http://chaos.com/product/blue_heelers_season_4_669439_147110.html). Chaos.com (http://chaos.com/). Retrieved 26 April 2008.

[58] Editors. *Blue Heelers*: Season 5, Part 2 DVD (http://www.ezydvd.com.au/item.zml/787193). EzyDVD.com (http://www.ezydvd.com.au/). Retrieved 26 April 2008.

[59] Editors. *Blue Heelers*: Season 6, Part 1 DVD (http://www.ezydvd.com.au/item.zml/787907). EzyDVD.com (http://www.ezydvd.com.au/). Retrieved 26 April 2008.

[60] Editors. *Blue Heelers*: Season 7, Part 1 DVD (http://www.ezydvd.com.au/item.zml/800172). EzyDVD.com (http://www.ezydvd.com.au/). Retrieved 14 July 2008.

[61] Editors. *Blue Heelers*: Season 8, Part 1 DVD (http://www.ezydvd.com.au/item.zml/801411). EzyDVD.com (http://www.ezydvd.com.au/). Retrieved 14 July 2008.

[62] Editors. *Blue Heelers*: Season 9, Parts 1 and 2 DVD (http://www.ezydvd.com.au/item.zml/808821). . Retrieved 7 September 2009.

[63] Editors. *Blue Heelers*: Season 10, Parts 1 and 2 DVD (http://www.ezydvd.com.au/item.zml/812098). . Retrieved 14 March 2010.

[64] Editors. *Blue Heelers*: Season 11, Parts 1 and 2 DVD (http://www.ezydvd.com.au/item.zml/813814). . Retrieved 27 May 2010.

[65] Editors. *Blue Heelers*: Season 12, Parts 1 and 2 DVD (http://www.ezydvd.com.au/item.zml/815405). . Retrieved 20 November 2010.

[66] AAP. Blue Heelers coming back (http://www.theage.com.au/news/tv--radio/blue-heelers-coming-back/2005/09/30/1127804637133. html), The Age, 30 September 2005. Retrieved 7 May 2008.

[67] "Blue Heelers" (1994) - Awards (http://imdb.com/title/tt0108709/awards)

[68] Australian Television: Blue Heelers: awards & nominations (http://australiantelevision.net/bh/awards.html)

[69] TV Week editors. History of the Gold Logie (http://tvweek.ninemsn.com.au/article.aspx?id=63394), TV Week. Retrieved 8 June 2008

[70] Zuk, Tim. List of Logie Award winners and nominees (http://australiantelevision.net/awards/awards.html), Australian Television Information Archive. Retrieved 8 June 2008.

[71] Television Awards 1986 - 2007 (http://www.afi.org.au/awards/pastwinners/Television Award Winners 1986-2007 .pdf). Australian Film Institute. Retrieved 26 April 2008.

[72] Australian Writers' Guild Awards. Australian Writers' Guild Awards of 1997 (http://www.australiantelevision.net/awards/awgie1997. html). @ Australian Television Information Archive (http://www.australiantelevision.net/). Retrieved 26 April 2008.

[73] Australian Writers' Guild Awards. Australian Writers' Guild Awards of 2002 (http://www.australiantelevision.net/awards/awgie2002. html). @ Australian Television Information Archive (http://www.australiantelevision.net/). Retrieved 26 April 2008.

[74] People's Choice Awards. People's Choice Awards of 1998 (http://www.australiantelevision.net/awards/people1998.html). @ Australian Television Information Archive (http://www.australiantelevision.net/). Retrieved 26 April 2008.

[75] People's Choice Awards. People's Choice Awards of 1999 (http://www.australiantelevision.net/awards/people1999.html). @ Australian Television Information Archive (http://www.australiantelevision.net/). Retrieved 26 April 2008.

[76] Tuohy, Wendy. True Blue and Loving It (http://australiantelevision.net/bh/articles/trueblue.html), The Age, 14 May 2000. Retrieved 16 June 2008.

[77] Zuk, Tim. Series Previously Aired in Canada (http://www.australiantelevision.net/now.html), Australian Television Information Archive (http://www.australiantelevision.net/). Retrieved 19 September 2008

External links

- *Blue Heelers* (http://www.imdb.com/title/tt0108709/) at the Internet Movie Database
- *Blue Heelers* (http://www.tv.com/show/3333/summary.html) at TV.com
- *Blue Heelers* (http://australiantelevision.net/bh/blueheelers.html) at the Australian Television Information Archive
- *Blue Heelers* (http://colsearch.nfsa.afc.gov.au/nfsa/search/display/display. w3p;adv=yes;group=;groupequals=;holdingType=;page=0;parentid=;query=255688;querytype=;rec=0;resCount=10) at the National Film and Sound Archive

The Man from Snowy River (TV series)

The Man from Snowy River / Snowy River: The McGregor Saga	
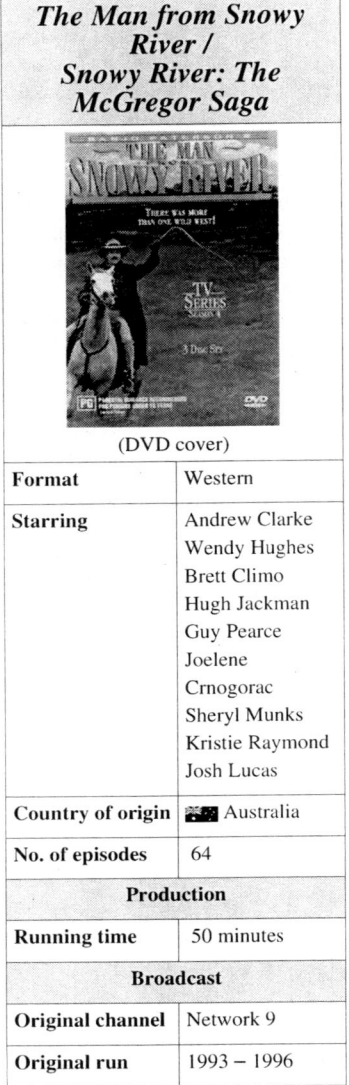	
(DVD cover)	
Format	Western
Starring	Andrew Clarke Wendy Hughes Brett Climo Hugh Jackman Guy Pearce Joelene Crnogorac Sheryl Munks Kristie Raymond Josh Lucas
Country of origin	Australia
No. of episodes	64
Production	
Running time	50 minutes
Broadcast	
Original channel	Network 9
Original run	1993 – 1996

The Man from Snowy River is an Australian television series based on Banjo Paterson's poem "The Man from Snowy River". Released in Australia as *Banjo Paterson's The Man from Snowy River*, the series was subsequently released in the United States as *Snowy River: The McGregor Saga*.

The television series concentrated on the adventures of Matt McGregor (Andrew Clarke), and his family, as a successful farmer. The series is based 25 years after his ride.[1]

Country	Title of "Snowy River" television series
Australia	*Banjo Paterson's The Man from Snowy River*
United States	*Snowy River: The McGregor Saga*
United Kingdom	*Snowy River: The McGregor Saga*
Vietnam	*Người đàn ông trên dòng sông băng*
Bosnia and Herzegovina	*McGregorovi*
Bulgaria	*Сноуи Ривър: Сага за Макгрегър* (*Snowy River: The McGregor Saga*)
Iran	*Rudkhaneye Barfi*
Gibraltar	*Snowy River*
Finland	*Lumisen virran mies*

See also

- "The Man from Snowy River" (poem)
- Snowy River

References

[1] *The Australian Film and Television Companion* — compiled by Tony Harrison — Simon & Schuster Australia, 1994
- *The Dictionary of Performing Arts in Australia* — Theatre . Film . Radio . Television — *Volume 1* — Ann Atkinson, Linsay Knight, Margaret McPhee — Allen & Unwin Pty. Ltd., 1996.

External links

- Snowy River: The McGregor Saga (The Man from Snowy River) (http://www.australiantelevision.net/snowyriver/snowyriver.html) — Australian Television Information Archive
- *Snowy River: The McGregor Saga* (http://www.imdb.com/title/tt0106136/) at the Internet Movie Database
- *Snowy River: The McGregor Saga* (http://www.tv.com/snowy-river-the-mcgregor-saga/show/3785/summary.html) - TV.com
- The Man From Snowy River (http://colsearch.nfsa.afc.gov.au/nfsa/search/display/display.w3p;adv=yes;group=;groupequals=;holdingType=;page=0;parentid=;query=322931;querytype=;rec=0;resCount=10) — at the National Film and Sound Archive (Australian Government website)
- La saga dei McGregor (http://www.antoniogenna.net/doppiaggio/telefilm/lasagadeimcgregor.htm) - Italian website

Erskineville Kings

Erskineville Kings	
Directed by	Alan White
Written by	Marty Denniss
Starring	Hugh Jackman
Music by	Soundtrack includes Louis Tillett
Release date(s)	1 January 1999
Country	Australia
Language	English

Erskineville Kings was a Radical Media production made for Palace Films on a minimal budget and directed by newcomer Alan White. It was released on 1 January 1999.[1] The lead actor, Hugh Jackman won the FCCA award for Best Actor - Male[2], for his performance as the brother of 25 year old Barky, played by Marty Denniss, who comes back home after he hears about his father's death.

Plot

The film deals with the story of two brothers. Barky, played by Marty Denniss, is 25 years old and returning home after two years of living in the northern sugar cane growing areas. He has returned home to attend the funeral of his father. The film begins with Barky's arrival at Central station at dawn, seeking the whereabouts of his brother, Wace. We learn from flashbacks that he left home two years ago to escape the clutches of his father's violent rages. Wace, the older brother, is not too happy about Barky's prolonged absence, having been left to manage looking after the father in his last years of life. After walking through the streets he finds an old mate of his, Wayne (Joel Edgerton), who assures him of the location of his brother. He succeeds in finding his brother through the help of Wayne and friends, who all end up a pub where it is revealed that Barky and Waces's mother left the family fifteen years earlier and that Wace hastened his father's death after he was struck down by a stroke. Barky also crosses paths with his ex-girlfriend, Lanny, and manages to rekindle the relationship. The film was filmed in the streets of Newtown and Erskineville, including inside Gould's Bookstore in Newtown. The title of the movie refers to the King's Hotel, a fictional hotel in which most of the movie takes place.

Cast

- Hugh Jackman
- Marty Denniss (also the screenwriter)
- Joel Edgerton
- Andrew Wholley
- Leah Vandenberg
- Aaron Blabey

Box Office

Erskineville Kings grossed $183,691 at the box office in Australia.[3]

See also

- Cinema of Australia

References

[1] Hollywood.com review (http://www.hollywood.com/movies/fulldetail/id/185377)

[2] FCCA Awards 2000 (http://www.imdb.com/Sections/Awards/Film_Critics_Circle_of_Australia_Awards/2000)

[3] *Film Victoria - Australian Films at the Australian Box Office* (http://film.vic.gov.au/resources/documents/AA4_Aust_Box_office_report. pdf)

External links

- *Erskineville Kings* (http://www.imdb.com/title/tt0212936/) at the Internet Movie Database

Paperback Hero (1999 film)

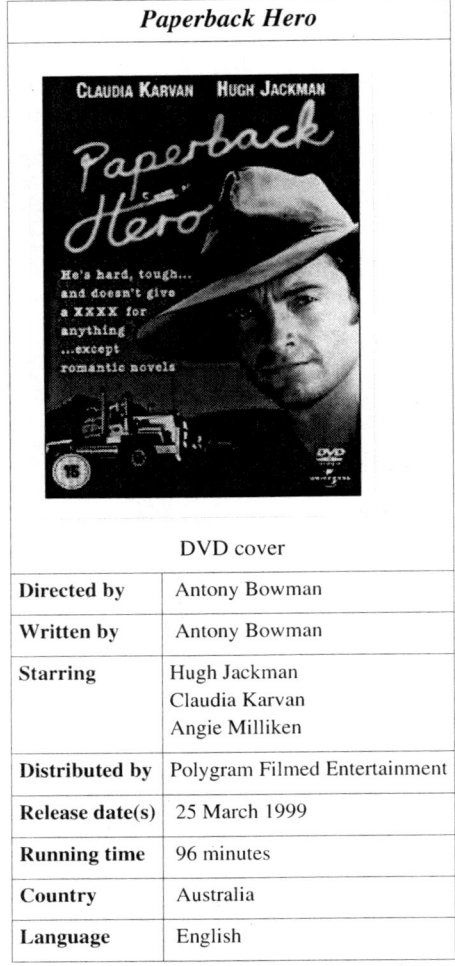

Paperback Hero	
DVD cover	
Directed by	Antony Bowman
Written by	Antony Bowman
Starring	Hugh Jackman Claudia Karvan Angie Milliken
Distributed by	Polygram Filmed Entertainment
Release date(s)	25 March 1999
Running time	96 minutes
Country	Australia
Language	English

Paperback Hero is a 1999 Australian comedy film starring Claudia Karvan and Hugh Jackman. It was directed by Antony Bowman who also wrote the screenplay.[1] The film was predominantly shot in Queensland.

Synopsis

The film follows the adventures of a truck driver, Jack Willis, from rural Australia after he writes a bestselling novel. Being embarrassed by its romantic content, he uses the name of his female friend as a pen name. When a publisher decides to take the author "Ruby Vale" on, he is suddenly faced with a problem. He tells his friend that he has used her name, and initially, she wants to tell the publisher the truth. However, Jack and the publisher convince her by telling her that they will organise her wedding, (as she is marrying Jack's best friend, Hamish) and so, Ruby is convinced.

Ruby and Jack then go to Sydney together, so that she can gain the book some more publicity. On the way, Ruby reads his book and finds that the lead female character is herself, and the main male character, Brian, is Jack. She is significantly touched by his book, even crying when she reads of Brian's death. The next few days go smoothly, although Ruby often voices her opinion that Jack should get the credit for writing such a story.

Things turn sour however, when the publisher finds out that Jack is indeed the author, but tells Jack not to let Ruby know. He doesn't, and that night the couple kiss after another publicity event. Hamish comes to Sydney, as he knows that Jack is the author, and tells Ruby, just before she is about to go on a satellite feed through to London, that he will stay for as long as it takes him to have a drink. That, coupled with the eventual knowledge that the knows who the real author is, sends Ruby back to Hamish and back to her rural hometown.

Jack does not follow her, instead staying and eventually making up his mind on what to do. While watching the T.V. in the local cafe, she hears Jack's voice on it. She finds that he has let the world know that he is the real author of the novel.

Soon after this, Hamish breaks up with her, knowing that she really loves Jack. As Ruby is wiping away the flys, and driving home, she sees a bird flying overhead, spelling the words, "I love you". She stops her car, and the plane lands in front of her. Jack hops out, and after some gentle sparring of words, they kiss and the story ends.

Box Office

Paperback Hero grossed $1,369,280 at the box office in Australia,[2] .

See also

- Cinema of Australia

References

[1] Urban Cinefile BOWMAN, ANTONY J.: Paperback Hero (http://www.urbancinefile.com.au/home/view.asp?a=2121&s=Interviews)

[2] *Film Victoria - Australian Films at the Australian Box Office* (http://film.vic.gov.au/resources/documents/AA4_Aust_Box_office_report. pdf)

External links

- *Paperback Hero (1999 film)* (http://www.imdb.com/title/tt0180037/) at the Internet Movie Database

X-Men (film)

X-Men	
 Theatrical release poster	
Directed by	Bryan Singer
Produced by	Lauren Shuler Donner Ralph Winter Avi Arad Tom DeSanto Richard Donner Stan Lee Kevin Feige Matthew Edelman Scott Nimerfro Joel Simon Bill Todman, Jr.
Screenplay by	David Hayter
Story by	Tom DeSanto Bryan Singer
Based on	*Uncanny X-Men* by Stan Lee and Jack Kirby
Starring	Patrick Stewart Hugh Jackman Ian McKellen Halle Berry Famke Janssen James Marsden Bruce Davison Rebecca Romijn-Stamos Ray Park Anna Paquin
Music by	Michael Kamen
Cinematography	Newton Thomas Sigel

Editing by	Steven Rosenblum Kevin Sitt John Wright
Studio	20th Century Fox Marvel Entertainment The Donners' Company Bad Hat Harry Productions Springwood Productions Genetics Productions
Distributed by	20th Century Fox
Release date(s)	July 13, 2000 (Australia) July 14, 2000 (United States)
Running time	104 minutes
Language	English
Budget	$75 million
Gross revenue	$296,339,527
Followed by	*X2*

X-Men is a 2000 superhero film based on the fictional Marvel Comics characters of the same name. Directed by Bryan Singer, the film stars Hugh Jackman, Patrick Stewart, Ian McKellen, Anna Paquin, Famke Janssen, Bruce Davison, James Marsden, Halle Berry, Rebecca Romijn, Ray Park and Tyler Mane. It introduces Wolverine and Rogue into the conflict between Professor Xavier's X-Men and the Brotherhood of Mutants, led by Magneto. Magneto intends to mutate world leaders at a United Nations summit with a machine he has built to bring about acceptance of mutantkind, but Xavier realizes this forced mutation will only result in their deaths.

Development for *X-Men* began as far back as 1989 with James Cameron and Carolco Pictures. The film rights went to 20th Century Fox in 1994. Scripts and film treatments were commissioned from Andrew Kevin Walker, John Logan, Joss Whedon and Michael Chabon. Singer signed to direct in 1996, with further rewrites by Ed Solomon, Singer, Tom DeSanto, Christopher McQuarrie and David Hayter. Start dates kept getting pushed back, while Fox decided to move *X-Men*'s release date from December to July 2000. Filming took place from September 22, 1999 to March 3, 2000, primarily in Toronto. *X-Men* was released to positive reviews and was a financial success, spawning the *X-Men* film series and a reemergence of superhero films.

Plot

In Congress, Senator Robert Kelly attempts to pass a "Mutant Registration Act", which would force mutants to publicly reveal their identities and abilities. Magneto begins his plans to level the playing field between mutants and humans. Meanwhile, a girl named Marie (a.k.a Rogue) runs away from her home in Meridian, Mississippi. She meets Wolverine in Canada. Suddenly, both of them are attacked by Sabretooth, a mutant and associate of Magneto. Cyclops and Storm arrive and save Wolverine and Rogue and bring them to the X-Mansion. Professor Charles Xavier runs the facility, and leads a group of mutants who are trying to seek peace with the human race, educate young mutants in the responsible use of their powers, and stop Magneto from starting a war with humanity.

Abducted by Mystique and Toad, Senator Kelly is brought to Magneto, who tests a machine on him that artificially induces mutation though Kelly manages to escape imprisonment with his new abilities. After an accident causes Rogue to use her powers on Wolverine, she is convinced by Mystique (disguised as Bobby Drake) that Xavier is angry with her and that she should leave the school. Xavier uses Cerebro to locate Rogue at a train station. Mystique infiltrates Cerebro and sabotages the machine. At the train station, Wolverine convinces Rogue to stay with Xavier but a fight ensues when Magneto, Toad and Sabretooth arrive to take Rogue. Arriving at Xavier's school Kelly dissolves into a puddle of water when his mutation becomes unstable.

The X-Men learn that Magneto intends to use Rogue's ability on himself to power his machine. Xavier attempts to use Cerebro to locate Rogue but falls into a coma. Jean Grey fixes it and uses Cerebro to find Magneto's machine on Liberty Island, which Magneto intends to use on the world leaders who are meeting for a summit on nearby Ellis Island. Just as the group arrives at the top of the statue and kill Toad, Magneto and Sabretooth incapacitate the group and continue with their plans. Magneto transfers his powers to Rogue who is forced to use them to start the machine. Wolverine breaks free and initiates a fight with Sabretooth but is thrown over the side of the statue.

Wolverine returns, and Cyclops, with Jean's help, blasts Sabretooth out of the statue. With Jean stabilizing him, Storm uses her abilities to send Wolverine to the top of Magneto's machine. With time running out, Wolverine attempts to stop the machine and save Rogue, but Magneto, now having regained some of his strength, halts Wolverine's claws. Cyclops manages to find a clean shot, wounding Magneto and allowing Wolverine to destroy the machine. Placing his hand to her face, Wolverine succeeds in transferring his regenerative abilities to a dying Rogue. Professor Xavier recovers from his coma and the group learns that Mystique is still alive (after Wolverine stabbed her at Liberty Island) when they see her impersonating Senator Kelly on a news broadcast. In an attempt to help Wolverine learn more about his past, Xavier sends him to a military base near Alkali Lake. Xavier visits Magneto in his plastic prison cell, and the two play chess. Magneto warns his friend that he will continue his fight, to which Xavier promises that he (and the X-Men) will always be there to stop him.

Cast

- Hugh Jackman as Logan / Wolverine: A tough, rugged, belligerent loner who makes a living in cage fights. He has lived for fifteen years without memory of who he is, apart from his dog tags marked "Wolverine" and an adamantium-encased skeleton (as well as adamantium claws). He has the ability to heal rapidly from numerous injuries, including the surgery that bonded the metal to his skeleton, which makes his age impossible to determine.

- Patrick Stewart as Professor Charles Xavier: Founder of the X-Men and the Xavier School for Gifted Youngsters, Xavier hopes for peaceful coexistence between mutantkind and mankind and is regarded as an authority on genetic mutation. Although he is restricted to a wheelchair, he is a powerful mutant with vast telepathic abilities. Along with Magneto, he is the inventor of the Cerebro supercomputer, which further amplifies his abilities.

- Ian McKellen as Erik Lehnsherr / Magneto: A Holocaust survivor, he and Xavier were once allies, and they built Cerebro together. However, his belief that humans and mutants could never co-exist lead to their separation. He has powerful magnetic abilities and a sophisticated knowledge in matters of genetic manipulation, which he uses to plan a mutation of the world leaders to allow mutant prosperity.

- Anna Paquin as Marie / Rogue: A seventeen-year-old girl, forced to leave her family in Mississippi after putting her boyfriend in a coma by kissing him. If she touches anyone, she absorbs their strength, memories and abilities, potentially killing them. During her travels, she meets Wolverine, who becomes her closest friend. She begins to have a romance with Bobby Drake.

- Famke Janssen as Dr. Jean Grey: She is in a relationship with Cyclops and works as the doctor of the X-Mansion. She has the powers of telekinesis and telepathy.

- Bruce Davison as Senator Robert Kelly: An anti-mutant politician that supports a Mutant Registration Act and wishes to ban mutant children from schools. He is kidnapped by Magneto in a test of his mutation machine, which causes his body to turn into a liquid-like substance.

- James Marsden as Scott Summers / Cyclops: He rescues Wolverine and Rogue from a truck explosion, taking them to safety to the X-Mansion where they live. He is the second leader of the X-Men behind Xavier, and is the team's field leader when they are out on missions as well as an instructor at the Institute. He is in love with Jean Grey and has a relationship with her. He produces a strong red beam of force from his eyes, which is only held in check by specialized ruby-quartz goggles and sunglasses.

- Halle Berry as Ororo Munroe / Storm: She works as a teacher at the X-Mansion and has the ability to manipulate the weather. Ororo has become bitter with other people's hatred for mutants, and while comforting a dying Senator Kelly says that she sometimes hates humans.

- Rebecca Romijn-Stamos as Mystique: Magneto's loyal second-in-command, her mutant ability to alter her shape and mimic any human being is almost secondary to her role as "the perfect soldier". She is an agile fighter, expert martial artist, and seems completely facile with modern technology. It is unknown whether her blue, scaly skin is her normal physical expression or if it is a choice which sets herself apart from "normal" humans.

- Ray Park as Toad: A very agile fighter with a menacing streak and a long, prehensile tongue, who can also spit a slimy substance onto others.

- Tyler Mane as Sabretooth: A ferocious, feline-like fighter who attacks Wolverine and Rogue in Canada before being stopped by Storm and Cyclops. He is a brutal and sadistic henchman of Magneto, and wields claws extending past each finger.

- Shawn Ashmore as Bobby Drake / Iceman: A student at Xavier's School For Gifted Youngsters who takes a liking to Rogue. He can change temperatures to subzero degrees and use the moisture in the air to create ice.

David Hayter, Stan Lee, and Tom DeSanto make cameo appearances. George Buza, the voice of Beast in *X-Men: The Animated Series*, appeared as the truck driver who drops Rogue off at the bar at which Wolverine works.[1] Gambit was considered for one of the students at the X-Mansion. Singer remembered, "We thought about Gambit as the young boy on the basketball field, but the feeling was that if he has the basketball and then releases it and it exploded, [then] people would be like 'What's wrong with those basketballs?'"[2] The success of *X-Men* (alongside *Blade*) started a reemergence for the comic book and superhero film genre.[3] A young Colossus appears sketching a picture in one scene.[2]

Production

Development

Throughout 1989 and 1990, Stan Lee and Chris Claremont were in discussions with James Cameron and Carolco Pictures for an *X-Men* film adaptation. The deal fell apart when Cameron went to work on *Spider-Man*, Carolco went bankrupt, and the film rights reverted to Marvel Studios.[5] In December 1992, Marvel discussed selling the property to Columbia Pictures to no avail.[6] Meanwhile, Avi Arad produced the animated *X-Men* TV series for Fox Kids. 20th Century Fox was impressed by the success of the TV show, and producer Lauren Shuler Donner purchased the film rights for them in 1994.[5] [7]

Andrew Kevin Walker was hired to write the script in early 1994.[8] Walker's draft involved Professor Xavier hiring Wolverine into the X-Men, which consists of Cyclops, Jean Grey, Iceman, Beast, and Angel. The Brotherhood of Mutants, which consisted of Magneto, Sabretooth, Toad, and the Blob, try to conquer New York City, while Henry Peter Gyrich and Bolivar Trask attack the X-Men with three 8 feet (2.4 m) tall Sentinels. The script focused on the rivalry between Wolverine and Cyclops, as well as the latter's self-doubt as a field leader. Part of the backstory invented for Magneto made him the cause of the Chernobyl disaster. The script also featured the X-Copter and the Danger Room. Walker turned in his second draft in June 1994.[9]

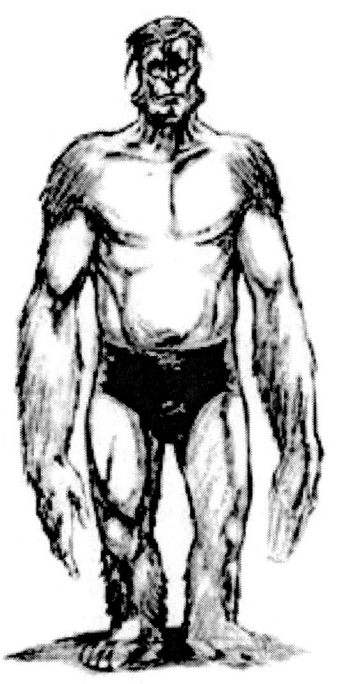

Concept art for Beast (before the character was deleted from subsequent scripts) by Industrial Light & Magic[4]

More scripts were written by John Logan, James Schamus,[1] and Joss Whedon. Whedon claimed his script was rejected because of its "quick-witted pop culture-referencing tone".[10] Only two dialogue exchanges from his draft appeared in the finished film.[11] [12] One of these scripts kept the idea of Magneto turning Manhattan into a "mutant homeland", while another hinged on a romance between Wolverine and Storm.[7] In 1996, Fox approached Michael Chabon to write a script. Chabon's six-page film treatment focused heavily on character development between Wolverine and Jubilee. It also included Professor X, Cyclops, Jean Grey, Nightcrawler, Beast, Iceman, and Storm. Under Chabon's plan, the villains would not have been introduced until the second film.[13]

Robert Rodriguez was approached to direct, but turned down the offer.[14] Bryan Singer was looking to do a science fiction film after the release of *The Usual Suspects*. Fox approached Singer for *Alien Resurrection*, but producer Tom DeSanto felt *X-Men* would be a better opportunity as he was impressed with how Singer directed an ensemble cast in *The Usual Suspects*.[5] Singer turned down the offer, believing that comic books were unintelligent literature. By July 1996, Singer had further turned down the film another two times,[7] and finally accepted after reading the comics and watching the animated series.[5] The themes of prejudice in the comic resonated with Singer.[1]

By December 1996, Singer was in the director's position, while Ed Solomon was hired to write the script in April 1997, and Singer went to film *Apt Pupil*. Fox then announced a Christmas 1998 release date.[15] [16] In late 1997, the budget was projected at $60 million.[2] In late 1998, Singer and DeSanto sent a treatment to Fox, which they believed was "perfect" because it took "seriously" the themes and the comparisons between Xavier and Magneto and Martin Luther King and Malcolm X, unlike the other scripts.[1] They made Rogue an important character because Singer recognized that her mutation, which renders her unable to touch anyone, was the most symbolic of alienation. Singer merged attributes of Kitty Pryde and Jubilee into the film's depiction of Rogue. Magneto's plot to mutate the world leaders into accepting his people is reminiscent of how Constantine I's conversion to Christianity ended the persecution of early Christians in the Roman Empire; the analogy was emphasized in a deleted scene in which Storm teaches history. Senator Kelly's claim that he has a list of mutants living in the United States recalls Joseph McCarthy's similar claim regarding communists.[1]

Fox, who had projected the budget at $75 million, rejected the treatment, which they estimated it would have cost $5 million more. Beast, Nightcrawler, Pyro, and the Danger Room had to be deleted before the studio greenlighted X-Men.[7] [17] Fox head Thomas Rothman argued that this would enhance the story,[7] and Singer concurred that removing the Danger Room allowed him to focus on other scenes he preferred. Elements of Beast, particularly his medical expertise, were transferred to Jean Grey.[1] Singer and DeSanto brought Christopher McQuarrie from *The Usual Suspects*, and together did another rewrite.[18] [19] David Hayter simultaneously rewrote the screenplay, receiving solo screenplay credit from the Writers Guild of America, while Singer and DeSanto were given story credit.[7] The WGA offered McQuarrie a credit, but he voluntarily took his name off when the final version was more in line with Hayter's script than his.[20]

Casting

Russell Crowe was Singer's first choice to play Wolverine. After Crowe turned the role down due to salary demands,[1] a number of actors offered their services for the role before Singer cast Dougray Scott. Part of Scott's contract included a sequel, but Scott backed out due to scheduling conflicts with *Mission: Impossible II* in early October 1999.[21] [22] [23] Hugh Jackman, who was an unknown actor at the time, was cast three weeks into filming.[24] Keanu Reeves also expressed interest in the role.[25]

Producer Richard Donner first suggested to Patrick Stewart that he play Xavier while filming 1997's *Conspiracy Theory*.[1] James Caviezel was originally cast as Cyclops, but backed out due to scheduling conflicts with *Frequency*.[26] James Marsden was unfamiliar with his character, but soon became accustomed after reading various comic books. Marsden modeled his performance similar to a Boy Scout.[27] Eric Mabius expressed interest for the role of Cyclops. Angela Bassett was approached to portray Storm in late 1997,[2] as was Janet Jackson.[28] Anna Paquin dropped out of the lead role in *Tart* in favor of *X-Men*.[29] Terence Stamp was considered for a part.[30] Thomas Jane turned down a role.[31]

Filming

The original start date was mid-1999,[32] with the release date set for Christmas 2000, but Fox moved *X-Men* to June. Steven Spielberg had been scheduled to film *Minority Report* for release in June 2000, but he had chosen to film *A.I. Artificial Intelligence*, and Fox needed a film to fill the void.[33] This meant that Singer had to finish *X-Men* six months ahead of schedule, although filming had been pushed back.[34] The release date was then moved to July 14.[35]

Filming took place from September 22, 1999 to March 3, 2000 in Toronto and in Hamilton, Ontario.[36] [37] Locations included Central Commerce Collegiate, Distillery District and Canadian Warplane Heritage Museum. Casa Loma, Roy Thomson Hall and Metro Hall were used for X-Mansion interiors, while Parkwood Estate (located in Oshawa, east of Toronto) was chosen for exteriors. For the train station scenes, Toronto Union Station and Hamilton GO Centre were set. Spencer Smith Park (in Burlington, Ontario) doubled for Liberty Island. A scale model was used for the Statue of Liberty.[38]

Design and effects

The filmmakers decided not to replicate the X-Men costumes as seen in the comic book. Stan Lee and Chris Claremont supported this decision. Claremont joked, "you can do that on a drawing, but when you put it on people it's disturbing!"[5] Producer/co-writer Tom DeSanto had been supportive of using the blue and yellow color scheme of the comics,[1] but once he saw tests of them, he declared, "No, that just doesn't work." Despite receiving positive feedback from various associates at Marvel Comics for the black costume design, fans on the internet still had negative emotions when *X-Men* was filming.[39] To acknowledge the fan complaints, Singer added Cyclops' line "What would you prefer, yellow spandex?" – when Wolverine complains about wearing their uniforms – during filming. Singer noted that durable black leather made more sense for the X-Men to wear as protective clothing.[1]

Wolverine's claws required a full silicone cast of Hugh Jackman's arm, and 700 versions for Jackman and his stunt doubles.[40] It took nine hours to apply Rebecca Romijn's prosthetic makeup.[41] She could not drink wine, use skin creams, or fly the day before filming, because it could have caused her body chemistry to change slightly, causing the 110 prosthetics applied to her skin fall off.[7] Between takes, the makeup department kept Romijn isolated in a windowless room to ensure secrecy. Romijn reflected, "I had almost no contact with the rest of the cast; it was like I was making a different movie from everyone else. It was hell."[7]

In the late 1990s, computer-generated imagery was becoming more commonly used. Singer visited the sets of *Star Wars Episode I: The Phantom Menace* and *Titanic* to understand practical and digital effects.[2] Filming had started without a special effects company hired. Digital Domain, Cinesite, Kleiser-Walczak Construction, Hammerhead Production, Matte World Digital, CORE and POP were all hired in December 1999.[42] Visual effects supervisor Mike Fink admitted to have been dissatisfied with his work on *X-Men* in 2003, despite nearly being nominated for an Academy Award.[43]

Digital Domain's technical director Sean C. Cunningham and lead compositor Claas Henke morphed Bruce Davison into a liquid figure for Kelly's mutation scene. Cunningham said, "There were many digital layers: water without refraction, water with murkiness, skin with and without highlights, skin with goo in it. When rendered together, it took 39 hours per frame."[44] They considered showing Kelly's internal organs during the transformation, "but that seemed too gruesome", according to Cunningham.[44]

Music

Singer approached John Williams to compose the film score, but Williams turned down the offer because of scheduling conflicts.[45] John Ottman was originally set as composer.[46] Michael Kamen was eventually hired.

Release

Promotion and gross

On June 1, 2000, Marvel published a comic book prequel to *X-Men*, entitled *X-Men: Beginnings*, revealing the backstories of Magneto, Rogue and Wolverine.[47] There was also a comic book adaptation based on the film.[48] Marvel Studios was depending on *X-Men*'s success to ignite other franchise properties (*Spider-Man*, *Fantastic Four*, *Hulk* and *Daredevil*).[49] *X-Men* was released in 3,025 theaters in North America on July 14, 2000, earning $54,471,475 in its opening weekend. The film eventually grossed $157,299,717 and made $139,039,810 in other countries, coming to a worldwide total of $296,339,527.[50] *X-Men* was the ninth highest-grossing film of 2000.[51] The film made over $50 million in home video sales.[2]

Reception

Based on 152 reviews collected by Rotten Tomatoes, 82% were positive, with the consensus that the "story [is] faithful to the comic books and, while the movie may be too Wolverine-centered, it packs a freaky punch that is sure to excite the average summer moviegoer".[52] 59% of 32 selected popular reviewers gave it positive reviews.[53] By comparison Metacritic collected an average score of 64/100 from 33 reviews.[54]

Kenneth Turan found "so much is happening you feel the immediate need of a sequel just as a reward for absorbing it all. While *X-Men* doesn't take your breath away wire-to-wire the way *The Matrix* did, it's an accomplished piece of work with considerable pulp watchability to it."[55] ReelReviews.net's James Berardinelli, an *X-Men* comic book fan, believed, "the film is effectively paced with a good balance of exposition, character development, and special effects-enhanced action. Neither the plot nor the character relationships are difficult to follow, and the movie avoids the trap of spending too much time explaining things that don't need to be explained. X-Men fandom is likely to be divided over whether the picture is a success or a failure".[56] Desson Thomson of *The Washington Post* commented, "[T]he movie's enjoyable on the surface, but I suspect many people, even die-hards, will be less enthusiastic about what lies, or doesn't, underneath".[57]

Roger Ebert of the *Chicago Sun-Times* said he "started out liking this movie, while waiting for something really interesting to happen. When nothing did, I still didn't dislike it; I assume the X-Men will further develop their personalities if there is a sequel, and maybe find time to get involved in a story. No doubt fans of the comics will understand subtle allusions and fine points of behavior; they should linger in the lobby after each screening to answer questions."[58] Peter Travers of *Rolling Stone* noted, "Since it's Wolverine's movie, any X-Men or Women who don't hinge directly on his story get short shrift. As Storm, Halle Berry can do neat tricks with weather, but her role is gone with the wind. It sucks that Stewart and McKellen, two superb actors, are underused."[59]

Awards

The film was nominated the Hugo Award for Best Dramatic Presentation, but lost to *Crouching Tiger, Hidden Dragon*.[60] *X-Men* was successful at the Saturn Awards. It won categories for Best Science Fiction Film, direction (Singer), writing, costume design, Best Actor (Hugh Jackman) and Supporting Actress (Rebecca Romijn). Nominations included Performance by a Younger Actor (Anna Paquin), Supporting Actor (Patrick Stewart), Special Effects and Make-up.[61] *Empire* readers voted Singer Best Director.[1]

References

[1] Hughes, David (2003). *Comic Book Movies*. Virgin Books. pp. 177–188. ISBN 0-7535-0767-6.

[2] "X-Men Archive" (http://www.comics2film.com/XMen.shtml). Comics2Film. . Retrieved 2008-08-09.

[3] Robert Levine (2004-06-27). "Does Whatever a Spider (and a C.E.O.) Can". *The New York Times* (The New York Times Company).

[4] Michael Dougherty, Dan Harris, David Hayter, Lauren Shuler Donner, Ralph Winter, X2 audio commentary, 2003, 20th Century Fox

[5] Stan Lee, Chris Claremont, Bryan Singer, Lauren Shuler Donner, Tom DeSanto, Avi Arad, The Secret Origin of The *X-Men*, 2000, 20th Century Fox

[6] "Marvel characters holding attraction for filmmakers" (http://www.variety.com/article/VR101955). *Variety*. 1992-12-09. . Retrieved 2008-08-09.

[7] Jeff Jensen (2000-07-21). "Generating X" (http://www.ew.com/ew/article/0,,276737,00.html). *Entertainment Weekly*. . Retrieved 2008-08-09.

[8] Steve Daly (1995-09-29). "Deadly Done Right" (http://www.ew.com/ew/article/0,,298924,00.html). *Entertainment Weekly*. . Retrieved 2007-05-22.

[9] Andrew Kevin Walker (1994-06-07). "X-Men First Draft" (http://www.dailyscript.com/scripts/x-men_walker3.html). Simplyscripts. . Retrieved 2007-07-13.

[10] Craig Seymour (2000-05-10). "X-Man Out" (http://www.ew.com/ew/article/0,,85186,00.html). *Entertainment Weekly*. . Retrieved 2007-05-22.

[11] Nazzaro, Joe (2002). *Writing Science Fiction and Fantasy Television*. Titan Books. ISBN 1840233834.

[12] Tasha Robinson (2001-09-05). "Interview - Joss Whedon" (http://www.avclub.com/articles/joss-whedon,13730/). *The A.V. Club*. The Onion. . Retrieved 2009-11-21.

[13] Kim Voynar (2006-07-09). "X-Men and Fantastic Four: What Would Chabon Have Written?" (http://www.cinematical.com/2006/07/09/x-men-and-fantastic-four-what-would-chabon-have-written/). *Cinematical*. . Retrieved 2007-09-23.

[14] "The Total Film Interview-Robert Rodriguez" (http://www.totalfilm.com/features/the_total_film_interview_-_robert_rodriguez). *Total Film*. 2003-10-01. . Retrieved 2007-10-07.

[15] Michael Fleming (1997-04-14). "A Mania For Marvel" (http://www.variety.com/article/VR1117434784). *Variety* . Retrieved 2008-03-25.

[16] Anita M. Busch (1996-12-10). "Singer set to direct Fox's *Men*" (http://www.variety.com/vstory/VR1117466461.html). *Variety*. . Retrieved 2008-03-25.

[17] Dan Cox (1998-07-29). "Col inks Solomon, Lynn" (http://www.variety.com/article/VR1117478916.html?categoryid=13&cs=1). *Variety*. . Retrieved 2008-03-25.

[18] Ed Solomon, Chris McQuarrie, Tom DeSanto, and Bryan Singer (1999-02-24). "February 1999 X-Men script" (http://www.scifiscripts.com/scripts/xmenscript.txt). Sci-Fi Scripts. . Retrieved 2007-07-01.

[19] Chris Petrikin (1999-01-20). "Rice gets Fox promotion" (http://www.variety.com/article/VR1117490409.html?categoryid=18&cs=1). *Variety*. . Retrieved 2008-03-25.

[20] Borys Kit (2009-08-13). "McQuarrie to pen 'Wolverine' sequel" (http://www.hollywoodreporter.com/hr/content_display/film/news/ e3i367bfce562b7ee624637405023e9228f). *The Hollywood Reporter*. . Retrieved 2009-08-13.

[21] Michael Fleming (1999-05-27). "Wahlberg a headbanger?; *X-Men* gets man" (http://www.variety.com/article/VR1117502566. html?categoryid=3&cs=1). *Variety*. . Retrieved 2008-03-25.

[22] Michael Fleming (1999-06-15). "*X* marks the Scott for Singer-helmed Fox pic" (http://www.variety.com/article/VR1117503085. html?categoryid=3&cs=1). *Variety*. . Retrieved 2008-03-25.

[23] Michael Fleming (1999-10-07). "NL scores Demme's *Blow*" (http://www.variety.com/article/VR1117756399). *Variety*. . Retrieved 2008-08-09.

[24] Chris Petrikin (1999-10-11). "Aussie Jackman jumps into Singer's *X-Men* pic" (http://www.variety.com/article/VR1117756476). *Variety*. . Retrieved 2008-08-09.

[25] Liane Bornin (1999-03-25). "Comic Relief" (http://www.ew.com/ew/article/0,,84258,00.html). *Entertainment Weekly*. . Retrieved 2007-09-23.

[26] Jeff Otto (2004-10-14). "IGN Interviews Jim Caviezel" (http://movies.ign.com/articles/556/556968p1.html). *IGN*. . Retrieved 2008-08-08.

[27] Scott Holleran (2006-06-02). "Close-Up: *X-Men*'s James Marsden" (http://boxofficemojo.com/features/?id=2082&p=.htm). *Box Office Mojo*. . Retrieved 2008-08-09.

[28] Janet Jackson (2008-02-22). "Janet Jackson, personal choice as 'Storm'" (http://www.youtube.com/watch?v=5rtEl-iuTKs). *Total Request Live*. . Retrieved 2009-03-22.

[29] Vanessa Torres (1999-10-18). "Swain signs to top *Tart* for Interlight" (http://www.variety.com/article/VR1117756727). *Variety*. . Retrieved 2008-08-09.

[30] Eric Vespe (2008-12-11). "Bryan Singer and Quint talk Nazis, Tom Cruise, Terence Stamp, VALKYRIE plus an update on SUPERMAN!!!" (http://www.aintitcool.com/node/39420). *Ain't It Cool News*. .

[31] Sean Cunningham (2004-04-04). "Capital Punishment: The Punisher's Tom Jane tells Slasherama about his "balls-to-the-wall, punk rock action movie"..." (http://www.slasherama.com/features/punisher.HTML). *Slasherama*. . Retrieved 2008-12-14.

[32] Chris Petrikin (1999-02-09). "Marvel, Fox pact for pix" (http://www.variety.com/article/VR1117491127.html?categoryid=13&cs=1). *Variety*. . Retrieved 2008-03-25.

[33] Chris Petrikin (1999-08-19). "Fox shifts actioner *X-Men* to June" (http://www.variety.com/article/VR1117750560.html?categoryid=13& cs=1). *Variety*. . Retrieved 2008-03-25.

[34] Josh Walk (1999-08-19). "Getting the 'Shaft'" (http://www.ew.com/ew/article/0,,84602,00.html). *Entertainment Weekly*. . Retrieved 2007-05-22.

[35] Chris Petrikin (1999-09-16). "Fox shuffles *X-Men* and *Anna*" (http://www.variety.com/article/VR1117755724). *Variety*. . Retrieved 2008-08-09.

[36] Greg Dean Schmitz. "Greg's Preview - X-Men" (http://web.archive.org/web/20070821124442/http://movies.yahoo.com/movie/ preview/1808406650). Yahoo!. Archived from the original (http://movies.yahoo.com/movie/preview/1808406650) on 2007-08-21. . Retrieved 2008-08-09.

[37] "X-Men filming locations: Hamilton, Ontario" (http://www.movie-locations.com/movies/x/xmen.html). Movie Locations. . Retrieved 2008-08-09.

[38] Scott Chitwood (2000-02-10). "X-Mens Sabretooth Scares Crap out of Kid, Toronto Set Visit, Wolvie Love Triangle, New Pics, & More" (http://movies.ign.com/articles/034/034940p1.html). *IGN*. . Retrieved 2008-08-10.

[39] Scott Chitwood (2000-02-10). "DeSanto talks about X-Men costumes" (http://movies.ign.com/articles/034/034827p1.html). *IGN*. . Retrieved 2008-08-10.

[40] Kris Abel (2006-10-26). "Making Wolverine's Claws" (http://krisabel.ctv.ca/blog/_archives/2006/10/26/2450347.html). *CTV*. . Retrieved 2006-10-26.

[41] Rob Worley (2003-04-21). "Bryan Singer's Mutant Agenda" (http://www.comicbookresources.com/news/newsitem.cgi?id=2135). Comic Book Resources. . Retrieved 2008-03-09.

[42] Marc Graser (1999-12-08). "Seven f/x houses will share *X-Men* duties" (http://www.variety.com/article/VR1117758743). *Variety*. . Retrieved 2008-08-09.

[43] *FX2* Visual Effects, 2003, 20th Century Fox

[44] Piers Bizony (2001). *Digital Domain: The Leading Edge of Visual Effects*. Billboard Books. p. 143. ISBN 0-8230-7928-7.

[45] Bill Ramey (2006-02-12). "Superman-on-Film" (http://www.batman-on-film.com/supermanonfilm/ article_singer_routh_wondercon2006.html). Batman-on-Film. . Retrieved 2007-05-22.

[46] Marc Graser (1999-06-21). "Ottman adds helming other duties" (http://www.variety.com/article/VR1117503313.html?categoryid=13& cs=1). *Variety*. . Retrieved 2008-03-25.

[47] "X-Men: Beginnings (Paperback)" (http://www.amazon.com/X-Men-Beginnings-Marvel-Comics/dp/0785107509). Amazon.com. . Retrieved 2008-02-09.

[48] "X-Men: The Movie (Paperback)" (http://www.amazon.com/X-Men-Movie-Marvel-Comics/dp/0785107495/ref=pd_sim_b_title_2). Amazon.com. . Retrieved 2008-02-09.

[49] Lew Irwin (2000-05-09). "Will The Movies Rescue Spidey et al.?" (http://www.imdb.com/news/ni0098691/). *Internet Movie Database*. . Retrieved 2008-08-09.

[50] "X-Men" (http://boxofficemojo.com/movies/?id=xmen.htm). Box Office Mojo. . Retrieved 2008-08-07.

[51] "2000 Worldwide Grosses" (http://boxofficemojo.com/yearly/chart/?view2=worldwide&yr=2000&p=.htm). Box Office Mojo. . Retrieved 2008-08-07.

[52] "X-Men" (http://www.rottentomatoes.com/m/xmen/). Rotten Tomatoes. . Retrieved 2008-08-08.

[53] "X-Men: Top Critics" (http://www.rottentomatoes.com/m/xmen/?critic=creamcrop). Rotten Tomatoes. . Retrieved 2008-08-08.

[54] "X-Men (2000): Reviews" (http://www.metacritic.com/video/titles/xmen?q=X-Men). Metacritic. . Retrieved 2008-08-08.

[55] Kenneth Turan (2000-07-14). "Gen-X" (http://www.calendarlive.com/movies/reviews/cl-movie000713-5,0,5945193.story). *Los Angeles Times*. . Retrieved 2008-08-08.

[56] "X-Men" (http://www.reelviews.net/php_review_template.php?identifier=760). James Berardinelli. . Retrieved 2008-08-08.

[57] Desson Thomson (2000-07-14). "*X-Men*: Tasty but Not Filling" (http://www.washingtonpost.com/wp-srv/entertainment/movies/reviews/xmenhowe.htm). *The Washington Post*. . Retrieved 2008-08-08.

[58] "X-Men" (http://rogerebert.suntimes.com/apps/pbcs.dll/article?AID=/20000714/REVIEWS/7140304/1023). Roger Ebert. . Retrieved 2008-08-08.

[59] Peter Travers (2000-12-10). "*X-Men*" (http://www.rollingstone.com/reviews/movie/5949101/review/5949102/xmen). *Rolling Stone*. . Retrieved 2008-08-08.

[60] "Hugo Awards: 2001" (http://www.imdb.com/Sections/Awards/Hugo_Awards/2001). Internet Movie Database. . Retrieved 2008-08-09.

[61] "Saturn Awards: 2001" (http://www.imdb.com/Sections/Awards/Academy_of_Science_Fiction_Fantasy_And_Horror_Films_USA/20011). Internet Movie Database. . Retrieved 2008-08-09.

External links

- *X-Men* (http://www.imdb.com/title/tt0120903/) at the Internet Movie Database
- *X-Men* (http://www.allmovie.com/work/187123) at Allmovie
- *X-Men* (http://www.rottentomatoes.com/m/xmen/) at Rotten Tomatoes
- *X-Men* (http://www.metacritic.com/film/titles/xmen) at Metacritic
- *X-Men* (http://www.boxofficemojo.com/movies/?id=xmen.htm) at Box Office Mojo
- X-Men on Marvel.com (http://marvel.com/movies/X-Men)

Kate & Leopold

Kate & Leopold	
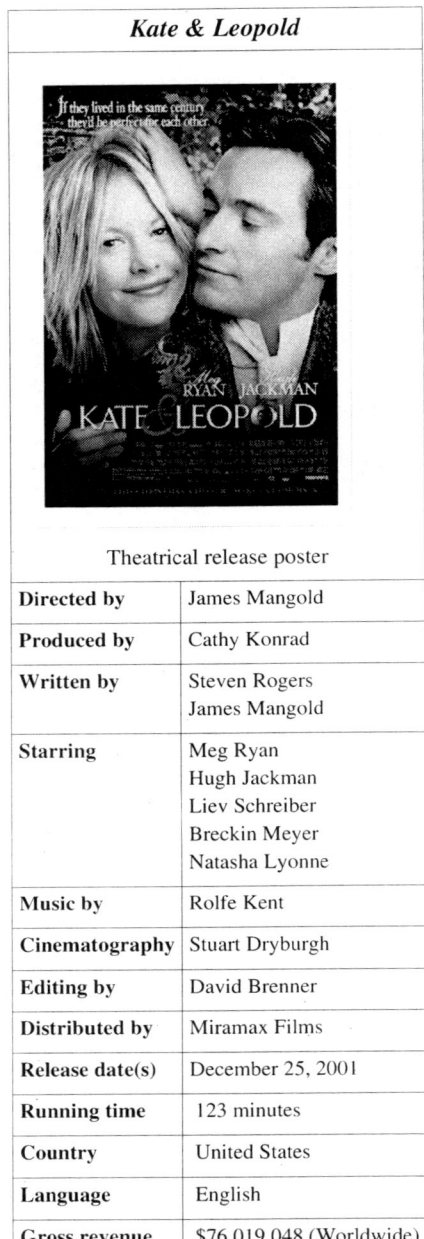	
Theatrical release poster	
Directed by	James Mangold
Produced by	Cathy Konrad
Written by	Steven Rogers James Mangold
Starring	Meg Ryan Hugh Jackman Liev Schreiber Breckin Meyer Natasha Lyonne
Music by	Rolfe Kent
Cinematography	Stuart Dryburgh
Editing by	David Brenner
Distributed by	Miramax Films
Release date(s)	December 25, 2001
Running time	123 minutes
Country	United States
Language	English
Gross revenue	$76,019,048 (Worldwide)

Kate & Leopold is a 2001 romantic comedy film that tells a story of a duke who travels through time from New York in 1876 to the present and falls in love with a career woman in the modern New York.

The film is directed by James Mangold and stars Meg Ryan, Hugh Jackman and Liev Schreiber. The DVD edition contains two versions of the film: one, the original theatrical release, runs for 118 minutes while the director's cut version runs for 122. One scene in the director's cut shows Ryan's character in a test screening for a new film and also features a cameo by Mangold.

Plot

In 1876, Leopold Alexis Elijah Walker Thomas Gareth Mountbatten, Duke of Albany, is a stifled dreamer. Strict Uncle Millard (Paxton Whitehead) has no patience for Leopold's disrespect for the monarchy, chastising him and telling him he must marry a rich American, as the Mountbatten family finances are depleted. His uncle has told him that on his "thirtieth birthday he had become a blemish to the family name".

The Duke finds Stuart Besser (Liev Schreiber), an amateur physicist (and descendant of Leopold, according to deleted scenes) perusing his schematic diagrams and taking photographs of them. He had seen him earlier at Roebling's speech about the Brooklyn Bridge. Leopold follows Stuart and tries to save him from what he thinks is a suicide, falling after him into the portal that brought the man there in the first place.

Leopold awakens in 21st century New York. He is at first confused and thinks that he has been kidnapped. Stuart says that he has created formulae to forecast portals in the temporal universe and that Leopold must stay inside his apartment until the portal opens again a week later. As Stuart takes his dog out, he is injured by falling into the elevator shaft, and is eventually institutionalized for speaking about his scientific discovery. (Apparently, Leopold's unintentional time travel to the 21st century has caused a disruption of all elevators.)

Leopold is intrigued by the cynical and ambitious Kate McKay (Meg Ryan), Stuart's ex-girlfriend, who comes to the apartment for her Palm Pilot stylus. He observes that she is a "career woman" and that her field, market research, is a fine avocation for a woman and states that he once dated a librarian from Sussex. Kate dismisses him and demands that he take Stuart's dog for a walk. Leopold is overwhelmed to see that Roebling's bridge is still standing. Back at the apartment, he befriends Charlie (Breckin Meyer), Kate's brother and an actor between gigs, who believes him to be an actor as well, steadfast to his character.

Kate and Leopold become romantically involved, as they dine and tour New York.

When shooting begins on the commercial in which Leopold has agreed to act, he finds the product, diet margarine, disgusting. He cannot understand how Kate would have him endorse a flawed item without qualms, and declares that "when someone is involved in something entirely without merit, one withdraws". Echoing his uncle, Kate says that sometimes one has to do things they don't want to. He chides her about integrity. She retorts, "I don't have time for pious speeches from two hundred year old men who have not worked a day in their life". Their dalliance seems at an end.

Stuart escapes from the mental hospital, and while Kate is accepting her promotion at a company banquet, he and Charlie are racing to meet her. Moments before she goes on stage, they arrive and produce pictures from Stuart's camera that show her in 1876. Stuart says that he had thought he disrupted the spacetime continuum, but actually "the whole thing is a beautiful 4-D pretzel of kismetic inevitability".

Kate chooses a life with Leopold over her career, and the three of them escape to the Brooklyn Bridge. There, catching the portal before it closes, Kate vanishes into 1876 where Leopold is himself about to announce Miss Tree as his bride. As he opens his mouth to speak, he sees Kate and announces *her* name, Kate McKay, as his bride.

In the closing scene, they kiss and the camera is drawn outward showing a wall clock depicting 12:15.

Cast

- Meg Ryan as Kate McKay
- Hugh Jackman as Leopold Alexis Elijah Walker Thomas Gareth Mountbatten
- Liev Schreiber as Stuart Besser
- Breckin Meyer as Charlie McKay
- Natasha Lyonne as Darci
- Bradley Whitford as J. J. Camden
- Paxton Whitehead as Millard Mountbatten
- Spalding Gray as Dr. Geisler
- Josh Stamberg as Bob
- Matthew Sussman as Phil
- Charlotte Ayanna as Patrice
- Philip Bosco as Otis
- Cole Hawkins as Hector
- Kristen Schaal as Miss Tree

Film score

1. A Clock in New York
2. I Want Him Resplendent
3. Leopold Chases Stuart to Brooklyn
4. That Was Your Best?
5. Let's Go!
6. Leopold Sees the Completed Bridge
7. You Did So Great (Kate's Theme)
8. Galloping
9. Dearest Kate...
10. Prolixin/Leopold and Charlie Buy Flowers
11. Charlie Wins Patrice, Leopold Wins Kate
12. Secret Drawer
13. Time for Bed
14. Charlie Realises Leopold Was For Real — 1876
15. Kate Goes to the Awards
16. Kate Sees the Pictures — "I have to Go"
17. You Have to Cross the Girder
18. Back in 1876 — Waltz
19. Back Where I Belong (song — Jula Bell)
20. Until... (song — Sting)

Award and nominations

Hugh Jackman was nominated in 2001 for the Golden Globe Award for Best Actor - Motion Picture Musical or Comedy. The film won the Golden Globe Award for Best Song for the song "Until", written and performed by Sting. The same song was also nominated for the Academy Award for Best Song.[1]

External links

[1] Awards for Kate & Leopold (http://www.imdb.com/title/tt0035423/awards)

- *Kate & Leopold* (http://www.imdb.com/title/tt0035423/) at the Internet Movie Database
- *Kate & Leopold* (http://www.rottentomatoes.com/m/kate_and_leopold/) at Rotten Tomatoes
- *Kate & Leopold* (http://www.currentfilm.com/dvdreviews3/kateleopolddvd.html) at currentfilm.com DVD reviews

Someone Like You (film)

Someone Like You	
Theatrical release poster	
Directed by	Tony Goldwyn
Produced by	Lynda Obst
Written by	Elizabeth Chandler Laura Zigman (novel)
Starring	Ashley Judd Greg Kinnear Hugh Jackman Marisa Tomei
Cinematography	Anthony B. Richmond
Distributed by	20th Century Fox
Release date(s)	March 30, 2001
Running time	97 minutes
Country	United States
Language	English
Budget	$23 million
Gross revenue	$27,338,033 (USA)

Someone Like You is a 2001 romantic comedy film, based on Laura Zigman's novel *Animal Husbandry* which tells a story of a heartbroken woman who is looking for the reason she was dumped. The film stars Ashley Judd, Greg Kinnear, Hugh Jackman and Marisa Tomei and was directed by Tony Goldwyn. The running time is 97 minutes.

Plot

The movie starts with a voiceover of Jane Goodale (Ashley Judd) over the images of a scientific experiment with a bull and a herd of cows, apparently the bull never mounts a cow twice, not even if her scent is changed. He prefers a new cow. Jane tells us that until recently she believed that men are all like the bull, but to understand what happened we have to go back in time.

Jane is a production assistant with a talk show that has recently been syndicated, which means that the host Diane Roberts (played by Ellen Barkin) who wants to be the best, is always looking for the ungettable guests, like Fidel Castro. Eddie Alden (Hugh Jackman) is the producer of the talk show and is a womaniser, much to the dismay of Jane and she comments on his actions with amicable critique.

Eddie is looking for a roommate, but his messages on the bulletin board are sabotaged by disgruntled exes. He wonders whether Jane would like to move in, but she turns him down with a vengeance. Then they meet the new producer of the show Ray Brown (Greg Kinnear), and Jane is immediately smitten. She tells her friend Liz (Marisa Tomei) and discuss her bad luck with men. Meanwhile her sister is trying to get pregnant with a fertility program.

Ray calls Jane and they spend an evening together and end up kissing. The next morning she calls Liz and is ecstatic. Liz gives her some advice as to how to deal with Ray and his girlfriend Dee (with whom he has trouble). Ray and Jane seem to be very much in love. The relationship evolves, and they decide to move in together. Jane puts in her notice; he goes to tell his girlfriend that it is over, but doesn't tell her about the new woman in his life.

Ray starts to get distant while Jane is packing to move over, and over dinner he breaks it off, leaving Jane in tears.

The next morning in the office Jane takes her revenge by announcing to move in with Eddie. She learns to deal with the many women in Eddie's life, they bond over scotch and old Chinese food. She reads an article about the old cow syndrome and starts researching for her theory of men. Liz works at a magazine for men and needs a columnist and persuades Jane to write a column about her theory, under a pen name Dr. Marie Charles.

The column that deals with the insecurity and dishonesty of men is a big hit, everybody wants to meet Dr. Charles, so does Diane. At a Christmas party Ray tells her he misses her and asks her out for New Year's Eve, but he doesn't show. When Jane shows up at a party looking for Eddie at midnight she can't find him and leaves in tears. Eddie tries to go after her but can't find her.

Back at the office, Ray tries to apologize, but Diane interrupts wearing a shirt Jane bought for Ray. Jane realizes she is "Dee," and Ray is back with her.

A board meeting is going to start and Eddie makes sure Jane isn't crying going in, but Jane is distracted so he covers for her. When Ray shows emotion over a Gérard Depardieu movie, Jane spills her guts over his inability to show empathy for her broken heart.

Diane, unaware of Jane's relationship with Ray, gives her advice on how to win her boyfriend back, telling her how she got hers back.

At a bar Liz follows Dr. Charles advice and is not going to fall for the same kind of guy anymore. Jane and Eddie get into a fight over the advice of Dr. Charles, back home she tells him she has to believe the theory because otherwise she is afraid that men don't leave women - they leave her. Eddie comforts her by saying Ray is not the last man she'll ever love, and they fall asleep together, the next morning Eddie wakes up happy and comfortable, Jane freaks out. Eddie tells her not to analyze this too. He is happy that he slept the whole night with her without it leading to sex. She tells Eddie he will show his true colours and will hurt her some time soon, Eddie tells her it is not about him, but it is her attitude that is the problem. Jane gets a call and it is her brother in law telling her that they lost the baby. At the hospital she sees the true love between them and decides to tell Diane that Dr. Charles is going to be on her show.

The interview is meant to be over the telephone, but Jane changes her mind and goes on the stage. She tells the audience that there is no Dr. Charles (we see Eddie leave at this point) and that the theory is ridiculous because she was hurt and needed to blame men for her pain. But not all men are animals, some will be there for you and tell you that Ray isn't the last one you'll ever love. By this time Eddie is long gone.

Jane goes after Eddie and finds him when he is taking a taxi, she gets him out of the taxi and tells him she found new love. He doesn't answer but kisses her with passion, with the dulcet tones of Van Morrison's "Someone Like You" playing in the background.

Cast

- Ashley Judd as Jane Goodale, a television show producer who is looking for love and the problems men have with giving it.
- Greg Kinnear as Ray Brown, the shows hunky executive producer. He dumps Jane right before they were supposed to move in together.
- Hugh Jackman as Eddie Alden, a womanizing coworker of Jane's.
- Marisa Tomei as Liz, Jane's best friend.
- Ellen Barkin as Diane Roberts, the star talent of Jane's show.
- Catherine Dent as Alice, Jane's sister.
- Peter Friedman as Stephen, Alice's husband.

Reception

The film opened at #2 at the North American box office making $10,010,600 USD in its opening weekend, behind *Spy Kids*. Rotten Tomatoes [1] consensus was "A light and predictable, if somewhat shallow, romantic comedy that's easy to sit through because of the charming leads." The score among critics was tallied at 41%.

External links

- Official website [2]
- *Someone Like You* [3] at the Internet Movie Database

References

[1] http://www.rottentomatoes.com/m/1106020-someone_like_you/
[2] http://www.someonelikeyoumovie.com/
[3] http://www.imdb.com/title/tt0244970/

Swordfish (film)

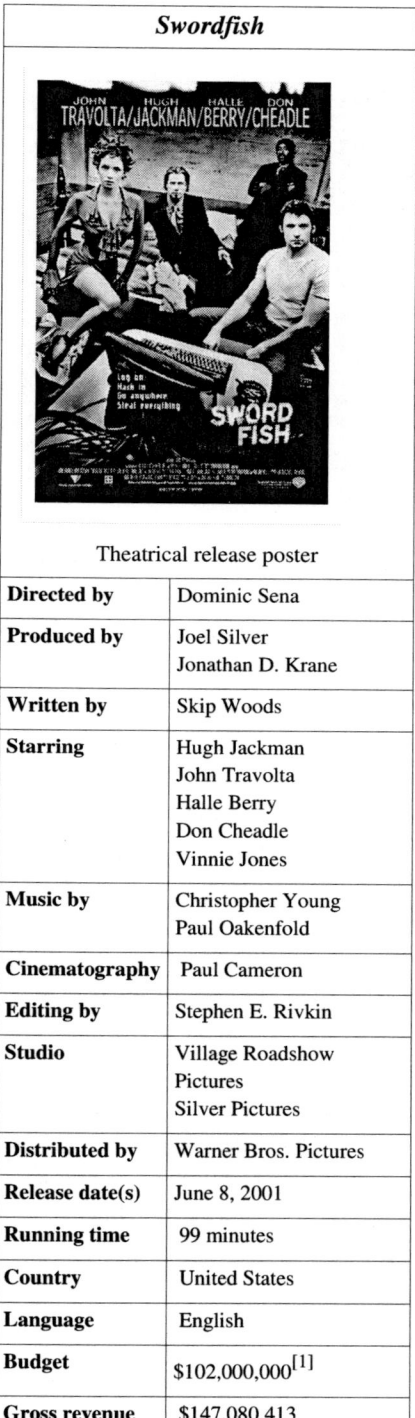

Swordfish	
Theatrical release poster	
Directed by	Dominic Sena
Produced by	Joel Silver Jonathan D. Krane
Written by	Skip Woods
Starring	Hugh Jackman John Travolta Halle Berry Don Cheadle Vinnie Jones
Music by	Christopher Young Paul Oakenfold
Cinematography	Paul Cameron
Editing by	Stephen E. Rivkin
Studio	Village Roadshow Pictures Silver Pictures
Distributed by	Warner Bros. Pictures
Release date(s)	June 8, 2001
Running time	99 minutes
Country	United States
Language	English
Budget	$102,000,000[1]
Gross revenue	$147,080,413

Swordfish is a 2001 crime-thriller film, directed by Dominic Sena and starring John Travolta, Hugh Jackman, Halle Berry, Don Cheadle and Vinnie Jones.

Plot

Stanley Jobson (Hugh Jackman) is an elite hacker who infected the FBI's Carnivore program with a potent computer virus, delaying its deployment by several years. For this, he was arrested by Agent Roberts (Don Cheadle), convicted of computer crimes and spent two years in Leavenworth. A condition of his parole is that he is forbidden from touching, much less using, a computer. His ex-wife, Melissa, has sole custody over their daughter Holly and a restraining order against Stanley from seeing Holly.

While Stanley is at home in rural Texas practicing his golf swing, Ginger Knowles (Halle Berry) shows up to solicit his hacking skills for her boss Gabriel Shear (John Travolta). Stanley is apparently recruited at the last minute as a replacement for Gabriel's first choice, Axl Torvalds, a European hacker of exceptional talent who was arrested by authorities at the airport. Torvalds is later assassinated by Gabriel's men before he can divulge anything about his assignment and who hired him to Agent Roberts. For an initial $100,000, Stanley agrees to meet with Gabriel. He and Ginger fly to Los Angeles and meet Gabriel in a night club. Gabriel pressures Stanley right then and there to hack a government system in 60 seconds while simultaneously being held at gun point by Gabriel's bodyguard and right hand man, Marco (Vinnie Jones) and receiving fellatio from a young woman. Although it was just a test (the gun was not loaded) Stanley succeeded in hacking the system, a feat that Gabriel had not anticipated.

At Gabriel's house he offers Stanley $10 million to write a worm that steals money from a secret government slush fund to the order of $9.5 billion. Gabriel reveals to Stanley that he works for an organization called the Black Cell that was started by J. Edgar Hoover in the 1950s, which is responsible for retaliatory attacks against terrorists who have attacked Americans. It is currently headed by Senator Reisman (Sam Shepard), who discovers that the FBI has caught onto Gabriel and attempts to pull the plug. After Gabriel refuses to terminate his plans, Reisman attempts to have Gabriel killed, which fails. Gabriel tracks the Senator down while he is fly fishing in Bend, Oregon and kills him.

Gabriel proceeds with his plan and raids the local branch of the WORLDBANC. He takes hostages, puts explosives on them and deploys Stanley's worm. After stealing the $9.5 billion he boards the hostages and his crew on a bus out of the bank. Gabriel demands a plane at the local airport (a hostage negotiation cliché) but it was a diversion. An S-64 Aircrane swoops down, lifts the bus and releases it on the rooftop of a skyscraper. From the rooftop, Gabriel seemingly departs with his team in a helicopter, which Stanley shoots down with a rocket-propelled grenade. At the morgue, Stanley and Agent Roberts learn that the body recovered from the helicopter is that of a former Mossad agent named Gabriel Shear, revealing that the fake Gabriel Shear is still alive.

The end of the film shows Ginger and Gabriel in Monte Carlo transferring the $9.5B into other accounts. The final scene shows a yacht being destroyed and a news anchor voice narrating that a suspected terrorist died on that yacht, the third such successful counter-terrorism operation in as many weeks.

Alternate endings

The DVD version contains an alternate ending wherein Ginger is told in the bank that the account is already empty, alluding to the possibility that Stanley has played one final trick on them and taken the money himself. In a companion scene to the alternate ending, Stanley is shown on a trip with his daughter in a brand new RV. While eating at a diner, Stanley is shown transferring many billion dollars to various charities before continuing his trip.

Cast

- John Travolta - Gabriel Shear
- Hugh Jackman - Stanley Jobson
- Halle Berry - Ginger Knowles
- Don Cheadle - Agent J.T. Roberts
- Sam Shepard - Senator James Reisman

- Vinnie Jones - Marco
- Drea de Matteo - Melissa
- Rudolf Martin - Axl Torvalds
- Zach Grenier - Assistant Director Bill Joy
- Camryn Grimes - Holly Jobson
- Angelo Pagan (as Angelo Pagán) - Torres
- Chic Daniel - SWAT Leader
- Kirk B.R. Woller - Axl's Lawyer
- Carmen Argenziano - Agent
- Tim DeKay - Agent
- Laura Lane - Helga

Reception

This film received a great deal of press initially because it featured Halle Berry's first nude scene. She was paid an extra $500,000 on top of her $2 million fee to appear topless in this film. Critics said the scene looked forced, thrown into the film just to garner press, but Berry said she did it just to overcome the fear of appearing nude onscreen (and obviously the extra $500,000 had nothing to do with it.)[2]

Only a quarter of the Rotten Tomatoes critics gave the film a positive review; the website's "Cream of the Crop" reviewers were even less positive.[3] In a review for *The New York Times*, Stephen Holden wrote:[4]

> With its blasé blend of bogus international intrigue and action-for-action's-sake, *Swordfish* suggests a James Bond movie stripped of humor. True, there are a few moments of wit, like the opening sequence. But the dominant tone masquerading as humor is a snide, rancid nihilism devoid of laughs, unless wholesale destruction and gloating stupidity are what tickle your funny bone.

According to *Box Office Mojo*, the film grossed over $147 million in worldwide box office receipts on a production budget of $102 million.[1]

Soundtrack

The soundtrack for *Swordfish* was produced by Paul Oakenfold, under Village Roadshow and Warner Bros. and distributed through London Sire Records, Inc. It contains 15 tracks.

The film's orchestral score was written by Christopher Young with several electronic additions by Paul Oakenfold. Fragments from the score were added to the official soundtrack, but were remixed by Oakenfold. A more complete release was issued as an award promo, which is known for its rarity.[5]

See also

- Swordfish (password) - Origin of the film's title.

References

[1] "SWORDFISH" (http://www.boxofficemojo.com/movies/?id=swordfish.htm). *Box Office Mojo*. .
[2] Kirkland, Bruce. "Halle Berry bares her soul" (http://jam.canoe.ca/Movies/Artists/B/Berry_Halle/2007/03/22/3804325.html). *Jam.canoe.ca*. . Retrieved July 20, 2009.
[3] "Swordfish (2001)" (http://www.rottentomatoes.com/m/swordfish/). *Rotten Tomatoes*. .
[4] "June 2001 Review" (http://movies.nytimes.com/movie/review?res=9E01E7DD1F3FF93BA35755C0A9679C8B63) (Registration required). *The New York Times*. . Retrieved July 20, 2009.
[5] http://www.soundtrack.net/albums/database/?id=5339

External links

- Official website (http://http://www2.warnerbros.com/operationswordfish/)
- *Swordfish* (http://www.imdb.com/title/tt0244244/) at the Internet Movie Database
- *Swordfish* (http://www.allmovie.com/work/244329) at Allmovie
- *Swordfish* (http://www.rottentomatoes.com/m/swordfish/) at Rotten Tomatoes
- *Swordfish* (http://www.boxofficemojo.com/movies/?id=swordfish.htm) at Box Office Mojo
- *Swordfish* (http://www.metacritic.com/film/titles/swordfish) at Metacritic
- Press Release (http://www.ericksonaircrane.com/press/SwordfishWebRelease.html) on helicopter sequence from the Erickson Air-Crane website

X2 (film)

X2	
 International theatrical poster	
Directed by	Bryan Singer
Produced by	Tom DeSanto Avi Arad Ralph Winter Lauren Shuler Donner Stan Lee Bryan Singer
Screenplay by	Michael Dougherty Dan Harris David Hayter
Story by	Bryan Singer David Hayter Zak Penn
Based on	*Uncanny X-Men* by Stan Lee and Jack Kirby
Starring	Hugh Jackman Patrick Stewart Ian McKellen Famke Janssen Brian Cox Alan Cumming Anna Paquin Halle Berry Shawn Ashmore James Marsden
Music by	John Ottman
Cinematography	Newton Thomas Sigel
Editing by	John Ottman Elliot Graham

Studio	20th Century Fox Marvel Entertainment Bad Hat Harry Productions The Donners' Company XF2 Canada Productions XM2 Productions
Distributed by	20th Century Fox
Release date(s)	May 2, 2003
Running time	133 minutes
Language	English
Budget	$110 million
Gross revenue	$407,711,549[1]
Preceded by	*X-Men*
Followed by	*X-Men: The Last Stand*

X2 (often promoted as ***X2: X-Men United***) is a 2003 superhero film based on the fictional characters the X-Men. Directed by Bryan Singer, it is the second film in the *X-Men* film series. It stars an ensemble cast including Hugh Jackman, Patrick Stewart, Ian McKellen, Alan Cumming, Famke Janssen, Anna Paquin, Shawn Ashmore, Aaron Stanford, Brian Cox, Rebecca Romijn, James Marsden, Halle Berry and Kelly Hu. The plot, inspired by the graphic novel *God Loves, Man Kills*, pits the X-Men and their enemies, the Brotherhood, against the genocidal Colonel William Stryker (Brian Cox). He leads an assault on Professor Xavier's school to build his own version of Xavier's mutant-tracking computer Cerebro, in order to destroy every mutant on Earth.

Development phase for *X2* began shortly after *X-Men*. David Hayter and Zak Penn wrote separate scripts, combining what they felt to be the best elements of both scripts into one screenplay. Michael Dougherty and Dan Harris were eventually hired for rewrite work, changing characterizations of Beast, Angel and Lady Deathstrike. Sentinels and the Danger Room were set to appear before being deleted because of budget concerns. Filming began in June 2002 and ended that November. Most of the filming took place at Vancouver Film Studios, the largest soundstage in North America. Production designer Guy Hendrix Dyas adapted similar designs of John Myhre from the previous film. *X2* was released in the United States on May 2, 2003 and became both a critical and financial success, earning eight nominations at the Saturn Awards and grossing approximately $407 million worldwide.

Plot

Nightcrawler, a teleporting mutant, attempts to assassinate the President of the United States in the White House, but he fails and escapes. Wolverine reappears after discovering nothing at Alkali Lake, while Storm and Jean find Nightcrawler with the help of Professor Xavier and Cerebro. Cyclops and the Professor visit Magneto in his plastic prison to see if he had any part in the attack on the president. Reading Magneto's mind, the Professor discovers that a covert government operative, William Stryker, has been extracting information from Magneto. A trap is sprung and Cyclops and the Professor are captured by Stryker and his assistant Yuriko Oyama. A military raid of the X-Mansion begins, with the soldiers sedating every student they find and Wolverine confronts Stryker, who fails to shed any light to his past.

Impersonating Senator Robert Kelly and Yuriko, Mystique gains information about Magneto's prison and provides a means for him to escape. Wolverine, along with Rogue, Iceman and Pyro, head to Iceman's (Bobby Drake's) parents' home in Boston. After a 9-1-1 call the police arrive just as the group is about to leave. The X-Jet arrives to pick them up but is soon attacked by a pair of F-16s. Using Storm's abilities they manage to defeat them and the X-Men team up with Magneto and Mystique. Magneto has learned Stryker orchestrated the attack on the president and has been experimenting on mutants, using a drug injected directly into the back of the neck to control them. Jean reads Nightcrawler's mind and determines that Stryker's base is located at Alkali Lake, inside the dam where he plans to kill the world's mutants by building a second Cerebro.

Through his son, Jason, Stryker gains control over the Professor. His son is able to project powerful visions in the mind, blinding a person to reality and through this the Professor is brainwashed to use Cerebro to find and kill all mutants. Mystique is able to infiltrate Stryker's base and as the X-Men enter by impersonating Wolverine, and Storm and Nightcrawler search for the kidnapped students. Jean, Magneto, and Mystique are attacked by a brainwashed Cyclops while trying to rescue the Professor and in the process cause damage to the generators that keep the dam from collapsing. The force of Jean's telekinetic blast awakens Cyclops from his brainwashing and at the same time Wolverine finds Stryker in an adamantium smelting room along with Lady Deathstrike. Wolverine manages to defeat Deathstrike and then finds Stryker on a landing pad, where Stryker attempts to bargain Wolverine for his life with stories of his past.

While disguised as Stryker, Mystique uses Jason to convince the Professor to kill all humans and Magneto and Mystique use Stryker's helicopter to escape Alkali Lake, chaining Stryker to concrete rubble. Meanwhile, Nightcrawler teleports Storm inside of Cerebro where she creates a snowstorm to free the Professor from his telepathic illusion. The dam bursts but a malfunction aboard the X-Jet prevents it from taking off. As the flood gets stronger, Stryker drowns and Jean leaves the jet and creates a telekinetic wall in order to stop the wave and raises the jet above the flood waters. Jean activates the X-Jet's primary engines, before releasing the torrent of water down on herself.

The X-Men are able to supply the president with files from Stryker's private offices, and the Professor warns him that humans and mutants must work together to build peace or they will destroy each other through war. The film ends with a voice-over by Jean Grey on the process of evolution (a speech originally made by the Professor in the introduction of the first film). The camera floats over Alkali Lake, showing a vague shape of a Phoenix in the lake.

Cast

- Hugh Jackman as Logan / Wolverine: A mutant who has no memory of his life before he was grafted with an indestructible adamantium skeleton. Wolverine is a gruff loner, but is in love with Jean Grey and acts as a father figure to Rogue. He wields three blades that come out of each of his fists, has keen animal-like senses, the ability to heal rapidly from virtually any injury, and is a ruthless and aggressive fighter.
- Sir Patrick Stewart as Professor Charles Xavier: A powerful telepathic mutant confined to a wheelchair who founded a School for "Gifted Youngsters", Xavier is a pacifist who believes humans and mutants can live together in harmony. He uses the Cerebro device, designed by Magneto and himself, to track and locate mutants across the world. A natural genius, Xavier is regarded as an authority on genetic mutation.
- Sir Ian McKellen as Eric Lehnsherr / Magneto: Once Xavier's ally, Magneto now believes mutants are superior to humans. Magneto wields the ability to manipulate metal magnetically, as well as the power to create magnetic fields. He wears a helmet that renders him immune to Xavier's powers and all related telepathic powers. Imprisoned after his scheme in the first film, he is drugged by William Stryker for information over Cerebro, before making his escape and forming an alliance with the X-Men to stop Stryker. He has demonstrated sophisticated knowledge in matters of genetic manipulation and engineering. The character's helmet was slightly redesigned as McKellen found wearing it uncomfortable in *X-Men*.[2]
- Famke Janssen as Dr. Jean Grey: A teacher at Xavier's school and the X-Mansion's doctor, Jean has begun to experience a growth in her telepathy and telekinetic powers since being affected by the radiation from Magneto's machine during the X-Men's battle with him. She is Cyclops' fiancé, even though she is attracted to Wolverine.
- Halle Berry as Ororo Munroe / Storm: A mutant and teacher at Xavier's School who can control the weather with her mind. Storm befriends Nightcrawler. Berry dropped out of Jennifer Lopez's role in *Gigli* to reprise the role.[3]

- James Marsden as Scott Summers / Cyclops: The field leader of the X-Men, and a teacher at Xavier's Institute, he shoots uncontrollable beams of concussive force from his eyes and wears a visor to control them. He is in a relationship with Jean. Cyclops is taken prisoner by Stryker.
- Rebecca Romijn as Mystique: Magneto's henchwoman, she is a shapeshifter. Mystique is blue, naked and covered in scales, and she acts as a spy. She injects a prison guard with metal, with which Magneto makes his escape, and also sexually tempts Wolverine. Romijn's makeup previously took nine hours to apply, however, the make-up department was able to bring it down to six hours for X2.[4]
- Anna Paquin as Marie / Rogue: A girl who can absorb any person's memories and abilities by touching them. As she cannot control this power, Rogue can easily kill anyone and thus is unable to be close to people.
- Shawn Ashmore as Bobby Drake / Iceman: Rogue's boyfriend, he can freeze objects and create ice. His family is unaware that he is a mutant and simply believe he is at a boarding school. After returning home, Bobby reveals to them what he actually is, much to his brother's derision.
- Aaron Stanford as John Allerdyce / Pyro: A friend of Bobby and Rogue, Pyro has anti-social tendencies and has the ability to control (although not create) fire. Magneto tells him that "You are a god amongst insects; never let anyone tell you different." The filmmakers cast Stanford in the role after they were impressed with his performance in *Tadpole*.[5]
- Brian Cox as Colonel William Stryker: A human military scientist who plans a worldwide genocide of mutants using Xavier and Cerebro. Stryker has experimented on mutants in the past, including Wolverine, and uses a serum to control them. Singer opted to cast Cox in the role as he was a fan of his performance as Hannibal Lecter in *Manhunter*.[6]
- Alan Cumming as Kurt Wagner / Nightcrawler: A kindly German mutant with a strong Catholic faith, yet ironically he has the appearance of a blue demon. Nightcrawler was used by Stryker in an assassination attempt on the President of the United States and gives help to the X-Men. He is capable of teleporting himself (and others) instantly from one location to another. On his body are many tattoos, one for every sin. Cumming had always been Singer's choice for the role, but Cumming could not accept the part due to scheduling conflicts.[7] Ethan Embry had been reported to be in contention for the role,[8] but the film labored in development long enough for Cumming to accept the part.[7] Singer also felt comfortable in casting Cumming since he is fluent in the German language.[9] The drawings of Adam Kubert were used as inspiration for Nightcrawler's makeup design,[10] which took four hours to apply.[11] For the scene where Nightcrawler has his shirt off, Cumming went through nine hours.[7] To best pose as Nightcrawler, Cumming studied comic books and illustrations of the character.[11]
- Kelly Hu as Yuriko Oyama / Deathstrike: A female mutant that has a healing ability like Wolverine's, and is controlled by Stryker. She wields long adamantium fingernails. Only her first name is mentioned in dialogue.
- Michael Reid McKay as Jason Stryker / Mutant 143: William Stryker's son. He was sent to Xavier's school in an attempt to "cure" his ability to create illusions. Returning home, Jason tortured his parents until his mother committed suicide. His father lobotomized him and uses a fluid from his brain to control mutants. Xavier's mind is too strong for the fluid, however, and Jason is instead used in order to manipulate him in Stryker's genocidal scheme.

Although the character of Senator Robert Kelly was killed in the first film, Bruce Davison reprised the role for scenes where Mystique uses his persona to infiltrate the government. In other cameos, Katie Stuart appeared as Kitty Pryde, a girl who can walk through walls, Bryce Hodgson as Artie, Kea Wong as Jubilee and Shauna Kain as Siryn, who is able to emit loud screams that alert the students to Stryker's attack. Also in the final scene with Xavier, a girl is seen dressed in a Native American style jacket, as well as a blond haired boy dressed in blue, played by Layke Anderson. These were confirmed to be Danielle Moonstar and Douglas Ramsey.[5] Daniel Cudmore appeared as Peter Rasputin / Colossus. Cudmore was set to use a Russian accent, but Singer dropped the idea for unknown reasons, and onset rewrites minimized the character's importance to a cameo.[12]

Jubilee, Psylocke and Multiple Man were to have cameos for the scene when Stryker and his troops storm the X-Mansion. Beast, Gambit and Marrow were to have appearances during the Dark Cerebro sequence. Gambit's cameo was actually shot, but the footage was not used in the final cut. Beast's scene was to show Dr. Hank McCoy transforming into his notable blue fur while Marrow was to be seen lying on a ground in New York City.[5] Hank McCoy appears on a television during the scene where Mystique drugs Magneto's prison guard. Michael Dougherty and Dan Harris, the film's writers, cameo in scenes of Wolverine's Weapon X flashbacks as surgeons.[13] Shaquille O'Neal wanted a role in the film but was ignored by the filmmakers.[14]

Development

Writing

The financial and critical success of *X-Men* persuaded 20th Century Fox to commission a sequel instantly. Starting in November 2000,[15] Bryan Singer researched various storylines (one of them being the Legacy Virus) of the *X-Men* comic book series, choosing *God Loves, Man Kills* as the premise.[16] Singer wanted to study, "the human perspective, the kind of blind rage that feeds into warmongering and terrorism,"[17] citing a need for a "human villain".[15] Singer and producer Tom DeSanto envisioned *X2: X-Men United* as the film series' *Empire Strikes Back*, in that the characters are "all split apart, and then dissected, and revelations occur that are significant... the romance comes to fruition and a lot of things happen."[18] Producer Avi Arad announced a planned November 2002 theatrical release date,[19] while David Hayter and Zak Penn were hired to write separate scripts.[20] Hayter and Penn combined what they felt to be the best elements of both scripts into one screenplay.[21] Singer and Hayter worked on another script, finishing in October 2001.[22]

Concept art of the Danger Room before the setpiece was stored due to budgetary concerns

Michael Dougherty and Dan Harris were hired to rewrite Hayter and Penn's script in February 2002,[23] turning down the opportunity to write *Urban Legends: Bloody Mary*.[24] Angel and Beast appeared in early drafts, but were deleted because there were too many characters. Dr. Hank McCoy, however, can be seen on a television interview in one scene. Beast's appearance was to resemble Jim Lee's 1991 artwork of the character in the series *X-Men: Legacy*.[10] Angel was to have been a mutant experiment by William Stryker, transforming into Archangel.[5] A reference to Dougherty's and Harris' efforts of Angel remains in the form of an X-ray on display in one of Stryker's labs.[16] Tyler Mane was to reprise as Sabretooth before the character was deleted.[25] In Hayter's script, the role eventually filled by Lady Deathstrike was Anne Reynolds, a character who appeared in *God Loves, Man Kills* as Stryker's personal assistant/assassin. Singer changed her to Deathstrike, citing a need for "another kick-ass mutant".[15] There was to be more development on Cyclops and Professor X being brainwashed by Stryker. The scenes were shot, but Fox cut them out because of time length and story complications. Hayter was disappointed, feeling that James Marsden deserved more screentime.[5]

Rewrites were commissioned once more, specifically to give Halle Berry more screentime. This was because of her recent popularity in *Monster's Ball*, earning her the Academy Award for Best Actress.[26] A budget cut meant that the Sentinels[16] and the Danger Room were dropped. Guy Hendrix Dyas and a production crew had already constructed the Danger Room set. In the words of Dyas, "The control room [of the danger room] was a large propeller that actually rotated around the room so that you can sit up [in that control room] and travel around the subject who is in the middle of the control room. The idea for the traveling is that if it's a mutant has some kind of mind control powers they can't connect."[11] Dyas and sculptor James Jones merged several Sentinel designs into a final maquette of an almost hollow robot who could compress into a disk shape. Animating the Sentinel would have cost $7 million.[27]

Production

Producer Lauren Shuler Donner had hoped to start filming in March 2002,[20] but production did not begin until June 17, 2002 in Vancouver and ended by November.[28] Over sixty-four sets were used in thirty-eight different locations.[11] The film crew encountered problems when not enough snow was produced in Kananaskis, Alberta. An excessive amount of fake snow was then applied.[29] The idea to have Jean Grey sacrifice herself at the end and to be resurrected in a third installment was highly secretive. Singer did not tell Famke Janssen until midway through filming.[30] Cinematographer Newton Thomas Sigel and two stunt drivers nearly died when filming the scene in which Pyro has a dispute with police officers.[6]

Michael Kamen, composer of *X-Men*, offered his services to compose the film score, but Singer opted for fellow collaborator John Ottman, who also assisted in editing the film.[31] Ottman established a new title theme, as well as themes specifically for Magneto, Jean Grey, Nightcrawler, Mystique and Pyro. Although Ottman tried his best to keep Kamen's basic approach of the previous film, Ottman also found inspiration from *X-Men: The Animated Series*.[32] Minor compositions of Mozart's *Requiem* were used for the opening scene with Nightcrawler at the White House.[33]

Design and effects

Cinematographer Newton Thomas Sigel and Singer credited *Road to Perdition* as a visual influence. Though Sigel filmed *X-Men* in the anamorphic 2.40:1 format, he opted to shoot *X2* in Super 35mm 2.35:1. Sigel felt the recent improvements in film stocks and optics increased the advantages of using spherical lenses, even if the blowup to anamorphic must be accomplished optically instead of digitally. Sigel noted, "If you think about it, every anamorphic lens is simply a spherical lens with an anamorphizer on it. They'll never be as good as the spherical lenses that they emulate."[34] Cameras that were used during filming included two Panaflex Millenniums and a Millennium XL, as well as an Aaton 35mm. Singer also used more zoom lens than he did in his previous films, while Sigel used a Frazier lens specifically for dramatic moments.[34]

The Blackbird was redesigned and increased in virtual size from 60–85 feet.[11] John Myhre served as the production designer on *X-Men*, but Singer hired Guy Dyas (*X2* was Dyas' first film as production designer).[35] For scenes involving Stryker's Alkali Base, Vancouver Film Studios, the largest sound stage in North America, was reserved.[10]

Nightcrawler's tail was mainly computer-generated, although Alan Cumming sometimes used one made of rubber.[6]

Visual effects supervisor Mike Fink was not satisfied with his work on the previous film, despite the fact it nearly received an Academy Award nomination. Up to 520 shots were created for *X-Men*, while *X2* commissioned roughly 800. A new computer program was created by Rhythm and Hues for the dogfight tornado scene. Cinesite was in charge of scenes concerning Cerebro, enlisting a 20-man crew. The

Alkali Lake Dam miniature was 25 ft (7.6 m) high and 28 ft (8.5 m) wide.[36] Cinesite created 300 visual effects shots, focusing on character animation, while Rhythm and Hues created over 100.[37]

Comic book references

One scene depicts Mystique going through files on Yuriko's computer. Bryan Singer purposely included various characters and hints of storylines in the *X-Men* comic book on Yuriko's computer screen. Singer "finds great difficulty in adapting all this stuff into a two—two and a half hour long movie".[6]

Among the following mutant files are of Gambit, Cannonball, Husk, Silver Samurai, Garrison Kane, Magneto, Artie Maddicks, Multiple Man, Karma, Quicksilver, Scarlet Witch, Proteus, Danielle Moonstar, Storm, Beast, Feral, Banshee, Black Tom Cassidy, Lila Cheney, Sabretooth, Sunspot, Polaris, Psylocke, Iceman, Blob, Skin and Wild Child. There are also folders seen on the desk, including Omega Red, Project Wideawake, Franklin Richards and Cerebro.

Closer inspection reveals that Stryker is keeping files on Pyro, Sabra, Dr. Cecilia Reyes, Synch, Penance, Nightcrawler, Mystique, Lady Deathstrike, Copycat, Deadpool, Cyclops, Dazzler, Fenris, Jamie Braddock, David North, Sunfire, Boom Boom, Mimic, Dr. Nathaniel Essex, Toad, Wolfsbane, Strong Guy, Kitty Pryde, Sauron and Forge. There are also files on Alpha, Beta and Gamma Flights, Weapon X, Project Wide Awake, Dept H, the Brotherhood, Graymalkin, Zero Tolerance, Massachusetts Academy, Blackbird, the Danger Room, Legacy, Morlocks, Xavier's School, Omega Red, Cerebro, the Salem Centre, Franklin Richards, Kevin McTaggart and Trash.

Reception

Release

The first cut of *X2* was rated R by the Motion Picture Association of America, due to more violent scenes concerning Wolverine when Stryker's army stormed the X-Mansion. A few seconds were cut to secure a PG-13 rating.[38]

X2 opened in America on May 2, 2003, accumulating $85,558,731 in its opening weekend in 3,749 theaters. The film grossed $214,949,694 in North America, while earning $192,761,855 worldwide, coming at a total of $407,711,549. *X2* was a financial success since it recouped its production budget three times.[1] *X2* debuted simultaneously in ninety-three countries, the largest North American and international opening ever at the time.[39] In addition, the film is the sixth highest grossing film based on a Marvel Comic book,[40] and was the sixth highest of 2003,[41] also earning $107 million in its first five days of DVD release.[30]

X2 had a video game tie-in on *X2: Wolverine's Revenge*, which has nothing to do with the events of the film, although Patrick Stewart voiced Professor X. *X-Men: The Official Game* bridges the storyline between *X2* and *X-Men: The Last Stand*. Specifically, it explains Nightcrawler's absence from *The Last Stand*. Chris Claremont wrote a novelization of the film, which left out its secretive cliffhanger.[42]

Critical response

Based on 221 reviews collected by Rotten Tomatoes, *X2* received a "Certified Fresh" 88% overall approval rating;[43] the film was more balanced with Rotten Tomatoes' 40 "Top Critics", receiving an 83% approval rating.[44] By comparison, Metacritic calculated an average score of 68/100 from 38 reviews.[45]

Roger Ebert wrote "the storyline did not live up to its potential" and was critical of plot holes. He was impressed, however, by how Singer was able to handle so many characters in one film. In addition, Ebert wrote that the film's closing was perfect for a future installment, giving *X2* three out of four stars.[46] Kenneth Turan of the *Los Angeles Times* wrote that it was rare for a sequel to be better than its predecessor. Turan observed that the film carried emotional themes that are present in the world today and commented that "the acting was better than usual [for a superhero film]".[47] Peter Travers of *Rolling Stone* wrote that Hugh Jackman heavily improved his performance, concluding "*X2* is a summer firecracker. It's also a tribute to outcasts, teens, gays, minorities, even Dixie Chicks."[48] Mick LaSalle of the *San Francisco Chronicle* was critical of the storyline, special effects and action scenes.[49] Joe Morgenstern of *The Wall Street Journal* specifically referred to the film as "fast-paced, slow-witted".[50] Stephen Hunter of *The Washington Post* quoted, "Of the many comic book superhero movies, this is by far the lamest, the loudest, the longest".[51] Richard Corliss of *Time* argued that Singer depended too much on seriousness and that he did not have enough sensibilities to communicate to an audience.[52] *Empire* called *X2* the best comic book movie of all time in 2006,[53] while *Wizard* named the film's ending as the twenty-second greatest cliffhanger of all time.[54] In May 2007, Rotten Tomatoes listed *X2* as the fifth greatest comic book film of all time.[55]

X2 won the Saturn Award for Best Science Fiction Film. In addition, Bryan Singer (Direction), Dan Harris and Michael Dougherty (Writing), and John Ottman (Music) all received nominations. It also received nominations with its costumes, makeup, special effects and DVD release, coming to a total of eight nominations.[56] The Political Film Society honored *X2* in categories of Human Rights and Peace,[57] while the film was nominated for the Hugo Award for Best Dramatic Presentation (Long Form).[58]

References

[1] "X2: X-Men United (2003)" (http://boxofficemojo.com/movies/?id=x2.htm). Box Office Mojo. . Retrieved 2008-03-06.

[2] Louise Mingenbach (http://www.imdb.com/name/nm0591281/s), United Colors of *X2*, 2003, 20th Century Fox

[3] Lew Irwin (2001-10-31). "Lopez Ousts Berry From *Gigli*" (http://www.imdb.com/news/wenn/2001-10-31#celeb4). Internet Movie Database. . Retrieved 2008-03-07.

[4] Rob Worley (2003-04-21). "Bryan Singer's Mutant Agenda" (http://www.comicbookresources.com/news/newsitem.cgi?id=2135). Comic Book Resources. . Retrieved 2008-03-09.

[5] Michael Dougherty, Dan Harris, David Hayter, Lauren Shuler Donner, Ralph Winter, DVD audio commentary, 2003, 20th Century Fox

[6] Bryan Singer, Newton Thomas Sigel, DVD audio commentary, 2003, 20th Century Fox

[7] Alan Cumming, Introducing the Incredible Nightcrawler, 2003, 20th Century Fox

[8] Stax (2002-05-30). "Nightcrawler Cumming This Way" (http://movies.ign.com/articles/361/361096p1.html). IGN. . Retrieved 2008-03-09.

[9] Rob Worley (2003-04-23). "That's Why They Call It The Blues: Stamos and Cumming Talk *X2*" (http://www.comicbookresources.com/news/newsitem.cgi?id=2147). Comic Book Resources. . Retrieved 2008-02-18.

[10] Rob Worley (2002-10-23). "Comics 2 Film" (http://www.comicbookresources.com/columns/index.cgi?column=comics2film&article=1467). Comic Book Resources. . Retrieved 2008-02-18.

[11] Rob Worley (2002-10-30). "X-Men 2" (http://www.comicbookresources.com/columns/index.cgi?column=comics2film&article=1475). Comic Book Resources. . Retrieved 2008-02-18.

[12] Tim Nydell (2006-07-28). "Interview with Daniel Cudmore" (http://www.hitrockbottom.org/danielcudmore.html). Rock Bottom. . Retrieved 2008-03-09.

[13] Heather Newgen (2006-06-16). "*Superman Returns* Screenwriters Dougherty and Harris" (http://www.superherohype.com/news/featuresnews.php?id=4393). Superhero Hype!. . Retrieved 2008-04-21.

[14] Army Archerd (2001-08-23). "Touchy topic addressed in upcoming pix" (http://www.variety.com/article/VR1117851683.html?categoryid=2&cs=1). *Variety*. . Retrieved 2008-04-06.

[15] The Second Uncanny Issue of *X-Men*: Making *X2*, 2003, 20th Century Fox

[16] Scott Brown (2003-05-09). "The NeXt Level" (http://www.ew.com/ew/article/0,,449160,00.html). *Entertainment Weekly*. . Retrieved 2008-02-18.

[17] "Comics 2 Film" (http://www.comicbookresources.com/columns/index.cgi?column=comics2film&article=1397). Comic Book Resources. 2002-08-14. . Retrieved 2007-05-01.

[18] Chris Hewitt (2003-03-28). "The *X* Factor". *Empire*. pp. 76.

[19] "*Fantastic Four*: The Comedy?!" (http://movies.ign.com/articles/057/057515p1.html). IGN. 2001-04-28. . Retrieved 2008-03-09.

[20] Stax (2001-06-15). "Lauren Shuler Donner Talks *X-Men 2* and *Constantine*" (http://movies.ign.com/articles/300/300581p1.html). IGN. . Retrieved 2008-03-09.

[21] Stax (2001-11-07). ""Closing In" on *X-Men 2*" (http://movies.ign.com/articles/315/315905p1.html). IGN. . Retrieved 2008-03-09.

[22] Michael Fleming (2001-10-14). "Aussie has bulk for *Hulk*" (http://www.variety.com/article/VR1117854264.html). *Variety*. . Retrieved 2008-06-01.

[23] Martin A. Grove (2003-04-11). "Fox's *X2* marks spot as presummer starts May 2" (http://web.archive.org/web/20070930201512/http://www.hollywoodreporter.com/hr/search/article_display.jsp?vnu_content_id=1863776). *The Hollywood Reporter*. Archived from the original (http://www.hollywoodreporter.com/hr/search/article_display.jsp?vnu_content_id=1863776) on 2007-09-30. . Retrieved 2007-04-15.

[24] Stax (2002-05-08). "Magneto Escapes!" (http://movies.ign.com/articles/358/358779p1.html). IGN. . Retrieved 2008-03-09.

[25] KJB (2000-08-10). "Tyler Mane Not in *Rollerball* Just Yet" (http://movies.ign.com/articles/034/034623p1.html). IGN. . Retrieved 2008-03-09.

[26] "The *X-Men 2* panel" (http://www.joblo.com/sandiegocon2002/con12.htm). JoBlo. 2002-07-30. . Retrieved 2008-03-12.

[27] James Jones. "Realized Art" (http://www.realized-art.com/). . Retrieved 2008-11-18. Click "Portfolio" and then "Movies" to find the Sentinel maquette.

[28] Greg Dean Schmitz. "Greg's Preview - *X2: X-Men United*" (http://web.archive.org/web/20080109062934/http://movies.yahoo.com/movie/preview/1808406654). Yahoo!. Archived from the original (http://movies.yahoo.com/movie/preview/1808406654) on 2008-01-09. . Retrieved 2008-08-09.

[29] "Let It Snow, Let It Snow" (http://www.imdb.com/news/sb/2002-11-13#film3). Internet Movie Database. 2002-11-13. . Retrieved 2008-03-12.

[30] Rob Allstetter (2003-12-01). "*X2* Update" (http://www.comicscontinuum.com/stories/0312/01/index.htm). Comics Continuum. . Retrieved 2008-02-18.

[31] Stax (2001-10-26). "Kamen Settles *X-Men 2* Score" (http://movies.ign.com/articles/315/315441p1.html). IGN. . Retrieved 2008-03-09.

[32] John Ottman, Requiem for Mutants: The Score of *X2*, 2003, 20th Century Fox

[33] Jonathan Jarry (2007-06-27). "Music for Superfantastic Invaders" (http://www.soundtrack.net/features/article/?id=237). Soundtrack.net. . Retrieved 2008-02-18.

[34] Jon Silberg (April 2003). "A Universe *X*-pands" (http://www.theasc.com/magazine/april03/cover/index.html). *American Cinematographer*. . Retrieved 2008-03-10.

[35] Guy Dyas, Evolution in the Details: Designing *X2*, 2003, 20th Century Fox

[36] *FX2* Visual Effects, 2003, 20th Century Fox

[37] "Comics 2 Film" (http://www.comicbookresources.com/columns/index.cgi?column=comics2film&article=1362). Comic Book Resources. 2002-07-10. . Retrieved 2007-05-01.

[38] Rob Worley (2003-04-28). "*X*-Producers: Lauren Shulder-Donner and Ralph Winter Talk About *X2*" (http://www.comicbookresources.com/news/newsitem.cgi?id=2181). Comic Book Resources. . Retrieved 2008-02-18.

[39] Brian Linder (2003-05-02). "This Weekend at the Movies: *X2* Debuts" (http://movies.ign.com/articles/400/400483p1.html). IGN. . Retrieved 2008-03-09.

[40] "Marvel Comics Movies" (http://boxofficemojo.com/franchises/chart/?id=marvelcomics.htm). Box Office Mojo. . Retrieved 2008-03-05.

[41] "2003 Yearly Box Office Results" (http://boxofficemojo.com/yearly/chart/?yr=2003&p=.htm). Box Office Mojo. . Retrieved 2008-03-05.

[42] Chris Claremont (March 2003). *X-Men 2* (http://www.randomhouse.com/delrey/catalog/display.pperl?isbn=9780345461964). Del Ray Books. pp. 416. ISBN 978-0-345-46196-4. .

[43] "X2: X-Men United" (http://www.rottentomatoes.com/m/x2_xmen_united/). Rotten Tomatoes. . Retrieved 2008-03-06.

[44] "X2: X-Men United: Top Critics" (http://www.rottentomatoes.com/m/x2_xmen_united/?critic=creamcrop&name_order=asc). Rotten Tomatoes. . Retrieved 2008-03-06.

[45] "X2: X-Men United (2003): Reviews" (http://www.metacritic.com/video/titles/x2xmenunited?q=X2: X-Men United). Metacritic. . Retrieved 2008-03-06.

[46] Roger Ebert (2003-05-02). "X2: X-Men United" (http://rogerebert.suntimes.com/apps/pbcs.dll/article?AID=/20030502/REVIEWS/305020306/1023). RogerEbert.com. . Retrieved 2008-03-06.

[47] Kenneth Turan (2003-05-02). "X2: X-Men United" (http://www.calendarlive.com/movies/reviews/cl-et-turan2may02,0,4985395.story). *Los Angeles Times*. . Retrieved 2008-03-06.

[48] Peter Travers (2003-05-29). "Mutants Gone Wild" (http://www.rollingstone.com/reviews/movie/5947779/review/5947780/x2_xmen_united). *Rolling Stone*. pp. 70. . Retrieved 2007-08-12.

[49] Mick LaSalle (2003-05-03). "The Inhuman Touch" (http://www.sfgate.com/cgi-bin/article.cgi?f=/c/a/2003/05/02/DD45234.DTL). *San Francisco Chronicle*. . Retrieved 2008-03-06.

[50] Joe Morgenstern (2003-05-02). "X2: X-Men United". *The Wall Street Journal*.

[51] Stephen Hunter (2003-05-02). "*X-Men United*: Missing a Why, It Spawns Zzzzs". *The Washington Post*.

[52] Richard Corliss (2003-04-27). "Pumping Up For The Sequel" (http://www.time.com/time/magazine/article/0,9171,1101030505-447216,00.html). *Time*. . Retrieved 2008-03-06.

[53] "The 20 Greatest Comic Book Movies" (http://www.empireonline.com/features/comicbookfilms/10-1.asp#comicbookfilms). *Empire*. . Retrieved 2006-10-20.

[54] Jake Rossen (2007-08-05). "The Top 25 Cliffhangers of All Time!". *Wizard*. pp. 23–8.

[55] "Comix Worst to Best" (http://www.rottentomatoes.com/features/special/2007/comic/?r=5&mid=1122256). Rotten Tomatoes. . Retrieved 2008-03-10.

[56] "Past Saturn Awards" (http://www.saturnawards.org/past.html#film). Saturnawards.org. . Retrieved 2007-04-14.

[57] "X2: X-Men United" (http://www.geocities.com/~polfilms/x2.html). Political Film Society. . Retrieved 2008-03-12.

[58] "The Hugo Awards By Year" (http://www.hugo.org/hy.html#94). Hugo.org. . Retrieved 2008-03-12.

External links

- *X2* (http://www.imdb.com/title/tt0290334/) at the Internet Movie Database
- *X2: X-Men United* (http://www.allmovie.com/work/278281) at Allmovie
- *X2: X-Men United* (http://www.rottentomatoes.com/m/x2_xmen_united/) at Rotten Tomatoes
- *X2: X-Men United* (http://www.boxofficemojo.com/movies/?id=x2.htm) at Box Office Mojo
- *X2: X-Men United* (http://www.metacritic.com/film/titles/x2xmenunited) at Metacritic
- MDP:X2 - Marvel Database Project (wiki)
- X-Men on Marvel.com (http://marvel.com/movies/X-Men)
- http://www.variety.com/article/VR1117887586

Van Helsing (film)

Van Helsing	

Theatrical release poster	
Directed by	Stephen Sommers
Produced by	Stephen Sommers Bob Ducsay
Written by	Stephen Sommers
Starring	Hugh Jackman Kate Beckinsale Richard Roxburgh David Wenham Will Kemp Kevin J. O'Connor Shuler Hensley
Music by	Alan Silvestri
Cinematography	Allen Daviau
Editing by	Bob Ducsay Kelly Matsumoto
Distributed by	Universal Pictures
Release date(s)	May 5, 2004 *United States* May 7, 2004
Running time	131 minutes
Country	United States
Language	English
Budget	$160 million
Gross revenue	$300,257,475
Preceded by	*Van Helsing: The London Assignment*

Van Helsing is a 2004 American action horror film about vigilante monster hunter Gabriel Van Helsing, written, produced, and directed by Stephen Sommers. The film stars Hugh Jackman and Kate Beckinsale. The film opened on May 7, 2004.

The film is a homage and tribute to the Universal Horror Monster films from the '30s and '40s (also produced by Universal Studios), of which director Stephen Sommers is a fan. The titular character was inspired by Abraham Van Helsing from Irish author Bram Stoker's novel *Dracula*. Distributed by Universal Pictures, the film includes a number of monsters such as Count Dracula and the Frankenstein's monster in a way similar to the multi-monster movies that Universal produced in the 1940s, such as *Frankenstein Meets the Wolf Man* and *House of Dracula*.

Plot

1887, Transylvania, Doctor Frankenstein (Samuel West) brings to life his Monster (Shuler Hensley) with the aid of his assistant Igor (Kevin J. O'Connor), and Count Dracula (Richard Roxburgh). Dracula kills Frankenstein after revealing that he helped him only so he could use the Monster to bring his undead children to life. The Monster then escapes to a windmill, which is burnt down by a pursuing mob. The mob flees as Dracula and his brides, Verona (Silvia Colloca), Aleera (Elena Anaya) and Marishka (Josie Maran), mourn the loss of the Monster and their chance to bring their children to life.

One year later, the Knights of the Holy Order, stationed at the Vatican, dispatch Gabriel Van Helsing, who has amnesia, to kill Dracula. He is also tasked with preventing the last of the Valerious family from falling into purgatory; the family swore to kill Dracula nine generations ago and is unable to enter Heaven until they succeed. He is given a torn piece of paper with an insignia on it. He is joined by Carl (David Wenham), a friar who provides support and weapons.

Arriving in Transylvania, the two meet Anna Valerious (Kate Beckinsale), who tells them her brother Velkan (Will Kemp) was recently killed by a werewolf. Van Helsing then saves her from Dracula's brides as they attack the village, ending with Van Helsing killing Marishka as the others escape. Anna then takes the pair back to her castle. Anna is determined to kill Dracula herself, but Van Helsing is unwilling for her to take the risk, knowing that she is the last of the Valerious family. When she resists, he gases her to sleep and puts her in her bed.

Later in the night, Anna awakens from her deep, dreamless sleep and encounters Velkan, now a werewolf himself. After Velkan flees, Van Helsing and Anna track him to Frankenstein's castle, only to find Dracula attempting to give life to his children using Velkan as a substitute for the Monster. Anna frees Velkan but he becomes a werewolf again. Dracula confronts Van Helsing, who recognizes him from his past.

While escaping, Van Helsing and Anna fall into a cave. There, they find Frankenstein's Monster alive. Van Helsing decides to take him to Rome so he can be protected. The brides and Velkan pursue the group as they flee in a carriage, but they use a decoy carriage full of stakes bundled against explosives, which kills Verona. Velkan is killed by Van Helsing, but not before he is bitten by him; when the next full moon occurs, Van Helsing will become a werewolf. Anna is then captured by Aleera and taken to Budapest.

In Budapest, Van Helsing hides the Monster before he and Carl head off to save Anna. They manage to rescue her, but the Monster is captured. Van Helsing, Anna, and Carl return to Frankenstein's castle, where they find all the equipment has been removed. At Anna's castle, Carl explains that Dracula was the son of Anna's ancestor. Dracula was murdered, but not before making a Faustian Bargain, which gave him new life. Carl explains that although Anna's ancestor made the vow to kill Dracula, he couldn't kill his own son. Instead, he banished Dracula to an icy fortress from which he should not have been able to return, but the Devil gave him wings and the power of flight, which allowed him to escape. Van Helsing then finds a portal to Dracula's castle disguised as a wall map, completed using the paper that Van Helsing brought from Rome. They enter the portal, emerging on a cliff near Castle Dracula.

As the trio sees the Monster being lifted to the laboratory, he tells them that Dracula has a werewolf cure. Carl realizes that only a werewolf can kill Dracula and that he uses werewolves to do his bidding, but needs a cure in case they have the willpower to turn against him. Making his way to the laboratory, Van Helsing frees the Monster, then becomes a werewolf and is attacked by Dracula, who turns into a giant bat creature. Anna and Carl retrieve the cure but are attacked by Aleera and Igor, the latter of whom are then killed.

Dracula reveals that Van Helsing is really Gabriel, the Left Hand of God - as well as the one who originally murdered him. He offers to restore Van Helsing's memories, but Van Helsing refuses as he bites into Dracula's throat, killing him and his offspring. Anna arrives with the cure and injects Van Helsing with it, only to be killed by him at the same time, much to his grief.

Van Helsing and Carl hold a quiet ceremony for Anna and cremate her as the Monster departs on a raft into the ocean, having been allowed a chance at life. As Anna's body burns, Van Helsing sees her and her family in Heaven, at peace thanks to Dracula's death. This sight cheers Van Helsing up as he and Carl depart for their next adventure.

Cast

- Hugh Jackman as Gabriel Van Helsing
- Kate Beckinsale as Anna Valerious
- Richard Roxburgh as Count Dracula
- David Wenham as Carl
- Shuler Hensley as Frankenstein's monster
- Elena Anaya as Aleera
- Will Kemp as Velkan Valerious
- Kevin J. O'Connor as Igor
- Alun Armstrong as Cardinal Jinette
- Silvia Colloca as Verona
- Josie Maran as Marishka
- Tom Fisher as Top Hat
- Samuel West as Dr. Victor Frankenstein
- Robbie Coltrane as the voice of Mr Hyde

Reception

The film opened at Number 1 in May 2004. Domestically, the film grossed $120,177,084. Worldwide, the film grossed $300,257,475. This amount was almost double the film's budget.[1] Despite this, critical reception was generally negative, and was classed by the website Rotten Tomatoes as "Rotten," with 23% of reviews counted as positive.

Soundtrack

The movie's original score was composed by Alan Silvestri. It was met with critical acclaim by both reviewers and fans.

Other media

Vivendi Universal Games published a *Van Helsing* video game for PlayStation 2, Xbox and Game Boy Advance. The game follows a similar plot to the movie, has gameplay similar to *Devil May Cry* and the PS2 and Xbox versions feature the voice talent of many of the actors including Hugh Jackman and Richard Roxburgh. Lavastorm Entertainment produced a mobile game that followed the plot of the movie, but was poorly received.[2]

Sommers expanded the story of Van Helsing in two direct spin-offs. The animated prequel titled *Van Helsing: The London Assignment* takes place before the main events of the film, focusing on Van Helsing's mission to try to stop Jack the Ripper, who turns out to actually be Mr. Hyde, from terrorizing London. There was also a one-issue comic book titled *Van Helsing: From Beneath the Rue Morgue*, that follows Van Helsing on a self-contained adventure that occurs during the events of the film, just after the death of Jekyll/Hyde in Paris but before Van Helsing returned to Rome. In the adventure, Van Helsing deals with Doctor Moreau and his hybrid mutants.

References

[1] Van Helsing (2004) (http://www.boxofficemojo.com/movies/?id=vanhelsing.htm)
[2] IGN: Van Helsing (http://wireless.ign.com/objects/681/681646.html)

External links

- Official website (http://http://www.vanhelsing.net/)
- *Van Helsing* (http://www.imdb.com/title/tt0338526/) at the Internet Movie Database
- *Van Helsing* (http://www.allmovie.com/work/286519) at Allmovie
- *Van Helsing* (http://www.rottentomatoes.com/m/van_helsing/) at Rotten Tomatoes
- *Van Helsing* (http://www.metacritic.com/film/titles/vanhelsing) at Metacritic
- *Van Helsing* (http://www.boxofficemojo.com/movies/?id=vanhelsing.htm) at Box Office Mojo
- Dark Horse Comics' Van Helsing one-shot comic book (http://www.darkhorse.com/profile/profile.php?sku=10-102)

Van Helsing: The London Assignment

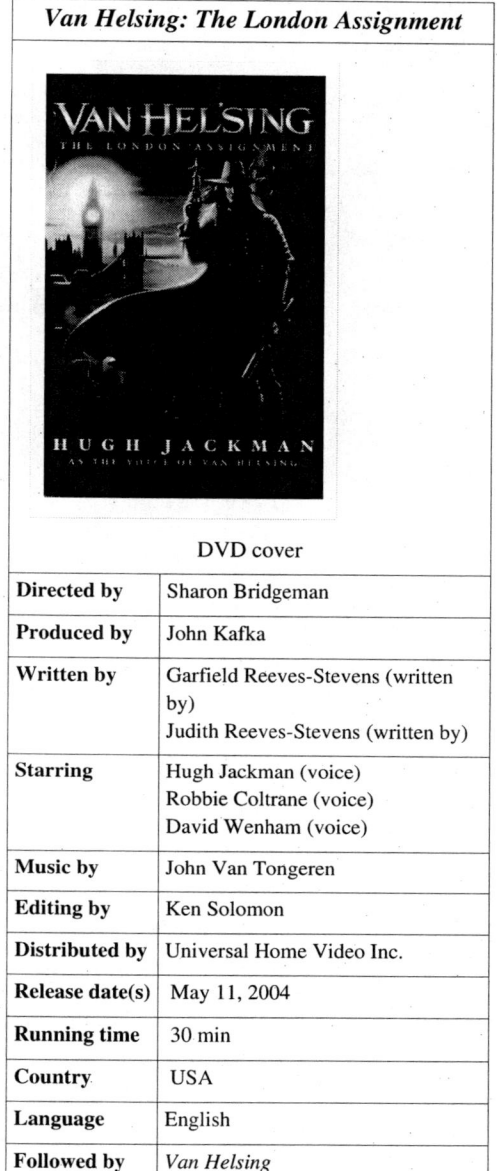

Van Helsing: The London Assignment	
DVD cover	
Directed by	Sharon Bridgeman
Produced by	John Kafka
Written by	Garfield Reeves-Stevens (written by) Judith Reeves-Stevens (written by)
Starring	Hugh Jackman (voice) Robbie Coltrane (voice) David Wenham (voice)
Music by	John Van Tongeren
Editing by	Ken Solomon
Distributed by	Universal Home Video Inc.
Release date(s)	May 11, 2004
Running time	30 min
Country	USA
Language	English
Followed by	*Van Helsing*

Van Helsing: The London Assignment is a 2004 animated film by Universal Home Entertainment Productions. This film features the voices of Hugh Jackman, Robbie Coltrane and David Wenham.

Plot

The London Assignment is an animated prequel to the 2004 motion picture *Van Helsing* (released the same year). It tells of the events before the film, in which monster hunter Gabriel Van Helsing travels to London to investigate a series of horrific, and decidedly supernatural murders, being committed by the mad scientist Dr. Jekyll, in the form of his evil alter-ego, Mr. Hyde. Van Helsing discovers that Dr. Jekyll is in love with the Queen and in order to keep her young and thus immortal has been placed under a spell by Dr. Jekyll that turns her into a young woman for one night. In order to create the potion which causes the transformations Dr. Jekyll needs the drained souls of his freshly killed victims and thus the killings will never stop. Helsing's confrontation with Dr. Jekyll with this information causes him to order his super natural servants to kidnap the Queen while he in Jekyll form fights Van Helsing and he eventually defeats the crazed doctor but still escapes. Van Helsing sends word back to the Vatican about what has happened while he tracks Jekyll to Paris resulting in the opening scene of the main movie.

Special features

- **Van Helsing: "Behind the Screams"**: A behind-the-scenes featurette on *Van Helsing*, hosted by actress Josie Maran.
- **The Making of the Van Helsing Game**: Tells about the creation of the film's official game for Xbox and PlayStation 2.
- **Animatic to Animation**: Moving storyboards revealing how four scenes from the film are taken from concept to final animation.

Voice cast

- Hugh Jackman - Gabriel Van Helsing
- David Wenham - Carl
- Robbie Coltrane - Mr. Hyde
- Dwight Schultz - Dr. Jekyll
- Tara Strong - Young Queen Victoria
- John DiMaggio - Carriage Driver

External links

- *Van Helsing: The London Assignment* [1] at the Internet Movie Database

References

[1] http://www.imdb.com/title/tt0406310/

Stories of Lost Souls

Stories of Lost Souls	
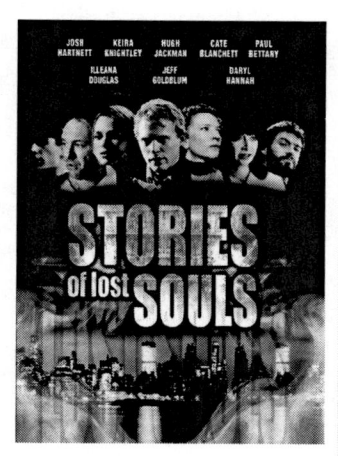 International Movie Poster	
Directed by	Mark Palansky Deborra-Lee Furness Andrew Upton Col Spector Toa Stappard William Garcia Illeana Douglas Paul Holmes
Produced by	Thomas Bannister
Starring	Josh Hartnett Hugh Jackman Cate Blanchett Keira Knightley Paul Bettany James Gandolfini Jeff Goldblum Daryl Hannah Billy Boyd
Distributed by	America Video Films
Release date(s)	**USA** 12 November 2004 **Japan** 25 August 2006 **Spain** 19 December 2006 **UK** 27 August 2007 **Germany** 28 September 2007
Running time	90 minutes

Country	United States United Kingdom Australia
Language	English

Stories of Lost Souls is a compilation of eight cinematic stories of lonely souls in unexpected situations starring many of cinema's biggest names including Josh Hartnett, Hugh Jackman, Keira Knightley, Cate Blanchett, James Gandolfini, Paul Bettany, Illeana Douglas and directed by eight different directors including Deborra-Lee Furness and Mark Palansky.

The collection was released at the 2005 Cannes Film Festival. *Stories of Lost Souls* was executive produced by Thomas Bannister.

Segments

Some versions of the film do not feature "Sniper 470" but start with "The Same" and feature "Supermarket".

The Same

Directed by Mark Palansky - Starring Josh Hartnett

A creepy house. Every night a dwarf awaits for his beautiful neighbor to return. He will do anything to win the girl of his dreams, including one terrible crime.

Standing Room Only

Directed by Deborra-Lee Furness - Starring Hugh Jackman, Michael Gambon, Joanna Lumley, and Mary Elizabeth Mastrantonio

The story revolves around a group of people waiting in line for a performance.

Bangers

Directed by Andrew Upton - Starring Cate Blanchett

The haunting story of a woman slipping into insanity. Julie-Anne, a marginally successful career woman, is preparing dinner for her gruff and unsympathetic mother. As she cooks the mashed potatoes and sausages, she tells an indifferent audience of her mother and cat about a recent promotion at work. As she rants about her job it becomes apparent that she is in the middle of a mental breakdown that culminates in burned sausage and mashed potatoes all over the floor.

New Year's Eve

Directed by Col Spector - Starring Keira Knightley

The story of a seductive temptress at a New Year's Eve party.

Euston Road

Written by Tristam Pye and Directed by Toa Stappard - Starring Paul Bettany

A fast car. Two men talking in a hotel bar. Seven questions in eight minutes. And it is 9 pm on Euston Road. Figure it out.

A Whole New Day

Directed by William Garcia - Starring James Gandolfini

The story of an abusive alcoholic who wakes up in an abandoned apartment after a black-out. A man comes to on the floor of an empty apartment - no furniture, no decor on the walls, no gas in the stove. He has only his cell phone, a jacket, and a hangover. Somewhere else in the city, his wife is in a kitchen, harried by three rambunctious children, angry at her husband. She leaves a message on his cell phone that the marriage is over. He calls his friend Jimmy and tells him to get over here and to bring some beer. Then, a young woman he does not know walks into the apartment.

What is going on?

Supermarket

Directed by Illeana Douglas - Starring Daryl Hannah, Jeff Goldblum and Illeana Douglas

The story of a woman who works at a supermarket where Daryl Hannah continually slacks off, nearly drooling fans stalk her, and Jeff Goldblum comes in to shop for pastries.

Sniper 470

Directed by Paul Holmes - Starring Billy Boyd

A futuristic tale of a lone sniper on a mission in outerspace.

External links

- *Stories of Lost Souls* [1] at the Internet Movie Database
- Official Trailer [2]
- International Sales [3] (America Video Films) *go to 03.library*
- *The Same* [4] at the Internet Movie Database
- *Standing Room Only* [5] at the Internet Movie Database
- *Bangers* [6] at the Internet Movie Database
- *New Year's Eve* [7] at the Internet Movie Database
- *Euston Road* [8] at the Internet Movie Database
- *A Whole New Day* [9] at the Internet Movie Database
- *Supermarket* [10] at the Internet Movie Database
- *Sniper 470* [11] at the Internet Movie Database

References

[1] http://www.imdb.com/title/tt0462721/
[2] http://www.youtube.com/watch?v=Hud_mCaNaQY
[3] http://www.americavideofilms.net/
[4] http://www.imdb.com/title/tt0365713/
[5] http://www.imdb.com/title/tt0185704/
[6] http://www.imdb.com/title/tt0303712/
[7] http://www.imdb.com/title/tt0378437/
[8] http://www.imdb.com/title/tt0436287/
[9] http://www.imdb.com/title/tt0300653/
[10] http://www.imdb.com/title/tt0409341/
[11] http://www.imdb.com/title/tt0358703/

Happy Feet

Happy Feet	
Promotional poster	
Directed by	George Miller Warren Coleman Judy Morris
Produced by	Bill Miller George Miller Doug Mitchell
Written by	Warren Coleman John Collee George Miller Judy Morris
Starring	Elijah Wood Robin Williams Brittany Murphy Hugh Jackman Nicole Kidman Hugo Weaving
Music by	John Powell Gia Farrell
Cinematography	David Peers
Editing by	Christian Gazal Margaret Sixel
Studio	Kennedy-Miller Productions Animal Logic Films
Distributed by	Warner Bros. Pictures Village Roadshow Pictures
Release date(s)	November 17, 2006 (United States) December 26, 2006 (Australia)
Running time	108 minutes

Country	United States Australia
Language	English
Budget	$100 million
Gross revenue	$384.3 million[1]
Followed by	*Happy Feet 2*

Happy Feet is a 2006 computer-animated family film with music, directed and co-written by George Miller. It was produced at Sydney-based visual effects and animation studio *Animal Logic* for Warner Bros., Village Roadshow Pictures and Kingdom Feature Productions and was released in North America on November 17, 2006. It is the first animated feature film produced by Kennedy Miller in association with visual effects/design company Animal Logic.

Though primarily an animated film, Happy Feet does incorporate live action humans in certain scenes. The film was simultaneously released in both conventional theatres and in IMAX 2D format.[2] The studio had hinted that a future IMAX 3D release was a possibility. However, Warner Bros., the film's production company, was on too tight a budget to release Happy Feet in IMAX digital 3D. [3]

Happy Feet won the Academy Award for Best Animated Feature and was nominated for the Annie Award for Best Animated Feature.

The film was dedicated in memory of Nick Enright, Michael Jonson, Robby McNeilly Green, and Steve Irwin.

Plot

Every penguin sings a unique song called a "heartsong" to attract a mate. If the female likes the male and his song, and if it completes the female's song, the two penguins mate. A penguin named Norma Jean sings the song "Kiss", whereupon a male penguin named Memphis sings "Heartbreak Hotel". Norma Jean chooses him as her mate. They couple and Norma Jean lays an egg. The egg is left with Memphis while Norma Jean leaves with the other females to fish. While the males struggle through the harsh winter, Memphis drops the egg, briefly exposing it to the freezing Antarctic temperatures. The resulting chick - the film's protagonist, Mumble (voiced by Elizabeth Daily) - has blue eyes, ever-lasting down feathers, and a terrible singing voice. However, Mumble has a talent that no other penguin has ever seen before: tap dancing. As a result, Mumble is ostracized, with only his mother and his best friend Gloria to turn to. One day Mumble wanders into a secluded area, where he is free to dance. Mumble is interrupted when Boss Skua and his posse Dino, Frankie, and Vinnie attempt to eat him. Mumble stalls by asking the leader of the pack about a yellow band that is attached to his right ankle. The Boss Skua tells Mumble that he had been abducted by "aliens". Mumble narrowly escapes the hungry birds by falling into a crevice.

Mumble grows into an adult (voiced by Elijah Wood), still half-covered in fluffy down. Mumble's class graduates, and although he has not graduated, he joins them on their first trip into the ocean. His class ends their day by partying on an iceberg. Mumble constantly interrupts their singing and is forced to enjoy the party on a small iceberg. Mumble dozes off and wakes to find himself alone. A leopard seal chases him off the iceberg, and the penguin finds himself far from his home. He finds some Adelie Penguins, small in stature, but fiercely loyal to those they call friends. He befriends a small group of bachelors who form a club called "the Amigos": the leader Ramon, the brothers Raul and Nestor, and twin brothers Rinaldo and Lombardo. The Amigos quickly embrace Mumble's dance moves and assimilate him into their misfit group. Mumble's joy is cut short when he accidentally starts an avalanche and causes a hidden human excavator to tumble out from a glacier. Driven by curiosity, he sets out to find the "aliens" responsible for the machine. Mumble has a lot of questions, and the group suggests that he ask Lovelace a Rockhopper or Macaroni Crested Penguin who answers questions in exchange for stones and is known as the guru,as well as being the leader of the Adelie penguins. Lovelace has the plastic rings of a six pack entangled around his neck, which he uses to project his guru image. When asked if the rings were from the aliens, Lovelace denies that aliens exists and claims that the plastic rings were bestowed upon him by mystic beings.

In Mumble's old home, it is mating season, and Gloria (voiced by Brittany Murphy) is the center of attention. Although she is surrounded by a large horde of suitors, none of their heartsongs interest her. Ramon tries to help Mumble by singing a Spanish version of "My Way". Gloria isn't fooled, however, for she knows Mumble can't sing. She notices Ramon behind Mumble and shoves him away to reveal the little penguin. Gloria becomes angry and turns her back on Mumble. As Mumble has no heartsong, Gloria continues towards the other males visibly distraught. As a last resort, Mumble tries to persuade her to sing along to his tapping rhythm. Because of her affection for him, she complies. As Mumble's beat speeds up, Gloria finds the chorus to her heartsong, and realizes it is "Boogie Wonderland". Overcome with happiness that they can now be mates, the pair begin dancing, along with the other penguins.

Noah the elder sees their lack of fish as punishment from the Great 'Guin for Mumble's dancing. Mumble tries to explain about the mysterious "aliens", and that they are the cause of the scarceness of fish, but only his mother and Gloria believe him. Noah exiles Mumble from the colony. Mumble vows that he will find the real cause of the famine. Mumble and the Amigos return to Lovelace only to find him being choked by the plastic rings. Lovelace confesses that he got stuck in the rings while swimming near the forbidden shores. He reveals that the forbidden shores are located past the land of elephant seals and beyond the blizzard country. Mumble, the Amigos and Lovelace start their journey. Gloria tries to come, but Mumble, fearing for her safety, drives her off by insulting her singing talents. They travel across vast territories till they reach the shore.

Mumble sees a boat and swims after it, leaving his friends behind. He ends up in a penguin exhibit at a marine park named Marine World. He tries to communicate with the "aliens" that surround him. When his pleas fail, Mumble nearly succumbs to madness after three months of confinement. Mumble starts dancing, and soon a large crowd gathers around the exhibit. He is released back into the wild, now with more adult feathers and a tracking device strapped to his back. He leads the humans to his native colony. The other penguins are skeptical at first, but when Gloria notices the tracking device, they realize that the "aliens" exist. Now convinced, the penguins (along with the once-stubborn elders) dance alongside Mumble in hopes of getting the humans' attention.

A research team arrives and film the penguins dancing. They bring this footage back to the human world, and a worldwide debate ensues. The world governments realize they are overfishing the Antarctic waters, and conclude that the penguins are trying to communicate that to them. Antarctic fishing is banned, and the fish population recovers. At this, the Emperor Penguins and the Amigos dance and celebrate their triumph. A dancing baby penguin seen at the end is implied to be the child of Mumble and Gloria.

In the credits, the characters reunite to dance for the final number, "The Song of the Heart."

Cast

- Elijah Wood as Mumble
- Brittany Murphy as Gloria
- Hugh Jackman as Memphis
- Nicole Kidman as Norma Jean
- Hugo Weaving as Noah the Elder
- Robin Williams as Ramón and Lovelace
- Carlos Alazraqui as Nestor
- Lombardo Boyar as Raul
- Jeffrey Garcia as Rinaldo
- Johnny Sanchez as Lombardo
- Miriam Margoyles as Mrs. Astrakhan
- Fat Joe as Seymour
- Elizabeth Daily as baby Mumble

- Alyssa Shafer as baby Gloria

Production

Miller cites as an initial inspiration for the film an encounter with a grizzled old camera-man, whose father was Frank Hurley of the Shackleton expeditions, during the shooting of Mad Max 2 say's Miller: "We were sitting in this bar, having a milkshake, and he looked across at me and said, 'Antarctica.'He'd shot a documentary there. He said, 'You've got to make a film in Antarctica. It's just like out here, in the wasteland. It's spectacular.' And that always stuck in my head."[4] *Happy Feet* was also partially inspired by earlier documentaries such as the BBC's *Life in the Freezer*.[5] In 2001, during an otherwise non-sequiter meeting, Doug Mitchell impulsively presented Warner Bros., studio president Alan Horn with an early rough draft of the film's screenplay, and asked them to read it while he and Miller flew back to Australia. By the time they'd landed, Warner Bros., had decided to provide funding on the film. Production was slated to begin sometime after the completion of the fourth Mad Max film, Fury Road, but geo-political complications pushed *Happy Feet* to the forefront in early 2003.

An earlier cut of the film seems to have included a large subplot regarding aliens in the extraterrestrial sense, whose presence was made gradually more and more known throughout, and who were planning to siphon off the planet's resources gradually, placing the humans in the same light as the penguins. At the end, through the plight of the main character, their hand is stayed, and instead, first contact is made. This was chopped out during the last year of production, and has yet to see the light of day in a finished form, although concept art from these sequences were showcased at the Siggraph 2007 demonstration [6] , and are available online, as well.

The animation in *Happy Feet* invested heavily in motion capture technology, with the dance scenes acted out by human dancers. The tap-dancing for Mumble in particular was provided by Savion Glover who was also co-choreographer for the dance sequences.[7] The dancers went through "Penguin School" to learn how to move like a penguin, and also wore head apparatus to mimic a penguin's beak.[8]

Happy Feet needed an enormous group of computers, and Animal Logic worked with IBM to build a server farm with sufficient processing potential. The film took four years to make. Ben Gunsberger, Lighting Supervisor and VFX Department Supervisor, says this was partly because they needed to build new infrastructure and tools.[9] The server farm used IBM BladeCenter framework and BladeCenter HS20 blade servers, which are extremely dense separate computer units each with two Intel Xeon processors. Rendering took up 17 million CPU hours over a nine month period.[10]

Music

Happy Feet is a jukebox musical, taking previously recorded songs and working them into the film's soundtrack to fit with the mood of the scene or character. Two soundtrack albums were released for the film; one containing songs from and inspired by the film, and another featuring John Powell's instrumental score. They were released on October 31, 2006 and December 19, 2006, respectively.

Awards

Won

Academy Awards

- Best Animated Feature

60th British Academy Film Awards

- Best Animated Feature Film

Golden Globes

- Best Original Song - "Song of the Heart" by Prince

American Film Institute Awards 2006

- Honored as one of the Top Ten Best Films of the Year

Los Angeles Film Critics Association Awards

- Best Animation

New York Film Critics Circle Awards

- Best Animated Film

Golden Trailer Awards[11]

- Best Music

Heartland Awards

- The Truly Moving Picture Award

Kids' Choice Awards

- Favorite Animated Movie

British Academy of Film and Television Arts - Children's Awards

- Best Feature Film

Nominations

Golden Globe Award

- Best Animated Feature

Annie Awards

- Best Animated Feature
- Best Writing in an Animated Feature Production

Satellite Awards

- Best Motion Picture, Animated or Mixed Media

Grammy Awards

- Best Score Soundtrack Album for Motion Picture, Television or Other Visual Media, John Powell, nominee
- Best Song Written for Motion Picture, Television or Other Visual Media: "The Song of the Heart", Prince, nominee

Top ten lists

The film appeared on numerous critics' top ten lists of the best films of 2006, including AFI's Annual list, which is listed above.[12] [13] AFI's jury said:

"*HAPPY FEET* is a one-of-a-kind motion picture experience. George Miller continues to paint outside the lines of traditional filmmaking, and his genius expands upon the animated art form to illuminate a world where penguins embrace dance and differences to survive and thrive. But that is just the tip of the iceberg, as the environment, religion and the chasm between generations enrich this sweet and subtle tale - one that is fun and funny, brilliant and beautiful, groundbreaking and global in its message."

- 1st - Jack Matthews, *The New York Daily News*
- 1st - Stan Urankar, *Sun News*
- 2nd - William Arnold, *Seattle Post-Intelligencer*
- 2nd - Mark Palermo, *The Coast*
- 3rd - Kirk Honeycutt, *Hollywood Reporter*

- 4th - Edward Douglas, *ComingSoon.net*
- 5th - Scott Foundas, *Village Voice*
- 5th - Peter Rainer, *Christian Science Monitor*
- 5th - Matthieu Santelli, *Critikat (Film review, in French)* [14]
- 5th - Kurt Loder, *MTV*
- 5th - Missy Thompson, *Tooele Transcript Bulletin*
- 6th - Constance Garfinkle, *The Patriot Ledger*
- 6th - Carole Wrona, *Critikat (Top 10 lists for 2006 films, in French)* [15]
- 6th - Lou Lumenick, *New York Post*
- 6th - Kyle Smith, *New York Post*
- 6th - Michael Wilmington, *Chicago Tribune*
- 6th - Keith Cohen, *Sun Newspapers*
- 8th - Rene Rodriguez, *Miami Herald*
- 9th - Schlomo Schwartzberg, *Box Office Magazine*

Home media release

Happy Feet was released on March 27, 2007[16] in the United States in three formats; DVD (in separate widescreen and pan and scan editions), Blu-ray Disc, and an HD DVD/DVD combo disc.[17]

Among the DVD's special features is a scene that was cut from the film where Mumble meets a blue whale and an albatross. The albatross was Steve Irwin's first voice role in the film before he voiced the elephant seal in the final cut. The scene was finished and included on the DVD in memory of Steve Irwin. This scene is done in Steve's classic documentary style, with the albatross telling the viewer all about the other characters in the scene, and the impact people are having on their environment.

Video games

A video game based on the film was developed by A2M and published by Midway Games. It has the same main cast as the film. It was released for the PC, PlayStation 2, GameCube, GBA, NDS, and Wii.[18]

Artificial Life, Inc. has also developed a Happy Feet mobile game for the Japan market.[19]

Reception

Box office

The film opened at #1 in the United States on its first weekend of release (November 17-19) grossing $41.6 million and beating *Casino Royale* for the top spot.[20] It remained #1 for the Thanksgiving weekend, making $51.6 million over the five-day period. In total, the film was the top grosser for three weeks, a 2006 box office feat matched only by *Pirates of the Caribbean: Dead Man's Chest*. As of June 8, 2008, *Happy Feet* has grossed $198.0 million in the U.S. and $186.3 million overseas, making about $384.3 million dollars worldwide. *Happy Feet* was the third highest grossing animated film in the U.S. , behind *Cars* and *Ice Age: The Meltdown*. *Happy Feet* also being the third highest grossing animated film worldwide, behind *Ice Age: The Meltdown* and *Cars*. The film has been released in about 35 international territories at the close of 2006.[21] [22] [23]

The production budget was $100 million.[24]

Critical reviews

Happy Feet has received better than average reviews from film critics, and received a 74% "Fresh" approval in the Rotten Tomatoes movie review aggregate site, with an 82% percent from the Top Critics.[25]

Analysis

The film has also garnered, since its release, quite a bit of analysis and dissection from various places. Film critic Yar Habnegnal has written an essay, published in *Forum on Contemporary Art and Society*, that examines the themes of encroachment presented throughout the film, as well as various other subtexts and themes, such as religious hierarchy and interracial tensions.[26] And, Vadim Rizov of the Independent Film Channel sees Mumble as just the latest in a long line of cinematic religious mavericks.

On a technical or formal level, the film has also been lauded in some corners for its innovative introduction of Miller's roving style of subjective cinematography into contemporary animation, among other things.

Sequel

Happy Feet 2 is currently in production at Dr. D Studios.[27] The estimated release date is November 18, 2011. Wood and Williams will reprise their roles for the sequel. But Murphy will not be able to reprise her role, due to her death. Matt Damon and Brad Pitt have reportedly signed on to provide voice work for the film also.[28]

Environmental message

As things progress there is increasing emphasis on environmental problems in the Antarctic.

The film's denouement shows a group of researchers taking video of the colony of dancing emperor penguins, and the footage is broadcast globally. After many heated arguments this publicity generates considerable pressure to stop commercial overfishing of the Antarctic.

According to the director, George Miller, the environmental message was not a major part of the original script, but "In Australia, we're very, very aware of the ozone hole," he said, "and Antarctica is literally the canary in the coal mine for this stuff. So it sort of had to go in that direction." This influence led to a film with a more environmental tone. Miller said, "You can't tell a story about Antarctica and the penguins without giving that dimension."[29]

References

[1] http://boxofficemojo.com/movies/?id=happyfeet.htm

[2] "Happy Feet: The IMAX Experience" (http://www.imax.com/ImaxWeb/filmDetail.do?type=comingSoon&movieID=code__.__30). IMAX. . Retrieved 2007-03-15.

[3] "Happy Feet Won't Debut in IMAX 3-D" (http://www.vfxworld.com/?sa=adv&code=3631a5a1&atype=news&id=17882). VFXWorld. . Retrieved 2007-03-15.

[4] The filmmaker behind the 'Mad Max' and 'Babe' franchises turns his attention to musical fowl (http://www.natoonline.org/infocus/06November/happyfeet.htm). *In Focus*. Retrieved 2010-11-13.

[5] "Penguin suits up for a cinema hit" (http://www.theaustralian.news.com.au/story/0,20867,20753501-2702,00.html). *The Australian*. . Retrieved 2008-03-28.

[6] (August 6, 2007). Live from the Happy Feet discussion at Siggraph 2007 (http://brooks.boyd.name/wordpress/2007/08/live-from-the-happy-feet-discussion-at-siggraph-2007). Retrieved 2010-11-13.

[7] Savion Glover. (2007). *Happy Feet*. [DVD]. Warner Brothers.

[8] Kelley Abbey. (2007). *Happy Feet*. [DVD]. Warner Brothers.

[9] UNSWorld (2007) *Bring on the dancing penguins* in UNSWorld, Issue 6, May 2007, pp. 14–15

[10] "Animal Logic builds rendering farm with IBM eServer BladeCenter" (http://www-01.ibm.com/software/success/cssdb.nsf/cs/mcag-6h2sr2?opendocument&site=corp). *IBM Australia*. . Retrieved 2010-02-01.

[11] Golden Trailer Awards (http://www.goldentrailer.com/gta7.html)

[12] "Film Critic Top Ten List, 2006 Critics' Picks" (http://www.metacritic.com/film/awards/2006/toptens.shtml). .

[13] "The Critics" (http://www.moviecitynews.com/awards/2007/top_tens/critics_01.html). .

[14] http://www.critikat.com/Happy-Feet.html

[15] http://www.critikat.com/Editorial-8.html

[16] Happy Feet (2006) - Elijah Wood, Nicole Kidman, Hugh Jackman (http://videoeta.com/movie.html?via=form&id=78865)

[17] *Happy Feet* to Dance on Blu-ray, HD DVD This March | High-Def Digest (http://www.highdefdigest.com/news/show/432)

[18] Happy Feet (http://www.midway.com/rxpage/Game_HappyFeet.html)

[19] Parthajit; "Happy Feet Goes Mobile"; Softpedia; April 24, 2007 (http://news.softpedia.com/news/Happy-Feet-Goes-Mobile-52871.shtml)

[20] Weekend Box Office Results for November 17–19, 2006 (http://www.boxofficemojo.com/weekend/chart/?yr=2006&wknd=46&p=.htm). *Box Office Mojo*. Retrieved 2010-11-13.

[21] Happy Feet (2006) - Weekend Box Office Results (http://www.boxofficemojo.com/movies/?page=weekend&id=happyfeet.htm). *Box Office Mojo*. Retrieved 2010-11-13.

[22] IMDb Charts (http://www.imdb.com/chart). *IMDb*. Retrieved 2010-11-13.

[23] Weekend Box Office Results for February 1–3, 2008 (http://www.boxofficemojo.com/weekend/chart). *Box Office Mojo*. Retrieved 2010-11-13.

[24] Happy Feet (2006) (http://www.boxofficemojo.com/movies/?id=happyfeet.htm). *Box Office Mojo*. Retrieved 2010-11-13.

[25] Happy Feet Movie Reviews, Pictures (http://www.rottentomatoes.com/m/happy_feet). *Rotten Tomatoes*. Retrieved 2010-11-13.

[26] Yar Habnegnal on Happy Feet (http://www.scribd.com/doc/2555518/Yar-Habnegnal-on-Happy-Feet). *Scribd.com*. Retrieved 2010-11-13.

[27] About Dr. D Studios (http://www.drdstudios.com). Retrieved 2010-11-13.

[28] (January 19, 2010). Matt Damon, Brad Pitt to Voice Characters in Happy Feet Sequel (http://www.showbizspy.com/article/198088/matt-damon-brad-pitt-to-voice-characters-in-happy-feet-sequel.html). *ShowbizSpy.com*. Retrieved 2010-11-13.

[29] Kelly, Kate (2006-11-17). "The New Animated Film *Happy Feet* Doesn't Dance Around Serious Issues" (http://online.wsj.com/public/article/SB116373257478225933-QS7Oc7yiEQI503rfJ2N42OUiVH8_20071119.html?mod=tff_main_tff_top). The Wall Street Journal. . Retrieved 2007-03-15.

External links

- Official website (http://http://www.happyfeetmovie.com/)
- *Happy Feet* (http://www.imdb.com/title/tt0366548/) at the Internet Movie Database
- *Happy Feet* (http://www.allmovie.com/work/322645) at Allmovie
- *Happy Feet* (http://www.rottentomatoes.com/m/happy_feet/) at Rotten Tomatoes
- *Happy Feet* (http://www.metacritic.com/film/titles/happyfeet) at Metacritic
- *Happy Feet* - Review (http://review-online.blogspot.com/2007/03/happy-feet.html)

Flushed Away

Flushed Away	
Promotional film poster.	
Directed by	David Bowers Sam Fell
Written by	Dick Clement Ian La Frenais
Starring	Hugh Jackman Kate Winslet Ian McKellen
Music by	Harry Gregson Williams
Studio	DreamWorks Animation Aardman Animations
Distributed by	Paramount Pictures
Release date(s)	November 3, 2006 (US)
Running time	85 mins
Country	United Kingdom
Budget	$149 million
Gross revenue	$178,120,010 (Worldwide)[1]

Flushed Away is a 2006 computer animated British film directed by David Bowers and Sam Fell. It is a partnership between Aardman Animations of Wallace and Gromit fame, and DreamWorks Animation, and is Aardman's first completely computer-animated feature as opposed to the usual stop-motion.[2]

The film stars the voice talents of Hugh Jackman, Kate Winslet, Andy Serkis, Bill Nighy, Ian McKellen, Shane Richie and Jean Reno. The story was by Sam Fell, Peter Lord, Dick Clement, and Ian La Frenais, and the screenplay was written by Dick Clement, Ian La Frenais, Christopher Lloyd, Joe Keenan, and William Davies.

The film was released in movie theatres on November 3, 2006, and is distributed by Paramount Pictures, except for Switzerland, Spain, and the Netherlands, which were handled by Universal Pictures.

Plot

Roddy St. James is a decidedly upper crust pet rat who makes his home in a posh Kensington flat. When a common sewer rat named Sid comes spewing out of the sink and decides to stay, especially as England are playing Germany in the FIFA World Cup final, Roddy schemes to get rid of Sid by luring him into the "jacuzzi", which is actually the toilet bowl. Sid may be an ignorant slob, but being a sewer rat, he knows his plumbing. He plays along and instead pushes Roddy in and flushes him away into the sewer.

There, Roddy meets Rita Malone, an enterprising scavenger rat who works the drains in her faithful boat, the *Jammy Dodger*. Rita does not like Roddy initially, but ends up taking him along as The Toad sends his henchmen, Spike and Whitey, after her because she had stolen back her father's prized ruby a long time ago. The Toad despises all rodents to the point of hateful obsession, blaming rats for his fall from grace (he was once Prince Charles' pet). He decides to have them frozen with liquid nitrogen. However, The Toad's plan fails. Worse, during their escape, Rita takes a unique electrical cable. The cable is required to control the Floodgates. The Toad's evil plan is to open the gates during halftime of the World Cup, drowning the rats and their underground city in sewage. He can then use the depopulated city as a home for millions of his own tadpole offspring.

Roddy (right) and Rita (left) arguing over the ruby.

Roddy finds that the ruby is a fake and breaks it in front of Rita, enraging her, for she can now not get the money she needs for her large family. Roddy offers her a real ruby if she takes him back to Kensington. Accepting the offer, the pair first stop to visit her family before setting off. During Roddy's stay, he overhears a conversation that causes him to think that Rita had double-crossed him, so he steals the *Jammy Dodger*. When Rita catches up to him, he is able to clear up the misunderstanding.

The pair evade Spike and Whitey pursuing in a remote-controlled toy boat, with Thimblenose Ted and others on eggbeater jet skis. During this scene, Roddy and Rita share a quick love moment. Incensed at his minions' repeated failures, The Toad sends to France for his cousin; an infamous, if somewhat laid back, mercenary known as Le Frog. Le Frog and his subordinates intercept the duo and retrieve the cable, but Roddy and Rita use a plastic bag to lift themselves out of the sewer (snatching away the cable during the ascent) and get Roddy home, though the *Jammy Dodger* has to be sacrificed.

Back home, Roddy pays Rita the promised ruby and an emerald, then proceeds to show her around his house. She at first believes he has family in the home, but noticing his cage, she realizes he's a pet. Roddy tries to pass Sid off as his brother, but Sid and Rita know each other. Rita tries to persuade Roddy to come with her, but he is too proud to admit that he is lonely. By now, they have fallen in love but have not told each other their feelings. She departs, both of them broken-hearted, but is soon captured by The Toad.

Talking to Sid about half-time, Roddy pieces together The Toad's plan. He gives Sid his cushy position and has Sid flush him back to the sewers to find Rita and save the city. Together, they defeat The Toad and freeze the wave of sewage generated by the flushing of countless toilets during the FIFA World Cup half-time with liquid nitrogen before it drowns the entire rat population.

Rita and Roddy build the *Jammy Dodger Mark Two* and set off in her with Rita's entire brood. A newspaper article reveals England had lost on penalties. Rita and Roddy become boyfriend and girlfriend. Later while the credits start, Roddy's former owner comes back with a new pet (a cat), which frightens Sid.

Cast

- Hugh Jackman as Roderick "Roddy" St. James, a lonely pampered pet rat living in a Kensington apartment with a wealthy English family.
- Kate Winslet as Rita Malone, a street smart scavenger and the oldest child of a large family. She is the captain of The Jammy Dodger.
- Ian McKellen as The Toad, a big, pompous amphibian wanting the entire rat population to be killed off so he can make room for his hundreds of offspring.
- Jean Reno as Le Frog, the Toad's French cousin. He masters martial arts and is the leader of a team of hench-frogs.
- Andy Serkis as Spike, one of the Toad's hench-rats. Being the Toad's hench-rat is Spike's first job, despite him being only a teenager. Spike is twitchy, and he is an accident-prone.
- Bill Nighy as Whitey, another of the Toad's hench-rats. Whitey is an albino rat, once working in a lab and he is Spike's partner. Unlike Spike, Whitey is gentle, and not as violent.
- Shane Richie as Sid, an over-weight and lazy rat from the sewers .
- Eric Dapkewicz and John Venzon edited the production.[3]

Production

The film's original concept involved pirates, and was pitched to DreamWorks soon after the release of *Chicken Run* in 2000. However, Aardman were told that there was no market for pirate films (this was before *Pirates of the Caribbean: The Curse of the Black Pearl* was released to great success in 2003), and were told to modernise the concept. By the time the rewrite was done, the project had to be postponed to make way for the production of *Wallace & Gromit: The Curse of the Were-Rabbit*; it was finally released after not only the original *Pirates of the Caribbean*, but also its first sequel.

The film's working title was *Ratropolis*, but it was changed due to its similarity to Disney-Pixar's *Ratatouille*. In Spain, the movie was released as *Ratónpolis* (*ratón* is Spanish for "mouse"). The Latin-American title for the film was *Lo que el agua se llevó* ("Gone with the Water"), a pun on *Gone with the Wind*.

Traditionally, Aardman have used stop-motion for their animated features, but it is very complex to render water with this technique, and using real water can damage plasticine models. It would have been very expensive to composite CGI into shots that include water, of which there are many in the movie, so they chose to make *Flushed Away* their first all-CGI production.[4] The characters still resemble Aardman's classic characters, as the designs were taken straight from the original plasticine models. Several techniques were employed to give the impression of stop-motion animation, such as using replacement mouths for lip-synch rather than the interpolation typically seen in computer animation.

The film underwent many changes and versions, resulting in an inflated budget. For example, Roddy originally had two hamster manservants named Gilbert and Sullivan that were featured heavily in early trailers.

This is the second of two Aardman-produced films released by Dreamworks. Aardman's experience with Dreamworks during the making of the film led to a split between the two studios.[5]

Home video release

Flushed Away was released on DVD February 20, 2007. It included behind the scenes, deleted info, Jammy Dodger videos and all new slug songs. It was released in the UK on April 2, 2007, where it was packaged with a plasticine 'Slug Farm' kit.[6] The film has yet to be released on Blu-ray.

Reaction

Critical response

Flushed Away has a 72% favorable rating on Rotten Tomatoes.[7]

Box office performance

Flushed Away collected $64,488,856 in the United States, which was below the average of other CGI films from Dreamworks Animation, but $111,814,663 from international markets for a worldwide total of $176,319,242.

References

[1] "Flushed Away at Box Office Mojo" (http://www.boxofficemojo.com/movies/?id=flushedaway.htm). . Retrieved 2010-09-29.

[2] Hornaday, Ann (2006-11-03). "Aardman Saves the Clay In Brilliant 'Flushed Away'" (http://www.washingtonpost.com/wp-dyn/content/article/2006/11/02/AR2006110201845_pf.html). The Washington Post. . Retrieved 2009-02-12.

[3] McCarthy, Todd (2006-10-15). "Flushed Away Review" (http://www.variety.com/review/VE1117931877.html?categoryid=31&cs=1). Variety. . Retrieved 2010-08-31.

[4] "First look at Aardman's rat movie" (http://news.bbc.co.uk/1/hi/entertainment/4720176.stm). *BBC News Online* (BBC). February 16, 2006. .

[5] Laura M. Holson (October 3, 2006). "Is Th-Th-That All, Folks?" (http://www.nytimes.com/2006/10/03/business/media/03animation.html?ex=1185940800&en=a4c0b1858b43f30d&ei=5070). *New York Times*. . Retrieved 2007-07-29.

[6] Buy Flushed Away [Exclusive With Slug Farm Kit!] - DVD Video from Woolworths.co.uk online shop (http://www.woolworths.co.uk/ww_p2/product/index.jhtml?pid=50903737)

[7] "Flushed Away Movie Reviews, Pictures - Rotten Tomatoes" (http://www.rottentomatoes.com/m/flushed_away/). . Retrieved 2009-02-12.

External links

- Official website (http://www.flushedaway.com)
- *Flushed Away* (http://www.imdb.com/title/tt0424095/) at the Internet Movie Database
- *Flushed Away* (http://www.bcdb.com/bcdb/cartoon.cgi?film=69569/) at the Big Cartoon DataBase
- *Flushed Away* (http://www.allmovie.com/work/319319) at Allmovie
- *Flushed Away* (http://www.rottentomatoes.com/m/flushed_away/) at Rotten Tomatoes
- *Flushed Away* (http://www.metacritic.com/film/titles/flushedaway) at Metacritic
- *Flushed Away* (http://www.boxofficemojo.com/movies/?id=flushedaway.htm) at Box Office Mojo
- *Flushed Away* (http://keyframeonline.com/Animation/Flushed_Away/454) at Keyframe - The Animation Resource

The Prestige (film)

The Prestige	
Promotional poster	
Directed by	Christopher Nolan
Produced by	• Christopher Nolan • Aaron Ryder • Emma Thomas
Screenplay by	• Jonathan Nolan • Christopher Nolan
Based on	• *The Prestige* by • Christopher Priest
Starring	• Hugh Jackman • Christian Bale • Michael Caine • Scarlett Johansson • David Bowie • Piper Perabo • Andy Serkis • Rebecca Hall
Music by	David Julyan
Cinematography	Wally Pfister
Editing by	Lee Smith
Studio	• Newmarket Films • Syncopy Films
Distributed by	Touchstone Pictures Warner Bros.
Release date(s)	October 20, 2006
Running time	130 minutes
Country	United States
Language	English

Budget	$40 million [1]
Gross revenue	$109,676,311

The Prestige is a 2006 mystery thriller film directed by Christopher Nolan, with a screenplay adapted from Christopher Priest's 1995 novel of the same name. The story follows Robert Angier and Alfred Borden, rival stage magicians in London at the end of the 19th century. Obsessed with creating the best stage illusion, they engage in competitive one-upmanship with tragic results.

The film features Hugh Jackman as Robert Angier, Christian Bale as Alfred Borden, and David Bowie as Nikola Tesla. It also stars Michael Caine, Scarlett Johansson, Piper Perabo, Andy Serkis, and Rebecca Hall. The film reunites Nolan with actors Bale and Caine from *Batman Begins*, and returning cinematographer Wally Pfister, production designer Nathan Crowley, film score composer David Julyan, and editor Lee Smith.

Priest's epistolary novel was adapted to the screen by Nolan and his brother, Jonathan Nolan, using Nolan's distinctive nonlinear narrative structure. Themes of duality, obsession, sacrifice, and secrecy pervade the conflict. The film was released on October 20, 2006, receiving good reviews and strong box office results, and obtained Academy Award nominations for Best Cinematography and Best Art Direction.

Plot

The movie opens with the trial of magician Alfred Borden (Christian Bale), accused of murdering his lifelong rival, Robert Angier (Hugh Jackman). Through flashbacks, the history of Angier and Borden is told, starting with their beginnings as plants for Milton the Magician (Ricky Jay), with John Cutter (Michael Caine) as his illusion engineer. Angier's wife Julia (Piper Perabo) tragically drowns while performing a predicament escape from a Chinese water torture cell, and Angier suspects that Borden bound her wrists with a new knot that he had suggested to Cutter before—one harder for her to undo than the customary one. At the funeral, Borden enrages Angier by saying he does not know which knot he tied.

The two men begin separate careers as magicians; Borden becomes "The Professor" and hires an engineer named Bernard Fallon, while Angier performs as "The Great Danton" with Cutter and new hire Olivia Wenscombe (Scarlett Johansson) as his assistants. During a parlor magic job, Borden meets a girl named Sarah (Rebecca Hall); they marry and have a daughter, Jess. Sarah feels uneasy about Borden and his apparent fickleness; she claims to know when he loves her "more than the magic" and when he does not. During Borden's performance of the bullet catch, a disguised Angier again demands to know which knot Borden used. Borden and Fallon quickly realize Angier has actually loaded the trick gun. At the last second, Fallon intervenes, and the bullet severs two of Borden's fingers instead of killing him. A disguised Borden later sabotages Angier's performance of the vanishing bird cage illusion, damaging Angier's reputation.

Borden soon astonishes crowds with a new trick called "The Transported Man", in which he bounces a ball across the stage before stepping through a door and instantly reappearing from a second door on the opposite side of the stage to catch the ball before it hits the ground. The new illusion amazes Angier and Olivia. Obsessed with beating Borden, Angier hires a double and steals Borden's trick, with a slight variation, as "The New Transported Man". The double enjoys the applause while Angier can only listen, hidden below the stage. Unhappy at missing the applause and obsessed with figuring out Borden's version of the teleportation illusion, Angier sends Olivia to become Borden's assistant and steal his secrets. Although Olivia provides Angier with Borden's enciphered diary, she falls in love with Borden and double-crosses Angier, allowing Borden to sabotage Angier's act, permanently crippling Angier's left leg by removing a crash mat. In return, Angier and Cutter capture Fallon and bury him alive inside a coffin, revealing his location to Borden in exchange for the key to Borden's illusion. Before rushing to dig out Fallon while he still has air, Borden gives Angier one word, "TESLA", and suggests that it is not merely the key to the transposition cipher of Borden's notebook, but also the key to the illusion.

Angier travels to Colorado Springs so he can meet Nikola Tesla (David Bowie) and learn the secret of Borden's illusion. Instead, Tesla constructs an actual teleportation machine that resembles a Magnifying Transmitter, but the device initially fails to work, leaving test objects lying exactly where they were beforehand. Angier learns from Borden's notebook that he has been sent on a wild goose chase. Feeling he has been cheated, he returns to Tesla's lab, but discovers the truth behind the machine: instead of teleporting an object from one spot to another, it creates an exact duplicate of the first object and leaves the original intact; the field behind the laboratory is full of identical hats and cloned black cats as a result of Tesla's numerous tests on those objects. Tesla is forced to leave Colorado Springs after his rival, Thomas Edison, sends henchmen to torch Tesla's lab, but he leaves Angier an improved version of the machine, as per their agreement. In a letter, however, he warns Angier to destroy it.

Borden's relationship with Olivia takes a heavy emotional toll on Sarah, driving her to drink. Borden's erratic behaviour and inconsistent affection, along with Sarah's suspicion of an extramarital relationship between Borden and Olivia, leads Sarah to hang herself in Borden's magic workshop. Angier returns to London to produce a final set of 100 performances of his new act, blatantly called "The Real Transported Man" as an insult to Borden. He insists that Cutter remain front stage for these shows and that only blind stagehands help backstage. In the new illusion, Angier disappears under huge arcs of electricity and instantaneously "teleports" 50 yards from the stage to the balcony. Borden is baffled but spots a trap door. After a show one night, Fallon follows Angier's stagehands. They move a large, concealed water tank across town to an abandoned building. Borden attends Angier's performance again. He slips backstage just in time to see Angier fall from the trap door into a locked water tank. Borden tries to save him, but Angier drowns before his eyes. Cutter subsequently catches Borden, who is accused of placing the tank there to kill Angier, convicted of murder, and sentenced to death.

In prison, Borden reads Angier's diary from Colorado which addresses him directly with hopes he will rot in prison for his murder. More troubling to him, his daughter Jess will become a ward of court, unless he accepts a mysterious offer. A man named Lord Caldlow sends his attorney to meet Borden in prison. An avid collector of illusionist paraphernalia, Caldlow asks for all of Borden's secrets and devices, including the truth of "The Transported Man". In exchange, he will adopt Jess, and raise her in a rich and comfortable lifestyle. Borden ultimately agrees to the arrangement, but refuses to reveal all unless he can see her before his execution. When Lord Caldlow visits Borden in person on the day of his hanging, with Jess in tow, Borden realizes that he is Angier. Beaten, Borden gives him a note containing the secret of the original Transported Man trick, but Angier tears it up without reading it. Cutter also meets the lord and realizes he is Angier and that Borden was innocent. Cutter then grasps the full grim cost of Angier's obsession when he sees he has adopted Jess. Cutter is furious that he was the one who indirectly framed Borden, who is subsequently hanged.

Cutter accompanies Angier to the abandoned building where the water tanks are stored, and helps him store the teleportation machine. Cutter leaves in disgust, silently acknowledging the arrival of a very-much-alive Borden, who fatally shoots Angier. Borden reveals that he and "Fallon" were identical twins, Albert and Frederick, who lived as a single individual, Alfred, alternating lives as needed. One twin was the husband of Sarah and father to daughter Jess, the one who loved Sarah more than the magic. The other was in love with Olivia, and it is he who volunteered to die in the gallows so that his niece may have her father. For the original Transported Man illusion, a twin acted as the double. They were so committed to hiding the truth of their illusion that after one twin's finger was shot off in Angier's attack, they amputated the other twin's finger to match his brother's injury. Similarly, flashbacks recount Angier's method: that each time he disappeared during his illusion, the machine would create a duplicate, with the first Angier falling through a trap door into a locked tank and drowning, and the duplicate teleporting to the balcony. Each tank stored in the warehouse contains a drowned duplicate of Angier for each time that he has performed the trick; Angier was in effect killing himself over and over. Before leaving, Alfred Borden looks back at the aisles of tanks containing the drowned duplicates and then leaves the dead final Angier as a fire begins to consume the building. Afterwards, Cutter reunites Borden with his daughter.

Cast

- Hugh Jackman as Robert Angier / The Great Danton, an aristocratic magician with a talent for performance. After reading the script, Jackman expressed interest in playing the part of Robert Angier. Christopher Nolan discovered Jackman was interested in the script, and after meeting with him, saw that Jackman possessed the qualities of stage showmanship that Nolan was looking for in the role of Angier. Nolan explained that Angier had "a wonderful understanding of the interaction between a performer and a live audience", a quality he believed that Jackman had. Nolan said that "[Jackman] has the great depth as an actor that hasn't really been explored. People haven't had the chance to really see what he can do as an actor, and this is a character that would let him do that."[2] Jackman based his portrayal of Angier on 1950s-era American magician Channing Pollock.[3]

- Christian Bale as Alfred Borden / The Professor, a working-class magician with an understanding of magic. Christian Bale expressed interest in playing the part of Alfred Borden, and was cast after Jackman. Although Nolan had previously cast Bale as Batman in *Batman Begins*, he did not consider Bale for the part of Borden until Bale contacted him about the script. Nolan said that Bale was "exactly right" for the part of Borden, and that it was "unthinkable" for anyone else to play the part.[2] Nolan described Bale as "terrific to work with", who "takes what he does very, very seriously".[4] Nolan suggested that the actors should not read the book, but Bale ignored his advice.[5]

- Michael Caine as John Cutter, the stage engineer who works for Angier. Caine had previously collaborated with Nolan and Bale in *Batman Begins*, where he played Alfred Pennyworth, the Wayne family butler. Nolan said that even though it felt like the character of Cutter was written for Caine, it was not. Nolan noted that the character "was written before I'd ever met him".[2] Caine describes Cutter as "a teacher, a father and a guide to Angier". Caine, in trying to create Cutter's nuanced portrait, altered his voice and posture. Nolan later said that "Michael Caine's character really becomes something of the heart of the movie. He has a wonderful warmth and emotion to him that draws you into the story and allows you to have a point of view on these characters without judging them too harshly."[6]

- Rebecca Hall as Sarah Borden: Borden's wife. Hall had to relocate from North London to Los Angeles in order to shoot the film, though the film itself takes place in North London. Hall said that she "was starstruck just to be involved in [the film]".[7]

- Scarlett Johansson as Olivia Wenscombe, Angier's assistant and Borden's lover. Nolan said that he was "very keen" for Johansson to portray the role, and when he met with her to discuss it, "she just loved the character".[2] Johansson praised Nolan's directing methods, saying that she "loved working with [him]"; he was "incredibly focused and driven and involved, and really involved in the performance in every aspect."[8]

- David Bowie as Nikola Tesla, the real life inventor who creates a device for Angier. For the role of Nikola Tesla, Nolan wanted someone who was not necessarily a film star, but was "extraordinarily charismatic". Nolan said that "David Bowie was really the only guy I had in mind to play Tesla because his function in the story is a small but very important role".[2] Nolan contacted David Bowie, who initially turned down the part. As a lifelong fan of his music, Nolan flew out to New York to pitch the role to Bowie in person, telling him that nobody else could possibly play the part;[9] Bowie accepted after a few minutes.[2]

- Piper Perabo as Julia McCullough, Angier's wife.

- Roger Rees as Owens.

- Andy Serkis as Mr. Alley, Tesla's assistant. Serkis said that he played his character with the belief that he was "once a corporation man who got excited by this maverick, Tesla, so jumped ship and went with the maverick". Serkis described his character as a "gatekeeper", a "conman", and "a mirror image of Michael Caine's character". Serkis, a big fan of Bowie, said that he was enjoyable to work with, describing him as "very unassuming, very down to earth... very at ease with himself and funny."[10]

- Ricky Jay as "Milton the Magician", an older magician Borden and Angier work for at the beginning of the story. Jay, a noted American stage magician, and Michael Weber trained Jackman and Bale for their roles with brief instruction in various stage illusions. The magicians gave the actors limited information, allowing them to know enough to pull off a scene.[5]

Production

Julian Jarrold's and Sam Mendes's producer approached Christopher Priest for an adaptation of his novel *The Prestige*. Priest was impressed with Nolan's films *Following* and *Memento*,[11] and subsequently, producer Valerie Dean brought the book to Christopher Nolan's attention.[12] In October 2000, Christopher Nolan traveled to the UK to publicize *Memento*, as Newmarket Films was having difficulty finding a U.S. distributor. While in London, Christopher Nolan read Priest's book and shared the story with his brother while walking around in Highgate (a location later featured in the scene where Angier ransoms Borden's ingénieur in Highgate Cemetery). The development process for *The Prestige* began as a reversal of their earlier collaboration: Jonathan Nolan had pitched his initial story for *Memento* to his brother during a road trip.[13]

A year later, the option on the book became available and was purchased by Aaron Ryder of Newmarket Films.[12] [13] In late 2001, Christopher Nolan became busy with the post-production of *Insomnia*, and asked Jonathan Nolan to help work on the script.[13] The writing process was a long collaboration between the Nolan brothers, occurring intermittently over a period of five years.[14] In the script, the Nolans emphasized the magic of the story through the dramatic narrative, playing down the visual depiction of stage magic. The three-act screenplay was deliberately structured around the three elements of the film's illusion: the pledge, the turn, and the prestige. "It took a long time to figure out how to achieve cinematic versions of the very literary devices that drive the intrigue of the story," Christopher Nolan told *Variety*. "The shifting points of view, the idea of journals within journals and stories within stories. Finding the cinematic equivalents of those literary devices was very complex."[15] Although the film is thematically faithful to the novel, two major changes were made to the plot structure during the adaptation process: the novel's spiritualism subplot was removed, and the modern-day frame story was replaced with Borden's wait for the gallows.[12] Priest approved of the adaptation, describing it as "an extraordinary and brilliant script, a fascinating adaptation of my novel".[12]

In early 2003, Nolan planned to direct the film before the production of *Batman Begins* accelerated.[5] [17] Following the release of *Batman Begins*, Nolan started up the project again, negotiating with Bale and Jackman in October 2005.[18] While the screenplay was still being written, production designer Nathan Crowley began the set design process in Nolan's garage, employing a "visual script" consisting of scale models, images, drawings, and notes. Jonathan and Christopher Nolan finished the final shooting draft on January 13, 2006, and began production three days later on January 16. Filming ended on April 9.[19]

The historic Tower Theatre in Los Angeles was used as the location for the Pantage Theatre in London[16]

Crowley and his crew searched Los Angeles for almost seventy locations that would resemble fin de siècle London.[16] Jonathan Nolan visited Colorado Springs to research Nikola Tesla and based the electric bulb scene on actual experiments conducted by Tesla.[13] Nathan Crowley helped design the scene for Tesla's invention; It was shot in the parking lot of the Mount Wilson Observatory.[16] Influenced by a "Victorian modernist aesthetic", Crowley chose four locations in the Broadway theater district in downtown Los Angeles for the film's stage magic performances: the Los Angeles Theatre, the Palace Theatre, the Los Angeles Belasco, and the Tower Theatre.[20] Crowley also turned a portion of the Universal back lot into Victorian London.[21] Nolan built only one set for the film, an "under-the-stage section that houses the machinery that makes the larger illusions work,"[22] preferring to simply dress various Los Angeles locations and sound stages to stand in for Colorado and Victorian England.[23] In contrast to most period pieces,

Nolan kept up the quick pace of production by shooting with handheld cameras,[23] and refrained from using artificial lighting in some scenes, relying instead on natural light on location.[5] Costume designer Joan Bergin chose attractive, modern Victorian fashions for Scarlett Johansson; cinematographer Wally Pfister captured the mood with soft earth tones as white and black colors provided background contrasts, bringing actors' faces to the foreground.[24]

Editing, scoring and mixing finished on September 22, 2006.[19] The song "Analyse" by Radiohead frontman Thom Yorke is played over the credits.[25]

Themes

The rivalry between Borden and Angier dominates the film. Obsession, secrecy, and sacrifice fuel the battle, as both magicians contribute their fair share to a deadly duel of one-upmanship, with disastrous results. Angier's obsession with beating Borden costs him Cutter's friendship, while Borden's obsession with maintaining the secrecy of his twin leads Sarah to question their relationship, eventually resulting in her suicide when she discovers the truth; in the end, Angier and Borden both lose Olivia's love because of their obsessions. Their struggle is also expressed through class warfare: Borden as The Professor, a working-class magician who gets his hands dirty, versus Angier as The Great Danton, a classy showman whose accent makes him appear American.[26] Film critic Matt Brunson observes a complex theme of duality exemplified by Angier and Borden, noting that the film chooses not to depict either magician as "good" or "evil".[27]

Angier's theft of Borden's teleportation illusion in the film echoes the many real-world examples of stolen tricks among magicians. Outside the film, similar rivalries include magicians John Nevil Maskelyne and Harry Kellar's dispute over a levitation illusion.[28] Gary Westfahl of *Locus Online* also notes a "new proclivity for mayhem" in the film over the novel, citing the murder/suicide disposition of Angier's duplicates and intensified violent acts of revenge and counter-revenge. This "relates to a more general alteration in the events and tone of the film" rather than significantly changing the underlying themes.[29]

Nor is this cutthroat competition limited to prestidigitation: engineering "wizards" Nikola Tesla and Thomas Edison engaged in a rivalry over electrical current, which appears in the film in parallel to Borden and Angier's competition for magical supremacy.[30] [31]

Den Shewman of *Creative Screenwriting* says the film asks how far one would go to devote oneself to an art. The character of Chung Ling Soo, according to Shewman, is a metaphor for this theme.[12] Film critic Alex Manugian refers to this theme as the "meaning of commitment."[32] For example, Soo's pretense of being slow and feeble misdirects his audience from noticing the physical strength required to perform the goldfish bowl trick, but the cost of maintaining this illusion is the sacrifice of individuality: Soo's true appearance and freedom to act naturally are consciously suppressed in his ceaseless dedication to the art of magic.

Nicolas Rapold of *Film Comment* addresses the points raised by Shewman and Manugian in terms of the film's "refracted take on Romanticism":

> Angier's technological solution – which suggests art as sacrifice, a phoenix-like death of the self - and Borden's more meat-and-potatoes form of stagecraft embody the divide between the artist and the social being.[33]

For Manugian the central theme is "obsession," but he also notes the supporting themes of the "nature of deceit" and "science as magic." Manugian criticizes the Nolans for trying to "ram too many themes into the story."[32]

Music

English musician and film score composer David Julyan penned the music for *The Prestige*. Julyan had previously collaborated with director Christopher Nolan on *Memento* and *Insomnia*. Like the film, the soundtrack was divided into three sections: the Pledge, the Turn, and the Prestige.[34]

Some critics were disappointed with the score, acknowledging that while it worked within the context of the film, it was not enjoyable by itself.[35] [36] Jonathan Jarry of SoundtrackNet described the score as "merely functional", establishing the atmosphere of dread but never taking over. Although the reviewer was interested with the score's notion, Jarry found the execution was "extremely disappointing".[35]

Christopher Coleman of Tracksounds felt that although it was "a perfectly fitting score", it was completely overwhelmed by the film itself, and was totally unnoticed at times.[36] Christian Clemmensen of Filmtracks recommended the soundtrack for those who enjoyed Julyan's work on the film, and noted that it was not for those who expected "any semblance of intellect or enchantment in the score to match the story of the film." Clemmensen called the score lifeless, "constructed on a bed of simplistic string chords and dull electronic soundscapes."[37]

Reception

Touchstone opted to move the release date up a week, from the original October 27, to October 20, 2006.[38] The film earned $14,801,808 on opening weekend in the United States, debuting at #1. It proceeded to gross $109 million, of which $53 million was from the US.[1] The film received nominations for the Academy Award for Best Art Direction and the Academy Award for Best Cinematography,[39] as well as a nomination for the Hugo Award for Best Dramatic Presentation, Long Form in 2007.[40]

The Prestige received generally favorable reviews from film critics,.[41] *Rotten Tomatoes* reported that 75% of critics gave the film positive reviews, with an average score of 7.1/10, based upon a sample of 179 reviews.[42] At *Metacritic*, which assigns a normalized rating out of 100 to reviews from mainstream critics, the film received an average score of 66, based on 36 reviews.[41] Claudia Puig of *USA Today* described the film as "one of the most innovative, twisting, turning art films of the past decade."[43] Drew McWeeny gave the film a glowing review, saying it demands repeat viewing,[44] with Peter Travers of *Rolling Stone* agreeing.[45] Richard Roeper and guest critic A.O. Scott gave the film a "two thumbs up" rating.[46] [47] Todd Gilchrist of IGN applauded the performances of Bale and Jackman whilst praising Nolan for making "this complex story as easily understandable and effective as he made the outwardly straightforward comic book adaptation (*Batman Begins*) dense and sophisticated... any truly great performance is almost as much showmanship as it is actual talent, and Nolan possesses both in spades."[48] *CNN.com* and *Village Voice* film critic Tom Charity listed it amongst his best films of 2006.[49] Philip French of *The Observer* recommended the film, comparing the rivalry between the two main characters to that of Mozart and Salieri in the highly acclaimed *Amadeus*.[50]

On the other hand, Dennis Harvey of *Variety* criticized the film as gimmicky, though he felt the cast did well in underwritten roles.[51] Kirk Honeycutt of *The Hollywood Reporter* felt that characters "are little more than sketches. Remove their obsessions, and the two magicians have little personality".[52] Nonetheless, the two reviewers praised David Bowie as Tesla, as well as the production values and cinematography. On a simpler note, Emanuel Levy has said: "Whether viewers perceive *The Prestige* as intricately complex or just unnecessarily complicated would depend to a large degree on their willingness to suspend disbelief for two hours." He gave the film a B grade.[53]

Roger Ebert gave the film three stars out of four, he described the revelation at the end a "fundamental flaw" and a "cheat". He wrote, "The pledge of Nolan's *The Prestige* is that the film, having been metaphorically sawed in two, will be restored; it fails when it cheats, as, for example, if the whole woman produced on the stage were not the same one so unfortunately cut in two."[54] R.J. Carter of *The Trades* felt, "I love a good science fiction story; just tell me in advance." He gave the film a B-.[55] Author Christopher Priest saw the film three times as of January 5, 2007, and his reaction was "'Well, holy shit.' I was thinking, 'God, I like that,' and 'Oh, I wish I'd thought of that.'"[56]

Blu-ray and DVD release

The Region 1 disc is by Buena Vista Home Entertainment, and was released on February 20, 2007, and is available on DVD and BD formats.[57] The Warner Bros. Region 2 DVD was released on March 12, 2007.[58] It is also available in both BD and regionless HD DVD in Europe (before HD DVD was canceled). Special features are minimal, with the documentary *Director's Notebook: The Prestige – Five Making-of Featurettes*, running roughly twenty minutes combined, an art gallery and the trailer. Nolan did not contribute to a commentary as he felt the film primarily relied on an audience's reaction and did not want to remove the mystery from the story.[59]

Notes

[1] "The Prestige (2006)" (http://boxofficemojo.com/movies/?id=prestige.htm). Box Office Mojo. . Retrieved 2007-03-03.

[2] Chris Carle (2006-10-12). "Casting The Prestige" (http://uk.movies.ign.com/articles/738/738782p1.html). IGN. . Retrieved 2007-03-05.

[3] White, Cindy (2006-10-18). "Christian Bale and Hugh Jackman square off as rival magicians in Christopher Nolan's The Prestige" (http://www.syfy.com/sfw/interviews/sfw13910.html). *Interviews. Sci Fi Weekly*. . Retrieved 2008-07-09.

[4] Murray, Rebecca. "Director Christopher Nolan Interview" (http://movies.about.com/od/theprestige/a/prestigcn101606.htm). About.com. . Retrieved 2008-06-29.

[5] Dan Jolin (2006-09-29). "You Won't Believe Your Eyes". Empire. pp. 134–140.

[6] Roberts, Sheila. "Interview: Michael Caine, *The Prestige*" (http://www.moviesonline.ca/movienews_10222.html). MoviesOnline. . Retrieved 2008-06-29.

[7] Lowe, Jaime (2006-11). "Rebecca Hall: for this Young Actress, Landing Choice Roles is like Pulling Rabbits out of a Hat" (http://findarticles.com/p/articles/mi_m1285/is_10_36/ai_n16850421). CNET Networks. . Retrieved 2008-06-29.

[8] Fischer, Paul (2006-07-26). "Interview: Scarlett Johansson for "Scoop"" (http://www.darkhorizons.com/interviews/1039/scarlett-johansson-for-scoop-). Dark Horizons. . Retrieved 2008-06-29.

[9] "Tricks of the Trade" (http://www.irishtimes.com/theticket/articles/2006/1110/1163059516890.html). *The Ticket (The Irish Times)*. 2006-11-10. . Retrieved 2008-04-21.

[10] Carnevale, Rob. "The Prestige – Andy Serkis interview" (http://www.indielondon.co.uk/Film-Review/the-prestige-andy-serkis-interview). Indie London. . Retrieved 2008-07-06.

[11] Toy, Sam (2006-09-29). "Magic marker". Empire. pp. 137.

[12] Shewman, Den. (Sept/Oct 2006). Nothing Up Their Sleeves: Christopher & Jonathan Nolan on the Art of Magic, Murder, and The Prestige. *Creative Screenwriting* (http://www.creativescreenwriting.com/index.html). Vol. 13:5.

[13] Jeff Goldsmith. *The Prestige Q&A: Interview with Jonathan Nolan* (http://cdn2.libsyn.com/creativescreenwritingmag/ThePrestigeQandA.mp3?nvb=20090804012227&nva=20090805013227&t=0177c850fb5969f409276) Creative Screenwriting Magazine Podcast. *Creative Screenwriting*. (2006-10-28). Podcast accessed on 2007-07-24.

[14] Stuart McGurk (2007-03-12). "How I made... The Prestige: Christopher Nolan" (http://www.thelondonpaper.com/staying-in/film-dvd-s/christopher-nolan). The London Night In. . Retrieved 2007-03-13.

[15] Cohen, David S. (2006-12-18). "Adapted Screenplay". Variety.

[16] Wada, Karen (2007-02-01). "Tricked Out: How production designer Nathan Crowley transformed modern Los Angeles into Victorian London for The Prestige". *Los Angeles Magazine* **52** (2): 94–97. ISSN 1522-9149.

[17] Michael Fleming (2003-04-16). "Nolan wants 'Prestige'" (http://www.variety.com/index.asp?layout=story&articleid=VR1117884751&categoryid=13&cs=1). Variety. . Retrieved 2007-03-04.

[18] Michael Fleming, David S. Cohen (2005-10-02). "Meet the men of magic" (http://www.variety.com/article/VR1117930078.html?categoryid=1236&cs=1&p=0). Variety. . Retrieved 2007-03-05.

[19] Nolan, Christopher (Director). (October 17, 2006). *The Prestige* (http://video.movies.go.com/theprestige/). [Motion picture]. USA: Touchstone Pictures. Event occurs at "Resonances" bonus feature. .

[20] Steffie Nelson (2007-01-09). "*Magic pics pull conjuring tricks*" (http://www.variety.com/awardcentral_article/VR1117956937.html?nav=look07). Variety. . Retrieved 2007-05-09.

[21] Idelson, Karen (2006-11-13). "H'wood back lots still work magic". **404**. Variety. pp. A4–A4.

[22] Lawson, Terry (2006-10-17). "'Batman' stars team in 'Prestige': Actors learned to perform magic for their roles". Detroit Free Press.

[23] Carle, Chris (2006-09-20). "The Prestige Edit Bay Visit" (http://uk.movies.ign.com/articles/733/733653p1.html). IGN. . Retrieved 2006-10-05.

[24] Nolan, Christopher (Director). (October 17, 2006). *The Prestige* (http://video.movies.go.com/theprestige/). [Motion picture]. USA: Touchstone Pictures. Event occurs at "Conjuring the Past" bonus feature. .

[25] Henriksen, Erik (October 19, 2006). "Ye Olde Dueling Magicians" (http://www.portlandmercury.com/portland/Content?oid=73234&category=22133). The Portland Mercury. . Retrieved 2006-10-23.

[26] Murray, Rebecca. "Christian Bale Talks About "The Prestige" - Page 2" (http://movies.about.com/od/theprestige/a/prestigcb101606_2.htm). About. . Retrieved 2006-11-01.

[27] Brunson, Matt. "Film/Now Showing" (http://www.connectsavannah.com/show_article.php?article_id=1448). Connect Savannah. . Retrieved 2006-11-03.

[28] Kawamoto, Wayne. "Film Review: The Prestige" (http://magic.about.com/od/magicinthemedia/fr/102206prestige.htm). About. . Retrieved 2006-11-01.

[29] Westfahl, Gary. "Seeing Double: A Review of The Prestige" (http://www.locusmag.com/2006/Features/Westfahl_ThePrestige.html). Locus Online. . Retrieved 2007-04-05.

[30] Difrancesco, Teresa (2006-10-20). "Jonathan Nolan on writing The Prestige" (http://www.movieweb.com/news/NEdUmdgicLhhgf). Movie Web. . Retrieved 2006-10-31.

[31] "'Prestige' is magical" (http://www.arktimes.com/Articles/ArticleViewer.aspx?ArticleID=aaac8060-5dbf-4877-a4bd-126f3f71f9b0). Arkansas Times. 2006-10-26. . Retrieved 2006-10-31.

[32] Manugian, Alex (2006-11-03). "Movie Review: Not dazzling, but still fascinating" (http://web.archive.org/web/20070930014459/http://www2.townonline.com/harvard/artsLifestyle/view.bg?articleid=609060&format=&page=1). The Harvard Post. Archived from the original (http://www2.townonline.com/harvard/artsLifestyle/view.bg?articleid=609060&format=&page=1) on 2007-09-30. . Retrieved 2006-11-03.

[33] Rapold, Nicolas (Jan-Feb 2007). "Dueling-Magician Pick:The Prestige". *Film Comment*: 77.

[34] Vincentelli, Elisabeth. "*The Prestige*: David Julyan: Music" (http://www.amazon.com/The-Prestige/dp/B000IFRQI6). Amazon.com. . Retrieved 2008-07-17.

[35] Jarry, Jonathan (2006-12-15). "SoundtrackNet: *The Prestige* Soundtrack" (http://www.soundtrack.net/albums/database/?id=4270&page=review). SoundtrackNet. . Retrieved 2008-07-26.

[36] Coleman, Christopher. "*The Prestige* by David Julyan" (http://www.tracksounds.com/reviews/the_prestige_david_julyan.htm). Tracksounds. . Retrieved 2008-07-17.

[37] Clemmensen, Christian. "Filmtracks: *The Prestige* (David Julyan)" (http://www.filmtracks.com/titles/prestige.html). Filmtracks. . Retrieved 2008-07-17.

[38] "*The Prestige* Changes the Date" (http://www.canmag.com/news/4/3/4493). Canmag.com. 2006-07-23. . Retrieved 2006-10-05.

[39] "79th Oscar Nominations Announced" (http://www.empireonline.com/news/story.asp?NID=20278). Empire. 2007-01-23. . Retrieved 2007-01-23.

[40] "Nippon 2007 Hugo Nominees" (http://www.nippon2007.us/hugo_nominees.php). Nippon 2007. 2001-04-01. . Retrieved 2007-05-20.

[41] "Prestige, The (2008): Reviews" (http://www.metacritic.com/film/titles/prestige). *Metacritic*. CNET Networks, Inc. . Retrieved 2008-07-11.

[42] "The Prestige reviews" (http://www.rottentomatoes.com/m/prestige/). *Rotten Tomatoes*. IGN Entertainment, Inc. . Retrieved 2008-07-11.

[43] Puig, Claudia (2006-10-20). "'The Prestige': Magical, marvelous filmmaking" (http://www.usatoday.com/life/movies/reviews/2006-10-19-review-prestige_x.htm). USA Today. . Retrieved 2007-03-04.

[44] McWeeny, Drew (2006-10-13). "Moriarty conjures up AICN's first review of The Prestige!" (http://www.aintitcool.com/?q=node/30390). Ain't It Cool News. . Retrieved 2006-10-15.

[45] Travers, Peter (2006-10-20). "The Prestige" (http://www.rollingstone.com/reviews/movie/9387671/review/12087204/the_prestige). Rolling Stone. . Retrieved 2007-03-04.

[46] Richard Roeper and A.O. Scott. (2006-10-20). *Ebert & Roeper*.

[47] A.O. Scott (2006-10-20). "Two Rival Magicians, and Each Wants the Other to Go Poof" (http://movies2.nytimes.com/2006/10/20/movies/20pres.html?ref=movies). The New York Times. . Retrieved 2007-02-16.

[48] Gilchrist, Todd (2006-10-15). "Elevating movie magic to new artistic heights" (http://uk.movies.ign.com/articles/740/740205p1.html). IGN. . Retrieved 2006-10-20.

[49] Charity, Tom (2006-12-28). "The best (and worst) films of the year" (http://www.cnn.com/2006/SHOWBIZ/Movies/12/27/best.films/index.html). CNN.com. .

[50] French, Philip (2006-11-12). "The Prestige" (http://www.guardian.co.uk/film/2006/nov/12/drama.sciencefictionandfantasy). *The Observer*. . Retrieved 2007-05-14.

[51] Harvey, Dennis (2006-10-13). "The Prestige" (http://www.variety.com/review/VE1117931858.html?categoryid=31&cs=1). Variety. . Retrieved 2006-10-15.

[52] Honeycutt, Kirk (2006-10-16). "The Prestige" (http://web.archive.org/web/20061103195022/http://www.hollywoodreporter.com/thr/reviews/review_display.jsp?vnu_content_id=1003254756). The Hollywood Reporter. Archived from the original (http://www.hollywoodreporter.com/thr/reviews/review_display.jsp?vnu_content_id=1003254756) on 2006-11-03. . Retrieved 2006-10-15.

[53] Levy, Emanuel (2006-10-15). "The Prestige" (http://www.emanuellevy.com/search/details.cfm?id=3427). Emanuel Levy.com. . Retrieved 2006-10-15.

[54] Roger Ebert (2007-09-07). "Atmospherically lovely, 'Prestige' is, alas, a cheat; Christopher" (http://rogerebert.suntimes.com/apps/pbcs.dll/article?AID=/20070906/REVIEWS/709060303/1023). Chicago Sun-Times. . Retrieved 2007-11-15.

[55] R.J Carer (2007-02-20). "The Prestige" (http://www.the-trades.com/article.php?id=5224). The Trades. . Retrieved 2007-11-15.

[56] Dawn, Randee (2007-01-05). "Source material" (http://www.hollywoodreporter.com/hr/search/article_display.jsp?vnu_content_id=1003528129). The Hollywood Reporter. . Retrieved 2007-03-04.

[57] Woodward, Tom (2007-01-08). "The Prestige" (http://www.dvdactive.com/news/releases/the-prestige.html). DVD Active. . Retrieved 2007-01-20.

[58] Gould, Chris (2007-01-16). "The Prestige" (http://www.dvdactive.com/news/releases/the-prestige2.html). DVD Active. . Retrieved 2007-01-20.

[59] Gilchrist, Todd (2007-02-20). "The Pledge, The Turn, The Prestige, The DVD" (http://dvd.ign.com/articles/766/766063p1.html). IGN. . Retrieved 2007-02-26.

External links

- Official website (http://http://theprestige.movies.go.com/)
- *The Prestige* (http://www.imdb.com/title/tt0482571/) at the Internet Movie Database
- *The Prestige* (http://www.boxofficemojo.com/movies/?id=prestige.htm) at Box Office Mojo
- *The Prestige* (http://www.allmovie.com/work/337176) at Allmovie
- *The Prestige* (http://www.rottentomatoes.com/m/prestige/) at Rotten Tomatoes

The Fountain

The Fountain	
Theatrical release poster	
Directed by	Darren Aronofsky
Produced by	Arnon Milchan Iain Smith Eric Watson
Written by	*Screenplay:* Darren Aronofsky *Story:* Darren Aronofsky Ari Handel
Starring	Hugh Jackman Rachel Weisz
Music by	Clint Mansell
Cinematography	Matthew Libatique
Editing by	Jay Rabinowitz
Studio	Regency Enterprises Protozoa Pictures
Distributed by	Warner Bros. (USA/Canada) 20th Century Fox (International)
Release date(s)	November 22, 2006
Running time	96 minutes
Country	United States
Language	English
Budget	$35 million
Gross revenue	$15,978,422

The Fountain is a 2006 American film directed by Darren Aronofsky and starring Hugh Jackman and Rachel Weisz. The film comprises three storylines where Jackman and Weisz play different sets of characters: a modern-day scientist and his cancer-stricken wife, a conquistador and his queen, and a space traveler who hallucinates his lost love. The storylines, interwoven with use of match cuts and recurring visual motifs, reflect the themes of love and mortality.

Aronofsky originally planned to direct *The Fountain* on a $70 million budget with Brad Pitt and Cate Blanchett in the lead roles, but Pitt's withdrawal and cost overruns led Warner Bros. to shut down production. The director rewrote the script to be sparser, and was able to resurrect the film with a $35 million budget with Jackman and Weisz in the lead roles. Production mainly took place on a sound stage in Montreal, and the director used macro photography to create key visual effects for *The Fountain* at a low cost.

The film was released theatrically in the United States and Canada on November 22, 2006. It grossed $10,144,010 in the United States and Canada and $5,761,344 in other territories for a worldwide total of $15,978,422. Critics' reaction to the film was divided. The consensus was that the film was visually strong but lacked focus in its ambition.

Narrative

The Fountain has three storylines, each separated by five centuries. The three periods are interwoven with match cuts and recurring visual motifs. In 16th century Central America in Mayan territory, conquistador Tomas quests for the tree of life. In 2005, medical researcher Tommy obsessively seeks a cure for the brain tumor killing his wife, Izzy. In 2500, space traveler Tom travels to a nebula in a bubble-shaped spacecraft that contains a garden and a dying tree of life. In all three periods, Hugh Jackman and Rachel Weisz play the main characters.[1] Director Darren Aronofsky emphasized that the storylines in their time periods and their respective convergences were open to interpretation. It is unclear what is "real": if the astronaut is meditating on his past; if the Conquistador is only a character in the wife's unfinished novel; or, it is intended to convey the psychodrama idea that re-imagining past events re-creates new meanings. The director said of *The Fountain*'s intricacy and underlying message, "[The film is] very much like a Rubik's cube, where you can solve it in several different ways, but ultimately there's only one solution at the end."[2]

Themes

Darren Aronofsky described the core of the film as, "...a very simple love story," about a man and a woman in love, with the woman dying young. The director researched people who were dying young, and learned from doctors and caregivers that such patients find new ways of coping. Aronofsky observed that the patients often die more alone because their families cannot recognize what happens with them, calling it, "an incredible tragedy":

> "Instead of facing this tragedy in terror, she is coming to terms with what is happening to her...Many patients actually start opening up to the possibility of what's happening to them, but there's very little vocabulary to help them deal...We decided to expand it with this woman [Izzy] offering a gift to her husband of a metaphor that tells him where she's come to. Hopefully through time he'll be able to understand it and basically get where she is."[3]

Judeo-Christian spirituality is a theme in the film—particularly the Fall of Man from the Book of Genesis' account of the story of Adam and Eve

The Fountain's theme of necrophobia (thanatophobia), or fear of death, is a "...movement from darkness into light, from black to white," that traces the journey of a man scared of death and moving toward it.[4] The film begins with a paraphrase of Genesis 3:24, the Biblical passage that reflects the fall of man. Hugh Jackman emphasized the importance of the fall in the film: "The moment Adam and Eve ate of the tree of knowledge, of good and evil, humans started to experience life as we all experience it now, which is life and death, poor and wealthy, pain and pleasure, good and evil. We live in a world of duality. Husband, wife, we relate everything. And much of our lives are spent not wanting to die, be poor, experience pain. It's what the movie's about."[5] Aronofsky also interpreted the story of Genesis as the definition of mortality for humanity. He inquired of the fall, "If they had drank from the tree of life [instead of the tree of knowledge] what would have separated them from their maker? So what makes us human is actually death. It's what makes us special."[6]

Production history

Director Darren Aronofsky

Director Darren Aronofsky sought to produce *The Fountain* after releasing *Requiem for a Dream* in 2000. In April 2001, he entered negotiations with Warner Bros. and Village Roadshow to direct the then-untitled film with actor Brad Pitt in the lead role.[7] *Requiem for a Dream* was screened for Pitt, and the preliminary script for *The Fountain* persuaded the actor to join the project.[8] Aronofsky prepared for production by traveling with a crew to Central America to consult with Mayan experts and to explore the ruins of Palenque. The group also visited to Tikal, a jungle location featured in the 1977 film *Star Wars*.[9] In addition to the trip, the films *Aguirre, the Wrath of God* and *The Holy Mountain* were screened for the crew to inspire it in designing a rain forest set for *The Fountain*.[10] In June 2001, actress Cate Blanchett entered talks to join Aronofsky's project.[11] Aronofsky, who wanted the film's actual title to be a secret, gave the project the working title of *The Last Man*.[12] Production was postponed to improve the script and to wait for Blanchett, pregnant when she joined, to give birth to her child in December 2001. The start date for production was tentatively set in summer 2002.[13]

In June 2002, Warner Bros. met with Aronofsky and producer Eric Watson, expressing concerns over an escalating budget and threatening to cease the project unless a co-financier was found. Watson petitioned independent production companies for support and was able to enlist Regency Enterprises for assistance.[8] Production was ultimately set for late October 2002 in Queensland and Sydney, Australia. The film, officially titled *The Fountain*, was 'greenlit' (approved for production) with a budget of $70 million, co-financed by Warner Bros. and New Regency, who filled the gap after Village Roadshow withdrew from the project.[14] Preparation for production of *The Fountain* cost $18 million.[15] Abruptly, Pitt, whose requested screenplay revisions were not met, left the project seven weeks before the first day of shooting.[9] The actor went on to star as Achilles in director Wolfgang Petersen's *Troy*.[16] With the studio threatening to shut down the project, Aronofsky sent the script to actor Russell Crowe as a potential replacement for Pitt. However, Crowe, worn out from recently completing *Master and Commander: The Far Side of the World*, declined.[8] In September 2002, Jeff Robinov, President of Production at Warner Bros. Pictures, announced that *The Fountain* would cease production,[16] with Blanchett receiving compensation for her time and the Australian crew being fired from the halted project.[8] Sets built for the production of the film, including a 10-story Mayan temple, were eventually auctioned off, in addition to props and other items.[17] Pitt said that he was disappointed to leave and added, "I remain encouraged that *The Fountain* will yet have its day."[16]

Aronofsky began to develop other projects. When he looked over the books he used to research for *The Fountain*, he decided to return to the project, feeling closer to it creatively more than the other possible projects. Without a studio and an actor, he decided to write a "no-budget" version of the film, using his experiences filming *Pi* and *Requiem for a Dream* with small budgets.[18] In February 2004, Warner Bros. resurrected Aronofsky's project and began to court actor Hugh Jackman to replace Pitt in the lead role. The film received a second greenlight with a budget of $35 million, in part because of the director's willingness to leave costly set pieces out of the screenplay.[19] In August, actress Rachel Weisz joined Hugh Jackman for the project, filling the vacancy left by Blanchett.[20] Filming lasted 60 days in early 2005 and took place mainly on a sound stage in Montreal.[21] [8]

Writing

Darren Aronofsky and his friend Ari Handel created the story for *The Fountain*, and Aronofsky wrote the screenplay. When Aronofsky saw *The Matrix* in 1999, he considered it a film that redefined the science fiction genre. He sought to make a science fiction film that would explore new territory in the genre like *The Matrix* and its predecessors *Star Wars* and *2001: A Space Odyssey*. Aronofsky had in mind a science fiction film that would go beyond the other films whose plots were driven by technology and science. The director said, "We've seen it all. It's not really interesting to audiences anymore. The interesting things are the ideas; the search for God, the search for meaning."[7]

In 1999, when Aronofsky turned 30 years old, his parents were diagnosed with cancer. He began reflecting on human mortality, "That was a really heavy-duty emotional time. I know it's a very young age, but turning thirty marks when your twenties are over and you could start considering, 'Wow, one of these days I'm actually going to die.'" While his parents overcame cancer, he began to focus on the concept of a young man saving a loved one from a life-threatening disease. He shared the concept with Handel, his undergraduate school roommate at Harvard University. Handel earned a Ph.D in neuroscience from New York University but was uncertain about a future in neuroscience. He

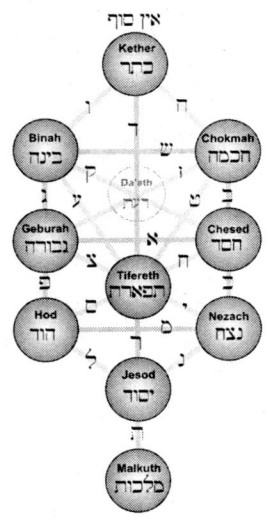

Jewish mysticism is a theme in Aronofsky's previous film *Pi*; the Tree of Life from the Book of Genesis and Kabbalah was an inspiration for *The Fountain*

recalled the discussion, "Darren and I just started talking about the story. We kept wanting to talk more about it as the story kept getting bigger. I decided to make some life choices to continue working with Darren, because it was so much fun."[22]

The director relied on a change of locale to inspire him to write *Pi* and *Requiem for a Dream*. For *The Fountain*, Aronofsky was inspired by a research trip he took to Guatemala with Handel to learn about Mayan history and philosophy.[23] The script for *The Fountain* was influenced by the accounts of Uruguayan journalist Eduardo Galeano, who wrote examples of myth from an indigenous perspective,[24] particularly Galeano's *Genesis* trilogy.[8] The film *Once Upon a Time in America* also served as an influence on the script.[25] Aronofsky, influenced by Bernal Díaz del Castillo's *The Conquest of New Spain*, applied the narrative in writing the film's conquistador scenes.[26]

Aronofsky realized that since writing in 2000 the battle scene between the armies of Mayans and conquistadors, *The Lord of the Rings* film trilogy, *Troy*, *King Arthur*, and other films had featured massive battle scenes. He felt less inclined to mimic the scale and rewrote the battle to be mainly between Jackman's conquistador character and the Mayans. The director realized that, with one man against the army, the rewrite was a suitable metaphor for his film's theme of a man defying odds to do the impossible and conquer death.[27]

The filmmakers researched space travel and Mayan culture, including its history, religion, and spirituality. They attended brain surgeries with the actors. With the research in place, Aronofsky said, "We decided which things we wanted to be purely factual and which things we wanted to bend."[28] The director did not strive to be historically accurate with the 16th century period, perceiving it as the setting of a fairy tale written by Izzi. He said, "It was more about painting a relationship between a queen and her warrior, and just using that for more fantasy reasons."[3]

Casting

Actor Hugh Jackman, who plays multiple characters in *The Fountain*

Aronofsky saw Hugh Jackman perform as Peter Allen in the Broadway musical *The Boy from Oz* and was impressed with his performance. The director met with Jackman, who sought "a role that could show a lot of dimension," and cast him into the lead role in *The Fountain*.[26] Jackman starred previously as the muscular character Wolverine in the *X-Men* films, so for *The Fountain*, he exercised to adopt a slimmer figure. Jackman practiced tai chi for seven months to demonstrate it in a 30-second scene. He also practiced yoga for over a year to achieve the lotus position for scenes set in space. For these scenes when he is seen in the position in mid-air, he was immersed in a swimming pool and harnessed to a rig that rotated him 360 degrees so his clothes floated freely about him.[29]

Jackman also watched a woman undergo brain tumor surgery and was shaken to see the woman have similar blond hair to his wife: "All I could think of was my wife on that table. As much as I'd read the script and theorized and practiced philosophy, I knew in that moment that I was so not ready for death."[5] For his various characters, the actor assumed a different posture for each persona. As the conquistador, Jackman was upright and forward-leaning to evoke an unstoppable nature. As the scientist, the actor hunched over with a dedicated focus on his character's work, being weighed down by the "world on his shoulders." As the space traveler, Jackman practiced the state of zen but also exhibited a continued persistence in his endeavor.[30]

Jackman suggested that Aronofsky cast Rachel Weisz as his character's wife. The director, who was in a relationship with the actress, had originally hesitated to show the studio signs of favoritism in casting Weisz. With Jackman's earnest recommendation, the actress was cast as Isabel.[31] For her role, Weisz read books and first-person accounts about people who had terminal illnesses.[30] The actress also visited hospitals to see young people who were dying and under hospice care. "There were a few days where I was in the headspace where I could say: 'I could go now'," said Weisz.[32]

The Fountain also stars Ellen Burstyn as Dr. Lillian Guzetti, Tommy's superior, and Mark Margolis as Father Avila, who accompanies Tomas the conquistador. Burstyn and Margolis appeared in Aronofsky's *Requiem for a Dream*, and the director wrote into the script roles for both of them.[26] Sean Patrick Thomas, Donna Murphy, and Ethan Suplee were cast as assistants to Tommy's lab work. Cliff Curtis was cast as Captain Ariel, a fellow conquistador, and Stephen McHattie was cast as Grand Inquisitor Silecio, a religious fanatic who threatens the Spanish queen.[33] Seventy extras were cast as Maya warriors, including twenty who had actual Guatemala Mayan backgrounds. One of the twenty, a real-life spiritual leader, was cast as the Maya spiritual leader in the film.[21]

Design

The film's locations, with the exception of scenes filmed at a museum and at a farmhouse, were built on the Montreal sound stage.[34] Production designer James Chinlund and his crew built sets for *The Fountain* in a large warehouse in Montreal. The sets included the 16th century jungle settings and the bubble-shaped spacecraft containing the tree of life and its garden.[35] The spacecraft set was placed against greenscreen, and the crew hung colored reflective material, which included green, black, gold, and silver, on three circular tracks around the set. One material would be moved into place instead of the heavy equipment, and with the other materials partitioned off, a light source was used with the preferred material. Silver was used for scenes in which the spacecraft moved through the stars, and gold was used for when it entered the nebula.[36]

The climax of the past storyline takes place at a Mayan ziggurat such as this one. To research the film, Darren Aronofsky took a trip to Guatemala and visited Mayan ruins.

In *The Fountain*, the Tree of Life was a central design and part of the film's three periods. The tree was based on Kabbalah's Sefirot, which depicts a "map" of creation to understand the nature of God and how he created the world ex nihilo (out of nothing). The Sefirot Tree, being two to three hundred feet tall in lore, had to be resized for *The Fountain* to fit in the camera's frame.[37] Pieces of driftwood and pieces from real trees in Canada were collected for the tree's branches and roots, and sculpted molds of the pieces were applied to a steel frame to create the tree's body.[38] According to production designer James Chinlund, the tree, part of an enormous set surrounded by green screens, and other sets presented difficult logistical problems because of the small budget given to the resurrected project. The tree set itself had been a collaboration between Chinlund, Aronofsky, and cinematographer Matthew Libatique to create the appropriate design, particularly the palette in comparison to the biospheric ship that carries the tree in the astronaut period.[39] Aronofsky described the astronaut period as a homage to David Bowie's "Space Oddity"; the protagonist's name "Tom" originating from the Major Tom of the popular song.[26] Co-writer Ari Handel researched biospherics, such as the Biosphere 2, to help design the ship that carried the protagonist and the tree through space.[39] With respect to the glass-sphered ship's design, Aronofsky argued, "There is no reason a spaceship would be built like a giant truck in space."[10]

Aronofsky and cinematographer Matthew Libatique also discussed using a limited palette of colors, an approach that started with Aronofsky's *Pi* and continued with *Requiem for a Dream*.[40] In *The Fountain*, the primary colors are gold and white. Gold represents "the Mayans, a sort of fool's gold, a false truth";[41] Aronofsky explained the choice, "When you see gold, it represents materialism and wealth and all these things that distract us from the true journey that we're on."[4] White was chosen to represent mortality and truth. Weisz's characters wear white or are enveloped in white light to accentuate this presentation. Secondary colors are green, representing the color of life, and red, representing death.[41] The director also used similar geometric constructs in the film to distinguish the three storylines. The 16th century conquistador's tale reflected triangles through pyramids and constellations, the 21st century researcher's period reflected rectangles through doors, windows, and computer screens, and the 26th century contemplative's journey reflected circles and spheres through the spacecraft and stellar bodies.[42]

Cinematography

Cinematographer Matthew Libatique shot *The Fountain* under Aronofsky's direction. Libatique, who worked with Aronofsky throughout the 1990s,[43] prepared for over a year for *The Fountain* when Aronofsky tried to produce the film for the first time. When production restarted on a smaller budget, Libatique felt that the more budget-conscious approach resulted in a better film, "I think the streamlining of the film helped us tell the story more effectively. It's been stripped down to its core, to what it's really about: a search for immortality, when the truth of life is mortality."[1]

Aronofsky planned to have a strong presentation of the thematic movement from darkness into light. He originally sought to show only a silhouette of the man until the second of the film's three acts, but he chose not to be so extreme, wanting to be more communicative to the audience. The movement was presented less aggressively in the film; Jackman's characters are seen in silhouette at the beginning, kept out of key light. In each of the three periods, the lighting on Jackman's characters is initially dim and gradually grows brighter as the storylines unfold.[41] Meanwhile, Weisz's characters are frequently awash with light in the storylines.[44] Libatique described the metaphoric change of the lighting on Jackman's characters, "We follow the arc of the Thomas character as he gets closer and closer to the truth."[41]

Aronofsky preferred to use one camera whenever possible, only using a second camera if the scene was more about the setting and could be shot from two distinctly different axes. Libatique said Aronofsky preferred the eyeline match, "Darren is big on eyelines, and if you sacrifice an eyeline on an angle, he feels it nullifies the shot and de-emphasizes the performances."[45] Aronofsky originally intended to have Jackman's characters always moving in an "unusual" left-right direction across the frame, but the plan was complicated by the spacecraft needing to move upward toward a light source.[40]

Visual effects

When production restarted in 2005, there was a more budget-conscious approach to filming *The Fountain*, whose original budget was mostly intended for visual effects. Libatique reflected, "Visual effects comprised of a lot of the budget in the original conception. The popcorn moments were in there to justify the budget and bring target audiences into the theater. Ultimately, I think the streamlining of the film helped us tell the story more effectively. It's been stripped down to the core, to what it's really about: a search for immortality, when the truth of life is mortality. I think at the end of the day, the theme of the film will be easier to feel."[46]

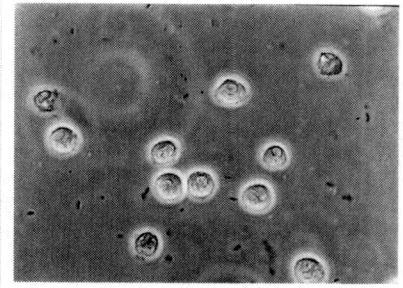

Rather than resort to CGI for special effects, Aronofksy preferred trick photography, such as enhancing photographs of microorganisms

To create a death scene, Aronofsky drew from Maya mythology the description of when valiant warriors die, flowers and butterflies emerge from their bodies. Aronofsky excluded butterflies from the death scene to minimize the film's computer-generated imagery but kept the effect of flowers bursting from the body.[37]

Jeremy Dawson and Dan Schrecker, who had provided visual effects for Darren Aronofsky's π and *Requiem for a Dream*, returned to *The Fountain* to help the director with the film's effects. The pair were assigned with the task of creating as little computer-generated imagery as possible, a difficult task with a third of the film taking place in deep space. Aronofsky chose to avoid effects that would make the film look dated in several decades but instead hold up as well as a film like *2001: A Space Odyssey*. Dawson said, "Using CG is really the easy route because it's so prevalent and the tools are great. What it did was really force us to come up with creative solutions to solve a lot of our problems." One creative solution was uncovering Peter Parks, a specialist in macro photography, who had retrieved deep-sea microorganisms and photographed them in 3-D under partial funding from the Bahamas government. Parks brewed chemicals and bacteria together to create reactions that Schrecker and Dawson shot 20,000 feet worth of film of over eight weeks.[39] To create the effects, Peter Parks took advantage of fluid dynamics, which affected the behavior of the substances that he photographed. "When these images are projected on a big screen, you feel like you're looking at infinity. That's because the same forces at work in the water—gravitational effects, settlement, refractive indices—are happening in outer space," Parks said. The specialist's talent convinced the film's creative department to go beyond computer-generated imagery and follow

Parks' lead. Instead of millions of dollars for a single special effects sequence, Parks generated all the footage for the film for just $140,000.[9]

The visual effects company Look Effects worked on 87 shots for *The Fountain* that included major set extensions, digital mattes, image enhancement, face replacement and blemish removal, as well as animating key elements to the film's story. Henrik Fett, the visual effects supervisor of Look Effects, said, "Darren was quite clear on what he wanted and his intent to greatly minimize the use of computer graphics... [and] I think the results are outstanding."[47]

Musical score

Clint Mansell—the composer for Aronofsky's previous films *Pi* and *Requiem for a Dream*—reprised his role for *The Fountain*. The San Francisco-based string quartet Kronos Quartet—who previously performed for the *Requiem for a Dream* soundtrack, and Scottish post-rock band Mogwai also contributed to the film score.[48] The soundtrack was released by Nonesuch Records in 2006 and received numerous award nominations.

Marketing

When Warner Bros. shut down pre-production of *The Fountain* in 2002, Aronofsky reserved rights to publish a graphic novel based on the script that was not produced. He said, "I knew it was a hard film to make, and I said at least if Hollywood fucks me over at least I'll make a comic book out of it."[49] He shopped the story to Vertigo Comics and met comic book artist Kent Williams, whose illustrations impressed him. Aronofsky hired Williams to create the graphic novel, and Ari Handel, co-writer for the film, provided Williams with research, photographs, and images on "Mayans, astronomy, pulsars, and all kinds of cool stuff" for the graphic novel's design. Aronofsky gave Williams the freedom to interpret the story as the artist saw fit.[49]

Singer David Bowie's song "Space Oddity" influenced one of *The Fountain*'s storylines

Composer Clint Mansell worked with post-rock band Mogwai and the classical string section Kronos Quartet to provide the film's music.

The Fountain was originally scheduled to be released on October 13, 2006, but the film was delayed to create a "long-lead campaign" and generate anticipation via word of mouth. The release date was ultimately set for November 22, 2006.[50] Aronofsky shared his screenplay with eleven artists: Phil Hale, Martin Wilner, Jason Shawn Alexander, Kostas Seremetis, Dave Gibbons, Barron Storey, James Jean, Jim Lee, Olivier Bramanti, Seth Fisher, and Bill Sienkiewicz. He invited them to interpret the screenplay in each one's chosen medium, and the interpretations were intended to be available on the film's website.[51] Aronofsky also published a book about the film that contained production stills, the original script, original art, and observations by the film's creators.[52] The content and research agency Ramp Industry launched The Fountain Remixed, an official website driven by user-generated content. Users could download freely provided audio parts from *The Fountain*'s film score, remix the music, and upload the work onto the website to be evaluated by other users.[53]

Reception

The film had its world premiere at the 63rd Venice International Film Festival on September 2, 2006.[54] Several critics booed *The Fountain* at the festival's press screening, while the film received a 10-minute standing ovation at the public screening the following evening.[15] *The Fountain* was released in 1,472 theaters in the United States and Canada on November 22, 2006, a day before the American Thanksgiving holiday. The film earned $3,768,702 in the U.S. and Canadian box office during the opening weekend of November 24. *The Fountain* earned $10,144,010 in the United States and Canada, and $5,761,344 in other territories. The film, which had a production budget of $35 million, grossed $15,978,422 in theaters worldwide.[55] The box office performance was considered a flop with the film only earning back 54% of its budget.[56]

The review aggregate website Rotten Tomatoes reported that 51% of 187 critics gave the film positive reviews and that it got a rating average of 5.9 out of 10.[57] At Metacritic, which assigns a weighted average score out of 100 to reviews from mainstream critics, the film received an average score of 51 based on 36 reviews.[58] Rotten Tomatoes reported the critics' consensus, "*The Fountain* — a movie about metaphysics, universal patterns, Biblical symbolism, and boundless love spread across one thousand years — is visually rich but suffers from its own unfocused ambitions."[57] *Newsweek* reported how people received the film, "Its supporters admire the film's beauty and daring; its detractors find it overblown and hokey."[59]

Michael Atkinson, writing for *Sight & Sound*, reviewed Aronofsky's endeavor, "It's difficult to recall another American film that, in pursuing a passionate and personal vision, goes so maddeningly, uproariously wrong." Atkinson said of the narrative, "The erratic and pointless leapfrogging between its storylines is torporific ... all three stories are assembled piecemeal, many of which repeat over and over as flashback and flashforwards." He complained of the numerous motifs, "It's difficult to swallow the amalgamation of Mayan, Biblical, Buddhist, Taoist and New Age iconography, all of it tossed as if into a stew."[60] In contrast, Glenn Kenny of *Premiere* wrote of the film, "*The Fountain* is probably the deftest stories-within-stories narrative film I've seen ... By *The Fountain*'s end, the multilayered meta-narrative... resolves (or does it?) into a kind of diegetic Möbius strip, to stunning effect." Kenny called the film "as demanding as it is dazzling" and compared Aronofsky's direction to Stanley Kubrick's "in terms of conceptual audacity and meticulousness of execution." He concluded, "It's a movie that's as deeply felt as it is imagined."[61]

Anthony Lane, reviewing for *The New Yorker*, called *The Fountain* "a gorgeous nimbus of confusion." Lane complained about the film's up-close and far-away shots, "What fails to concern or attract Aronofsky is the place where most of us hang out—the in-between, the midshot of everyday existence." He summarized, "The movie may have significant truths to impart, although I have my doubts, but it feels too inexperienced, too unworldly, to have earned the right to them."[62] Roger Ebert, who admired Aronofsky's previous films, conceded in the *Chicago Sun-Times* that *The Fountain* was "not a great success." He identified the film's issues: "too many screens of blinding lights," "too many transitions for their own sake," and "abrupt changes of tone." He believed that the scaling down of the film from Aronofsky's original ambition lost some elements and anticipated a director's cut truer to Aronofsky's vision.[63]

In 2009, Aronofsky reflected on the reception of *The Fountain*, "There are a lot of Fountain-haters out [at the Venice Film Festival]. The film's about the fact that it's OK that we die, and we should come to terms with it. But many, many people don't want to think about that, so why pay money for a meditation on losing someone you love? Everything about western culture denies that." He also believed the film was released at the wrong time, "It was pre-Obama, smack in the middle of Paris Hilton time. But there has been a serious turn now, people are starting to realise that the party's over, finally. So we can stop thinking about the culture of superficiality, start to remember there are other things going on."[64]

In the book *Positive Psychology At The Movies: Using Films to Build Virtues and Character Strengths*, Ryan M. Niemiec and Danny Wedding cite the film as one which depicts the development of perspective. "[Jackman's character's] denial and work addiction are obstacles to the development of the strength of perspective, but he is able to confront those obstacles as he develops acceptances and wisdom, represented by themes drawn from both Buddhism (meditation, rebirth, reincarnation) and Christianity (eternal life, faith, and love)."[65]

Home video

The Fountain was released on DVD, HD DVD, and Blu-ray in the United States on May 15, 2007. The included extras were the theatrical trailer and a six-part featurette gallery about the film's periods and settings.[66] Aronofsky was disappointed with the limited extras available on home video. He reported that Warner Bros. did not want to have the director record a commentary track because it felt the commentary would not help sales. He hoped to petition for the film to be re-released in the Criterion Collection with extras that were not made available on the initial media.[67] Aronofsky recorded a commentary track on his own and made the track available on his personal website.[68] In December 2008, he expressed interest in reassembling *The Fountain*, not as a director's cut, but as an alternate story that combined theatrical footage and unused footage.[69]

See also

Similar works listed at Allmovie:[70]

- *Solaris* (2002)
- *Altered States* (1980)
- *A.I. Artificial Intelligence* (2001)
- *What Dreams May Come* (1998)
- *The Nines* (2007)
- *Youth Without Youth* (2007)
- *Sunshine* (2007)

Notes

[1] Calhoun 2006, pp. 51–52

[2] Kolakowski, Nick (November 24, 2006). "Director Darren Aronofsky: A 'Fountain' Quest Fulfilled" (http://www.washingtonpost.com/wp-dyn/content/article/2006/11/23/AR2006112300534.html). *Washington Post*. . Retrieved November 27, 2006.

[3] Macaulay 2006, p. 44

[4] Murray, Rebecca (October 20, 2006). "Darren Aronofsky Talks About "The Fountain"" (http://movies.about.com/od/thefountain/a/fountain101906_2.htm). *About.com*. .

[5] Schneller, Johanna (August 31, 2006). "Hugh Jackman: Cover Story" (http://archive.premiere.com/actors/3060/cover-story-hugh-jackman.html). *Premiere*. . Retrieved November 11, 2006.

[6] Sciretta, Peter (November 21, 2006). "Interview: Darren Aronofsky, director of The Fountain, Part 2" (http://www.slashfilm.com/article.php/20061121aronofskyinterview2). */FILM*. . Retrieved December 19, 2006.

[7] Linder, Brian (April 5, 2001). "Aronofsky, Pitt Team for Sci-Fi Epic" (http://movies.ign.com/articles/050/050987p1.html). *IGN*. . Retrieved November 1, 2006.

[8] Fierman, Daniel (December 1, 2006). "From Here to Eternity" (http://www.ew.com/ew/article/0,,1557390,00.html). *Entertainment Weekly*. . Retrieved February 18, 2007.

[9] Silberman, Steve (November 1, 2006). "The Outsider" (http://wired.com/wired/archive/14.11/outsider_pr.html). *Wired News*. . Retrieved November 11, 2006.

[10] Dollar, Steve (November 6, 2006). "The Fountain of youth..." (http://www.pastemagazine.com/action/article/3493/feature/film/the_fountain_of_youth). *Paste*. . Retrieved November 11, 2006.

[11] Linder, Brian (June 28, 2001). "Blanchett Joining Pitt in Aronofsky's Next" (http://movies.ign.com/articles/300/300933p1.html). *IGN*. . Retrieved November 10, 2006.

[12] Topel, Fred (November 27, 2006). "Crave talks to Darren Aronofsky" (http://web.archive.org/web/20070927195728/http://www.craveonline.com/filmtv/articles/04647134/crave_talks_to_darren_aronofsky.html). *CraveOnline.com*. Archived from the original (http://www.craveonline.com/filmtv/articles/04647134/crave_talks_to_darren_aronofsky.html) on September 29, 2007. . Retrieved December 18, 2006.

[13] Linder, Brian (August 31, 2001). "Aronofsky's Sci-Fi Epic Postponed" (http://movies.ign.com/articles/305/305442p1.html). *IGN*. . Retrieved November 10, 2006.

[14] Linder, Brian (July 25, 2002). "*Fountain* Flows at Warner Bros." (http://movies.ign.com/articles/365/365914p1.html). *IGN.* . Retrieved November 10, 2006.

[15] Macnab, Geoffrey (September 7, 2006). "'I knew we were going to get attacked ... '" (http://www.guardian.co.uk/film/2006/sep/07/festivals1). *Guardian Unlimited.* . Retrieved October 8, 2006.

[16] Linder, Brian (September 13, 2002). "Brad Pitt: Achilles Heel" (http://movies.ign.com/articles/370/370982p1.html). *IGN.* . Retrieved November 10, 2006.

[17] Linder, Brian (August 26, 2003). "*The Fountain* Auctioned Off" (http://movies.ign.com/articles/435/435434p1.html). *IGN.* . Retrieved November 10, 2006.

[18] Macaulay 2006, p. 42

[19] Linder, Brian (February 27, 2004). "*The Fountain* Flows Again" (http://movies.ign.com/articles/495/495272p1.html). *IGN.* . Retrieved November 10, 2006.

[20] Linder, Brian (August 5, 2004). "Weisz Wades Into *Fountain*" (http://movies.ign.com/articles/536/536252p1.html). *IGN.* . Retrieved November 10, 2006.

[21] Carr, David (March 20, 2005). "A Reincarnation Story That Won't Stay Dead" (http://www.nytimes.com/2005/03/20/movies/20carr.html). *The New York Times.* . Retrieved November 10, 2006.

[22] Goldsmith 2006, p. 53

[23] Goldsmith 2006, p. 54

[24] Wright, Andrew (November 22, 2006). "Long Strange Trip" (http://www.thestranger.com/seattle/Content?oid=110172). *The Stranger.* . Retrieved February 17, 2007.

[25] Morris, Clint (January 29, 2007). "Ask a Celeb: Darren Aronofsky's Answers!" (http://web.archive.org/web/20071011154256/http://www.moviehole.net/news/20070129_ask_a_celeb_darren_aronofskys.html). *Moviehole.net.* Archived from the original (http://www.moviehole.net/news/20070129_ask_a_celeb_darren_aronofskys.html) on 2007-10-11. . Retrieved February 17, 2007.

[26] Daniel Robert Epstein (2005-04-01). "Darren Aronofsky - The Fountain" (http://suicidegirls.com/interviews/Darren+Aronofsky+-+The+Fountain/). SuicideGirls. . Retrieved 2006-11-10.

[27] Macaulay 2006, pp. 42–43

[28] Macaulay 2006, p. 43

[29] Wood, Gaby (January 28, 2007). "Here's looking at Hugh". *The Sun-Herald.*

[30] Server, David (November 17, 2006). "CD Exclusive: 'The Fountain' Cast and Crew Q&A!" (http://www.countingdown.com/features?feature_id=3917457). *CountingDown.com.* .

[31] Roberts, Sheila (November 17, 2006). "Hugh Jackman Interview, The Fountain" (http://www.moviesonline.ca/movienews_10478.html). *MoviesOnline.ca.* . Retrieved December 19, 2006.

[32] ""The Fountain" makes a splash at Venice" (http://www.channelnewsasia.com/stories/entertainment/view/228648/1/.html). *Channel NewsAsia.* September 5, 2006. . Retrieved November 11, 2006.

[33] "The Fountain – Cast" (http://movies.nytimes.com/movie/312594/The-Fountain/cast). *The New York Times.* . Retrieved December 7, 2009.

[34] Douglas, Edward (November 17, 2006). "Exclusive: Filmmaker Darren Aronofsky" (http://www.comingsoon.net/news/movienews.php?id=17542). *ComingSoon.net.* . Retrieved December 19, 2006.

[35] Calhoun 2006, p. 54

[36] Calhoun 2006, p. 55

[37] Peter Sciretta (2006-11-20). "Interview: Darren Aronofsky, director of The Fountain" (http://www.slashfilm.com/article.php/20061120darreninterview). /FILM. . Retrieved 2006-11-28.

[38] Blair, Iain (January 8, 2007). "Design spotlight: 'The Fountain'" (http://www.variety.com/awardcentral_article/VR1117956944.html?nav=news&categoryid=1985&cs=1). *Variety.* . Retrieved February 17, 2007.

[39] Weiland, Jonah (April 11, 2005). "Talking with the Makers of "The Fountain"" (http://www.comicbookresources.com/news/newsitem.cgi?id=5080). *Comic Book Resources.* . Retrieved November 10, 2006.

[40] Calhoun 2006, p. 53

[41] Calhoun 2006, pp. 53–54

[42] "Capone and Darren Aronofsky Discuss THE FOUNTAIN!!!"" (http://www.aintitcool.com/node/30768). *Ain't It Cool News.* November 20, 2006. . Retrieved November 27, 2006.

[43] Calhoun 2006, p. 50

[44] Faraci, Devin (November 22, 2006). "Devin's Exclusive Interview: Darren Aronofsky (The Fountain)" (http://web.archive.org/web/20070218234251/http://chud.com/interviews/8081). *CHUD.com.* Archived from the original (http://chud.com/interviews/8081) on February 18, 2007. . Retrieved November 28, 2006.

[45] Calhoun 2006, p. 62

[46] Calhoun 2006, p. 51

[47] "Look Effects Does More With Less CG on The Fountain" (http://www.awn.com/news/visual-effects/look-effects-does-more-less-cg-fountain). Animation World Network. October 23, 2006. . Retrieved April 23, 2010.

[48] "Mogwai Contribute to Film Score on Aronofsky Film 'The Fountain'" (http://www.thespacelab.tv/spaceLAB/2006/08August/MusicNews-05-Mogwai.htm). *Spacelab Music News.* August 1, 2006. . Retrieved November 10, 2006.

[49] Weiland, Jonah (April 6, 2005). "Talking "The Fountain" Graphic Novel with Darren Aronofsky and Ari Handel" (http://www.comicbookresources.com/?page=article&id=4853). *Comic Book Resources*. . Retrieved November 10, 2006.

[50] Stax (August 1, 2006). "*Fountain, Accepted* Shift" (http://movies.ign.com/articles/722/722494p1.html). *IGN*. . Retrieved November 11, 2006.

[51] Gustines, George Gene (November 5, 2006). "Six Ways of Looking at 'The Fountain'" (http://www.nytimes.com/2006/11/05/movies/moviesspecial/05gust.html). *The New York Times*. . Retrieved November 11, 2006.

[52] "Rizzoli New York - Catalog - The Fountain by Darren Aronofsky" (http://www.rizzoliusa.com/catalog/display.pperl?isbn=9780789314956). *rizzoliusa.com*. Rizzoli. . Retrieved November 11, 2006.

[53] "Ramp to create UGC site for launch of Fox's 'The Fountain'" (http://www.brandrepublic.com/bulletins/digital/article/603142/ramp-create-ugc-site-launch-foxs-the-fountain/). *Brand Republic*. November 7, 2006. . Retrieved November 11, 2006.

[54] "'The Fountain' makes a splash at Venice". Agence France-Presse. September 4, 2006.

[55] "The Fountain (2006)" (http://www.boxofficemojo.com/movies/?page=main&id=fountain.htm). *Box Office Mojo*. . Retrieved May 18, 2007.

[56] "Hollywood's Biggest Flops" (http://www.forbes.com/2010/01/22/sean-penn-eddie-murphy-business-entertainment-star-flops.html). *forbes.com*. Forbes. January 22, 2010. . Retrieved April 23, 2010. "*The Fountain* earned $16 million on a budget of $35 million. It failed to earn back 54% of its budget."

[57] "The Fountain (2006)" (http://www.rottentomatoes.com/m/the_fountain/). *Rotten Tomatoes*. . Retrieved December 4, 2009.

[58] "Fountain, The" (http://www.metacritic.com/film/titles/fountain). *Metacritic*. . Retrieved December 4, 2009.

[59] Gordon, Devin (November 27, 2006). "2006: A Space Oddity". *Newsweek* **148** (20): 56. ISSN 0028-9604.

[60] Atkinson, Michael (March 2007). "The Fountain". *Sight & Sound* **17** (3): 56. ISSN 0037-4806.

[61] Kenny, Glenn (November 22, 2006). "The Fountain" (http://www.premiere.com/Review/Movies/The-Fountain). *Premiere*. . Retrieved December 4, 2009.

[62] Lane, Anthony (December 4, 2006). "The Current Cinema: High Hopes". *The New Yorker* **82** (40): 104–105. ISSN 0028-792X.

[63] Ebert, Roger (September 14, 2007). "'The Fountain' spews forth lots of babble" (http://rogerebert.suntimes.com/apps/pbcs.dll/article?AID=/20070913/REVIEWS/709130305/1023). *Chicago Sun-Times*. . Retrieved December 4, 2009.

[64] "Darren Aronofsky: 'Everyone gets cheques now'". *The Guardian*. June 24, 2009.

[65] Niemiec, Ryan M.; Wedding, Danny (2008). "Wisdom II: Open Mindedness, Love of Learning and Perspective". *Positive Psychology At The Movies: Using Films to Build Virtues and Character Strengths*. Hogrefe Publishing. pp. 49. ISBN 0889373523.

[66] "Warner Brings 'The Fountain' to Blu-ray, HD DVD" (http://www.highdefdigest.com/news/show/Warner/Disc_Announcements/Warner_Brings_The_Fountain_to_Blu-ray,_HD_DVD/515). *High-Def Digest* (Internet Brands, Inc.). March 7, 2007. . Retrieved March 19, 2007.

[67] Sciretta, Peter (May 30, 2007). "Darren Aronofsky Blames Warner Bros For Fountain DVD" (http://www.slashfilm.com/2007/05/30/darren-aronofsky-blames-warner-bros-for-fountain-dvd/). */FILM*. . Retrieved December 8, 2009.

[68] Sciretta, Peter (September 17, 2007). "Darren Aronofsky Releases The Fountain Audio Commentary Online" (http://www.slashfilm.com/2007/09/17/darren-aronofsky-releases-the-fountain-audio-commentary-online/). */FILM*. . Retrieved December 8, 2009.

[69] Loder, Kurt (December 4, 2008). "Mickey Rourke And Darren Aronofsky: Party People" (http://moviesblog.mtv.com/2008/12/04/mickey-rourke-and-darren-aronofsky-party-people-by-kurt-loder/). *MTV Movies Blog* (MTV). . Retrieved December 8, 2009.

[70] "The Fountain > Overview" (http://www.allmovie.com/work/the-fountain-312594). *Allmovie*. . Retrieved August 19, 2010.

References

- Calhoun, John (November 2006). "Eternal love". *American Cinematographer* **87** (11): 50–60,62–63. ISSN 0002-7928.

- Goldsmith, Jeff (September 2006). "The Fountain". *Creative Screenwriting* **13** (5): 53–57. ISSN 1084-8665.

- Macaulay, Scott (October 2006). "Death defying". *Filmmaker* **15** (1): 40–45,128,130–131. ISSN 1063-8954.

Further reading

- Aronofsky, Darren (2006). *The Fountain*. Universe. ISBN 0789314959

External links

- Official website (http://http://thefountainmovie.warnerbros.com/)
- *The Fountain* (http://www.imdb.com/title/tt0414993/) at the Internet Movie Database

Scoop (2006 film)

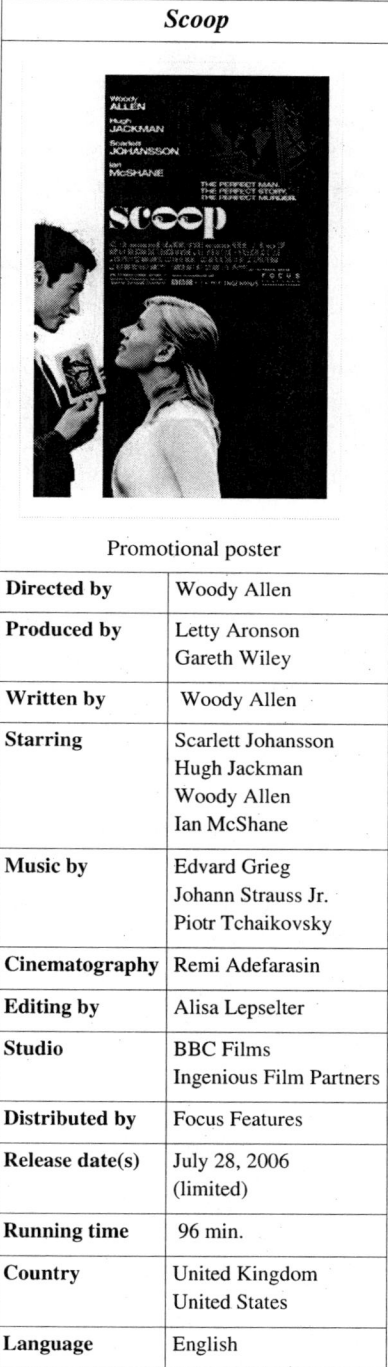

Scoop	
Promotional poster	
Directed by	Woody Allen
Produced by	Letty Aronson Gareth Wiley
Written by	Woody Allen
Starring	Scarlett Johansson Hugh Jackman Woody Allen Ian McShane
Music by	Edvard Grieg Johann Strauss Jr. Piotr Tchaikovsky
Cinematography	Remi Adefarasin
Editing by	Alisa Lepselter
Studio	BBC Films Ingenious Film Partners
Distributed by	Focus Features
Release date(s)	July 28, 2006 (limited)
Running time	96 min.
Country	United Kingdom United States
Language	English

Budget	US$4 million[1] [2]
Gross revenue	US$39,215,642

Scoop is a 2006 American-British romantic comedy/murder mystery written and directed by Woody Allen and starring Hugh Jackman, Scarlett Johansson, Ian McShane, and Allen himself. Focus Features released the film, which was rated PG-13 by the MPAA for "some sexual content."

Plot

Following the memorial service for irrepressible investigative reporter Joe Strombel (McShane), Strombel's spirit finds himself on the barge of death with several others, including a young woman who believes she was poisoned by her employer, Peter Lyman (Jackman). The woman tells Strombel she thinks Lyman, a handsome British aristocrat with political ambitions, may be the Tarot Card Killer, a notorious serial killer of prostitutes, and that he killed her when she stumbled onto his secret. The Tarot Card Killer left a card on each dead body after each murder.

Sondra Pransky (Johansson) is a beautiful but somewhat awkward American college journalist on vacation in London. Pransky attends a performance given by magician Sid Waterman (Allen), aka "The Great Splendini," and agrees to participate on the stage. While in a booth known as The Dematerializer, Pransky encounters Strombel's ghost who has escaped the Grim Reaper himself to impart his suspicions of Lyman to a journalist who can investigate the story (a scene influenced by a similar scene in Federico Fellini's *Nights of Cabiria*, where when Cabiria (Giulietta Masina) is about to expose a stage magician as a fraud, he performs actual magic). Sondra decides to infiltrate Lyman's privileged world and find out if he truly is the dreaded criminal, enlisting Sid in the process and taking advantage of his powers of deception.

Sondra catches Lyman's attention by pretending to drown near him at a swimming pool. When he rescues her, she introduces herself as Jade Spence, daughter of a wealthy oil family from Palm Beach. While Sid poses as her father, "Jade" begins dating Lyman. As the deception begins, Sondra is convinced Lyman is the murderer while Sid finds it impossible to believe. But as the film progresses and Sondra falls in love with Lyman, she begins to trust him as well. Meanwhile, Sid becomes less sanguine about Lyman as he notices more and more inconsistencies, especially after he and Sondra find a Tarot deck hidden under a French horn in Peter's vault, a climate-controlled music room containing expensive musical instruments. Sid finally prevails upon Sondra to write a news story implicating Lyman, but the newspaper editor refuses the story because of Sondra's lack of proof. Throughout their investigations, Sid and Sondra have a relationship that is in turns friendly, paternal, and also antagonistic—fueled largely by Sondra's annoyance that her smooth "Jade Spence" charade is being compromised by Sid's obnoxious attempts to act the part of a nouveau riche oil baron.

Soon thereafter, however, the police arrest the real Tarot Card Killer. Sondra, relieved that her suspicions were for naught, reveals her real name and the deception she and Sid had practiced. Lyman is surprisingly gracious, and tells Sondra he desires to keep seeing her. They plan to spend the weekend at Lyman's isolated country estate. Later, Sid (at Strombel's urging) suggests that Peter used the Tarot Card murders to cover up a murder he committed.

While Sondra and Lyman vacation in the country, Sid continues to investigate this theory. He finds that Lyman did frequent a prostitute, Betty Gibson, who was later killed, apparently by the Tarot Card Killer. Gibson is described as a "baby-faced blonde" (just like Sondra) before Peter convinced her to dye her hair, presumably to match the profile of the other Tarot victims. When Sid calls Sondra with his findings, she waves them off. Unbeknownst to her, Peter is ominously listening in on another extension.

As the film approaches its climax, Sid breaks in to Lyman's vault again, this time finding the key to Betty Gibson's flat. Meanwhile, out on a canoe in Lyman's lake, Peter confesses to Sondra that he killed Gibson to stop her blackmailing him, and he used the Tarot Card pattern to allay suspicion, just as Strombel had told Sid. Peter comments on the irony that he first met Sondra by saving her from drowning, and now she really would drown. He would kill Sid later; no one would connect an obscure stage magician's death to that of a clumsy journalism student. This scene is intercut with shots of Sid driving madly to the Lyman estate to rescue Sondra, a shot interrupted by an off camera crash.

After his confession, Peter throws Sondra into the lake and watches her go under. He then calls the police. When they question him, he tells them of how Sondra was a terrible swimmer and how she almost drowned that first day at the pool. Suddenly, Sondra enters, soaking wet but smiling cheerfully. She informs Peter and the police that the drowning had been an act to get his attention, and actually she was a very good swimmer.

The penultimate scene of the film takes place back in the newspaper offices. The editor who previously rejected Sondra's article now congratulates Sondra on a brilliant piece of investigative journalism, the start of a promising career. This scene also reveals that the appearance of Peter's cufflink at the earlier murder was a coincidence resulting from the fact that he regularly visited prostitutes.

Sondra seems flattered, and says she must also credit Joe Strombel and the late Sid Waterman, Splendini. The final scene of the film shows Sid, now himself a passenger on the Reaper's ship, performing the same magical gags and comedy routines he did in life for his fellow spirits.

Cast

- Scarlett Johansson as Sondra Pransky
- Woody Allen as Sid Waterman
- Hugh Jackman as Peter Lyman
- Ian McShane as Joe Strombel
- Charles Dance as Mr. Malcom
- Romola Garai as Vivian
- Kevin R. McNally as Mike Tinsley
- Julian Glover as Lord Lyman
- Victoria Hamilton as Jan
- Fenella Woolgar as Jane Cook
- Geoff Bell as Strombel's Co-Worker

Production

- As is often the case with Allen's films, there is no original score. Most of the music pieces heard in the film are ones composed by Pyotr Ilyich Tchaikovsky, Johann Strauss Jr., and Edvard Grieg.
- The lead character (originally an adult journalist) was tailored specifically to Johansson, whom Allen observed as having an unused "funny" quality about her while working on the previous film, *Match Point*.
- The film is the second of Allen's films (the other being *Hollywood Ending*) not to have a UK theatrical release. However, it was given a British TV premiere on February 7, 2009 on BBC Two

Critical reception

The film received generally mixed reviews from critics. As of January 21, 2008, the review aggregator Rotten Tomatoes reported that the film received 38 percent positive reviews, based on 132 reviews.[3] Metacritic reported the film had an average score of 48 out of 100, based on 35 reviews.[4] On IMDb, it has a score of 6.8 out of 10.

Stephen Hunter, of *The Washington Post* called it the "worst movie Woody Allen has ever made":

> Basically the movie decodes into a Hardy Boys-level mystery. It's not, of course, that comedies must display documentary realism on this sort of thing. You forgive anything in a movie if it's funny. *Scoop* is never funny enough — except for the odd, whiny Allen gibe, mainly because it recalls better days — to achieve this dispensation; the lack of realism becomes a crippling attribute. This gives nobody, least of all me, any pleasure, but a truth must be faced: *Scoop* is the worst movie Woody Allen has ever made.[5]

At the other extreme, Mick LaSalle of the *San Francisco Chronicle*, who also gave positive reviews to Allen's *Melinda and Melinda*, called it "the funniest movie of the year so far" and Allen's funniest film in a decade. He also said:

> *Scoop* has something *Match Point* didn't, something that none of Allen's films have had to quite this degree in 10 years. It's really, really funny. Not funny "heh-heh," but laugh-out-loud funny. Funny like you walk out wanting to tell your friends its best lines. Funny like you're walking down the street and remember a moment and start laughing like an idiot. Woody Allen has written himself an ideal role, creating a character and a situation that result in a continuous stream of winning bits. And he's paired himself with a partner in Scarlett Johansson who brings deftness and freshness to Allen's familiar comic universe.[6]

Manohla Dargis of *The New York Times* called it "not especially funny yet oddly appealing":

> Mr. Allen doesn't seem to be working terribly hard in *Scoop*, and while that makes for some apparent goofs and lots of ragged edges, it gives the whole thing a pleasantly carefree vibe. After the first 20 or so clunky minutes, the film settles into a groove and then, ever so slightly, deepens. Mr. Allen's invocation of the *Thin Man* films in an interview makes sense, even if he's no William Powell and Ms. Johansson is certainly no Myrna Loy. *Scoop* was made by someone who understands that what makes the "Thin Man" series enduring isn't whodunit and why, but the way Nick and Nora look at each other as they sip their martinis, Asta nipping at their heels.[7]

Ty Burr of *The Boston Globe* called it "fluffy, fatally implausible farce":

> You can assume this kind of humor goes over well with the Europeans who are the director's financial backers and primary audience these days. Like Charlie Chaplin in his final years, Allen has found refuge in exile, far from the US audiences who have turned their backs on him (because we're lowbrow slobs or because his movies have stopped being very good; your call). When we see him onstage as The Great Splendini, Allen even eerily resembles Chaplin in "Limelight," shyly smiling out at the audience with the comedian's eternal hope of unconditional love. Does he see anything besides the beautiful young woman and himself? Sweet and woebegone, "Scoop" says no.[8]

Box office

Scoop opened in 538 American theatres on July 28, 2006. In its first three days, it grossed $3,046,924 for a per-theatre-average of $5,663. *Box Office Mojo* listed its opening as the biggest limited release premiere of 2006.[9] By the time the film's domestic run had ended on September 28, 2006, it grossed $10,525,717 in the U.S. and $39,212,510 worldwide.[10] The film had a $4 million budget, not including prints and advertising expense.

References

[1] Business Data for *Scoop* (http://imdb.com/title/tt0457513/business) from IMDb

[2] http://www.washingtontimes.com/news/2006/aug/03/20060803-084654-8657r/

[3] "Scoop - Movie Reviews, Trailers, Pictures - Rotten Tomatoes" (http://www.rottentomatoes.com/m/scoop/). Rotten Tomatoes. . Retrieved 2008-01-21.

[4] "Scoop (2006): Reviews" (http://www.metacritic.com/film/titles/scoop). Metacritic. . Retrieved 2008-01-21.

[5] *Scoop*: Just Kill the Story (http://www.washingtonpost.com/wp-dyn/content/article/2006/07/27/AR2006072700447.html), a review by Stephen Hunter for *The Washington Post*

[6] *Scoop* is Allen's funniest film in years (http://www.sfgate.com/cgi-bin/article.cgi?f=/c/a/2006/07/28/DDGG5K5KIL1.DTL), a review by Mick LaSalle for the *San Francisco Chronicle*

[7] *Scoop*: Shades of Nick and Nora, With Woody Allen's Shtick (http://movies2.nytimes.com/2006/07/28/movies/28scoo.html?ref=arts), a review by Manohla Dargis for *The New York Times*

[8] *Scoop*: Allen's 'Scoop' is fatally fluffy (http://www.boston.com/movies/display?display=movie&id=9089), a review by Ty Burr for *The Boston Globe*

[9] Box Office Mojo report on *Scoop* (http://www.boxofficemojo.com/movies/?id=scoop.htm)

[10] *Scoop* (http://www.boxofficemojo.com/movies/?id=scoop.htm) at Box Office Mojo

External links

- *Scoop* (http://www.imdb.com/title/tt0457513/) at the Internet Movie Database
- *Scoop* (http://www.metacritic.com/film/titles/scoop) at Metacritic

X-Men: The Last Stand

X-Men: The Last Stand	
 Theatrical release poster	
Directed by	Brett Ratner
Produced by	Lauren Shuler Donner Ralph Winter Avi Arad Stan Lee Kevin Feige David Gorder Ross Fanger Lee Cleary James M. Freitag Kurt Williams John Palermo
Written by	Simon Kinberg Zak Penn
Based on	*Uncanny X-Men* by Stan Lee and Jack Kirby
Starring	Hugh Jackman Halle Berry Ian McKellen Patrick Stewart Famke Janssen Anna Paquin James Marsden Rebecca Romijn Ellen Page
Music by	John Powell
Cinematography	Dante Spinotti
Editing by	Mark Helfrich Mark Goldblatt Julia Wong

Studio	20th Century Fox
	Marvel Entertainment
	The Donners' Company
	Ingenious Film Partners
	Dune Entertainment
	Major Studio Partners
	X3 Canada Productions
	X3 U.S. Productions
	XM3 Service
Distributed by	20th Century Fox
Release date(s)	May 26, 2006
Running time	104 minutes
Language	English
Budget	$210 million[1]
Gross revenue	$459,359,555[2]
Preceded by	X2
Followed by	X-Men Origins: Wolverine

X-Men: The Last Stand (also known colloquially as **X-Men 3** or **X3**) is a 2006 superhero film and the third in the X-Men series. It is directed by Brett Ratner, who took over when Bryan Singer dropped out to direct *Superman Returns*. The movie revolves around a "mutant cure" that causes serious repercussions among mutants and humans, and on the mysterious resurrection of Jean Grey, who appeared to have died in *X2*. The film is loosely based on two X-Men comic book story arcs: writer Chris Claremont's and artist John Byrne's "The Dark Phoenix Saga" in *The Uncanny X-Men* and writer Joss Whedon's and artist John Cassaday's six-issue "Gifted" arc in *Astonishing X-Men*.

The film was released on May 26, 2006 in the United States and Canada. Despite mixed reviews from critics and fans, the film performed well at the box office. Its opening-day gross of $45.5 million is the fourth-highest on record while its opening weekend gross of $103 million is the fifth highest ever.

Plot

The film opens twenty years earlier with Magneto and Professor Charles Xavier visiting a young Jean Grey to recruit her to Xavier's School. Ten years later, a boy named Warren Worthington III is scratching his back with knives to remove the wings sprouting from his shoulders. Xavier worries about Cyclops, who is still heartbroken about the loss of Jean Grey. Mystique is captured by government agents leading Hank "Beast" McCoy to discover that a potential cure for the mutant X-Gene has been invented from the DNA of a mutant boy called Jimmy, who is being held in a facility in Alcatraz Island. The project is financed by Warren Worthington II, following the discovery of his son's mutation.

Cyclops returns to Alkali Lake, where Jean appears to him. Sensing trouble, Xavier sends Wolverine and Storm to investigate, but when they arrive, they encounter telekinetically floating rocks, Cyclops' glasses, and an unconscious Jean. When Magneto launches a raid to rescue Mystique she blocks a cure shot aimed at Magneto, losing her mutant ability, and is abandoned by Magneto, who sadly states she is no longer one of them. As a result of this betrayal, Mystique later spills everything she knows about Magneto's plans to the US authorities.

Back at the mansion, Xavier explains to Wolverine that when Jean was younger, she was so powerful that he had to put telepathic blocks on her mind to help keep her powerful telepathic and telekinetic powers and abilities under control. Her "bottled-up" powers manifested themselves as an alternate personality Jean called the Phoenix, a purely instinctual creature ruled only by its violent desires. Wolverine is initially skeptical but is more convinced when Jean reawakens, different than before. He confronts Jean about Cyclops, but she cannot remember and fears she killed him. Jean pleads with Wolverine to kill her before she harms anybody else, but when he refuses and offers to have Xavier help her, Jean flees to her childhood home, with Xavier, Wolverine and Storm in pursuit. Magneto, also aware that Jean's powers are loose, meets Xavier at Jean's house. The two men plead for Jean's loyalty until the Phoenix resurfaces, unleashing her devastating power. Furious, Jean lifts and destroys her family's house and engages in a psychic battle with Xavier, whom she overpowers and telekinetically tears apart before leaving with Magneto.

Following the losses of Xavier and Cyclops, Xavier's students are left despondent and overcome by his death. Rogue leaves to take the cure after seeing her boyfriend, Iceman, ice-skating with Kitty Pryde. Wolverine leaves the school to find Jean and finds out that Magneto and his army plan to attack Alcatraz and goes back to the school, leading the X-Men to assemble and head there. Meanwhile, the troops guarding Alcatraz are armed with cure weapons while Magneto moves the Golden Gate Bridge to allow his army to reach the island.

The Brotherhood's first charge is ineffective, and the first wave of mutants are hit with the cure cartridges and overpowered: Magneto initially tries to magnetically destroy the weapons, but fails since the guns are plastic instead of metal. However, Magneto's minion Arclight is able to take out the cure weapons, leaving the soldiers defenseless. The X-Men arrive as another attack is about to begin, and while they confront the Brotherhood, Kitty Pryde goes inside the facility to save Jimmy, defeating Juggernaut in the process. Meanwhile, Storm engages in a fight with Callisto, defeating her. Near the end of the battle, Iceman and Pyro have a one-on-one showdown, which Iceman wins by transforming into his solid ice form and knocking Pyro out.

With the help of Colossus, Wolverine distracts Magneto to enable Beast to inject him with the cure. After this, Wolverine nearly coaxes Jean back to sanity; however, army reinforcements arrive and open fire on all present. The Phoenix resurfaces and, in her rage, begins to destroy everything around her. While the X-Men, soldiers and the remnants of the Brotherhood flee from the Phoenix's terrible fury, Wolverine tells Storm that only he can stop her, and instructs her to lead everyone away safely. Wolverine fights his way to Jean, relying upon his self-healing powers and abilities to protect himself from her. When he reaches her, the Phoenix shows contempt for Wolverine's willingness to die for the others, to which he retorts that he would only die for her. Momentarily stunned at this reply, the true Jean regains control of herself and begs him to save her. Wolverine confesses his love for Jean, and reluctantly stabs her in the stomach. Jean dies with a peaceful smile.

The school continues without Xavier, with Storm now as headmistress and Logan as a teacher; the President appoints Beast as ambassador to the United Nations; Rogue returns, telling Iceman she has taken the "cure." The underpowered Magneto sits at a chessboard in a park and reaches out toward a metal chess piece that moves slightly, indicating that the mutant cure may possibly be only temporary.

In a scene following the credits, Dr. Moira MacTaggert checks on a comatose patient who greets her with Xavier's voice. This is a reference to a statement Xavier made earlier on in the film while teaching a class, where he discussed the ethics of transferring one's consciousness into the body of another, who, in this case, had no consciousness to speak of, although all organs and circulation were functioning normally. The film ends as Moira, shocked, whispers, "Charles?"

Cast

The X-Men

The X-Men are a special ops team from The Xavier Institute, charged with protecting both humans and mutants and trying to prevent a war between the two.

- Hugh Jackman as Logan / Wolverine: Logan can regenerate spontaneously, a talent which allowed the painful implantation of a adamantium metal coating on his bones and metal claws that emerge from each hand.

- Halle Berry as Ororo Munroe / Storm: One of Xavier's original students, Storm can influence the weather around her with her mind. Halle Berry stated during interviews for *X2* that she would not return as Storm in the third film unless the character had a significant presence comparable to the comic-book version. Brett Ratner also felt Storm required a larger role and there was little difficulty reaching an agreement.[3]

- Sir Patrick Stewart as Professor Charles Xavier: The founder of The Xavier Institute for Gifted Youngsters who has uncharted telepathic powers and uses a wheelchair. He is an authority on genetic mutation as well as an advocate of peaceful relations between human and mutant kind. He is destroyed by Phoenix. After the credits of the movie commence, Dr. Moira MacTaggert is shown with a body whose face you cannot see. The body speaks, and Dr. MacTaggert says "Charles" indicating that there is a slight possibility that Professor Charles Xavier may somehow still be alive, though they do not show his face, it is his voice. His grave is seen next to Cyclops' and Jean's.

- James Marsden as Scott Summers / Cyclops: The X-Men's field leader. He emits powerful energy blasts from his eyes, and has to keep them in check with a ruby-quartz visor or sunglasses. He may have been killed by Phoenix; since she kills people by taking them apart on the molecular level, his body is never shown. His grave can be seen, next to Jean's and Xavier's. Despite appearing in his X-Men leather uniform and battle visor in the film's promotional posters, Cyclops is never seen wearing it in the actual film.

- Kelsey Grammer as Dr. Henry "Hank" McCoy / Beast: A former student of Xavier's School who became the Secretary of Mutant Affairs in the U.S. Government. Beast is covered in blue fur and has a genius level I.Q., as well as heightened strength and agility. He is a brilliant scientist and researcher with vast intelligence and insight into mutant genetics.

- Anna Paquin as Marie / Rogue: A teenage runaway mutant who has found a home at Xavier's school and falls in love with Bobby Drake. When she touches someone she absorbs their life force, their powers (if they are a mutant) and, if she holds on too long, she ends their life. She only uses her powers one time in the film, when she absorbs Colossus' power to protect herself from the Sentinel.

- Shawn Ashmore as Bobby Drake / Iceman: He can control the temperature of the moisture in the air around him to create constructs of ice or blasts of cold. Under extreme conditions his body may take on many of the characteristics of ice in addition to those of a human.

- Ellen Page as Kitty Pryde / Shadowcat: She can "phase" through matter which allows her to walk through solid objects.

- Ben Foster as Warren Worthington III / Angel: He has feathered wings which allow him to fly. Cayden Boyd plays Warren as a child. Although seen in the leather X-Men uniform in promotional posters, Warren does not wear it and is seen in civilian clothes most of the time. He does not wish to take the cure, although he admits his wings have often been of great inconvenience to him.

- Daniel Cudmore as Peter Rasputin / Colossus: He can transform his skin into an organic steel, granting superhuman strength and a resistance to damage and temperature. He has only one line in the movie.

The Brotherhood of Mutants

The Brotherhood is Magneto's personal strike force, whose goal is to ensure mutant supremacy.

- Sir Ian McKellen as Eric Lehnsherr / Magneto: Leader and founder of The Brotherhood, this incredibly powerful mutant can manipulate any form of metal. He is a Holocaust survivor who wages war against humanity in the name of mutant superiority, a goal that often pits him against his old friend Charles Xavier. Has very little interest in or regard for non-mutant human life. He has sophisticated knowledge in matters of genetic manipulation and engineering and has used radiation to mutate humans.

- Famke Janssen as Jean Grey: A former member of the X-Men who sacrificed herself to save her comrades. Her former self, Jean Grey, died when she did this, but her powers wrapped her in a cocoon of energy, which allowed her to survive. Now a Class 5 mutant, she possesses limitless telepathic powers as well as limitless telekinetic powers (that even surpass that of Magneto's and Xavier's) that can be used at a sub-atomic level, making her the

Jean Grey/Phoenix unleashing her devastating power.

most powerful and most dangerous mutant in the film. It is revealed that when she was young, Xavier locked away a large portion of her power, which created two personalities within her, and that after the incident at the end of *X2: X-Men United*, the dark side of Jean's persona known as The Phoenix is unleashed. Combined with her lack of control over her powers, this means she can disintegrate people and objects at will.

- Rebecca Romijn as Raven Darkholme / Mystique: Magneto's blue-skinned right-hand woman can shape shift to match anyone's appearance and can fight with incredible agility and strength. She saves Magneto from a cure dart, loses her powers and is subsequently abandoned by The Brotherhood, later choosing to inform on them.

- Aaron Stanford as John Allerdyce / Pyro: Former Xavier Institute student Pyro can manipulate fire, although he cannot start it (he carries a lighter — attached to a cuff on his wrist — with him at all times). He holds a grudge against his former friend Bobby Drake.

- Vinnie Jones as Cain Marko / Juggernaut: The Juggernaut is a new recruit to the Brotherhood. He is incredibly strong, fast, and once he gains momentum, he becomes unstoppable. Despite being the stepbrother of Xavier in the comics, there is no mention of his relation in the film. Also in the comics he is an enchanted human as opposed to a mutant. He is responsible for what was perhaps the most well known line in the film, "Don't you know who I am? I'm the Juggernaut, bitch!", which was actually inspired by an internet meme which came to fruition prior to the film's release.

- Eric Dane as James Madrox / Multiple Man: Multiple Man can split himself into multiple copies. He is a criminal who joins the Brotherhood upon their releasing him.

The Omegas

A group of mutant outcasts which exists as part of an underground network that stretches across the nation.[4]

- Dania Ramirez as Callisto: Callisto is the leader of the Omegas, a group of mutant outcasts. In the comics, as well as the 90's and Evolution cartoons, she led a similar group called The Morlocks. She possesses superhuman speed, strength, reflexes, agility and senses. She can detect electrical energy spikes from miles away, and can sense the presence, locations, and powers of other mutants. Throughout the film she is constantly battling Storm. In the comic book storyline Storm and Callisto had to battle to see who was the true leader of The Morlocks, where Storm was victorious.

- Ken Leung as Kid Omega: This character resembles the comic books' character Quill; however, the official cast credits read "Kid Omega". He has the ability to eject spikes from his body, most notably his face.

- Omahyra Mota as Arclight: Arclight has the power to create and generate powerful shock waves of concussive force by clapping her hands together. She can modulate her power, targeting specific materials to be destroyed.

- Meiling Melançon as Psylocke: Psylocke has the ability to teleport herself through areas of shadow. Her primary ability of creating psionic blades was left out in the film.

Other characters

- Cameron Bright as Jimmy / Leech: A mutant boy whose power neutralizes the powers of nearby mutants. His DNA is the basis for the "cure". After being rescued, he is admitted to The Xavier Institute.

- Michael Murphy as Warren Worthington II: The head of Worthington Labs, the corporation developing the "cure". He is Angel's father, and wants to rid his son of his mutant abilities. He changes his mind when he is saved from Magneto's and Phoenix's attack by his son.

- Shohreh Aghdashloo as Dr. Kavita Rao: Rao is a scientist working at Worthington Labs on the mutant cure, which was created with the DNA of Leech. She is killed by Quill in the film's climax.

- Josef Sommer as The President: The mutant-tolerating President of the United States. He nominates Hank McCoy to be a Cabinet member and later as the U.S. Ambassador to the United Nations.

- Bill Duke as Bolivar Trask: The head of the Department of Homeland Security, he aids the President during the Mutant War. Unlike his counterpart in the comics he has no connections with the creation of the Sentinels.

- Olivia Williams as Moira MacTaggert: On a video shown at The Xavier Institute, she talks about mutant ethics, such as whether it would be right to transfer the mind of a dying father of four into the body of a man born with no higher brain functions. After the film's ending credits, it appears that Xavier has transferred his mind into the physical body of Moira's patient.

Production

Bryan Singer, the director of the first two *X-Men* films, left the project during pre-production in order to direct the film *Superman Returns*. He was joined by *X2* screenwriters Dan Harris and Michael Dougherty and composer / editor John Ottman. Though Singer, Harris and Dougherty had yet to complete a script, the director has revealed that at the time of his departure they had partially completed a story treatment for the film which would have focused exclusively on Jean Grey's resurrection[5] with the new villain Emma Frost, a role intended for Sigourney Weaver.[6] Frost was an empath manipulating Jean's emotions in the treatment, and like the finished film Magneto desires to control her. Overwhelmed by her powers, Jean kills herself, but Jean's spirit survives and becomes a god-like creature, which Dougherty compared to the star child in *A Space Odyssey*.[7]

Simon Kinberg was hired as writer soon after Singer's departure, and speculation arose to Joss Whedon directing the film.[8] Whedon turned down the offer because he was working on a *Wonder Woman* film.[9] Rob Bowman[10] and Alex Proyas[11] were also rumored, though Proyas personally turned it down.[12] Zack Snyder was also approached, though he turned it down due to his commitment to *300*.[13] Despite the controversy over Singer's departure, the cast and producers were still clearly keen to return.[14] Matthew Vaughn was hired as the new director for the project. He cast Kelsey Grammer as Beast and Vinnie Jones as Juggernaut, but family issues reportedly led Vaughn to withdraw before shooting began.[15] Vaughn was replaced by Singer's friend Brett Ratner.[16] Ratner had coincidentally been set to direct *Superman: Flyby*.

On June 13, 2005, a review of an incomplete early draft of the screenplay posted by Drew McWeeny from Ain't It Cool News sparked controversy from fans, due to certain main characters' storylines;[17] however, that was the very first of over two dozen drafts of the script. Most notably the Golden Gate Bridge sequence was originally in the middle of the film, but Ratner decided it would create a more dramatic climax if moved to the end,[18] which was originally to take place in Washington, D.C.[19]

X-Men: The Last Stand began shooting in August 2005 and ended in January 2006. Much of *X-Men: The Last Stand* was filmed in Vancouver, British Columbia, Canada. According to associate producer Dave Gordon, "This is the biggest production ever filmed in Canada. It used to be *X2*, now it's *X3*."[20]

The visual effects crew started working on April 2005, before the director had even been announced.[1] Special effects supervisor John Bruno estimates one sixth of the effects budget was spent on the Golden Gate Bridge scene, which employed both computer-generated imagery and a miniature of the bridge.[1] Other notable effect was "digital skin-grafting", which "de-aged" the faces of senior actors Patrick Stewart and Ian McKellen by complex keyframing, though CGI was not used.[21]

The film has extensive wirework, where many of the actors performed some of their own stunts. The whirlwind wire-stunt performed by Halle Berry during one fight scene reportedly caused Berry to become so nauseated that she vomited, with the crew bringing in buckets for her before shooting her scenes. Angel's wings were initially too heavy for Ben Foster, and were remade from foam.[22] Despite his fear of heights, Foster performed a single second-unit stunt where he escapes Worthington's facility by jumping from the tall building.[23] The shot was completed by flying a stuntman swooping from the window using a crane rig, with the harness and wires removed and wings added digitally.

Reception and box office

X-Men: The Last Stand grossed $45.1 million domestically for the seventh-highest opening day after *The Dark Knight* ($68.7 million), *Spider-Man 3* ($59 million), *Pirates of the Caribbean: Dead Man's Chest* ($55.8 million), and *Star Wars Episode III: Revenge of the Sith* ($50 million).[2] (All figures here not adjusted for inflation.) It is ranked fourth among film debuts having generated an estimated $122.9 million in the North American box office during its four-day Memorial Day opening weekend and the number one Memorial Day movie of all time until the record was broken by *Pirates of the Caribbean: At World's End* which earned $142 million during its four-day Memorial Day opening. The website *The Numbers* notes that the film's weekend gross "equals the record for the fewest number of days taken to earn $100 million, joining four other movies that achieved the feat in three days."[24] However, the film suffered a significant drop of 66.9% in its second weekend, when its box office take fell to $34.0 million.[25] Nevertheless, the film has grossed over $234 million in North America (fourth-highest of 2006) and over $459 million globally (fifth-highest of 2006).[2] It is the ninth-highest-grossing comic book adaptation, and the highest grossing of the X-Men series.[2] It became the first film of 2006, and the 67th film on record, to pass the $200 million mark at the North American box office, which it accomplished on the weekend of June 9, 2006. It is the first X-Men movie to surpass $200 million outside the United States. *X-Men: The Last Stand* is one of the few third installments in a series to outgross its predecessors, *Spider-Man 3* and *The Lord of the Rings: The Return of the King* being examples.

Reviews of the film have been generally mixed, with the film-review website Rotten Tomatoes giving the film a 57% approval rating.[26] The film review aggregate site Metacritic also reported mixed reviews with a score of 58/100.[27] Ebert and Roeper gave the film a "two thumbs up" rating, with Ebert stating "I liked the action, I liked the absurdity, I liked the incongruous use and misuse of mutant powers, and I especially liked the way it introduces all of those political issues and lets them fight it out with the special effects."[28] Some film critics did however consider the third film to be of lesser quality than the previous two. Justin Chang from *Variety* said the film is "a wham-bam sequel noticeably lacking in the pop gravitas, moody atmospherics and emotional weight that made the first two Marvel comicbook adaptations so rousingly successful."[29] Frank Lovece of *Film Journal International* said, "A risk-taking script with genuine consequences elevates this ... above the lackluster direction of Brett Ratner, whose competent mechanics move the story efficiently but with very little soul."[30] At the 2007 Saturn Awards, Famke Janssen won the Best Supporting Actress award for her portrayal of Jean Grey.[31] Also impressed with Janssen's performance were *Total Film*, who said, "playing the super-freaky mind-control goddess like *GoldenEye*'s Xenia Onatopp's all-powerful psycho sister, her scenes — particularly that one with the house — crackle with energy and tragedy. If only the rest of *X3* had followed suit."[32] Halle Berry received a People's Choice Award for "Favorite Female Action Star" for her role as Storm. During her acceptance speech, she asked all fans who wanted to see an "X-Men 4" to write letters to producer Tom Rothman asking for another movie.[33] Matthew Vaughn, who was once set to direct the film, heavily responded with negative feedback to Ratner's direction.[34]

Adaptations

Novelization

The novelization of the film, written by comic book writer Chris Claremont, was released on May 16, 2006.[35]

The novelization of the movie differs in some areas from the film. In the novel, young Jean Grey discovers her powers after an accident that takes her best friend's life (taken directly from the comic book incarnation's origin). Angel officially joins the X-Men and travels with them to Alcatraz Island instead of going on his own. Storm spares Callisto's life, and Rogue decides to keep her powers in the end, and Beast stays at the school as a teacher, the latter two of which were alternate versions of the film. Iceman takes an unconscious Pyro away from Alcatraz. The attack on Alcatraz is referred to as M-Day, a reference to the "Decimation of mutantkind" storyline in the comic books. Moira MacTaggert visits Magneto in the park, presumably offering an antidote to the "cure", which he refuses because as the book says: "He couldn't go back. That path had brought nothing but grief, to those he cared for, those who trusted him, to himself." Unlike the film, the novel does not allude to Xavier's resurrection. In the end of the novel Wolverine is in the basement of the Institute training the new X-Men, which includes Gambit, Sage, Danielle Moonstar and Cannonball.

The novel also makes a reference to *X3* scriptwriter Zak Penn, whose name is given to a sergeant in the middle of the novel, and to the X-Men co-creator and writer Stan Lee as Mr. Lee, one of Jean's neighbors portrayed by Stan Lee in the film. The president's name in the novelization is David Cockrum, a reference to comics artist Dave Cockrum. McCoy asks the president about his wife Paty, who in real life is David Cockrum's wife who used to work at Marvel. Two other references are made towards the end of the book, the first is Hollywood planning a film about the Battle of Alcatraz (a possible reference to the actual movie) along with a British Shakespearean actor, who is also a Knight playing Magneto (a possible reference to Sir Ian McKellen who played Magneto in all three films). Other references include the mutant Bishop as police officer after Pyro attacks a cure facility, and Rogue mentions Dust.

The book also briefly references Kitty Pryde's political ambitions when she is shown hanging up a homemade "Pryde for President" poster. In a few possible futures seen in the comics, Pryde has ended up President (*X-Men: The End*) and her plans to run for office were a sub-plot during the *X-Treme X-Men* series.

Video games

Games publisher Activision released *X-Men: The Official Game*, the official video game tie-in to the film across all major video game platforms on May 16, 2006. The various editions of the game bridge the events of the films *X2* and *X-Men: The Last Stand* and feature many of both films' prominent characters. Hugh Jackman, Patrick Stewart, Alan Cumming, Eric Dane, Shawn Ashmore and Tyler Mane reprise their film roles in this game. Sentinels, Lady Deathstrike, Sabretooth and Silver Samurai also appear in the game. It also provides an explanation of Nightcrawler's absence from the film. An *X-Men: The Last Stand* game was also released for mobile phones.

Home media

X-Men: The Last Stand was released in the United States and Canada on DVD in both standard and collector's edition formats on October 3, 2006. The single-disc standard DVD, in either widescreen or fullscreen, features two menu settings: "Join The Brotherhood" and "Take A Stand". These choices change the menu's design and the deleted scenes available. The DVD also features commentaries featuring the director, writers, and producers; 10 deleted scenes; three alternate endings; and two easter eggs. On the first day of its release, errors were reported with the DVD. About 60% of the DVDs currently in circulation have errors in them. Some DVDs come with only 10 deleted scenes while others come with 21, amongst other errors.[36]

The "Stan Lee Collector's Edition" DVD is a widescreen standard DVD that was packaged in a slipcase with a 100-page booklet featuring a completely new *X-Men* comic by Stan Lee. *The Hollywood Reporter* announced that 20th Century Fox will make films available to buy online the same day as the DVD, through Direct2Drive, with *X-Men: The Last Stand* among the first such available. Also, Wal-Mart stores included a special exclusive DVD titled "X-Men Revealed" with 50 minutes of behind-the-scenes look at the evolution of the *X-Men* franchise. The Wal-Mart exclusive DVD disc is not what it seems however. From the information of the exclusive DVD front and back cover, it is supposed to be a behind-the-scenes look of the *X-Men* movie franchise but instead it is a brief history of the *X-Men* comics. Target also has an exclusive that comes in a tin case with the single-disc DVD plus a reprint of *Giant-Size X-Men* #1 and four collectible cards from the movie. There are also other versions.

The DVD sold 5 million copies in its first week in stores.[37] In other countries, such as the United Kingdom and Australia, the DVD package is a 2-Disc Special Edition and has a bonus disc containing three documentaries (*Brett Ratner's Production Diary*, *X-Men: Evolution Of A Trilogy*, and *X-Men: The Excitement Continues*) as well as various featurettes, character guides and pre-visualization sequences. This version is not planned for a Region 1 release.

X-Men: The Last Stand has also been released on Blu-ray Disc. The video was encoded in 1080p with 6.1 DTS ES HD Master Audio. The film was released on Universal Media Disc as well.

Soundtrack

X-Men: The Last Stand: Original Motion Picture Soundtrack	
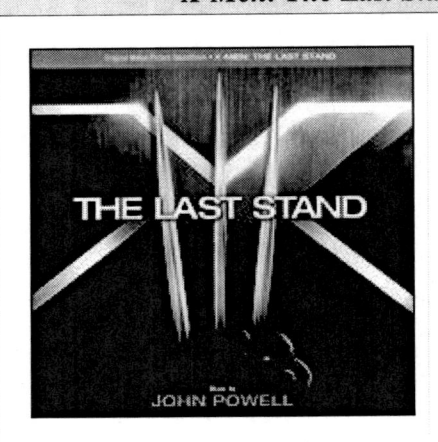	
Film score by John Powell	
Released	May 23, 2006
Genre	Soundtracks Film scores
Length	60:26

Label	Varèse Sarabande
Producer	John Powell
Professional reviews	

- Allmusic ★ ★ ★ ★ ★ link [38]
- Score Reviews ★ ★ ★ ★ ★ link [39]
- Tracksounds ★ ★ ★ ★ ★ link [40]

Marvel Comics film series soundtrack chronology

Fantastic 4: The Album (2005)	**X-Men: The Last Stand: Original Motion Picture Soundtrack** (2006)	*Music from and Inspired by Spider-Man 3* (2007)

X-Men: The Last Stand: Original Motion Picture Soundtrack was released on May 23, 2006 by Varèse Sarabande. It has received generally positive reviews.

1. "20 Years Ago" (1:10)
2. "Bathroom Titles" (1:09)
3. "The Church of Magneto, Raven is My Slave Name" (2:40)
4. "Meet Leech, Then off to the Lake" (2:37)
5. "Whirlpool of Love" (2:04)
6. "Examining Jean" (1:12)
7. "Dark Phoenix" (1:28)
8. "Angel's Cure" (2:34)
9. "Jean and Logan" (1:39)
10. "Dark Phoenix Awakes" (1:45)
11. "Rejection is Never Easy" (1:09)
12. "Magneto Plots" (2:05)
13. "Entering the House" (1:18)
14. "Dark Phoenix's Tragedy" (3:18)
15. "Farewell to X" (0:30)
16. "The Funeral" (2:52)
17. "Skating on the Pond" (1:12)
18. "Cure Wars" (2:57)
19. "Fight in the Woods" (3:06)
20. "St. Lupus Day" (3:03)
21. "Building Bridges" (1:16)
22. "Shock and No Oars" (1:15)
23. "Attack on Alcatraz" (4:36)
24. "Massacre" (0:31)
25. "The Battle of the Cure" (4:21)
26. "Phoenix Rises" (4:21)
27. "The Last Stand" (5:29)

Sequel

Producer Lauren Shuler Donner reported in August 2006 that renegotiations would be required to continue the primary film series. Newer cast members were signed, while the older cast members, including Halle Berry, Rebecca Romijn, Famke Janssen, and Anna Paquin, were not.[41] Berry, James Marsden,[42] and Patrick Stewart[43] have expressed interest in returning, and Bryan Singer was approached once more to direct, but he was busy.[44] Shawn Ashmore stated that he is still contracted for another film featuring Iceman.[45] Tyler Mane and Ray Park have both expressed interest in reprising their roles from *X-Men* as Sabretooth and Toad, respectively, in future films, although it is unlikely Mane would be asked due to Liev Schreiber taking over the Sabretooth role in *X-Men Origins: Wolverine* and his commitment to the *Halloween* franchise. However, as of July 2007, there was no script for a fourth film, and none was in the works.[46]

Later in the month, however, Kevin Feige, president of production at Marvel Studios said that another X-Men film was possible.[47] Donner admitted, "There is forty years worth of stories. I've always wanted to do 'Days of Future Past' and there are just really a lot of stories yet to be told."[48] At a Fox Blu-ray press event in Beverly Hills in September 2009, Lauren Shuler Donner stated that she is currently "cooking up plans for" an *X-Men 4*. However she stressed that it has yet to be pitched to the studio.[49] As of March 2010, Shuler Donner also has pitched Bryan Singer on doing a fourth installment of the previously established X-Men franchise, following the completion of *X-Men: First Class*.[50]

References

[1] "X Marks the Shots" (http://www.ew.com/ew/article/0,,1201520,00.html). *Entertainment Weekly*. 2006-06-06. . Retrieved 2009-09-12.

[2] "X-Men: The Last Stand (2006)" (http://www.boxofficemojo.com/movies/?page=main&id=x3.htm). Box Office Mojo. . Retrieved 2009-03-06.

[3] Daniel Robert Epstein (2006-05-24). "Halle Berry of X-Men: The Last Stand" (http://web.archive.org/web/20060718103731/http://www.ugo.com/summermovies/Content/ProductViewer.aspx?BlogsPageNumber=3&ProductID=172). *ugo.com*. UGO Networks. Archived from the original (http://www.ugo.com/summermovies/Content/ProductViewer.aspx?BlogsPageNumber=3&ProductID=172) on 2006-07-18. . Retrieved 2006-06-06.

[4] X-Men: The Last Stand Official Site (http://www.x-menthelaststand.com/)

[5] "Quint" (2006-07-22). "Quint on Superman Returns gag reel & sequel talk with Singer" (http://www.aintitcool.com/node/23943). Ain't It Cool News. . Retrieved 2006-10-06.

[6] Franklin, Garth (2006-09-14). "Sigourney was considered for "X3"" (http://www.darkhorizons.com/news04/040916e.php). *DarkHorizons.com*. . Retrieved 2006-10-06.

[7] David Bentley (2008-11-26). "Screenwriter reveals ideas for Singer's planned third X-Men film" (http://blogs.coventrytelegraph.net/thegeekfiles/2008/11/x3lit.html). *Coventry Telegraph*. . Retrieved 2008-11-26.

[8] Stax (2004-08-12). "Whedon wants X-Men 3" (http://uk.movies.ign.com/articles/538/538233p1.html). IGN. . Retrieved 2006-10-11.

[9] Erik Davis (2007-04-24). "Joss Whedon Talks X-Men 4, Wonder Woman Woes and Batman Heartache" (http://www.cinematical.com/2007/04/24/joss-whedon-talks-x-men-4-wonder-woman-woes-and-batman-heartach/). *Cinematical*. . Retrieved 2008-10-05.

[10] Stax (2006-10-12). "Three for X3?" (http://uk.movies.ign.com/articles/556/556650p1.html). IGN. . Retrieved 2006-10-11.

[11] Stax (2006-10-13). "X3 Director Update" (http://uk.movies.ign.com/articles/556/556859p1.html). IGN. . Retrieved 2006-10-11.

[12] Stax (2005-02-17). "X3 trailer with FF?" (http://uk.movies.ign.com/articles/588/588539p1.html). IGN. . Retrieved 2006-10-11.

[13] Robert Sanchez (2007-02-13). "Exclusive Interview: Zack Snyder Is Kickin' Ass With 300 and Watchmen!" (http://iesb.net/index.php?option=com_content&task=view&id=1883&Itemid=99). IESB. . Retrieved 2007-02-14.

[14] Stax (2004-09-28). "The Status of X-Men 3" (http://uk.movies.ign.com/articles/552/552000p1.html). IGN. . Retrieved 2006-10-11.

[15] "Director quits X-Men 3 for family" (http://news.bbc.co.uk/1/hi/entertainment/film/4600291.stm). *bbc.co.uk*. BBC NEWS. 2005-06-01. . Retrieved 2006-09-18.

[16] Scott Bowles (2005-05-24). "Franchise's fans reverse stand on new director" (http://www.usatoday.com/life/movies/news/2006-05-24-xmen-ratner_x.htm). *usatoday.com*. USA Today. . Retrieved 2006-06-05.

[17] Moriaty (2005-06-13). "AICN EXCLUSIVE! X3 Script Review! Plus An Open Letter To Tom Rothman And Fox Stockholders!!" (http://www.aintitcool.com/display.cgi?id=20443). *Ain't It Cool News*. . Retrieved 2006-06-05.

[18] Hugh Hart (2006-04-23). "INDUSTRY BUZZ" (http://www.sfgate.com/cgi-bin/article.cgi?f=/c/a/2006/04/23/PKGU9GIREH1.DTL). *sfgate.com*. San Francisco Chronicle. . Retrieved 2006-06-05.

[19] Tom Russo (May 2006). "Cover Story: X-Men: The Last Stand (Page 3 of 4)" (http://web.archive.org/web/20071226013420/http://www.premiere.com/behindthescenes/2748/cover-story-x-men-the-last-stand-page3.html). *premiere.com*. Premiere. Archived from the original (http://www.premiere.com/behindthescenes/2748/cover-story-x-men-the-last-stand-page3.html) on 2007-12-26. . Retrieved

2007-12-21.

[20] George A. Tramountanas (2006-02-23). ""X-Men: The Last Stand" – Dave Gorder - The Super-Associate Producer" (http://www.comicbookresources.com/news/newsitem.cgi?id=6747). Comic Book Resources. . Retrieved 2006-06-05.

[21] Daniel Robert Epstein (2006-05-25). "Brett Ratner, Director of X-Men: The Last Stand" (http://www.ugo.com/summermovies/Content/ProductViewer.aspx?BlogsPageNumber=2&ProductID=172). ugo.com. UGO Networks. . Retrieved 2006-06-06.

[22] IANS (2006-05-25). "Gear up to meet mutant heroes in 'X Men 3'" (http://209.85.129.104/search?q=cache:w5pwrhjHYQUJ:nowrunning.com/news/news.asp?it=6703+"Gear+up+to+meet+mutant+heroes"&hl=en&ct=clnk&cd=3). *nowrunning.com*. nowrunning.com. Archived from the original (http://nowrunning.com/news/news.asp?it=6703) on 2007-10-30. . Retrieved 2006-06-06.

[23] Brett Ratner, Simon Kinberg. Zak Penn. (2006). *Audio Commentary*. [DVD]. 20th Century Fox.

[24] "The Numbers" (http://www.the-numbers.com/interactive/newsStory.php?newsID=1937). *The Numbers*. Nash Information Services. . Retrieved 2006-06-06.

[25] "X-Men Broken Up By Rom-Com Defeat" (http://www.comingsoon.net/news/movienews.php?id=14831). Comingsoon.net. . Retrieved 2006-06-05.

[26] "X-Men: The Last Stand (2006)" (http://www.rottentomatoes.com/m/x_men_3_the_last_stand). *Rotten Tomatoes*. IGN. . Retrieved 2009-06-20.

[27] "Metacritic - X-men: The Last Stand (2006)" (http://www.metacritic.com/film/titles/xmenthelaststand). *Metacritic*. . Retrieved 6 June 2006.

[28] Roger Ebert. "X-Men: The Last Stand (PG-13)" (http://rogerebert.suntimes.com/apps/pbcs.dll/article?AID=/20060525/REVIEWS/60509005/1023). rogerebert.com. . Retrieved 2006-06-05.

[29] Justin Chang (2006-05-22). "X-Men: The Last Stand" (http://www.variety.com/review/VE1117930584?categoryId=31&cs=1). *Variety* (Reed Business Information).

[30] Frank Lovece (2006-05-22). "X-Men: The Last Stand" (http://filmjournal.com/filmjournal/reviews/article_display.jsp?vnu_content_id=1002576_27). *Film Journal International*. filmjournal.com. .

[31] David S. Cohen (2007-05-10). "'Superman' tops Saturns" (http://www.variety.com/awardcentral_article/VR1117964717.html?nav=news&categoryid=1983&cs=1). *Variety*. . Retrieved 2007-05-11.

[32] "X-Men: The Last Stand - Film Review" (http://www.totalfilm.com/cinema_reviews/x-men_the_last_stand). *Total Film*. . Retrieved 2007-10-11.

[33] http://www.youtube.com/watch?v=BWu1EbVeAVQ

[34] Brent Sprecher (2007-10-09). "*Stardust* Director Matthew Vaughn Blasts Brett Ratner's *X-Men 3: The Last Stand*!" (http://comicbookmovie.com/news/articles/3994.asp). ComicBookMovie.com. . Retrieved 2007-10-11.

[35] Claremont, Chris. *X-Men: The Last Stand*. Del Rey. ISBN 0-345-49211-0.

[36] "Region 1 X-Men 3 DVD Error" (http://www.comics2film.com/FanFrame.php?f_id=22333). Comics2Film. . Retrieved 2006-10-06.

[37] "*X-Men: The Last Stand* Tops with 5 million DVDs sold" (http://www.superherohype.com/news/x-mennews.php?id=4798). SuperHeroHype.com. 2006-10-11. . Retrieved 2006-10-14.

[38] http://www.allmusic.com/cg/amg.dll?p=amg&sql=10:gpdayl66xppb

[39] http://www.scorereviews.com/reviews/review.aspx?id=539

[40] http://www.tracksounds.com/reviews/xmen_last_stand.htm

[41] Marilyn Beck; Stacy Jenel Smith (2006-08-13). "Major renegotiations possible stumbling block for new 'X-Men'" (http://www.dailynews.com/search/ci_4177414). *Los Angeles Daily News*. . Retrieved 2007-07-11.

[42] Steve Chupnick (2006-08-10). "James Marsden Talks Cyclops and X-Men Spinoffs" (http://www.movieweb.com/news/40/14040.php). Moviehole.net. . Retrieved 2007-08-06.

[43] "Patrick Stewart's Last Stand" (http://www.empireonline.com/news/story.asp?NID=18710). *Empire*. 2006-05-08. . Retrieved 2007-08-07.

[44] Michael Tsai (2006-11-08). "Sequel to 'Superman Returns' due in 2009" (http://the.honoluluadvertiser.com/article/2006/Nov/08/br/br0948627351.html). *The Honolulu Advertiser*. . Retrieved 2007-08-06.

[45] "Shawn Ashmore ready and signed to reprise X-Men's Iceman" (http://scifiwire.com/2009/04/shawn-ashmore-ready-and-s.php). Sci-Fi Wire. 2009-04-29. . Retrieved 2009-06-18.

[46] Stephen Galloway (2007-07-10). "Studios are hunting the next big property" (http://web.archive.org/web/20070815233220/http://www.hollywoodreporter.com/hr/content_display/film/news/e3if727c623f03c782b8ad564866c828796). *The Hollywood Reporter*. Archived from the original (http://www.hollywoodreporter.com/hr/content_display/film/news/e3if727c623f03c782b8ad564866c828796) on 2007-08-15. . Retrieved 2007-07-11.

[47] Jake Coyle (2007-07-19). "Hollywood Studios Go Sequel Crazy" (http://apnews.myway.com/article/20070719/D8QFQ3SO0.html). MyWay. . Retrieved 2007-07-19.

[48] Robert Sanchez (2006-11-19). "Exclusive Interview: Part II With Mega Producer Lauren Shuler Donner" (http://www.iesb.net/index.php?option=com_content&task=view&id=677&Itemid=99). IESB.net. . Retrieved 2007-08-06.

[49] Rorschach01. "*X Men 4* And New Mutants Movies In The Works!" (http://www.comicbookmovie.com/fansites/rotyetamovie/news/?a=10241). Comic Book Movie. .

[50] Bryan Singer on 'X-Men: First Class': It's got to be about Magneto and Professor X (http://latimesblogs.latimes.com/herocomplex/2010/03/bryan-singer-and-the-xmen-together-again.html)

External links

- Official website (http://http://www.xmenthelaststanddvd.com/)
- *X-Men: The Last Stand* (http://www.imdb.com/title/tt0376994/) at the Internet Movie Database
- *X-Men: The Last Stand* (http://www.allmovie.com/work/291112) at Allmovie
- *X-Men: The Last Stand* (http://www.rottentomatoes.com/m/x_men_3_the_last_stand/) at Rotten Tomatoes
- *X-Men: The Last Stand* (http://www.boxofficemojo.com/movies/?id=x3.htm) at Box Office Mojo
- *X-Men* on Marvel.com (http://marvel.com/movies/X-Men)

Viva Laughlin

Viva Laughlin	
Viva Laughlin intertitle	
Genre	Comedy-drama Musical
Created by	Peter Bowker Bob Lowry
Written by	Elizabeth Davis Michael Gans Bob Lowry Richard Register
Directed by	Matt Earl Beesley Brian Dannelly Tamra Davis John Fortenberry Don Kurt Leslie Libman John Peters John Showalter
Starring	Lloyd Owen Mädchen Amick Ellen Woglom Carter Jenkins Eric Winter D.B. Woodside Hugh Jackman Melanie Griffith P. J. Byrne
Theme music composer	Trevor Morris
Composer(s)	Patrick Milligan John E. Nordstrom
Country of origin	United States
Language(s)	English
No. of seasons	1
No. of episodes	8 (6 unaired)
Production	
Executive producer(s)	Peter Bowker Hugh Jackman Bob Lowry Gabriele Muccino John Palermo Paul Telegdy

Producer(s)	Don Kurt
Editor(s)	Quincy Z. Gunderson Keith Henderson Hughes Winborne
Cinematography	Paul M. Sommers
Running time	42 min
Broadcast	
Original channel	CBS
Original run	October 18, 2007 – October 21, 2007
Status	Ended

Viva Laughlin is an American musical-dramedy series adapted by Bob Lowry and Peter Bowker (creator of the original series) from the popular BBC British serial, *Blackpool*. They also served as executive producers alongside Hugh Jackman, John Palermo, Paul Telegdy and Gabriele Muccino. The latter also directed the pilot.[1] It was filmed on location in part at the Morongo Casino Resort & Spa in Cabazon, California for most of the inside casino shots.

Produced by BBC Worldwide, CBS Paramount Network Television, Sony Pictures Television and Seed Productions, the series was greenlit and given a thirteen-episode order on May 14, 2007.[2] Excerpts from the series were aired in subsequent previews throughout the CBS telecast of the 61st Annual Tony Awards on June 10, 2007.[3] CBS aired a preview of the pilot on October 18, 2007 following an episode of *CSI: Crime Scene Investigation* before broadcasting its official season premiere on October 21, 2007 in its regular timeslot on Sunday nights at 8:00/7:00c, following *60 Minutes*.[4] [5]

CBS cancelled *Viva Laughlin* on October 22, 2007 after airing two episodes, with the Nine Network (in Jackman's home country of Australia) following suit the next day by canceling the show after airing only one episode[6] [7] Both CBS and Nine filled the show's time slot with episodes of *CSI*, with *The Amazing Race* then taking *Viva Laughlin's* place on CBS on November 4.[8] [9]

Plot

Viva Laughlin is a mystery drama musical about businessman Ripley Holden, whose ambition is to run a casino in Laughlin, Nevada. It occasionally has the actors break into contemporary song. Ripley has invested all his money into opening a casino that is nowhere near completion, when his financing suddenly falls through. Needing an investor, Ripley approaches his rival, wealthy casino owner Nicky Fontana; but Fontana wants to own the casino himself, and Ripley turns down the deal. Ripley becomes embroiled in a murder investigation after the body of his ex-business partner is found at his casino.[1]

Cast

- Lloyd Owen - Ripley Holden
- Mädchen Amick - Natalie Holden
- Ellen Woglom - Cheyenne Holden
- Carter Jenkins - Jack Holden
- Eric Winter - Peter Carlyle
- D.B. Woodside - Marcus Henckman
- Hugh Jackman - Nicky Fontana
- Melanie Griffith - Bunny Baxter
- P. J. Byrne - Jonesy

Critical reception

Critical reaction to the show was mostly negative. The musical numbers themselves were not criticized as much as the plot, the dialogue and the acting.

The opening line of *The New York Times* review said, "*Viva Laughlin* on CBS may well be the worst new show of the season, but is it the worst show in the history of television?"[10]

Newsday's review started with, "The stud is a dud. And that's only the first of a dozen problems with CBS' admirably ambitious but jaw-droppingly wrongheaded new musical/murder mystery/family drama *Viva Laughlin*. Let us count the ways it bombs..."[11]

International broadcasters

The following broadcasters purchased the series:

Country	TV Network(s)	Series Premiere	Weekly Schedule
Australia	Channel Nine	22 October 2007	Cancelled after first episode[6] [7]
Canada	E!	October 2007	Cancelled after second episode; was seen Sundays at 7PM ET
United Kingdom	Virgin 1 Living	Virgin 1:2007 Living: 2008	Virgin 1: To be announced Living: TBA
United States	CBS	October 18, 2007	Cancelled after second episode

In Pop Culture

- A few days after the cancellation, a clip of *Viva Laughlin* was featured on *The Soup*. The show's host Joel McHale described it as "the show that was loved by hundreds". McHale also sarcastically remarked that "we need that" for easy jokes.

See also

- *Cop Rock* - A poorly received 1990 ABC series which attempted to combine the genres of musical theater and police procedural
- *Hull High* - A 1990 NBC "musical soap opera"
- List of television series cancelled after one episode

References

[1] "Viva Laughlin at The Futon Critic" (http://www.thefutoncritic.com/showatch.aspx?id=viva_laughlin). . Retrieved 2006-06-26.

[2] Sullivan, Brian Ford (2007-05-14). "CBS picks up *Bang, Power,* plus four dramas" (http://www.thefutoncritic.com/news.aspx?id=7387). . Retrieved 2007-06-26.

[3] "CBS to use *The American Theatre Wing's 61st Annual Tony Awards*" to showcase multiple promos for Viva Laughlin, *a new drama premiering in the fall, executive produced by Tony Award and Emmy Award winner Hugh Jackman*" (http://www.thefutoncritic.com/news.aspx?id=20070607cbs01). The Futon Critic. 2007-06-07. .

[4] Andreeva, Nellie (2007-07-18). "CBS announces premiere week lineup" (http://web.archive.org/web/20070820093134/http://www.hollywoodreporter.com/hr/content_display/television/news/e3ie5f8bddafc23b9d8cd631f69e4234572). Archived from the original (http://www.hollywoodreporter.com/hr/content_display/television/news/e3ie5f8bddafc23b9d8cd631f69e4234572) on 2007-08-20. . Retrieved 2007-07-19.

[5] "CBS announces 2007-2008 primetime schedule" (http://www.thefutoncritic.com/news.aspx?id=20070516cbs02). The Futon Critic. 2007-05-16. . Retrieved 2007-06-26.

[6] ""Hugh Jackman's show Viva Laughlin dumped by Channel Nine"" (http://www.news.com.au/perthnow/story/0,21598,22634823-5012990,00.html). The Daily Telegraph. 2007-10-23. . Retrieved 2007-10-29.

[7] ""Back from the dud"" (http://www.smh.com.au/news/tv--radio/we-took-a-gamble--furness/2007/10/24/1192941127545.html). The Sydney Morning Herald. 2007-10-25. . Retrieved 2007-10-29.

[8] Schneider, Michael (2007-10-22). "CBS cancels *Viva Laughlin*" (http://www.variety.com/article/VR1117974484.html?categoryid=14& cs=1). Variety. . Retrieved 2007-10-22.

[9] . http://www.news.com.au/perthnow/story/0,21598,22634823-5012990,00.html.

[10] Alessandro Stanley (2007-10-18). "Singing in the Casino? That's a Gamble" (http://www.nytimes.com/2007/10/18/arts/television/ 18stan.html). *New York Times*. . Retrieved 2007-10-24.

[11] Diane Werts (2007-10-18). "Review: CBS' *Viva Laughlin* a train wreck" (http://web.archive.org/web/20071020034800/http://www. newsday.com/entertainment/tv/ny-ettell5415699oct18,0,5351094.story). *Newsday*. Archived from the original (http://www.newsday. com/entertainment/tv/ny-ettell5415699oct18,0,5351094.story) on 2007-10-20. . Retrieved 2007-10-30.

External links

- *Viva Laughlin* (http://www.imdb.com/title/tt0878801/) at the Internet Movie Database
- *Viva Laughlin* (http://www.tv.com/show/68672/summary.html) at TV.com
- *Viva Laughlin* (http://epguides.com/VivaLaughlin) at epguides.com

Deception (2008 film)

Deception	
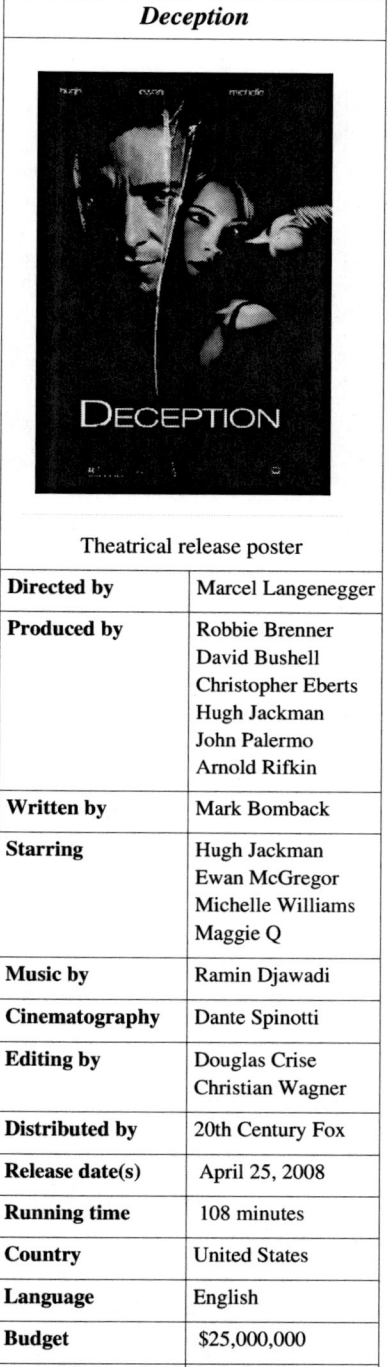 Theatrical release poster	
Directed by	Marcel Langenegger
Produced by	Robbie Brenner David Bushell Christopher Eberts Hugh Jackman John Palermo Arnold Rifkin
Written by	Mark Bomback
Starring	Hugh Jackman Ewan McGregor Michelle Williams Maggie Q
Music by	Ramin Djawadi
Cinematography	Dante Spinotti
Editing by	Douglas Crise Christian Wagner
Distributed by	20th Century Fox
Release date(s)	April 25, 2008
Running time	108 minutes
Country	United States
Language	English
Budget	$25,000,000
Gross revenue	$17,741,298

Deception is a 2008 drama/thriller film, directed by Marcel Langenegger and written by Mark Bomback. It stars Ewan McGregor, Hugh Jackman, and Michelle Williams. The film was released on April 25, 2008 in the United States.

Plot

Accountant Jonathan McQuarry (Ewan McGregor) is an auditor with little to no social life. One night while working late in a boardroom he is interrupted by a lawyer, Wyatt Bose (Hugh Jackman), who befriends him and offers him marijuana. After a long conversation, Jonathan takes the subway home where he has a brief encounter with a blond woman (Michelle Williams) while waiting on the train. Upon returning home he notices a pipe in his bedroom is leaking and leaving a stain.

Jonathan contacts Wyatt the next day and they play tennis after work. Afterward they stop by Wyatt's lavish apartment where Jonathan borrows an expensive suit. They meet again for lunch the next day and upon leaving, Wyatt intentionally takes Jonathan's mobile phone instead of his own, forcing a trade. He mentions he will be in London on business for the next few weeks.

When Jonathan realizes the phones have been switched he attempts to contact Wyatt but does not reach him. He is soon contacted by a woman (Natasha Henstridge) who asks if he is free that night. He informs her that he is and agrees to meet her. When she arrives, they proceed directly to a hotel room to have sex and Jonathan realizes that Wyatt must be on some type of exclusive sex club list.

When Wyatt calls the next day, he encourages Jonathan to continue his participation with other list members. Upon doing so he has an encounter with an older woman (Charlotte Rampling) who explains more of the list's rules: the initiator pays for the room, no names are exchanged, there is no conversation and no rough play. Participants are always anonymous, although Jonathan does spot the older woman on the cover of *Forbes*. He continues to participate over the next few weeks with several partners.

One night after initiating another encounter, Jonathan is surprised to find that his partner is the blond woman he met while waiting for the train. When she begins to undress he stops her and tells her that they had met once before. He requests that she have dinner with him and they order room service and talk for hours. The next day Jonathan rejects other callers from the list but when the blond woman calls again they agree to meet for dinner in Chinatown. They then proceed to a hotel where she requests some ice. When Jonathan returns to the room she is gone and there is blood on the bedsheets. Someone knocks him out from behind and when he wakes up the bed has been made. He contacts the police and explains to the Detective (Lisa Gay Hamilton) that the woman is missing but that he has little to no information about her. She doubts his story and his sanity. Jonathan tries to trace Wyatt and is told that he is not known at the law firm or the apartment.

Upon returning home Jonathan is surprised to find Wyatt waiting for him and demanding that he steal $20 million from Clute-Nichols, an investment firm he will begin to audit in a few days. Jonathan having a level 4 access and the money being dirty and belongs in the CEO's slush fund. Jonathan agrees to do so but only because he fears for the safety of the blond woman. The following night at work, Jonathan receives a call asking if he's free, from a woman named Tina (Maggie Q), an investment banker with the Chicago branch of Clute-Nichols, who was "his (Wyatt's) first", and introduced Wyatt to the exclusive sex club list. She reveals that Wyatt's real name is Jamie Getz, and that they met when he was attending a private corporate event as a guest of Rudolph Holloway, a junior partner at the Chicago branch and someone Jamie Getz played tennis with. Jonathan then calls the NYPD Central Records posing as Detective Russo, and finds out that Jamie Getz murdered Rudolph Holloway via strangulation with tennis strings, and also did three years for insurance fraud and arson. Jonathan is later notified by the detective that a blond woman matching his earlier description was discovered dead. When he comes in to identify her, he sees that it is actually the first woman that called him, and that she was also strangled by tennis strings.

He goes on to complete a wire transfer to a bank in Spain in his name, but secretly adds Wyatt's name as co-signer. When he returns home he notices that a picture Wyatt had sent of the blond woman being held captive was taken in his apartment before the pipe started leaking. He realizes that she must have been a conspirator and wisely avoids his apartment which explodes when the superintendent enters to fix the pipe.

Now in Madrid, Wyatt impersonates Jonathan and attempts to withdraw the funds from the bank, but he is denied access because of the co-signer.

Wyatt leaves the bank without any money and outside the bank receives a call asking him if he was "available tonight?", realizing that Jonathan was not dead, Jonathan appears from behind. The plot unfolds. Jonathan agrees to help him withdraw the funds but only if Wyatt splits it with him. Jonathan and Wyatt having swapped identities cash in the $20 million in two $10 million suitcase. (A deleted scene reveals that Jonathan encountered a black market operator in Chinatown, who offered a variety of items, including fake passports; Jonathan presumably obtained a passport with his image in the name of Wyatt Bose and used this in his scheme to obtain half of the money).

After the transaction is complete, Jonathan offers Wyatt half of his money if Wyatt tells him where the blond woman is. Wyatt pretends to agree and lures Jonathan to an uncrowded area where he attempts to shoot Jonathan but before he is able to do so he is shot by the blond woman who quickly leaves. Jonathan leaves a dying Wyatt and the money behind to pursue her and asks her to talk to him but the girl tells him that she wants to call it off and apologizes to him as she didn't know Wyatt was going to kill him. The girl gets into a cab and leaves as Jonathan watches her go.

On the other hand when the detective checks the death investigation report of Mr. Lewman (superintendent who enters to fix the pipe) is surprised to find the reality.

In Madrid, Jonathan again crosses path with the blond woman and they exchange smiles. The film comes to a close as Jonathan walks to her and she stands waiting for him.

Cast

- Hugh Jackman as Jamie Getz a.k.a. Wyatt Bose
- Ewan McGregor as Jonathan McQuarry
- Michelle Williams as "S"
- Maggie Q as Tina
- Lisa Gay Hamilton as Detective J. Russo
- Natasha Henstridge as Simone Wilkinson
- Charlotte Rampling as Wall Street Belle
- Javier Godino as Spanish Bank Manager

Critical reception

The film received substantially negative reviews from critics. As of April 27, 2008, the review aggregator Rotten Tomatoes reported that 13% of critics gave the film positive reviews, based on 63 reviews - with the consensus that the film is "a middling, predictable potboiler."[1] Metacritic reported the film had an average score of 32 out of 100, based on 22 reviews.[2]

Box office

In its opening weekend, the film grossed $2.3 million in 2,001 theaters in the United States and Canada, averaging only $1,155 per theater and ranking #10 at the box office.[3] As of September 22, 2009, the film has grossed $4,598,506 in the United States and Canada while grossing $13,114,439 in foreign countries adding to a total of $17,712,945.

See also

- Gerhard Richter, whose painting is featured

References

[1] "Deception Movie Reviews, Pictures - Rotten Tomatoes" (http://www.rottentomatoes.com/m/10009724-deception/). Rotten Tomatoes. . Retrieved June 20, 2010.
[2] "Deception (2008): Reviews" (http://www.metacritic.com/film/titles/deception). Metacritic. . Retrieved April 27, 2008.
[3] "Deception (2008) (2008) - Weekend Box Office Results" (http://www.boxofficemojo.com/movies/?page=weekend&id=deception.htm). Box Office Mojo. . Retrieved April 29, 2008.

External links

- Official website (http://http://www.deception-movie.com/site/index.html)
- *Deception* (http://www.imdb.com/title/tt0800240/) at the Internet Movie Database
- *Deception* (http://www.allmovie.com/work/358058) at Allmovie
- *Deception* (http://www.boxofficemojo.com/movies/?id=deception.htm) at Box Office Mojo
- *Deception* (http://www.rottentomatoes.com/m/10009724-deception/) at Rotten Tomatoes
- *Deception* (http://www.metacritic.com/film/titles/deception) at Metacritic

Australia (2008 film)

Australia	
 Australian promotional poster	
Directed by	Baz Luhrmann
Produced by	Baz Luhrmann Catherine Knapman G. Mac Brown
Screenplay by	Baz Luhrmann Ronald Harwood Stuart Beattie Richard Flanagan
Story by	Baz Luhrmann
Starring	Nicole Kidman Hugh Jackman David Wenham
Music by	David Hirschfelder
Cinematography	Mandy Walker
Editing by	Dody Dorn
Distributed by	20th Century Fox
Release date(s)	26 November 2008
Running time	165 minutes
Country	Australia
Language	English
Budget	$130 million ($78 million after Australian tax rebates)[1] [2]
Gross revenue	$211,342,221 (worldwide)[3] [4]

Australia is a 2008 epic romance film directed by Baz Luhrmann and starring Nicole Kidman and Hugh Jackman. It is the second-highest grossing Australian film of all time, behind *Crocodile Dundee*. The screenplay was written by Luhrmann and screenwriter Stuart Beattie, with Ronald Harwood. The film is a character story, set between 1939 and 1942 against a dramatised backdrop of events across northern Australia at the time, such as the bombing of Darwin during World War II. Production took place in Sydney, Darwin, Kununurra, and Bowen. The movie was to be released on 13 November 2008 in Australia[5] and 16 November 2008 in the United States;[6] however, Fox announced that it had pushed back the release dates in both Australia and the United States to 26 November 2008,[7] with subsequent worldwide release dates throughout late December 2008 and January and February 2009.

Plot

In 1939, Lady Sarah Ashley (Nicole Kidman) travels from England to northern Australia to force her philandering husband to sell his faltering cattle station, Faraway Downs. Her husband sends an independent cattle drover (Hugh Jackman), called simply "Drover", to Darwin to transport her to Faraway Downs.

Lady Sarah's husband is murdered shortly before she arrives, and the authorities tell her that the killer is an Aboriginal elder with magical powers, "King George" (David Gulpilil). Meanwhile, cattle station manager Neil Fletcher (David Wenham) is trying to gain control of Faraway Downs, so that Lesley 'King' Carney (Bryan Brown) will have a complete cattle monopoly in the Northern Territory, giving him negotiating leverage with an Australian army officer, Captain Dutton (Ben Mendelsohn).

The childless Lady Sarah is captivated by the boy Nullah (Brandon Walters), who was born to an Aboriginal mother and an unknown white father. Nullah tells her that he has seen her cattle being driven onto Carney's land — in other words, stolen from her. Because of this Fletcher mistreats Nullah and threatens him and his mother, after which Lady Sarah fires Fletcher and decides to try and run the cattle station herself. When Nullah and his mother hide from the white authorities in a water tower, his mother drowns. Lady Sarah comforts Nullah by singing the song "Over the Rainbow" from the film *The Wizard of Oz*. Nullah tells her that "King George" is his grandfather, and that like "King George" he too is a "magic man".

Lady Sarah persuades Drover to take the cattle to Darwin for sale. Drover, a white man, is friendly with the Aborigines, and therefore shunned by many of the other whites in the territory. It is revealed that he was married to an Aboriginal woman, who died after being refused medical treatment in a local hospital because of her race. Lady Sarah also reveals she is barren and can not have children.

Drover leads a team of six other riders, including Lady Sarah, Drover's Aboriginal brother-in-law Magarri (David Ngoombujarra), Nullah, and the station's accountant Kipling Flynn (Jack Thompson), to drive the 1,500 cattle to Darwin. They encounter various obstacles along the way, including a fire set by Carney's men that scares the cattle, resulting in the death of Flynn when the group tries to stop the cattle from stampeding over a cliff. Lady Sarah and Drover fall in love, and she gains a new appreciation for the Australian territory. The team drive the cattle through the dangerous Never Never desert. Then, when at last delivering the cattle in Darwin, the group has to race them onto the ship before Carney's cattle are loaded.

Afterwards, Lady Sarah, Nullah, and Drover live together happily at Faraway Downs for two years. Meanwhile, Fletcher kills Carney, marries his daughter Cath Carney, takes over Carney's cattle empire, and continues to menace Lady Sarah. It is established that Fletcher was the actual murderer of Lady Sarah's husband, and is also almost certainly Nullah's father.

Nullah is drawn to perform a walkabout with his grandfather "King George", but is instead taken by the authorities and sent to live on Mission Island with the other half-Aboriginal children (dubbed the "Stolen Generations"). Lady Sarah, who has come to regard Nullah as her adopted son, vows to rescue him. Meanwhile, she works as a radio operator in Darwin during the escalation of World War II. When the Japanese attack the island and Darwin in 1942, Lady Sarah fears that Nullah has been killed.

Drover, who had quarrelled with Lady Sarah and left, apparently never to return, returns to Darwin and hears (mistakenly) that she has been killed in the bombing. Drover learns of Nullah's abduction to Mission Island, and goes with Magarri and a young priest to rescue him and the other children. Meanwhile, Lady Sarah has sold Faraway Downs to Fletcher, and is leaving for England that day, since she believes there is nothing more to hold her in Australia. But when Drover and the children sail back into port at Darwin, and Nullah plays "Over the Rainbow" on his harmonica, Lady Sarah hears the music and the three are reunited.

Fletcher, who is distraught at the death of his wife, attempts to shoot Nullah, but is speared by King George and falls dead. Lady Sarah, Drover, and Nullah return to the safety of remote Faraway Downs. There, King George calls for Nullah, who returns to the Outback with his grandfather.

Soundtrack

Recurring motifs

A recurring motif in the film is the Harold Arlen/E.Y. Harburg song "Over the Rainbow" from *The Wizard of Oz (1939 film)*. The song bonds Lady Ashley and Nullah, and relates to the Aboriginal concepts of Rainbow Serpent, songlines, Dreamtime, and "magic men" like Nullah's grandfather and Nullah himself. In a scene set in October 1939, Nullah is seen raptly watching *Oz* in a Darwin cinema.

Bach's aria "*Schafe können sicher weiden* ("Sheep may safely graze")" from the Hunting Cantata BWV 208 is another recurring motif in the film.

Additional music

David Hirschfelder composed the score to *Australia*. Interpolated musical numbers include the jazz standards "Begin the Beguine," "Tuxedo Junction," "Sing Sing Sing (With a Swing)," and "Brazil." Edward Elgar's "Nimrod" from "Enigma" Variations is heard in the final scene of the film.[8] Luhrmann hired singer Rolf Harris to record his wobble board for the opening credits,[9] and Elton John composed and performed a song called "The Drover's Ballad," to lyrics by Luhrmann, for the end credits. Also used in the end credits is "By the Boab Tree," a song nominated for a 2008 Satellite Award,[10] again with Luhrmann lyrics, performed by Sydney singer Angela Little. Little's rendition of "Waltzing Matilda" completes the end credits in some versions of the film. The jazz sound track to "Australia" was performed by the Ralph Pyle big band with clarinet solos by Andy Firth.[11]

Cast

- Nicole Kidman as Lady Sarah Ashley, an English aristocrat who inherits the cattle station Faraway Downs in Australia.
- Hugh Jackman as the Drover, a drover who helps Lady Sarah Ashley move the cattle across the property.
- David Wenham as Neil Fletcher, a station manager who plans to take Faraway Downs from Lady Sarah Ashley.
- Bryan Brown as Lesley 'King' Carney, a cattle baron who owns much of the land in northern Australia.
- Jack Thompson as Kipling Flynn, an alcoholic accountant who enjoys a luxurious lifestyle.
- David Gulpilil as King George, a magic tribal elder, grandfather of Nullah.
- Brandon Walters as Nullah, a young Aboriginal boy whom Lady Sarah Ashley finds at Faraway Downs.
- David Ngoombujarra as Magarri, the Drover's colleague and friend.
- Ben Mendelsohn as Captain Emmett Dutton, a Darwin-based Australian Army officer in charge of beef supply.
- Sandy Gore as Gloria Carney, King Carney's wife, and Catherine's mother.
- Essie Davis as Catherine 'Cath' Carney Fletcher, wife of Neil Fletcher and daughter of King Carney.
- Barry Otto as Administrator Allsop, the King's representative in the Northern Territory.
- Ursula Yovich as Daisy, the mother of Nullah.
- Yuen Wah as Sing Song, a Cantonese chef at Faraway Downs.

- Jacek Koman as Ivan, the saloonkeeper and innkeeper in Darwin.
- Tony Barry as Sergeant Callahan, the head of the Northern Territory police who tries to take Nullah to Mission Island.

Production

Originally, Baz Luhrmann was planning to make a film about Alexander the Great starring Leonardo DiCaprio and Nicole Kidman, with a screenplay by David Hare.[12] The director had built a studio in the northern Sahara but a rival film made by Oliver Stone was released first and after several years in development, Luhrmann abandoned the project to make a film closer to home.[12]

The visual effects were done by the Animal Logic films and The LaB Sydney.

Luhrmann spent six months researching general Australian history.[12] At one point he considered setting his film during the First Fleet, 11 ships that sailed from Britain in 1787 and set up the first colony in New South Wales. The director wanted to explore Australia's relationship with England and with its indigenous population.[12] He decided to set the film between World Wars I and II in order to merge a historical romance with the Stolen Generations, where thousands of mixed-race Aboriginal children were forcibly removed from their families by the state and integrated into white society. Luhrmann has said that his film depicts "a mythologised Australia".[12]

Casting

In May 2005, Russell Crowe and Nicole Kidman entered negotiations to star in an untitled 20th Century Fox project written by director Baz Luhrmann and screenwriter Stuart Beattie, with Luhrmann directing the film.[13] For her role, Kidman learned to round up cattle.[14] In May 2006, due to Crowe's demanding personal script approval before signing onto the project, Luhrmann sought to replace the actor with Heath Ledger.[15] Crowe said he didn't want to work in an environment that was influenced by budgetary needs.[16] About this casting issue, Luhrmann said, "it was hard pinning [Crowe] down. Every time I was ready, Russell was in something else, and every time he was ready, I would be having another turmoil".[12] The following June, Luhrmann replaced Crowe with actor Hugh Jackman.[17]

Australia sign board

In January 2007, actors Bryan Brown, Jack Thompson, and David Wenham were cast into *Australia*.[18] In November 2006, Luhrmann began searching for an actor to play an Aboriginal boy of 8–10 years old and by April 2007, 11-year-old Brandon Walters was cast into the role.[19]

Pre-production

The untitled project was scheduled to begin production in September 2006, but scheduling conflicts and budget issues postponed the start of production to February 2007.[16] In November 2006, Luhrmann explored The Kimberley to determine the amount of production to be shot there. In December 2006, Bowen was chosen as a filming location for a third of the production, portraying the look of Darwin.[20] Bowen

Filming of *Australia* at Stokes Hill Wharf

was chosen as a prospect due to the financing of $500,000 by the Queensland government.[21] In April, Kununurra was chosen as another location for *Australia*, this time to serve as Faraway Downs, the homestead owned by Kidman's character.[22] Entire sets were built from scratch, including a stand-alone set in the Queensland town of Bowen, the re-creation of war scenes near Darwin Harbour, and the construction of an outback homestead in

Western Australia.[23]

Costumes

Academy Award winning costume designer Catherine Martin did extensive research for the film's outfits, studying archival images and newspapers from the 1930s and 1940s Australia. She also interviewed descendants of the original Darwin stockmen in order to find out if they "wore socks with his boots when he rode a horse, that's something you either get through a snapshot, or something you have to go talk to the people who lived there about".[24] The Asian-inspired costumes of the film were intended to evoke the romanticism of the era, and one of the centrepieces of the film's costuming is a red chrysanthemum-printed Chinese cheongsam or qipao that was made for Nicole Kidman's character.[25] The film received an Academy Award nomination for Best Costume Design.

Principal photography

The director planned to begin filming in March 2007.[26] However, principal photography began on 30 April 2007 in Sydney,[27] and Kidman found out that she was pregnant. She instantly withdrew from her next film, *The Reader*.[28] Afterwards, the production moved to Bowen on 14 May.[22]

Filming in Kununurra was a gruelling experience for the cast and crew with temperatures soaring to 43 °C (109 °F) which, one day, caused Kidman to faint while on a horse.[28] In addition, she worked 14 and 15-hour days while dealing with morning sickness.[28] While shooting in a remote region of Western Australia, the shoot had to be rescheduled when the Faraway Downs set, the homestead central to the film's story, was reduced to mud from torrential rain – the first in 50 years.[29] The cast and crew went back to Sydney to shoot interior scenes until the expensive set dried out.[23] In addition, at one point, the entire country's horses were in lock down over equine flu.[12]

Filming lasted five months, wrapping up at Fox Studios, Sydney, on 19 December 2007.[30] In late April, Luhrmann titled his project *Australia*. Two other titles that he considered for the film had been *Great Southern Land* and *Faraway Downs*.[31] On 11 August 2008, eight months after filming wrapped, several members of the cast and crew were back at Fox Studios, Sydney, to film pick up shots.[32]

Post-production

Two weeks before the film's premiere, the *Daily Telegraph* erroneously reported that Luhrmann gave in to studio pressure after "intense" talks with executives and re-wrote and then re-shot the ending of *Australia* for a happier conclusion after "disastrous reviews" from test screenings.[33] To counter these negative reports, the studio had Jackman and Kidman promoting *Australia* on *The Oprah Winfrey Show*, which dedicated an entire episode of the program to the film,[34] and Fox Co-Chairman Tom Rothman spoke to the *Los Angeles Times* where he described the *Telegraph* article as "patently nonsensical. It's all too typical of the way the world works today that everybody picked up an unsourced, anonymous quote-filled story in a tabloid from Sydney and nobody ever bothered to check to see if it was accurate".[33] Rothman also said that Luhrmann had final cut on his film. The director admitted that he wrote six endings in the drafts he authored, and shot three of them.[35]

Tourism tie-in

Tourism Western Australia spent $1 million on a campaign linked with the release of *Australia* in the United States, Canada, Japan, Europe and South Korea that ties in with an international Tourism Australia plan.[36] Concerned about the recession and fluctuating international fuel prices, the tourism industry hoped that Luhrmann's film would deliver visitors from all over the world in the same kind of numbers that came to the country following the 1986 release of *Crocodile Dundee*, and follow the significant increase in visitors to New Zealand since 2001 after the release of the *Lord of the Rings* films. Federal Tourism Minister Martin Ferguson said, "This movie will potentially be seen by tens of millions of people, and it will bring life to little-known aspects of Australia's extraordinary natural environment, history and indigenous culture".[36] Tourism Australia worked with Luhrmann and 20th Century Fox on a publicity campaign titled, "See the Movie, See the Country", based on movie maps and location guides, to transform the film into "a real-life travel adventure".[36] In addition, the director made a $50 million series of commercials promoting the country.[29] [37]

Critical reception

Summary

Early reviews in the Australian press were mixed with the general consensus that *Australia* was a good but not great film.[38] Review aggregator *Rotten Tomatoes* reported that as of 4 October 2010, 55% of critics gave the film a positive write-up, based upon a sample of 199, with an average score of 5.9/10. The site reported that the consensus was that while the film features "lavish vistas" and "impeccable production," it suffers due to its "lack of originality" and "thinly-drawn characters."[39] At *Metacritic*, which assigns a normalised rating out of 100 to reviews from mainstream critics, the film has received an average score of 53, based on 31 reviews, denoting "mixed or average reviews."[40]

Positive

Chris Tookey, in his review for the *Daily Mail* wrote, "Kidman and Jackman have great sexual chemistry, as well as the glamour of Forties cinema idols." He also rated the film the maximum five stars.[41] The *News of the World* followed suit by rating the film with five stars, the reviewer Robie Collin praised the casting and camerawork; "The jaw-dropping, picture postcard camerawork, that will have your eyes scouring each scene for every last delicious detail.The uproarious comic interludes (Nicole's rendition of Somewhere Over The Rainbow, and the build-up to it, is one of the best-played comic set pieces of the year)..The magnetic and irksomely handsome Hugh Jackman, the undisputed star of the show."[42]

Claire Sutherland, in her review for the *Herald Sun* wrote, "A love letter to the Australian landscape and our history, *Australia* has international blockbuster written all over it".[43] In his review for *The Australian*, David Stratton wrote, "It's not the masterpiece that we were hoping for, but I think you could say that it's a very good film in many ways. While it will be very popular with many people I think there's a slight air of disappointment after it all. Despite its flaws — and it certainly has flaws — I think *Australia* is an impressive and important film."[44]

Anne Barrowclough of *The Times* (United Kingdom) gave the film four out of five stars, and states the film defies expectation and "in what turns out to be a multi-layered story it describes an Australia of the 1940s that is at once compellingly beautiful and breathtakingly cruel".[45]

Megan Lehmann, writing in *The Hollywood Reporter*, said that the film "defies all but the most cynical not to get carried away by the force of its grandiose imagery and storytelling", and it is "much less earnest than the trailer suggests, layered with a thin veneer of camp and a nod and a wink to accompany the requisite Aussie clichés", and the bottom line is "In epic style, Baz Luhrmann weaves his wizardry on Oz".[46]

Roger Ebert gave the film 3 stars out of 4, noting "Baz Luhrmann dreamed of making the Australian *Gone With the Wind*, and so he has, with much of that film's lush epic beauty and some of the same awkwardness with a national legacy of racism".[47]

David Ansen, in his review for *Newsweek*, wrote, "Kidman seems to blossom under Luhrmann's direction: she's funny, warm and charming, and the erotic charge between her and the gruff, hunky Jackman is delicious. In a solemn season, *Australia*'s bold, kitschy, unapologetic artifice is a welcome respite".[48]

In her review for the *New York Times*, Manohla Dargis wrote, "this creation story about modern Australia is a testament to movie love at its most devout, cinematic spectacle at its most extreme, and kitsch as an act of aesthetic communion".[49]

Neutral

Writing for *The Age*, Jim Schembri had problems with the length of the film: "The film is fine, and never boring but, boy, is it overlong. At a mammoth 165 minutes it feels too much like a work-in-progress. There is a lot of narrative flab and longueurs in the first two hours and the film often has the pace of a steamroller with engine trouble".[50]

In her review for the *New York Times*, Manohla Dargis wrote, "this creation story about modern Australia is a testament to movie love at its most devout, cinematic spectacle at its most extreme, and kitsch as an act of aesthetic communion".[49]

Andrew Sarris, in his review for the *New York Observer*, wrote, "*Australia* is clearly a labor of love, and a matter of national pride. It is also a bit of a mess. I must confess that I might have been harder on Mr Luhrmann's film if I had not remained entranced by Ms Kidman ever since I first saw her in Phillip Noyce's *Dead Calm* in 1989; in my opinion, she has lost none of her luster in the 20 years since".[51]

In his review for *Time*, Richard Schickel wrote, "Have you seen everything *Australia* has on offer a dozen times before? Sure you have. Its a movie less created by director and co-writer Baz Luhrmann than assembled, Dr Frankenstein-style, from the leftover body parts of earlier movies. Which leaves us asking this question: How come it is so damnably entertaining?"[52]

Ann Hornaday, in her review for the *Washington Post*, wrote, "A wildly ambitious, luridly indulgent spectacle of romance, action, melodrama and revisionism, *Australia* is windy, overblown, utterly preposterous and insanely entertaining".[53]

Negative

Mark Naglazas of *The West Australian* accused positive reviews from News Ltd press outlets of being manipulated by 20th Century Fox, calling *Australia* a film of "unrelenting awfulness" that "lurches drunkenly from crazy comedy to Mills and Boonish melodrama in the space of a couple of scenes".[54]

Bonnie Malkin of *The Daily Telegraph* stated: "Local critics had worried that the much-anticipated film *Australia* would present to the world a series of time-honoured Antipodean clichés. Their fears were well founded".[55]

In her review for Salon.com, Stephanie Zacharek wrote, "The second half of *Australia*, Luhrmann's attempt to pull off a wartime weeper, is so aggressively sentimental that it begins to feel more like punishment than pleasure. I left *Australia* feeling drained and weakened, as if I'd suffered a gradual poisoning at the hands of a mad scientist".[56]

Box office and DVD sales

The film has been a box office success worldwide, despite a disappointing gross in the U.S. — a pattern similar to Luhrmann's three previous films. As of November 2009, the film has grossed $211,342,221 in its worldwide releases.[3] [4]

In Australia, the film grossed $AU6.37 million in its opening weekend, setting the record for the highest grossing opening weekend for an Australian film and bumping the latest James Bond movie *Quantum of Solace* to second place.[57]

Australia performed less well in the U.S., where it surprised box office analysts by opening only at #5, behind *Quantum of Solace*, *Twilight*, *Bolt*, and *Four Christmases*, and grossed $20 million opening weekend.[57] However, Fox officials were reportedly happy with the numbers, as they said they were expecting only an $18 million opening gross for the movie.[1] [2] They further pointed out that Baz Luhrmann's other films, like *Moulin Rouge!*, *Strictly Ballroom*, and *Romeo + Juliet*, started slowly and then built momentum.[58] *Australia* eventually grossed $49,554,002 in the U.S., 23.4% of its total worldwide gross.[3]

Australia's ticket sales outside of the U.S. are $161,788,219 from 51 countries.[3] It opened at No. 1 in Spain, France, and Germany, and at No. 3 in Britain.[57] *Australia* grossed $87,555,757 at the box office in Australia.[59]

The DVD was released in the U.S. on 3 March 2009, opening at #2, and sold 728,000 units in the opening weekend, translating to revenue of $12.3 million.[60] *Australia* sold almost two million DVDs in one month, 80% of what the studio predicted it would sell altogether. As of 15 November 2009, Australia has sold 1,739,700 units in the U.S., for a revenue of $27.9 million.[60] Since being released in Australia, the DVD has sold double what the studio expected.[61]

Awards and nominations

Awards			
Award	**Category**	**Recipient(s)**	**Outcome**
Satellite Awards	Satellite Award for Best Art Direction and Production Design	Catherine Martin	Won
	Satellite Award for Best Cinematography	Mandy Walker	Won
	Satellite Award for Best Visual Effects	Chris Godfrey	Won
	Satellite Award for Best Original Screenplay	Baz Luhrmann	Nominated
	Satellite Award for Best Original Score	David Hirschfelder	Nominated
	Satellite Award for Best Original Song	'By the Boab Tree'	Nominated
	Satellite Award for Best Editing	Dody Dorn	Nominated
	Satellite Award for Best Sound	Wayne Pushley	Nominated
	Satellite Award for Best Costume Design	Catherine Martin	Nominated
81st Academy Awards	Academy Award for Best Costume Design	Catherine Martin	Nominated
Film Critics Circle of Australia	Best Cinematography	Mandy Walker	Won
	Best Supporting Actor	Brandon Walters	Won
	Best Film	*Australia*	Nominated
	Best Music Score	David Hirschfelder	Nominated
Young Artist Award	Best Performance in an International Feature Film – Leading Young Performers –	Brandon Walters	Won
Best Young Performer	Critics' Choice Awards	Brandon Walters	Nominated
Chicago Film Critics	Best Cinematography	Mandy Walker	Nominated
	Most Promising Performer	Brandon Walters	Won

See also

- Cinema of Australia

References

[1] "Hollywood Studios Turn Hopeful Eye Toward Holiday." (http://www.reuters.com/article/industryNews/idUSTRE4AM1T520081125) *Reuters*, 25 November 2008

[2] "Hollywood Stuffs Thanksgiving Slate." (http://www.variety.com/article/VR1117996415.html?categoryId=13&cs=1) *Variety*, 24 November 2008

[3] BoxOfficeMojo.com (http://www.boxofficemojo.com/movies/?id=australia.htm)

[4] *Australia* release dates (http://www.imdb.com/title/tt0455824/releaseinfo)

[5] Val Morgan Cinema Network - : Details view (http://www.valmorgan.com.au/au/movie-planner/details-view/movieid/20009864/moviesdate/0/)

[6] Pamela McClintock (31 March 2008). "2008 awards season shaping up" (http://www.variety.com/index.asp?layout=awardcentral&jump=article&articleid=VR1117983222). *Variety*. . Retrieved 1 April 2008.

[7] Michaela Boland (28 August 2008). "Nicole Kidman's 'Australia' Pushed Back" (http://www.variety.com/article/VR1117991269.html?categoryid=13&cs=1). *Variety*. . Retrieved 29 August 2008.

[8] Reel Soundtrack *Australia* (http://www.reelsoundtrack.com/index.php?act=movie_details&id=52543)

[9] Richard Luscombe (10 November 2008). "Kidman's outback adventure gets happy ending after studio pressure" (http://www.guardian.co.uk/film/2008/nov/10/australia-nicole-kidman-hugh-jackman-baz-luhrmann). *The Guardian* (London). . Retrieved 11 November 2008.

[10] Awards Daily - Satellite Awards Nominees (http://www.awardsdaily.com/?p=4414), Retrieved 22 December 2008.

[11] *Australia* – The Soundtrack (http://www.australiamovie.net/2008/12/australia-the-soundtrack/), Retrieved 22 December 2008.

[12] Killian Fox (2 November 2008). "How we made the epic of Oz" (http://www.guardian.co.uk/film/2008/nov/02/baz-luhrmann-nicole-kidman-australia). *The Guardian* (London). . Retrieved 11 November 2008.

[13] Michael Fleming (4 May 2005). "Inside Move: All the Aussies gathering together" (http://www.variety.com/article/VR1117922158.html?categoryid=1238&cs=1). *Variety*. . Retrieved 28 April 2007.

[14] Baz Bamigboye (2 March 2007). "Kidman follows the herd" (http://www.dailymail.co.uk/pages/live/articles/showbiz/bazbamigboye.html?in_page_id=1794&in_article_id=439603). *Daily Mail*. . Retrieved 29 April 2007.

[15] Reardanz, Karen (30 May 2006). "Crowe Dumped for Ledger" (http://www.sfgate.com/cgi-bin/blogs/sfgate/detail?blogid=7&entry_id=5642). *San Francisco Chronicle*. . Retrieved 28 April 2007.

[16] Reardanz, Karen (26 September 2006). "Crowe: 'I Don't Do Charity Work for Studios'" (http://www.sfgate.com/cgi-bin/blogs/sfgate/detail?blogid=7&entry_id=9252). *San Francisco Chronicle*. . Retrieved 28 April 2007.

[17] "Jackman taking over for Crowe" (http://web.archive.org/web/20080309063437/http://www.cnn.com/2006/SHOWBIZ/06/09/showbuzz/#2). CNN. 9 June 2006. Archived from the original (http://www.cnn.com/2006/SHOWBIZ/06/09/showbuzz/#2) on March 9, 2008. . Retrieved 28 April 2007.

[18] "An epic showcase" (http://www.news.com.au/entertainment/story/0,23663,21116465-7485,00.html). Sydney Confidential. 25 January 2007. . Retrieved 29 April 2007.

[19] Katie Hampson (18 April 2007). "Broome boy rides high in Aussie blockbuster" (http://web.archive.org/web/20070930013110/http://www.thewest.com.au/default.aspx?MenuID=23&ContentID=26307). *The West Australian*. Archived from the original (http://www.thewest.com.au/default.aspx?MenuID=23&ContentID=26307) on September 30, 2007. . Retrieved 29 April 2007.

[20] "Luhrmann epic to be shot in Bowen" (http://www.thewest.com.au/aapstory.aspx?StoryName=340410). *The West Australian*. 12 December 2006. . Retrieved 28 April 2007.

[21] Des Partridge; Rosanne Barrett (13 December 2006). "Grant lures Baz" (http://www.news.com.au/couriermail/story/0,23739,20917320-3102,00.html). *The Courier-Mail*. . Retrieved 29 April 2007.

[22] Rachel Browne (16 April 2007). "Other Tom gives Nic saddle tips" (http://www.theage.com.au/news/film/nic-gets-saddle-tips/2007/04/15/1176575723647.html). *The Age* (Melbourne). . Retrieved 29 April 2007.

[23] Christine Sams (1 July 2007). "Muddy hell as Kidman homestead set flooded" (http://www.smh.com.au/news/film/muddy-hell/2007/06/30/1182624229314.html). *Sydney Morning Herald*. . Retrieved 11 November 2008.

[24] Eric Wilson (31 October 2008). "Socks to Blouses, a Film Finds Its Look" (http://www.nytimes.com/2008/11/02/movies/moviesspecial/02mart.html?_r=1&oref=slogin). *The New York Times*. . Retrieved 11 November 2008.

[25] "The Look of 'Australia'" (http://www.nytimes.com/slideshow/2008/10/31/movies/20081102_MARTIN_SLIDESHOW_5.html). *The New York Times*. 31 October 2008. . Retrieved 25 April 2010.

[26] "Luhrmann epic to start filming in March" (http://www.abc.net.au/news/newsitems/200611/s1778649.htm). Australian Broadcasting Corporation. 1 November 2006. . Retrieved 29 April 2007.

[27] Johnathon Moran (29 April 2007). "Nicole and Hugh film *Australia*" (http://www.news.com.au/dailytelegraph/story/0,,21638026-5001026,00.html?from=public_rss). *The Daily Telegraph*. . Retrieved 29 April 2007.

[28] John Powers (1 July 2008). "Days of Heaven" (http://www.style.com/vogue/feature/061708VFEA/). *Vogue*. . Retrieved 11 November 2008.

[29] Jeff Dawson (14 September 2008). "Nicole Kidman returns to Australia for Baz Luhrmann" (http://entertainment.timesonline.co.uk/tol/arts_and_entertainment/film/article4731651.ece). *Sunday Times* (London). . Retrieved 11 November 2008.

[30] australiamovie.net (16 April 2007). "That's a Wrap, People!" (http://www.australiamovie.net/12/2007/thats-a-wrap-people/). . Retrieved 19 December 2007.

[31] Garry Maddox (23 November 2006). "Luhrmann to parade Australia's epic scale" (http://www.theage.com.au/news/entertainment/luhrmann-to-parade-australias-epic-scale/2006/11/22/1163871482154.html). *The Age* (Melbourne). . Retrieved 28 April 2007.

[32] australiamovie.net (11 August 2008). "Pick Ups Commence At Fox Studios" (http://www.australiamovie.net/2008/08/pick-up-shoots-commence-at-fox-studios/). . Retrieved 16 August 2008.

[33] Patrick Goldstein (11 November 2008). "Fox says it hasn't tampered with *Australia*" (http://latimesblogs.latimes.com/the_big_picture/2008/11/fox-says-it-has.html). *Los Angeles Times*. . Retrieved 13 November 2008.

[34] Richard Jinman (11 November 2008). "Battling Baz wobbles into home stretch" (http://www.smh.com.au/news/entertainment/film/battling-baz-wobbles-into-home-stretch/2008/11/10/1226165477503.html). *Sydney Morning Herald*. . Retrieved 11 November 2008.

[35] Scott Feinberg (11 November 2008). "Baz Luhrmann addresses big questions about *Australia*—and remains confident in his film" (http://latimesblogs.latimes.com/files/2008/11/baz-luhrmann.html). *Los Angeles Times*. . Retrieved 13 November 2008.

[36] Elizabeth Gosch (16 June 2008). "See the film, then come visit" (http://www.theaustralian.com.au/news/see-the-film-then-come-visit/story-e6frgcs6-1111116642284). *The Australian*. . Retrieved 11 November 2008.

[37] Kathy Marks (18 September 2008). "Down under - the movie" (http://www.independent.co.uk/news/world/australasia/down-under--the-movie-but-can-baz-nicole-and-hugh-persuade-us-to-go-to-australia-935433.html). *The Independent* (London). . Retrieved 11 November 2008.

[38] Tom O'Neil (18 November 2008). "First Aussie reviews of 'Australia': 'Good, but no classic'" (http://goldderby.latimes.com/awards_goldderby/2008/11/australian-baz.html). *Los Angeles Times*. . Retrieved 18 November 2008.

[39] "Australia Movie Reviews" (http://www.rottentomatoes.com/m/australia/). IGN Entertainment, Inc. . Retrieved 26 November 2008.

[40] Metacritic. "Australia(2008): Reviews" (http://www.metacritic.com/film/titles/australia). CNET Networks, Inc. . Retrieved 26 November 2008.

[41] Australia: Barmy Baz is the Wizard of Oz - unique, magical and endearingly bonkers (http://www.dailymail.co.uk/tvshowbiz/reviews/article-1101728/Australia-Barmy-Baz-Wizard-Oz--unique-magical-endearingly-bonkers.html) Daily Mail. 25 December 2008

[42] Australia (12A) (http://www.newsoftheworld.co.uk/entertainment/film/104829/Australia-12A.html) News of the World. 21 December 2008

[43] Claire Sutherland (18 November 2008). "Baz Luhrmann's movie *Australia* is a winner for Nicole Kidman and Hugh Jackman" (http://www.news.com.au/entertainment/story/0,26278,24668203-7485,00.html). *Herald Sun*. . Retrieved 18 November 2008.

[44] David Stratton (18 November 2008). "Baz Luhrmann's Australia is good, but not a masterpiece" (http://www.theaustralian.news.com.au/story/0,25197,24670334-601,00.html). *The Australian*. . Retrieved 18 November 2008.

[45] Anne Barrowclough (18 November 2008). "Review: *Australia*, the movie" (http://entertainment.timesonline.co.uk/tol/arts_and_entertainment/film/article5178513.ece). *The Times* (London). . Retrieved 18 November 2008.

[46] Megan Lehmann (18 November 2008). "Film Review: *Australia*" (http://www.hollywoodreporter.com/hr/film/reviews/article_display.jsp?&rid=11975). The Hollywood Reporter. . Retrieved 18 November 2008.

[47] Roger Ebert (25 November 2008). "*Australia*" (http://rogerebert.suntimes.com/apps/pbcs.dll/article?AID=/20081125/REVIEWS/811259991). *Chicago Sun-Times*. . Retrieved 27 November 2008.

[48] David Ansen (28 November 2008). "It's Epic" (http://www.newsweek.com/id/171193). *Newsweek*. . Retrieved 8 December 2008.

[49] Manohla Dargis (26 November 2008). "Oh Give Me a Home Where the Cowboys and Kangaroos Roam" (http://movies.nytimes.com/2008/11/26/movies/26aust.html?ref=movies). *The New York Times*. . Retrieved 27 November 2008.

[50] Jim Schembri (18 November 2008). "Good, but no classic, and way, way too long" (http://www.theage.com.au/articles/2008/11/18/1226770367495.html). *The Age* (Melbourne). . Retrieved 18 November 2008.

[51] Andrew Sarris (25 November 2008). "Luminous Kidman Finds Home on the Range With Dirty, Sexy Jackman" (http://www.observer.com/2008/o2/luminous-kidman-finds-home-range-dirty-sexy-jackman). *New York Observer*. . Retrieved 27 November 2008.

[52] Richard Schickel (25 November 2008). "*Australia*: Epic Romance Down Under" (http://www.time.com/time/arts/article/0,8599,1862279,00.html). *Time*. . Retrieved 27 November 2008.

[53] Ann Hornaday (26 November 2008). "An Aussome Spectacle" (http://www.washingtonpost.com/wp-dyn/content/article/2008/11/25/AR2008112502454.html). *Washington Post*. . Retrieved 27 November 2008.

[54] Mark Naglazas (19 November 2008). "Luhrmann's red dirt epic will leave a nation red-faced" (http://www.thewest.com.au/default.aspx?MenuID=23&ContentID=108983). *The West Australian*. . Retrieved 19 November 2008.

[55] Bonnie Malkin (18 November 2008). "First review of *Australia* the movie" (http://www.telegraph.co.uk/news/worldnews/australiaandthepacific/australia/3477400/First-review-of-Australia-the-movie.html). *The Daily Telegraph* (London). . Retrieved 18 November 2008.

[56] Stephanie Zacharek (26 November 2008). "'Australia*"* (http://www.salon.com/ent/movies/review/2008/11/26/australia/index.html). Salon.com. . Retrieved 27 November 2008.

[57] "*Australia* heads Aussie box office, dies in US" (http://www.news.com.au/couriermail/story/0,23739,24732238-5003420,00.html). *Courier Mail*. 1 December 2008. . Retrieved 2 December 2008.

[58] Ronald D. White (1 December 2008). "*Four Christmases* adds up to No. 1 at the box office" (http://www.latimes.com/entertainment/ news/movies/la-fi-boxoffice1-2008dec01,0,1906482.story). *Los Angeles Times*. . Retrieved 2 December 2008.

[59] *Film Victoria - Australian Films at the Australian Box Office* (http://film.vic.gov.au/resources/documents/ AA4_Aust_Box_office_report.pdf)

[60] The-numbers.com (http://www.the-numbers.com/movies/2008/AUSTL-DVD.php)

[61] Natasha Robinson (4 April 2009). "Baz Luhrmann's Australia's takings are still growing steadily" (http://www.theaustralian.news.com. au/story/0,,25286999-16947,00.html). *The Australian*. . Retrieved 6 April 2009.

External links

- Official website (http://http://www.australiamovie.com)
- *Australia* (http://www.imdb.com/title/tt0455824/) at the Internet Movie Database
- *Australia* (http://www.allmovie.com/work/387021) at Allmovie
- *Australia* (http://www.rottentomatoes.com/m/australia/) at Rotten Tomatoes
- *Australia* (http://www.metacritic.com/film/titles/australia) at Metacritic
- *Australia* (http://www.boxofficemojo.com/movies/?id=australia.htm) at Box Office Mojo
- *Australia* soundtrack (listenable) (http://www.reelsoundtrack.com/index.php?act=movie_details&id=52543)
- Tourism Australia's campaign produced by Baz Luhrmann (http://www.australia.com/campaigns/walkabout/ au/index.htm?ta_cid=au:brand:20081008:hp:flash)
- Slide show of costume designs for *Australia* by Catherine Martin (http://www.nytimes.com/slideshow/2008/ 10/31/movies/20081102_MARTIN_SLIDESHOW_index.html) from the *New York Times*

The Burning Season (2008 film)

Directed by	Cathy Henkel
Produced by	Jeff Canin, Cathy Henkel and Trish Lake
Written by	Cathy Henkel
Narrated by	Hugh Jackman
Starring	Lone Drøscher Nielsen, Dorjee Sun, Achmadi
Music by	Nicolette Boaz
Cinematography	Leonard Retel Helmrich, Ismail Fahmi Lubis
Editing by	Jane St Vincent Welch
Distributed by	National Geographic International
Release date(s)	August 2, 2008 (BIFF) September 10, 2009 (New Zealand)
Running time	90 minutes
Country	Australia
Language	English

The Burning Season is a 2008 cinema documentary about the burning of rainforests in Indonesia. The main characters featured in the film are; Dorjee Sun from Australia; Achmadi, a small-scale palm oil farmer from Jambi province in Indonesia; and Lone Drøscher Nielsen, a Danish conservationist based in Kalimantan, Indonesia.

Synopsis

Every year, there is a burning season in Indonesia. Areas of rainforest the size of Denmark are cut down and set alight by farmers and corporations to develop palm oil plantations. As well as destroying the habitat of critically endangered orangutans, new scientific evidence shows that deforestation comprises 20% of global carbon emissions, contributing significantly to climate change.

A 30-year-old Australian environmental entrepreneur, Dorjee Sun, sets out to find a solution. Using expertise gained during the dot-com boom, Dorjee forms a small carbon-trading firm and signs up three pioneering Indonesian governors to partner in his venture. His idea involves selling the carbon credits represented by large forest areas in Aceh and Papua to big carbon emitters in the West. Despite the scepticism surrounding carbon trading, Dorjee's quest for a 'big deal' takes him from Sydney to New York, Washington DC, San Jose, San Francisco and London.

Meanwhile, another burning season is underway. Achmadi, a small-scale Indonesian farmer, sets fire to his newly acquired piece of forest to clear it for palm oil. But he too has to face up to the impact of his burning on the global climate. And in Borneo, Danish-born Lone Drøscher-Nielsen rescues and cares for orangutans injured or orphaned by the fires. As she prepares for the release of rehabilitated orangutans back into the wild, the UN Climate Change Conference in Bali commences. Everything hinges on whether all the countries of the world can agree on the wording of a new climate change protocol and whether protection of forests will be included. As the drama of this historic moment plays out, Dorjee relentlessly pursues his deal. Is he a pioneer or a profiteer? What value does his concept offer to the remaining forests of the world and to the challenges of climate change?.[1]

Premiere

Tribeca Film Festival, New York, NY USA, 2009

Awards

- Brisbane International Film Festival Audience Choice Award 2008 [Preview Cut]
- Inside Film Award for Best Documentary

See also

- Deforestation in Indonesia
- Environmental impact of palm oil
- Asian brown haze

References

[1] "The Burning Season press kit" (http://www.theburningseasonmovie.com/media/docs/The_Burning_Season_Press_Kit.pdf). 2009. . Retrieved 2009-09-08.

External links

- *The Burning Season* (http://www.theburningseasonmovie.com/) website
- *The Burning Season* (http://www.imdb.com/title/tt1321813/) at the Internet Movie Database

X-Men Origins: Wolverine

X-Men Origins: Wolverine	
 Theatrical release poster	
Directed by	Gavin Hood
Produced by	Hugh Jackman Lauren Shuler Donner Ralph Winter Peter MacDonald Richard Donner Stan Lee John Palermo Louis G. Friedman Marsha L. Swinton Whitney Thomas Kurt Williams
Written by	David Benioff Skip Woods
Starring	Hugh Jackman Liev Schreiber Danny Huston Will.i.am Lynn Collins Taylor Kitsch Ryan Reynolds Daniel Henney Tahyna Tozzi Dominic Monaghan
Music by	Harry Gregson-Williams
Cinematography	Donald McAlpine
Editing by	Nicolas De Toth Megan Gill

Studio	20th Century Fox
	Marvel Entertainment
	The Donners' Company
	Seed Productions
	Ingenious Film Partners
	Big Screen Productions
	Dune Entertainment
Distributed by	20th Century Fox
Release date(s)	April 29, 2009 (Australia)
	May 1, 2009 (United States)
Running time	107 minutes
Language	English
Budget	$150 million[1]
Gross revenue	$373,062,864[1]
Preceded by	X-Men: The Last Stand
Followed by	X-Men: First Class

X-Men Origins: Wolverine is a 2009 American superhero action thriller based on the Marvel Comics' fictional character Wolverine. The fourth installment in the X-Men series, it was released worldwide on May 1, 2009. The film is directed by Gavin Hood and stars Hugh Jackman as the title character, along with Liev Schreiber, Danny Huston, Will.i.am, Lynn Collins, Taylor Kitsch, Daniel Henney, and Ryan Reynolds. The film acts as a prequel to the *X-Men* film series, focusing on the violent past of the mutant Wolverine and his relationship with his half-brother Victor Creed. The plot also details Wolverine's early encounters with Major William Stryker, his time with Team X, and the bonding of Wolverine's skeleton with the indestructible metal adamantium during the Weapon X program.

The film was mostly shot in Australia and New Zealand, with Canada also serving as a location. Production and post-production was troubled, with conflicts arising between director Hood and Fox's executives, and an unfinished workprint being leaked in the internet one month before the film's debut. Reviews for *X-Men Origins: Wolverine* were mixed, with critics considering the film and its screenplay uninspired, but praising Hugh Jackman's performance. It opened at the top of the box office, and has grossed $179 million in the United States and Canada and over $373 million worldwide.

Plot

In 1845 Canada, young James Howlett sees his father killed by groundskeeper Thomas Logan. The trauma activates the boy's mutation: bone claws protrude from James' hands, and he kills his father's murderer. With his dying breath, Thomas Logan reveals that he, not John Howlett, is James' real father. James flees with Victor Creed, the abused son of their father who is thus James' brother. They spend the next century as soldiers, fighting in the American Civil War, both World Wars and the Vietnam War. In Vietnam, Victor attempts to rape a local village woman, but is stopped after killing a senior officer. Despite his objections to Victor's actions, James defends his brother, and the two are sentenced to execution by firing squad, which they survive. Major William Stryker approaches them, now in military custody, and offers them membership in Team X, a group of mutants including marksman Agent Zero, swordsman Wade Wilson, teleporter John Wraith, invincible Fred Dukes and electropathic Chris Bradley. They join the team, but the group's questionable actions and disregard for human life cause James to leave.

Six years later, James, now going by the name Logan, lives in Canada with his girlfriend, Kayla Silverfox. Colonel Stryker locates Logan and warns him that someone is killing members of the team; both Wilson and Bradley are dead. Shortly afterward, Victor murders Kayla and attacks Logan. Stryker offers Logan a way to beat Victor; Logan undergoes an operation to reinforce his skeleton with adamantium, a virtually indestructible metal. Before the procedure, Logan asks for new dog tags inscribed with "Wolverine", based on a story that Kayla told him. Once the procedure is complete, Stryker orders Logan's memory erased, but Logan overhears and fights his way out. Logan hides at a farm, but the next day Zero tracks him down. Zero attacks Logan, killing the owners of the farm, but later he defeats Zero and continues his revenge.

Logan locates Wraith and Dukes and asks them about the location of Stryker's new laboratory, referred to as "The Island". They tell him to find Remy LeBeau, who escaped and knows the location of The Island. Logan locates Gambit in New Orleans, and asks for the Island's location, but Gambit suspects Logan was sent to recapture him and attacks. Creed manages to find Logan, and after killing Wraith, he attacks him. When Logan is about to kill Victor, Gambit interrupts, giving Victor the chance to escape. Logan and Gambit fight one last time before Logan convinces him he is not working for Stryker. Gambit takes him to Stryker's facility on Three Mile Island. Logan learns that Kayla is alive and conspired with Stryker in exchange for her sister's safety.

Logan leaves, enraging Victor. When Victor demands the adamantium bonding promised for his service, Stryker refuses on the basis that Victor would not survive the procedure. Victor attempts to kill Kayla when she tries to persuade him Stryker betrayed them both, but Logan hears her screams and returns. Logan defeats and nearly kills Victor, but stops when Kayla reminds him of his humanity. Kayla and Logan free the imprisoned mutants.

Stryker activates Weapon XI, originally Wade Wilson, but now a "mutant killer" with the abilities of other mutants, which Stryker refers to as "The Deadpool". Logan holds Weapon XI off while the mutants flee. The party is greeted by Professor Charles Xavier, who offers them shelter at his school.

Kayla, mortally wounded, decides to stay. Logan lures Weapon XI to the top of one of the plant's cooling towers. Logan is almost killed until Victor intervenes. Logan decapitates Weapon XI and kicks him into the base of the cooling tower. Victor departs and Logan is saved from the collapsing tower by Gambit. As Logan carries Kayla to safety, Stryker shoots him in the forehead with adamantium bullets, rendering him unconscious. Kayla uses her persuasion powers to make Stryker drop the gun and commands him to walk away before dying from her wounds. Gambit returns as Logan regains consciousness, but the bullets that were shot at his brain have triggered amnesia. Gambit tries convincing Logan to come with him, but he declines, wanting to go his own way.

In a post-credits scene, it is revealed that Weapon XI is still alive in the rubble of the cooling tower. In an alternate post-credits scene, Logan is revealed to have traveled to Japan. Also during the credits Stryker is shown to continue walking along a road with his shoes ripped, damaged and worn out before he is found by the military.

Cast

- Hugh Jackman as James Howlett / Logan / Wolverine: The mutant and future X-Men member. Jackman, who played Wolverine in the previous films, has also become producer of the film via his company Seed Productions, and earned $25 million for the film.[2] Jackman underwent a high intensity weight training regimen to improve his physique for the role. He altered the program to shock his body into change and also performed cardiovascular workouts. Jackman noted no digital touches were applied to his physique in a shot of him rising from the tank within which Wolverine has his bones infused with adamantium.[3]

  - Troye Sivan as Young James Howlett: Casting directors cast Sivan as the young Wolverine after seeing him sing at the Channel Seven Perth Telethon, and he was accepted after sending in an audition tape.[4] Kodi Smit-McPhee was originally cast in the role, when filming was originally beginning in December 2007,[5] but he opted out to film The Road.[6]

- Liev Schreiber as Victor Creed: Logan's half-brother and fellow soldier. Jackman and Hood compared Wolverine and Sabretooth's relationship to the Borg-McEnroe rivalry in the world of tennis: Victor hates him because he loved and needed his brother, but is too proud to admit he needs him back.[7] Tyler Mane, who played him in X-Men, had hoped to reprise the role.[8] Jackman worked with Schreiber before, in the 2001 romantic comedy Kate & Leopold and described him as having a competitive streak necessary to portray Sabretooth. They "egged" each other on set to perform more and more stunts. Schreiber put on 40 lb (18 kg) of muscle for the part,[7] and described Sabretooth as the most monstrous role he ever played. As a child, he loved the Wolverine comics because of their unique "urban sensibility". Schreiber had studied to be a fight choreographer and wanted to be a dancer like Jackman, so he enjoyed working out their fight scenes.[9]

- Michael James Olsen as Young Victor Creed

- Danny Huston as William Stryker: Schreiber was originally in negotiations for the part,[10] while Brian Cox, who played the character in *X2*, wanted to reprise the role. He believed computer-generated imagery, similar to the program applied to Patrick Stewart and Ian McKellen in the opening flashback of *X-Men: The Last Stand*, would allow him to appear as the younger Stryker.[11] Huston liked the complex Stryker, who "both loves and hates mutants because his son was a mutant and drove his wife to suicide. So he understands what they're going through, but despises their destructive force." He compared the character to a racehorse breeder, who rears his mutant experiments like children but abandons them when something goes wrong. His son is shown to be frozen at the Weapon X facility and the reason Stryker starts the Weapon XI program.[7]

- Lynn Collins as Kayla Silverfox: Wolverine's love interest and later captive of Stryker. She has the powers of tactile telepathy/hypnosis.[7] However, it is shown that Victor is immune to her powers. Describing her role, Collins said that "I had to play off all the guys and their testosterone-heavy abilities. But I learned that the female powers of persuasion easily trump fangs and knives and guns."[12] Michelle Monaghan turned down the role because of scheduling conflicts, despite her enthusiasm to work with Jackman.[13]

- Taylor Kitsch as Remy LeBeau / Gambit: A Cajun thief who has the ability to charge any object he touches with kinetic energy, forcing it to explode. The size of the object determines the magnitude of the resulting explosion.[7] He is also skilled in the use of a staff, and happens to be very agile. Due to the nature of his power, he displays supernatural durability, being able to take Wolverine's elbow to his face and return to fight moments later. When asked about his thoughts on the character, Kitsch had said, "I knew of him, but I didn't know the following he had. I'm sure I'm still going to be exposed to that. I love the character, I love the powers, and I love what they did with him. I didn't know that much, but in my experience, it was a blessing to go in and create my take on him. I'm excited for it, to say the least."[14]

- Will.i.am as John Wraith: A teleporting mutant. It is will.i.am's major live-action film debut. Although he initially did not get on with the casting director, he got the role because he wanted to play a mutant with the same power as Nightcrawler. He enrolled in boot camp to get into shape for the part.[15] When filming a fight, he scarred his knuckles after accidentally punching and breaking the camera.[16]

- Kevin Durand as Fred J. Dukes / The Blob: A mutant with an nearly indestructible layer of skin and the ability to create his own gravitational field. In the film's early sequences, he is a formidable fighting man, but years later, due to a poor diet, has gained an enormous amount of weight that gives him an invulnerability.[7] A fan of the *X-Men* movies, Durand contacted the producers for a role as soon as news of a new film came out.[17] The suit went through six months of modifications, and had a tubing system inside to cool Durand down with ice water.[18]

- Ryan Reynolds as Wade Wilson: A wisecracking mercenary with lethal swordsmanship skill and athleticism, who later becomes Deadpool. Reynolds had been interested in playing the character in his own film since 2003.[19] Originally, Reynolds was only going to cameo as Wilson but the role grew after he was cast.[20] Reynolds did sword-training for the character, and also worked out to get his physique comparable to Jackman's.[21]

- Scott Adkins as Weapon XI / Deadpool: Weapon XI is the final antagonist of the film, having been genetically altered to be the ultimate mutant killer. He has powers taken from other mutants killed or kidnapped in the film, as well as retractable blades in his arms. Ryan Reynolds portrays Weapon XI for close-ups, standing shots, and simple stunts while Scott Adkins is used for the more complicated and dangerous stunt work.[22]

- Daniel Henney as Agent Zero: A member of the Weapon X program and an expert tracker with lethal sniper skills.[7] An X-Men fan, Henney liked the role of a villain because "there are no restrictions playing it, allowing you freely to express it, so you can act how you want to".[23] He described the film as more realistic and cruder than the *X-Men* trilogy.[24]

- Dominic Monaghan as Chris Bradley: A mutant who can manipulate electricity and a technopath.[25] It was originally reported that Monaghan was going to play Barnell Bohusk / Beak.[26]

- Tim Pocock as Scott Summers: A mutant capable of emitting powerful beams of energy from his eyes, who will later become Cyclops, leader of the X-Men. He is shown as a Weapon X captive as he is caught by Victor Creed. Pocock is a debuting screen actor who previously worked with Opera Australia, who decided to play the character as "his own" instead of following James Marsden's performance in the *X-Men* trilogy, feeling that "he's a very different human being at that point in time. He's a teenager. What teenager is the same when they're 30 years old?" Pocock also described *Wolverine* as being Cyclops' "big transition moment", with the character going from a troubled teenager to a leader throughout the course of the film.[27]

- Tahyna Tozzi as Emma Frost: A mutant with the power to turn her skin into diamond, who in the film is Silverfox's sister.[28] *X2* writer Dan Harris said that Sigourney Weaver would have played Emma Frost in *X-Men: The Last Stand* if Bryan Singer had stayed on to direct.[29] The film depiction of Emma does not exhibit the character's traditional telepathic abilities. Film credits list the character as "Kayla's sister/Emma" as opposed to "Emma Frost"; however, trailers and television ads identify her by full name as "Emma Frost".

- Peter O'Brien as John Howlett: James' alleged father, shot by Thomas Logan in the film's opening.

- Alice Parkinson as Elizabeth Howlett: James' mother.

- Aaron Jeffery as Thomas Logan: Victor and James' real father, who ends up getting killed by James.

- Max Cullen and Julia Blake as Travis Hudson and Heather Hudson: An elderly couple who take care of Wolverine after his adamantium bonding. The Hudsons are heavily adapted from the comics' James MacDonald and Heather Hudson.

The film includes numerous cameo appearances of younger versions of characters from the previous films, including Jason Stryker (William Stryker's lobotomized telepathic son whom he keeps in cryogenic suspension).[30] There was a cameo for a young Storm, which can be seen in the trailer, but it was removed from the released film.[31] A digitally rejuvenated Patrick Stewart also makes an uncredited cameo as a younger Charles Xavier who had not yet lost the use of his legs.[32]

Asher Keddie played Dr. Carol Frost.[33] Poker player Daniel Negreanu has a cameo. Phil Hellmuth wanted to join him but was unable because he committed to an event in Toronto.[34] X-Men co-creator Stan Lee said he would cameo, but ended up not appearing in the film.[35]

Production

Development

David Benioff, a comic book fan, pursued the project for almost three years before he was hired to write the script in October 2004.[36] [37] In preparing to write the script, he reread Barry Windsor-Smith's "Weapon X" story, as well as Chris Claremont and Frank Miller's 1982 limited series on the character (his favorite storyline).[36] [38] Also serving as inspiration was the 2001 limited series *Origin*, which reveals Wolverine's life before Weapon X.[39] Jackman collaborated on the script, which he wanted to be more of a character piece compared with the previous *X-Men* films.[40] Skip Woods, who had written *Hitman* for Fox, was later hired to revise and rewrite Benioff's script.[41] Benioff aimed for a "darker and a bit more brutal" story, writing it with an R rating in mind, although he acknowledged the film's final tone would rest with the producers and director.[36] Jackman did not see the need for an R-rating.[42] The film's final rating was PG-13.[43]

Deadpool had been developed for his own film by Reynolds and David S. Goyer at New Line Cinema in 2003, but the project fell apart as they focused on *Blade: Trinity* and an aborted spin-off.[19] Benioff wrote the character into the script in a manner Jackman described as fun, but would also deviate from some of his traits. Similarly, Gambit was a character who the filmmakers had tried to put in the previous *X-Men* films. Jackman liked Gambit because he is a "loose cannon" like Wolverine, stating their relationship echoes that of Wolverine and Pyro in the original trilogy.[3] David Ayer contributed to the script.[44] Benioff finished his draft in October 2006, and Jackman stated there would be a year before shooting,[45] as he was scheduled to start filming *Australia* during 2007.[46] Before the 2007–2008 Writers Guild of America strike began, James Vanderbilt and Scott Silver were hired for a last-minute rewrite.[47]

Gavin Hood was announced as director of the project in July 2007 for a 2008 release.[48] Previously, *X-Men* and *X2* director Bryan Singer and *X-Men: The Last Stand* director Brett Ratner were interested in returning to the franchise,[49] [50] while Alexandre Aja and Len Wiseman also wanted the job.[51] [52] Zack Snyder, who was approached for *The Last Stand*, turned down this film because he was directing *Watchmen*.[53] Jackman saw parallels between Logan and the main character in Hood's previous film *Tsotsi*.[7] Hood explained that while he was not a comic book fan, he "realized that the character of Wolverine, I think his great appeal lies in the fact that he's someone who in some ways, is filled with a great deal of self-loathing by his own nature and he's constantly at war with his own nature".[54] The director described the film's themes as focusing on Wolverine's inner struggle between his animalistic savagery and noble human qualities. Hood enjoyed the previous films, but set out to give the spin-off a different feel.[55] In October, Fox announced a May 1, 2009, release date and the *X-Men Origins* prefix.[10]

Filming

Preliminary shooting took place at the Fox Studios Australia in Sydney, during late 2007.[56] Principal photography began on January 18, 2008[57] in New Zealand. One of the filming locations that was selected was Dunedin.[58] Controversy arose as the Queenstown Lakes District Council disputed the Department of Labour's decision to allow Fox to store explosives in the local ice skating rink. Fox moved some of the explosives to another area.[59] The explosives were used for a shot of the exploding Hudson Farm, a scene which required four cameras.[60] Jackman and Palermo's Woz Productions reached an agreement with the council to allow recycling specialists on set to advise the production on being environmentally friendly.[61]

Filming continued at Fox (where most of the shooting was done) and New Orleans, Louisiana.[10] Cockatoo Island was used for Stryker's facility; the enormous buildings there saved money on digitally expanding a set.[7] Production of the film was predicted to generate AUD$60 million for Sydney's economy.[62] Principal photography ended by May 23. The second unit continued filming in New Zealand until March 23, and were scheduled to continue filming for two weeks following the first unit's wrap.[63] This included a flashback to Logan during the Normandy Landings, which was shot at Blacksmiths, New South Wales.[64]

Hood and Fox were in dispute on the film's direction. One of the disputes involved the depiction of Wolverine as an Army veteran with post-traumatic stress disorder, with the executives arguing that audiences would not be interested in such heavy themes.[65] The studio had two replacements lined up before Richard Donner, husband of producer Lauren Shuler Donner, flew to Australia to ease on-set tensions.[66] Hood remarked, "Out of healthy and sometimes very rigorous debate, things get better. [...] I hope the film's better because of the debates. If nobody were talking about us, we'd be in trouble!"[7] Hood added he and Thomas Rothman were both "forceful" personalities in creative meetings but they had never had a "stand-up" argument.[67] In January 2009, after delays due to weather and scheduling conflicts, such as Hugh Jackman's publicity commitments for *Australia*, production moved to Vancouver, mostly at Lord Byng Secondary School and in University of British Columbia.[68] [69] Work there included finishing scenes with Ryan Reynolds, who had been working on two other films during principal photography.[70]

Gavin Hood has announced that multiple "secret endings" exist for the film and that the endings will differ from print to print of the film.[71] One version shows Wolverine drinking in a Japanese bar. The bartender asked if he is drinking to forget, Logan replies that he is drinking to remember.[72] The other shows Weapon XI on the rubble of the destroyed tower, trying to touch his severed head.[73]

Effects

More than 1,000 shots of *Wolverine* have visual effects in them, which required three effects supervisors and seventeen different companies to work on the film.[74] The most prominent was Hydraulx, who had also worked in the *X-Men* trilogy and was responsible for the battle in Three Mile Island and Gambit's powers. Many elements were totally generated through computer-generated imagery, such as the adamantium injection machine, the scene with Gambit's plane and Wolverine tearing through a door with his newly-enhanced claws.[74] CG bone claws were also created for some scenes because the props did not look good in close-ups.[75] Extensive usage of matte paintings was also made, with Matte World Digital creating five different mattes for the final scene of the film—a pullback depicting the destroyed Three Mile Island—and Gavin Hood handing company Hatch Productions pictures of favelas as reference for the Africa scenes.[74] [75]

Music

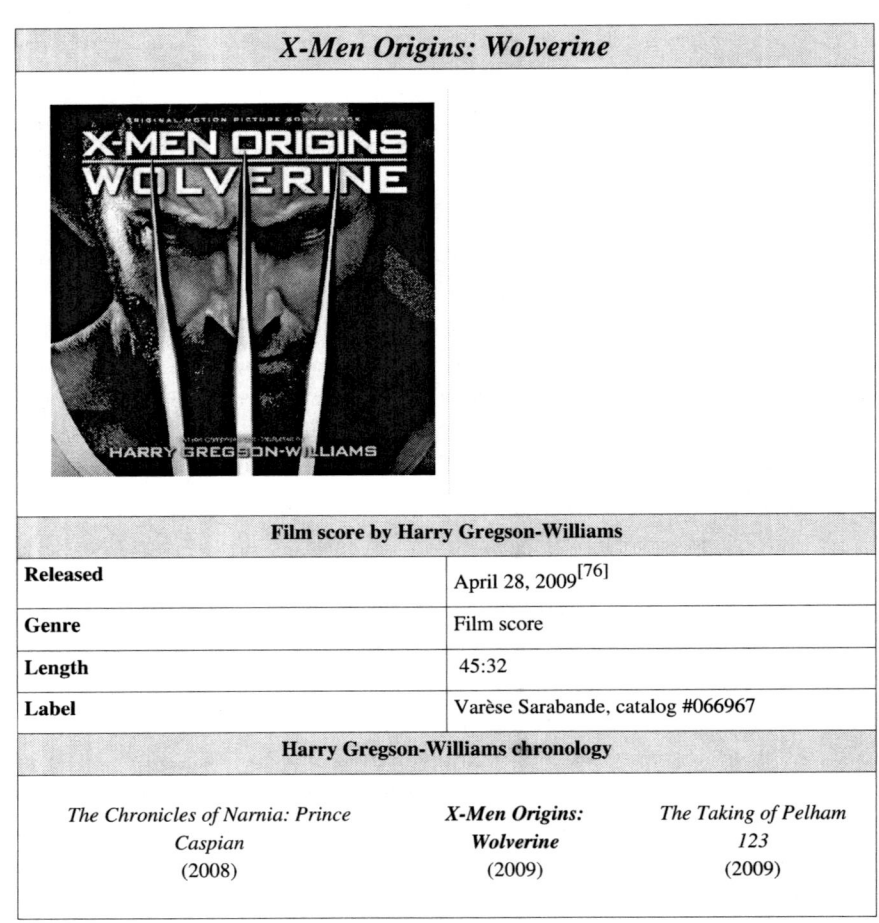

X-Men Origins: Wolverine		
Film score by Harry Gregson-Williams		
Released	April 28, 2009[76]	
Genre	Film score	
Length	45:32	
Label	Varèse Sarabande, catalog #066967	
Harry Gregson-Williams chronology		
The Chronicles of Narnia: Prince Caspian (2008)	***X-Men Origins: Wolverine*** (2009)	*The Taking of Pelham 123* (2009)

Composed by Harry Gregson-Williams, the score for *X-Men Origins: Wolverine* was mixed by Malcolm Luker, engineered by Costa Kotselas, and featured Martin Tillman on the electric cello.[77]

In a 2008 interview with Christopher Coleman of *Tracksounds.com*, Gregson-Williams said that Gavin Hood attracted him to the project, adding: "I happened to meet him at the Golden Globes dinner about three years ago. That night we were both nominees, but both losers. He had been nominated for *Tsotsi* and during the dinner I had spoken to him and he seemed like a really smart and creative guy...and into music. So I was really delighted when I got a call to meet him and discuss the possibilities for *Wolverine*."[78]

In late March 2009, Jon Burlingame of *Variety* was at the Newman Scoring Stage at 20th Century-Fox to listen and report on the recording of the score.[79] Gregson-Williams conducted "a 78-piece orchestra and a 40-voice choir (20 male, 20 female)" to achieve the sound.[79] At the time of his visit, Burlingame noted that the choir was singing "stanzas from an ancient Norse poem in Old Icelandic" to underscore what would be first track. "Logan Through Time."[79] Director Gavin Hood commented on Gregson-Williams' style, saying: "Harry's challenge is to give us operatic scale, but also keep it intimate and human. Harry's music has a kind of muscular confidence and strength that is very useful for the action, but he also has tremendous soul."[79] Hood also called the recording performance "frigging brilliant!"[79]

Release

Leaked workprint

On March 31, 2009, a full-length DVD-quality workprint of the film without a timecode or watermark, with some unfinished effects shots, a different typeface for titles and casting, and alternate sound effects was leaked online.[80] [81] [82] The studio said it would be able to determine the source of the leak using forensic marks in the workprint. The FBI and MPAA began investigating the illegal posting.[81] Fox estimated the workprint was downloaded roughly 4.5 million times by the time *Wolverine* was released in theaters.[83]

The print contained a reference to Rising Sun Pictures, an Australian visual effects company working on the film.[80] The company denied that they ever had a full copy of the film.[84] Executive producer Thomas Rothman noted the leaked version lacked the ten minutes added during pick-ups in January 2009.[82] [84] However, the theatrical version of the film has no extra scenes that were not included in the leaked workprint.[85] Both versions run exactly 107 minutes, but director Gavin Hood said "another ending exists that features the film's villain."[82]

Roger Friedman, a gossip reporter for Fox News—a channel also owned by Fox's parent company News Corporation—was fired for writing a review of the film using the leaked copy he downloaded over the internet.[86] He described how easy it was to find and download the film even if the original source of the leak was no longer available on the web. The article he wrote for his column on the Fox News website was immediately removed.[87]

Marketing

Among the companies which provided tie-in merchandising were 7-Eleven,[88] Papa John's Pizza,[89] and Schick.[90] Hugh Jackman also posed as Wolverine for the Got Milk? campaign.[91] In February 2009, Hasbro released a film-related toyline, featuring action figures and a glove with retractable claws.[92] In April, Marvel debuted a new comic series, *Wolverine: Weapon X*, which writer Jason Aaron said that while not directly influenced by the film, was written considering people who would get interested in *Wolverine* comics after watching the film.[93]

Raven Software developed a video game based on the film with the same name, which Activision Blizzard published.[94] Marc Guggenheim wrote the script,[95] while Hugh Jackman, Liev Schreiber,[96] and will.i.am voiced their characters from the film.[97] The storyline goes beyond the one from the film, including other villains from the comics such as the Sentinels and the Wendigo,[98] as well as the appearance of Mystique, who was in the other three *X-Men* films.[99]

In December 2009, Hot Toys released the 12 inch highly detailed figure of Wolverine based on the movie with Hugh Jackman's likeness.

Theatrical run

X-Men Origins: Wolverine was released on April 29, 2009, in the UK, Denmark, South Africa, and Australia; April 30, 2009 in the Philippines and in the Dominican Republic; and May 1, 2009 in the United States and Canada. A contest was held on the official website to determine the location of the world premiere on April 27. In the end, the Harkins at the Tempe Marketplace in Tempe, Arizona won the premiere.[100] The release in Mexico was delayed until the end of May due to an outbreak of H1N1 flu in the country.[101] On April 22, nine days before the release of the film, it was reported that *X-Men Origins: Wolverine* was outselling *Iron Man* "3-to-1 at the same point in the sales cycle (nine days prior to the film's release)."[102]

Hugh Jackman, Ryan Reynolds, Taylor Kitsch, Liev Schreiber, Lynn Collins, and will.i.am at the premiere in Tempe, Arizona.

Hugh Jackman at the Tempe Premiere.

During its first day of wide release, *Wolverine* took in an estimated $35 million,[103] with almost $5 million of that from midnight showings.[104] The earnings placed the film as the 16th highest-grossing opening day ever (22nd with ticket-price inflation).[103] It went on to be number one film at the box office with a total of $85 million.[105] [106] Among summer kick-offs, it ranked fifth behind *Spider-Man*, *X2*, *Spider-Man 3*, and *Iron Man* and it was in the top ten of comic book adaptations.[106] The opening was lower than the last film in the franchise, *X-Men: The Last Stand*, as well as *X2*, but higher than *X-Men*, the first film in the series.[106]

The worldwide opening was over $158.1 million, but Fox stated that some markets underperformed, mostly due to the leaked workprint in countries with illegal downloading problems.[83] However, in an article for the "piracy issue" of *Screen International* magazine, film critic John Hazelton was doubtful of this explanation, writing that the film's initial performance was "uncertain" as the outbreak of swine flu in territories with the worst piracy problems means that other territories didn't compare at all.[107]

While it has received mixed reviews from critics, the film has been a financial success at the box office. According to Box Office Mojo *Wolverine* has grossed approximately $179,883,157 in the United States and Canada. It took in another $193,179,707 in other territories, giving it a worldwide total of $373,062,864.[1]

Home media

On September 15, 2009, Fox Home Entertainment released *X-Men Origins: Wolverine* on DVD and Blu-ray disc.[108] The two-disc Blu-ray includes commentary by Hood, another commentary by producers Lauren Shuler Donner and Ralph Winter, the featurette "The Roots of Wolverine: A Conversation with X-Men creators Stan Lee and Len Wein", the featurette "Wolverine Unleashed: The Complete Origins", 10 character chronicles, two more featurettes, a trivia track, deleted scenes with commentary from Hood, two alternate sequences, a Fox Movie Channel premiere featurette and imdb BD Live technology. Disc two of the set includes a digital copy.[109] In addition, a Wal-Mart exclusive 3-disc set, which includes a standard DVD copy of the film was also released.[110] The two-DVD special edition includes the two commentaries, the featurette with Stan Lee and Len Wein, an origins featurette, deleted and alternate scenes, and an anti-smoking PSA on disc one; disc two has a digital copy of the film. The single-disc DVD release has the origins featurette and anti-smoking PSA.[109]

Wolverine was the highest selling and most rented DVD release of the week, selling over three million copies,[111] 850,000 of them on Blu-Ray.[112] Through its first six weeks the DVD has sold 3.79 million copies, generating $64.27 million in sales.[113]

Reception

Critical reception was decidedly mixed. Rotten Tomatoes currently reports a 37% rating—or 17% when filtered for their "Top Critics"—with 245 reviews (90 "fresh", 155 "rotten").[114] Metacritic reports a "metascore of 43 out of 100 from 36 critic reviews."[115] Comparatively, Yahoo! Movies currently reports a grade of "C+" averaged from 13 critic reviews.[116]

Richard Corliss of *Time* commented on the film's standing among other Marvel films, saying that it is "an O.K., not great, Marvel movie that tells the early story of the prime X-Man, and attempts to make it climax in a perfect coupling with the start of the known trilogy." He also said that "superhero mythologies can be so complicated, only a lonely comic-book-reading kid could make sense of it all."[117] James Mullinger of *GQ* also commented on the structure of the story in saying that the "film clumsily tries to explain the origins of James [Howlett], AKA Wolverine, which had wisely only ever been briefly referred to in the original *X-Men* saga. In doing so, it creates a fairly bland plot which is full of holes."[118] Lou Lumenick of the *New York Post* was generally more favorable towards *Origins*, stating "Fortunately, Jackman is well-matched with Schreiber, who can sneer with the best of them and wears fangs well. The two have three spectacular battles together before squaring off against a formidable enemy atop a nuclear reactor."[119] Peter Rainer of *The Christian Science Monitor* also praised Jackman's performance, saying that "Hugh Jackman demonstrates that you can segue effortlessly from a tuxedoed song-and-dance man at the Oscars to a feral gent with adamantium claws and *berserker rage.*"[120] Claudia Puig of *USA Today* considered the movie "well-acted, with spectacular action and witty one-liners".[121]

Roger Ebert gave the film two stars out of four and expressed his views on the title character: "Why should I care about this guy? He feels no pain and nothing can kill him, so therefore he's essentially a story device for action sequences."[43] James Berardinelli gave *Wolverine* two and a half stars out of four, calling the action scenes competently executed but not memorable, and considering that when dealing with Wolverine's past "there's little creativity evident in the way those blanks are filled in", and that the revelations made Wolverine "less compelling".[122] Comparatively, Bill Gibron of AMC's Filmcritic.com website gave the film a positive "4.0 out of 5 stars," saying that although Hugh Jackman is "capable of carrying even the most mediocre effort, he singlehandedly makes *X-Men Origins: Wolverine* an excellent start to the summer 2009 season." He did however predict that "there will be purists who balk at how Hood and his screenwriters mangle and manipulate the mythology;" and further said that "any ending which leaves several characters unexplained and unaccounted for can't really seal the full entertainment deal."[123]

Regarding *Wolverine* within the context of the *X-Men* film series, Tom Charity of CNN commented: "Serviceable but inescapably redundant, this *Wolverine* movie does just enough to keep the *X-Men* franchise on life support, but the filmmakers will have to come up with some evolutionary changes soon if it's going to escape X-tinction."[124] Similarly, A. O. Scott of *The New York Times* expressed that "*X-Men Origins: Wolverine* will most likely manage to cash in on the popularity of the earlier episodes, but it is the latest evidence that the superhero movie is suffering from serious imaginative fatigue."[125] On a more negative note, Philip French of *The Observer* said that the film's "dull, bone-crushing, special-effects stuff" are "of interest only to hardcore fans who've probably read it all in Marvel comics."[126]

Sukhdev Sandhu of *The Daily Telegraph* stated that "*Wolverine* is an artificial stimulus package of the most unsatisfying kind. Aggressively advertised and hyped to the hills, it will no doubt attract full houses at first; after that though, when word-of-mouth buzz-kill goes into overdrive, there's bound to be widespread deflation and a palpable feeling of being conned."[127] Similarly, Orlando Parfitt of IGN (UK) praised the performances of the actors and the action scenes, but stated that the film felt underdeveloped: "There's an enjoyable time to be had with *Wolverine*, but it's also somewhat unsatisfying."[128] Furthermore, Scott Mendelson of *The Huffington Post* gave the film a grade of "D", noting that "Wolverine was the lead character of [the *X-Men*] films, and we've already learned everything we need to know from the films in said franchise," adding that "the extra information given here actually serves to make the character of Logan/Wolverine less interesting."[129] Trevan McGee of *Ink* also commented on the supporting cast, saying "the movie bends over backward trying to inject as many cameos and secondary characters into the movie as possible. The mutants invented for the movie are uninspired and boring..."[130]

Sequel

"I won't lie to you, I have been talking to writers... I'm a big fan of the Japanese saga in the comic book."

Hugh Jackman[131]

In September 2009, Hood speculated that there will be a sequel, which will be set in Japan.[54] During one of the post credits scenes Logan is seen drinking at a bar in Japan. Such a location was the subject of Claremont and Miller's series, which was not in the first film as Jackman felt "what we need to do is establish who [Logan] is and find out how he became Wolverine".[45] Jackman stated the Claremont-Miller series is his favorite Wolverine story.[132] Of the Japanese arc, Jackman also stated that:

> ...there are so many areas of that Japanese story, I love the idea of this kind of anarchic character, the outsider, being in this world - I can see it aesthetically, too - full of honor and tradition and customs and someone who's really anti-all of that, and trying to negotiate his way. The idea of the samurai, too - and the tradition there. It's really great. In the comic book he gets his ass kicked by a couple of samurai - not even mutants. He's shocked by that at first.[131]

Jackman added that another Wolverine film would be a follow-up rather than continuing on from *X-Men: The Last Stand*.[133] The inclusion of Deadpool and Gambit also leads to the possibilities of their own spin-offs.[134] Before *Wolverine*'s release, Lauren Shuler Donner approached Simon Beaufoy to write the script, but he did not feel confident enough to commit.[135] On May 5, 2009, just four days after its initial weekend run, the sequel was officially confirmed.[136] A Deadpool spin-off has also been confirmed with Ryan Reynolds attached to reprise the role of Wade Wilson,[137] but producer Shuler Donner stated that she wants to "ignore the version of Deadpool that we saw in *Wolverine* and just start over again. Reboot it."[138]

Christopher McQuarrie, who went uncredited for his work on *X-Men*, was hired to write the screenplay for the *Wolverine* sequel in August 2009.[139] According to Lauren Schuler-Donner, the sequel will focus on the relationship between Wolverine and Mariko, the daughter of a Japanese crime lord, and what happens to him in Japan. Wolverine will have a different fighting style due to Mariko's father having "this stick-like weapon. There'll be samurai, ninja, katana blades, different forms of martial arts - mano-a-mano, extreme fighting." She continued: "We want to make it authentic so I think it's very likely we'll be shooting in Japan. I think it's likely the characters will speak English rather than Japanese with subtitles."[140] In January 2010, at the People's Choice Awards, Jackman stated that the film will start shooting sometime in 2011,[141] and in March 2010 McQuarrie declared that the screenplay was finished for production to start in January the following year.[142] Sources indicated Darren Aronofsky was in negotiations to direct the film.[143]

In October 2010, it was confirmed that Aronofsky will direct the film.[144] Jackman commented that with Darren Aronofsky directing that *Wolverine 2* will not be "usual" stating, "This is, hopefully for me, going to be out of the box. It's going to be the best one, I hope... Well, I would say that, but I really do feel that, and I feel this is going to be very different. This is Wolverine. This is not Popeye. He's kind of dark... But, you know, this is a change of pace. Chris McQuarrie, who wrote *The Usual Suspects*, has written the script, so that'll give you a good clue. [Aronofsky's] going to make it fantastic. There's going to be some meat on the bones. There will be something to think about as you leave the theater, for sure".[145]

In November 2010, Aronofsky stated that the title of the film will be *The Wolverine* and described the film as a "one-off" rather than a sequel.[146] Also in November, Fox Filmed Entertainment sent out a press release stating that they have signed Darren Aronofsky and his production company Protozoa Pictures to a new two-year, overall deal. Under the deal, Protozoa will develop and produce films for both 20th Century Fox and Fox Searchlight Pictures. Aronofsky's debut picture under the pact will be *The Wolverine*.[147] It has been reported that the film will begin principal photography in March 2011 in New York City before the production moves to Japan for the bulk of shooting.[148]

References

[1] "*X-Men Origins: Wolverine* (2009)" (http://boxofficemojo.com/movies/?page=main&id=wolverine.htm). Box Office Mojo. . Retrieved October 1, 2009.

[2] Galloway, Steven (2007-07-10) "Studios Are Hunting the Next Big Property" (http://www.hollywoodreporter.com/hr/content_display/film/news/e3if727c623f03c782b8ad564866c828796). *The Hollywood Reporter*. . Retrieved 2010-01-16.

[3] Sam Ashurst (2008-12-10). "Hugh Jackman's First Full Wolverine Interview" (http://www.totalfilm.com/features/hugh-jackman-s-first-full-wolverine-interview). *Total Film*. . Retrieved 2008-12-15.

[4] Harvey, Shannon (2008-10-18). "Howling success" (http://www.perthnow.com.au/news/howling-success/story-e6frg303-1111117790075). *The Sunday Times*. . Retrieved 2010-07-26.

[5] Sutherland, Claire (2007-10-25). "Romulus, My Father Set for AFIs — Four Films Dominated at the Announcements of This Year's L'Oreal Paris AFI Awards Nominees in Sydney Yesterday" (http://www.heraldsun.com.au/entertainment/confidential/father-set-for-afis/story-e6frf96x-1111114719070). *Herald Sun*. . Retrieved 2010-01-16.

[6] Simmons, Leslie (2008-02-06). "Smit-McPhee Takes 'Road' Less Traveled" (http://www.hollywoodreporter.com/hr/content_display/film/news/e3i67f661e87c3de3d37045f375a72cb938). *The Hollywood Reporter*. . Retrieved 2010-01-16.

[7] O'Hara, Helen (January 2009). "Weapon X". *Empire*: pp. 85–90.

[8] Adler, Shawn; Carroll, Larry (2007-03-21). "Movie File: Chris Brown, *Ocean's Thirteen*, Michelle Trachtenberg & More — Brown Reveals Next Project; Don Cheadle Exits 'Ocean's' Series; Trachtenberg Goes Goth" (http://www.mtv.com/news/articles/1555168/20070320/brown_chris_18_.jhtml). *MTV*. . Retrieved 2010-01-16.

[9] Topel, Fred (2008-12-08). "Wolverine's Schreiber Is Feral" (http://www.superherohype.com/features/articles/97911-liev-schreiber-gets-feral-in-wolverine). *Sci Fi Wire*. . Retrieved 2008-12-08.

[10] McClintock, Pamela (2007-10-17). "*Wolverine* Claws on May '09 Date — Liev Schreiber in Final Talks for 'X-Men' Role" (http://www.variety.com/article/VR1117974247.html?categoryid=13&cs=1). *Variety*. . Retrieved 2010-01-17.

[11] Purdin, Rickey (2007-08-02). "Dig Your Claws into 'Wolverine: The Movie' — Wizard Serves Up the Full Scoop as Hugh Jackman Slices and Dices His Way Back to the Big Screen as Wolverine" (http://web.archive.org/web/20070930165257/http://www.wizarduniverse.com/movies/wolverinemovie/005458455.cfm). *Wizard*. Archived from the original (http://www.wizarduniverse.com/movies/wolverinemovie/005458455.cfm) on 2007-07-30. . Retrieved 2010-01-16.

[12] Kahn, Howie (April 2009). "Wolverine Has a Girlfriend" (http://www.gq.com/women/photos/200904/lynn-collins-wolverine-x-men). *GQ*. . Retrieved 2010-07-26.

[13] Heather Newgen (2008-01-18). "Michelle Monaghan Talks *Wolverine*" (http://www.iesb.net/index.php?option=com_content&task=view&id=4138&Itemid=99). *IESB*. . Retrieved 2008-01-19.

[14] "Taylor Kitsch on Being Gambit in X-Men Origins: Wolverine" (http://www.movieweb.com/news/NEh0tojn6wmWki). Movie Web. 2008-10-13. . Retrieved 2009-06-19.

[15] Shawn Adler (2008-02-21). "Will.I.Am Sings On 'Wolverine,' Becomes Teleporting Mutant" (http://moviesblog.mtv.com/2008/02/21/william-sings-on-wolverine-becomes-teleporting-mutant/). *MTV*. . Retrieved 2008-02-21.

[16] Larry Carroll (2008-06-19). "Will.I.Am Reveals Details About His Big-Screen Debut In *X-Men Origins: Wolverine*' (http://www.mtv.com/news/articles/1589665/20080619/black_eyed_peas.jhtml). *MTV*. . Retrieved 2008-06-19.

[17] "Kevin Durand Talks Wolverine's Blob" (http://www.iesb.net/index.php?option=com_content&task=view&id=5172&Itemid=99). IESB.net. 2008-07-08. . Retrieved 2009-07-04.

[18] "Wolverine Week: Kevin Durand chats about playing Blob" (http://whosnews.usaweekend.com/2009/04/wolverine-week-kevin-durand-chats-about-playing-blob/). *USA Weekend*. 2009-04-28. . Retrieved 2009-07-04.

[19] Rick Marshall (2008-12-11) "Deadpool And Gambit: The Long Road To 'X-Men Origins: Wolverine'... And Beyond?" (http://splashpage.mtv.com/2008/12/11/deadpool-and-gambit-the-long-road-to-x-men-origins-wolverine-and-beyond/). *MTV Movies Blog*. . Retrieved 2008-12-12.

[20] Steve Weintraub (2009-03-14). "Ryan Reynolds talks about playing DEADPOOL in X-Men Origins: Wolverine" (http://www.collider.com/entertainment/interviews/article.asp?aid=11252&tcid=1). *Collider*. . Retrieved 2009-03-15.

[21] Murray, Rebecca. "'X-Men Origins: Wolverine' Press Conference - The Cast and Director Gavin Hood" (http://movies.about.com/od/xmenoriginswolverine/a/jackman-reynolds.htm). About.com. . Retrieved 2009-06-27.

[22] "EXCLUSIVE: Ryan Reynolds On Deadpool & Mystery Mutant In 'Wolverine' Movie Trailer: 'That's Me'" (http://splashpage.mtv.com/2009/03/17/exclusive-ryan-reynolds-on-deadpool-mystery-mutant-in-wolverine-movie-trailer-thats-me/). MTV. 2009-03-17. . Retrieved 2009-05-08.

[23] "Daniel Henney exclusive interview: Most wants to act in a romance film with Zhang Ziyi" (http://ent.sina.com.cn/m/f/2009-06-14/08352563168.shtml) (in Chinese). Sina.com. 2009-06-14. . Retrieved 2009-07-04.

[24] "X-Men Origins: Wolverine Daniel Henney Interview" (http://www.movieweb.com/video/VIgYVijmiDeSkh). MovieWeb. . Retrieved 2009-07-04.

[25] "Monaghan allies with "Wolverine"" (http://www.reuters.com/article/idUSN2252955120080222). *Reuters*. 2008-02-22. . Retrieved 2009-05-09.

[26] Seigel, Tatiana (2008-02-21). "Dominic Monaghan joins 'Wolverine'" (http://www.variety.com/article/VR1117981281. html?categoryid=1350). *Variety*. . Retrieved 2009-05-10.

[27] Murray, Rebecca. "X-Men Origins Wolverine - Tim Pocock Interview" (http://video.about.com/movies/Tim-Pocock-Wolverine.htm). About.com. . Retrieved 2009-06-27.

[28] "Cast of X-Men Origins: Wolverine" (http://movies.yahoo.com/movie/1808665084/cast). Yahoo! Movies. . Retrieved 2009-05-08.

[29] Sauriol, Patrick (September 16, 2004). "What might have been for X-MEN 3" (http://www.mania.com/might-for-xmen-3_article_42506. html). Mania.com. . Retrieved 11 July 2009.

[30] "'X-Men Origins: Wolverine': A Shot-By-Shot Analysis Of Exclusive New Trailer" (http://www.mtvasia.com/News/200903/06017669. html). MTV Asia. 2009-03-06. . Retrieved 2009-07-11.

[31] "Producer talks X-MEN ORIGINS: WOLVERINE - Storm not in the movie" (http://www.widescreen-online.de/aid,675743/ EXCLUSIVE-Producer-talks-X-MEN-ORIGINS-WOLVERINE-Storm-not-in-the-movie/News/). *Widescreenvision.de*. 2009-02-10. . Retrieved 2009-02-10.

[32] Lovece, Frank (2009-04-30). "Film Review: X-Men Origins: Wolverine" (http://www.filmjournal.com/filmjournal/content_display/ reviews/major-releases/e3id5be315f15f95c42d5b30a4d0852820f). Film Journal International. . Retrieved 2009-05-04.

[33] Emily Dunn, Josephine Tovey (2008-04-21). "A little offstage bonding" (http://www.smh.com.au/news/stay-in-touch/ a-little-offstage-bonding/2008/04/20/1208629722259.html). *The Sydney Morning Herald*. . Retrieved 2008-04-24.

[34] Rob Worley (2008-03-18). "'Wolverine' to duke it out...in the World Series of Poker?" (http://www.mania.com/ wolverine-to-duke-out-in-world-series-poker_article_90769.html). *Comics2Film*. . Retrieved 2008-03-18.

[35] Sandy Cohen (2008-07-25). "Stan Lee to make a cameo in new 'X-Men' movie" (http://www.usatoday.com/life/movies/ 2008-07-25-3338403900_x.htm). Associated Press. . Retrieved 2008-07-25.

[36] Matt Brady (2005-04-15). "*Wolverine* screenwriter keeps it real" (http://forum.newsarama.com/showthread.php?s=&threadid=31765). *Newsarama*. . Retrieved 2007-10-07.

[37] Michael Fleming (2004-10-04). "'X' marks spinoff spot" (http://www.variety.com/article/VR1117911455.html?categoryId=13&cs=1). *Variety*. . Retrieved 2006-09-01.

[38] Daniel Robert Epstein (2004-12-28). "David Benioff" (http://suicidegirls.com/interviews/David+Benioff/). *SuicideGirls*. . Retrieved 2008-02-09.

[39] Vaughan, Owen (2009-04-29). "Chris Claremont, Len Wein: the men who created Wolverine" (http://entertainment.timesonline.co.uk/ tol/arts_and_entertainment/film/article6191387.ece). *The Times* (London). . Retrieved 2009-05-12.

[40] "Interview - Hugh Jackman" (http://www.canmag.com/news/4/3/5413). *CanMag*. 2006-10-15. . Retrieved 2006-10-15.

[41] Stax (2007-09-28). "New Wolverine Screenwriter" (http://movies.ign.com/articles/823/823830p1.html). IGN. . Retrieved 2009-07-09.

[42] "Hugh Jackman on *The Prestige*!" (http://www.latinoreview.com/news/video-interview-hugh-jackman-on-the-prestige-1056) (Quicktime video). *Latino Review*. 2006-10-20. . Retrieved 2009-06-27.

[43] Ebert, Roger (April 29, 2009). "X-Men Origins: Wolverine" (http://rogerebert.suntimes.com/apps/pbcs.dll/article?AID=/20090429/ REVIEWS/904299978). *Chicago Sun-Times*. . Retrieved May 3, 2009.

[44] "*X-Men Origins: Wolverine* Script Review" (http://filmbuffonline.com/ReadingRoom/Wolverine.htm). FilmBuffOnLine. . Retrieved 2009-01-16.

[45] Karl Schneider (2006-10-15). "Jackman says *Wolverine* script is ready" (http://www.mania.com/ jackman-says-wolverine-script-set_article_52545.html). *Mania Entertainment*. . Retrieved 2006-10-15.

[46] Marilyn Beck; Stacy Jenel Smith (2006-08-13). "Major renegotiations possible stumbling block for new *X-Men*" (http://www.dailynews. com/search/ci_4177414). *Los Angeles Daily News*. . Retrieved 2007-07-11.

[47] Michael Fleming, Pamela McClintock (2007-10-30). "Studios prep back-up plan" (http://www.variety.com/article/VR1117975064. html?categoryId=13&cs=1). *Variety*. . Retrieved 2007-10-31.

[48] Michael Fleming, Peter Gilstrap (2007-07-19). "Fox says Hood good for *Wolverine*" (http://www.variety.com/article/VR1117968868. html?categoryid=13&cs=1). *Variety*. . Retrieved 2007-07-20.

[49] Michael Tsai (2006-11-08). "Sequel to *Superman Returns* due in 2009" (http://the.honoluluadvertiser.com/article/2006/Nov/08/br/ br0948627351.html). *The Honolulu Advertiser*. . Retrieved 2007-10-18.

[50] Carroll, Larry (2006-03-14). "Juggernaut Weighs In On 'X-Men' Spinoffs" (http://www.mtv.com/movies/news/articles/1526112/story. jhtml). *MTV*. . Retrieved 2009-07-11.

[51] Sean Elliott (2006-03-11). "*The Hills Have Eyes* Director Alexandre Aja gets grisly" (http://web.archive.org/web/20071130193111/ http://ifmagazine.com/feature.asp?article=1444). *iF Magazine*. Archived from the original (http://ifmagazine.com/feature. asp?article=1444) on 2007-11-30. . Retrieved 2007-11-01.

[52] Edward Douglas (2007-07-22). "Len Wiseman on *Wolverine*" (http://www.mania.com/len-wiseman-wolverine_article_107546.html). *Mania Entertainment*. . Retrieved 2007-07-09.

[53] Robert Sanchez (2007-02-13). "Exclusive Interview: Zack Snyder Is Kickin' Ass With *300* and *Watchmen*!" (http://iesb.net/index. php?option=com_content&task=view&id=1883&Itemid=99). *IESB*. . Retrieved 2008-02-09.

[54] Kyle Braun and Jordan Riefe (2007-09-29). "Rendition Interviews" (http://www.ugo.com/ugo/html/article/?id=17949). *UGO*. . Retrieved 2007-09-30.

[55] Larry Carroll (2007-10-03). "*Wolverine* Director, Hugh Jackman Digging Their Claws Into *X-Men* Spinoff" (http://www.mtv.com/ movies/news/articles/1571060/20070301/story.jhtml). *MTV*. . Retrieved 2007-10-03.

[56] Staff writer (2008-01-22). "X-Men Cameras Set To Roll Down South" (http://www.stuff.co.nz/entertainment/229636). *The Dominion Post.* . Retrieved 2010-01-17.

[57] "Domestic Film: In Production" (http://www.hollywoodreporter.com/hr/tools_data/production_listings/search_results.jsp?d=y&f=y&s=production). *The Hollywood Reporter.* . Retrieved 2008-01-27.

[58] "Shooting for *Wolverine* Set to Commence in South Island" (http://www.3news.co.nz/Video/Shooting-for-Wolverine-set-to-commence-in-South-Island/tabid/303/articleID/44401/cat/100/Default.aspx#top) (video requires Adobe Flash). *TV3.* 2008-01-27. . Retrieved 2008-11-27.

[59] Button, Katie (2008-01-24). "*X-Men* Film Upsets Local Council" (http://www.digitalspy.co.uk/movies/news/a87256/x-men-film-upsets-local-council.html). *Digital Spy.* . Retrieved 2010-01-17.

[60] Williams, David (2007-11-03). "Explosive End for SI Blockbuster" (http://www.stuff.co.nz/entertainment/11223). *The Press.* . Retrieved 2010-01-17.

[61] Morris, Chris (2008-01-29). 'Film Crew Commits to Green Ethic". *Otago Daily Times.*

[62] Staff writer (2008-02-25). "Jackman's 'Wolverine' Starts Shooting in Sydney — Australian Actor Hugh Jackman Will Start Filming His New Movie, *X-Men Origins: Wolverine*, in Sydney Today" (http://www.abc.net.au/news/stories/2008/02/25/2171933.htm). *ABC News.* . Retrieved 2010-01-17.

[63] Robert Sanchez (2008-05-23). "X-Men Origins: Wolverine Wraps Principal Photography!" (http://www.iesb.net/index.php?option=com_content&task=view&id=4940&Itemid=99). *IESB.net.* . Retrieved 2008-05-23.

[64] David Bentley (2008-06-12). "Hugh Jackman films war scenes for Wolverine" (http://blogs.coventrytelegraph.net/thegeekfiles/2008/06/new-set-pictures-hugh-jackman.html). *Coventry Telegraph.* . Retrieved 2008-06-12.

[65] "'X-Men Origins: Wolverine': Summer Movie Preview" (http://www.ew.com/ew/article/0,,20272960_2,00.html). *Entertainment Weekly.* 2009-04-11. . Retrieved 2009-07-11.

[66] Tatiana Siegel (2008-09-05). "Fox's not-so-hot summer at the movies" (http://www.variety.com/article/VR1117991696.html?categoryId=2520&cs=1). *Variety.* . Retrieved 2008-09-10.

[67] "Wolverine: Gavin Hood" (http://link.brightcove.com/services/player/bcpid17054225001?bclid=18291076001&bctid=18039014001) (Video). *The Hollywood Reporter.* . Retrieved 2009-04-03.

[68] "No Reshoots for Wolverine" (http://movies.ign.com/articles/946/946193p1.html). *IGN.* 2009-01-19. . Retrieved 2009-07-11.

[69] "Hollywood North on campus" (http://ubyssey.ca/news/hollywood-north-on-campus). *The Ubyssey.* 2009-03-12. .

[70] Fred Topel (2009-03-14). "Wolverine's Ryan Reynolds reveals Deadpool secrets" (http://scifiwire.com/2009/03/wolverines-ryan-reynolds.php). *Sci Fi Wire.* . Retrieved 2009-03-15.

[71] Billington, Alex (2009-04-24). "X-Men Origins: Wolverine Will Have Multiple Secret Endings!" (http://www.firstshowing.net/2009/04/24/x-men-origins-wolverine-will-have-multiple-secret-endings/). First Showing. . Retrieved 2009-04-25.

[72] "Movie Review: X-Men Origins: Wolverine" (http://www.slashfilm.com/2009/04/27/movie-review-x-men-origins-wolverine/). SlashFilm. 2009-04-29. . Retrieved 2009-05-17.

[73] "Ryan Reynolds to headline 'Wolverine' spin-off 'Deadpool'" (http://news-briefs.ew.com/2009/05/reynolds-to-hea.html). *Entertainment Weekly.* 2009-05-06. . Retrieved 2009-05-17.

[74] Bielik, Alain (2009-05-04). "Wolverine Gets Indestructible in X-Men Origins" (http://www.awn.com/articles/production/wolverine-gets-indestructible-ix-men-originsi). *VFXWorld.* . Retrieved 2009-05-24.

[75] Seymour, Mike (2009-05-05). "Wolverine : The Making of an X-man" (http://www.fxguide.com/article530.html). *FXguide.* . Retrieved 2009-05-26.

[76] "X-Men Origins: Wolverine [Original Motion Picture Soundtrack (http://www.allmusic.com/cg/amg.dll?p=amg&sql=10:acftxzw0ldje)]". *Allmusic.* . Retrieved 2010-07-06.

[77] "X-Men Origins - Wolverine soundtrack Harry Gregson-Williams (2009)" (http://www.hans-zimmer.com/fr/disco_detail.php?id=864). www.hans-zimmer.com. . Retrieved 2009-05-08.

[78] Christopher Coleman (2003-05-08). "Composer Harry Gregson-Williams: What Goes Around, Comes Around" (http://www.tracksounds.com/specialfeatures/Interviews/interview_harry_gregson_williams_2008_page1.htm). Tracksounds.com. . Retrieved 2009-05-05.

[79] Jon Burlingame (2009-04-22). "Recording the 'Wolverine' score: A look at Gregson-Williams in the studio" (http://www.variety.com/article/VR1118002758.html?categoryid=3604&cs=1&nid=2564). *Variety.* . Retrieved 2009-05-05.

[80] "New Wolverine film leaked online" (http://news.bbc.co.uk/2/hi/entertainment/7977265.stm). *BBC News Online.* 2009-04-01. . Retrieved 2009-04-01.

[81] "X-Men pic "Wolverine" leaks online" (http://www.reuters.com/article/filmNews/idUSTRE53113T20090402). Reuters. April 2, 2009. . Retrieved April 2, 2009.

[82] "Leak doesn't keep fans away from 'Wolverine'" (http://www.allbusiness.com/media-telecommunications/movies-sound-recording/12435709-1.html). *Associated Press.* May 4, 2009. . Retrieved May 5, 2009.

[83] McClintock, Pamela (2009-05-06). "'X-Men' takes hit in foreign markets" (http://www.variety.com/article/VR1118003285.html?categoryid=1278&cs=1). *Variety.* . Retrieved 2009-07-11.

[84] Christine Spines (2009-04-02). "Fox chairman says leaked 'Wolverine' is an 'unfinished version' and 'a complete misrepresentation of the film'" (http://hollywoodinsider.ew.com/2009/04/03/exclusive-fox-c/). *Entertainment Weekly.* . Retrieved 2009-04-03.

[85] Goldstein, Patrick (2009-04-29). "Fox on 'Wolverine' whopper: No fibbing involved" (http://latimesblogs.latimes.com/the_big_picture/2009/04/fox-on-wolverine-whopper-no-fibbing-involved.html). *Los Angeles Times.* . Retrieved 2009-05-04.

[86] Child, Ben (2009-04-07). "Wolverine review leads to Fox News writer's dismissal" (http://www.guardian.co.uk/film/2009/apr/07/roger-friedman-fox-news-wolverine). *The Guardian* (London). . Retrieved 2009-07-11.

[87] Eric D. Snider (2009-04-04). "Roger Friedman Brags About Downloading 'Wolverine'" (http://www.cinematical.com/2009/04/04/roger-friedman-brags-about-downloading-wolverine/). *Cinematical*. . Retrieved 2009-05-20.

[88] "Get Your XMO: Wolverine Slurpee Cups at 7-Eleven" (http://marvel.com/news/moviestories.7817.Get_Your_Wolverine_Slurpee_Cups). Marvel.com. 2009-04-30. . Retrieved 2009-06-27.

[89] "X-MEN ORIGINS: WOLVERINE - Only in Theaters" (http://www.papajohns.com/wolverine/). Papa John's. . Retrieved 2009-06-27.

[90] "Schick Quattro Wolverine Razor" (http://www.schickquattro.com/xmenorigins/). Schick. . Retrieved 2009-06-27.

[91] "Wolverine Rocks the Milk Mustache" (http://marvel.com/news/moviestories.7751.wolverine_rocks_the_milk_mustache). Marvel.com. 2009-04-23. . Retrieved 2010-07-26.

[92] Hasbro (2009-02-13). "MARVEL'S X-MEN ORIGINS: WOLVERINE MOVIE TOYS TEAR THROUGH RETAIL AISLES THIS SPRING" (http://www.hasbro.com/corporate/media/press-releases/Marvel-X-Men-Origins-Wolverine.cfm). Press release. . Retrieved 2009-07-09.

[93] Schedeen, Jesse (2009-04-06). "The Return of Wolverine's Weapon X" (http://comics.ign.com/articles/969/969975p1.html). IGN. . Retrieved 2009-06-27.

[94] César A. Berardini (2008-07-15). "X-Men Origins: Wolverine and Transformers: Revenge of the Fallen Movie Tie-ins Announced" (http://news.teamxbox.com/xbox/17079/XMen-Origins-Wolverine-and-Transformers-Revenge-of-the-Fallen-Movie-Tieins-Announced/). *TeamXbox*. . Retrieved 2008-07-15.

[95] Scott Rosenberg (2008-04-07). "Cursed to Write: TV & Comics Scribe Marc Guggenheim" (http://expressnightout.com/content/2008/04/cursed_to_write_tv_comics_scribe_marc_gu.php). *ReadExpress*. . Retrieved 2008-04-100.

[96] "Wolverine's Liev Schreiber on video games and parenting" (http://shine.yahoo.com/channel/parenting/wolverines-liev-schreiber-on-video-games-and-parenting-454865/). Yahoo!. 2009-05-01. . Retrieved 2009-05-11.

[97] Marshall, Rick (2009-05-01). "Will.I.Am Makes Double Debut With 'X-Men Origins: Wolverine' Movie, Video Game" (http://www.mtv.com/news/articles/1610489/20090501/will_i_am.jhtml). MTV. . Retrieved 2009-05-11.

[98] "X-Men Origins: Wolverine - Game Detail Page" (http://www.xbox.com/en-US/games/x/xmenoriginswolverine/default.htm). Xbox.com. . Retrieved 2009-05-12.

[99] Goldstein, Hilary (2009-05-05). "X-Men Origins: Wolverine -- Another Take" (http://xbox360.ign.com/articles/979/979886p1.html). IGN. . Retrieved 2009-05-12.

[100] Goodykoontz, Bill (April 19, 2009). "Tempe wins *Wolverine* premiere" (http://www.azcentral.com/thingstodo/movies/articles/2009/04/19/20090419wolverine0420.html). The Arizona Republic. . Retrieved May 1, 2009.

[101] Jim, Vejvoda (2009-04-29). "Hasta Luego, Wolverine" (http://uk.movies.ign.com/articles/977/977717p1.html). IGN. . Retrieved 2009-04-29.

[102] ""Wolverine" Outselling "Iron Man" in Advance Ticket Sales" (http://www.worstpreviews.com/headline.php?id=13157). Worst Preview. April 23, 2009. . Retrieved July 11, 2009.

[103] Gray, Brandon (May 2, 2009). "Friday Report: *Wolverine* Rages on First Day" (http://www.boxofficemojo.com/news/?id=2582). Box Office Mojo. . Retrieved May 2, 2009.

[104] McClintock, Pamela (May 1, 2009). "*Wolverine* wolfs down nearly $5 mil" (http://www.variety.com/article/VR1118003083.html?categoryid=13&cs=1). *Variety*. . Retrieved May 2, 2009.

[105] ""Wolverine" weekend box office nudged lower" (http://www.reuters.com/article/idUSN0445884220090505). *Reuters*. 2009-05-04. . Retrieved 2009-05-10.

[106] Gray, Brandon (May 4, 2009). "Weekend Report: *Wolverine* Roars" (http://boxofficemojo.com/news/?id=2583&p=.htm). Box Office Mojo. . Retrieved May 8, 2009.

[107] Hazelton, John (2009-07-10). "Attack on the Wolf" (http://www.screendaily.com/news/analysis/-attack-on-the-wolf/5003335.article). *Screen International* (1696): pp. 14–15. . Retrieved 2009-08-27.

[108] "Get X-Men Origins: Wolverine Now on DVD" (http://marvel.com/news/moviestories.9327.Get_X-Men_Origins~colon~_Wolverine_Now_on_DVD). Marvel.com. 2009-09-10. . Retrieved 2009-09-21.

[109] Marshall, Rick (2009-07-28). "'X-Men Origins: Wolverine' To Hit DVD And Blu-Ray September 15" (http://splashpage.mtv.com/2009/07/28/x-men-origins-wolverine-to-hit-dvd-and-blu-ray-september-15/). MTV. . Retrieved 2009-09-21.

[110] "X-Men Origins: Wolverine (Exclusive) (3-Disc) (Blu-ray) (With BD-Live + Digital Copy + DVD)" (http://www.walmart.com/catalog/product.do?product_id=12177171). Wal-Mart. . Retrieved 2009-09-21.

[111] Arnold, Thomas K. (2009-09-23). "'Wolverine' Slashes Up the Charts" (http://www.homemediamagazine.com/research/wolverine-slashes-charts-17121). *Home Media Magazine*. . Retrieved 2010-07-26.

[112] 'Wolverine' is year's top selling Blu-ray (http://www.afterdawn.com/news/article.cfm/2009/10/26/wolverine_is_year_s_top_selling_blu_ray)

[113] X-Men Origins: Wolverine - DVD Sales (http://www.the-numbers.com/movies/2009/WOLVE-DVD.php)

[114] "X-Men Origins: Wolverine reviews" (http://www.rottentomatoes.com/m/wolverine/). Rotten Tomatoes. . Retrieved 2009-12-16.

[115] "X-Men Origins: Wolverine reviews" (http://www.metacritic.com/film/titles/wolverine). Metacritic. . Retrieved 2009-05-09.

[116] "X-Men Origins: Wolverine (2009)" (http://movies.yahoo.com/movie/1808665084/info;_ylt=AqKBWDnBOZX3V_0qQtA2Az5fVXcA). Yahoo! Movies. . Retrieved 2009-05-08.

[117] Corliss, Richard (April 30, 2009). "Wolverine: There Ain't No Sanity Claws" (http://www.time.com/time/arts/article/ 0,8599,1894905,00.html). *Time.* . Retrieved May 3, 2009.

[118] Mullinger, James. "X-Men Origins: Wolverine" (http://www.gqmagazine.co.uk/entertainment/entertainment/articles/ 090421-wolverine-film-review.aspx). GQ.com. . Retrieved May 3, 2009.

[119] Lumenick, Lou (May 4, 2009). "HUGH GOTTA BELIEVE!" (http://www.nypost.com/seven/04292009/entertainment/movies/ hugh_gotta_believe__166736.htm). *New York Post.* . Retrieved May 21, 2009.

[120] Rainer, Peter (May 1, 2009). "Review: 'X-Men Origins: Wolverine'" (http://www.csmonitor.com/2009/0501/p17s01-almo.html). *The Christian Science Monitor.* . Retrieved May 21, 2009.

[121] Puig, Claudia (2009-05-01). "Hugh Jackman springs to life in sharply directed 'Wolverine'" (http://www.usatoday.com/life/movies/ reviews/2009-04-29-wolverine_N.htm). *USA Today.* . Retrieved 2009-05-24.

[122] Berardinelli, James (2009-05-01). "X-Men Origins: Wolverine" (http://www.reelviews.net/php_review_template.php?identifier=1616). Reelviews. . Retrieved 2009-05-24.

[123] Gibron, Bill. "X-Men Origins: Wolverine" (http://www.filmcritic.com/misc/emporium.nsf/reviews/X-Men-Origins-Wolverine). FilmCritic.com. . Retrieved May 3, 2009.

[124] Charity, Tom (May 1, 2009). "Review: *Wolverine* doesn't cut it" (http://www.cnn.com/2009/SHOWBIZ/Movies/05/01/review.xmen. wolverine/). CNN. . Retrieved May 3, 2009.

[125] Scott, A. O. (May 1, 2009). "I, Mutant, Red in Face and Claw" (http://movies.nytimes.com/2009/05/01/movies/01wolv.html). *The New York Times.* . Retrieved May 3, 2009.

[126] French, Philip (May 3, 2009). "X-Men Origins: Wolverine" (http://www.guardian.co.uk/film/2009/may/03/ x-men-origins-wolverine-review). London: *The Observer.* . Retrieved May 3, 2009.

[127] Sandhu, Sukhdev (2009-04-30). "X-Men Origins: Wolverine review" (http://www.telegraph.co.uk/culture/film/filmreviews/5251255/ X-Men-Origins-Wolverine-review.html). *The Daily Telegraph* (London). . Retrieved 2009-05-08.

[128] Parfitt, Orlando. "X-Men Origins: Wolverine review" (http://movies.ign.com/articles/977/977183p1.html). IGN UK. . Retrieved 2009-05-08.

[129] Mendelson, Scott. "Huff Post Review -- X-Men Origins: Wolverine (2009)" (http://www.huffingtonpost.com/scott-mendelson/ huff-post-review---x-men_b_194311.html). *The Huffington Post.* . Retrieved 2009-05-08.

[130] "'X-Men Origins: Wolverine' fumbles the story, action sequences" (http://www.inkkc.com/article/5214). Ink. 2009-05-06. . Retrieved 2009-05-08.

[131] Seijas, Casey (April 29, 2009). "EXCLUSIVE: Hugh Jackman 'Talking To Writers' About 'Wolverine' Sequel Set In Japan" (http:// splashpage.mtv.com/2009/04/29/exclusive-hugh-jackman-talking-to-writers-about-wolverine-sequel-set-in-japan/). MTV.com. . Retrieved April 30, 2009.

[132] "SDCC 08: Hugh Jackman" (http://uk.media.movies.ign.com/media/034/034461/vids_1.html) (Video). *IGN.* 2008-07-24. . Retrieved 2008-07-25.

[133] Stephanie Sanchez (2008-11-21). "Hugh Jackman on Australia and Wolverine!" (http://www.iesb.net/index.php?option=com_content& task=view&id=5804&Itemid=99). *IESB.* . Retrieved 2008-11-22.

[134] Graser, Marc, and Tatiana Siegel (2008-02-19). "Reynolds, will.i.am join 'Wolverine'" (http://www.variety.com/article/VR1117981136. html?categoryid=13&cs=1). *Variety.* . Retrieved 2008-02-19.

[135] Sean Smith (2009-03-25). "'Wolverine 2': Will 'Slumdog' writer tackle the script?" (http://hollywoodinsider.ew.com/2009/03/ wolverine-2-wil.html). *Entertainment Weekly.* . Retrieved 2009-03-27.

[136] "Wolverine Sequel Already in the Works" (http://www.eonline.com/uberblog/b122213_wolverine_sequel_already_in_works.html). *E! Online.* 2009-05-05. . Retrieved 2009-05-08.

[137] "UPDATE: Deadpool Spin-Off Moving Forward" (http://www.comingsoon.net/news/movienews.php?id=55139). *The Hollywood Reporter.* 2008-05-06. . Retrieved 2009-05-08.

[138] De Semlyen, Nick (2009-10-16). "The Future of the X-Men Franchise: Deadpool" (http://www.empireonline.com/features/ future-of-x-men-franchise/3.asp). *Empire.* . Retrieved 2010-10-23.

[139] Borys Kit (2009-08-13). "McQuarrie to pen 'Wolverine' sequel" (http://www.hollywoodreporter.com/hr/content_display/film/news/ e3i367bfce562b7ee624637405023e9228f). *The Hollywood Reporter.* . Retrieved 2009-08-13.

[140] De Semlyen, Nick (2009-10-16). "The Future of the X-Men Franchise: Wolverine 2" (http://www.empireonline.com/features/ future-of-x-men-franchise/default.asp). *Empire.* . Retrieved 2010-10-23.

[141] Marnell, Blair (2010-01-11). "'Wolverine' Sequel To Shoot In 2011?" (http://splashpage.mtv.com/2010/01/11/ wolverine-sequel-to-shoot-within-a-year/). MTV. . Retrieved 2010-03-28.

[142] Friedman, Roger (2010-03-03). "Wolverine Japan Adventure Is a Go" (http://buzz.hollywoodreporter.com/2010/03/03/ wolverine-japan-adventure-is-a-go/). *The Hollywood Reporter.* . Retrieved 2010-03-28.

[143] "Darren Aronofsky in Talks for Wolverine 2" (http://www.superherohype.com/news/articles/ 108795-darren-aronosfky-in-talks-for-wolverine-2). Superhero Hype!. 2010-10-13. . Retrieved 2010-10-13.

[144] "Jackman Talks Wolverine 2, Confirms Aronofsky" (http://www.superherohype.com/news/articles/ 109165-jackman-talks-wolverine-2-confirms-aronofsky). Superhero Hype!. 2010-10-19. . Retrieved 2010-10-19.

[145] "Hugh Jackman Promises Aronofsky's Wolverine 2 Will Be 'Thoughtful,' 'Meaty'" (http://nymag.com/daily/entertainment/2010/10/ hugh_jackman_promises_aronofsk.html). *Vulture.* 2010-19-10. . Retrieved 2010-10-20.

[146] McWeeny, Drew (2010-11-13). "Darren Aronofsky confirms a new title for 'Wolverine 2'" (http://www.hitfix.com/blogs/
      motion-captured/posts/darren-aronofsky-confirms-a-new-title-for-wolverine-2). *HitFix*. . Retrieved 2010-11-14.

[147] Fleming, Mike (2010-11-18). "Fox Brings 'Wolverine' Director Darren Aronofsky In With 2-Year Deal" (http://www.deadline.com/
      2010/11/fox-brings-wolverine-director-darren-aronofsky-in-with-2-year-deal/). Deadline.com. . Retrieved 2010-11-18.

[148] Fleming, Mike (October 17, 2010). "As 'Wolverine 2' Closes, Is Hot Helmer Job 'Pride, Prejudice, Zombies' With Scarlett Johansson And
      Bradley Cooper?" (http://www.deadline.com/2010/10/
      as-wolverine-2-closes-is-next-hot-helmer-job-pride-prejudice-and-zombies-with-scarlett-johansson-and-bradley-cooper/). Deadline.com. .
      Retrieved 2010-10-18.

External links

- Official website (http://http://www.x-menorigins.com/us/)

  - *X-Men Origins: Wolverine* (http://www.myspace.com/x-menorigins) on Myspace

- *X-Men Origins: Wolverine* (http://www.imdb.com/title/tt0458525/) at the Internet Movie Database

- *X-Men Origins: Wolverine* (http://www.allmovie.com/work/396429) at Allmovie

- *X-Men Origins: Wolverine* (http://www.boxofficemojo.com/movies/?id=wolverine.htm) at Box Office Mojo

- *X-Men Origins: Wolverine* (http://www.rottentomatoes.com/m/wolverine/) at Rotten Tomatoes

Real Steel

	Real Steel
	 Shawn Levy and Hugh Jackman on a film set in July 2010
Directed by	Shawn Levy
Produced by	Shawn Levy Susan Montford
Screenplay by	Leslie Bohem John Gatins
Story by	Richard Matheson
Starring	Hugh Jackman Dakota Goyo Evangeline Lilly Kevin Durand Anthony Mackie James Rebhorn Rima Fakih
Cinematography	Mauro Fiore
Editing by	Dean Zimmerman
Studio	Angry Film ImageMovers
Distributed by	DreamWorks Pictures (through Touchstone Pictures/Paramount Pictures)
Release date(s)	October 7, 2011
Country	United States
Language	English
Budget	$80 million

Real Steel is an upcoming action drama film inspired by Richard Matheson's short story "Steel". The story was first adapted for television by Matheson as an episode of *The Twilight Zone*. The film stars Hugh Jackman and is directed by Shawn Levy.[1]

Synopsis

Hugh Jackman plays Charlie Kenton, a washed-up fighter who lost his chance at a title when 2000-pound, 8-foot-tall steel robots took over the ring. Now nothing but a small-time promoter, Charlie earns just enough money piecing together low-end bots from scrap metal to get from one underground boxing venue to the next. When Charlie hits rock bottom, he reluctantly teams up with his estranged son Max (Dakota Goyo) to build and train a championship contender. As the stakes in the brutal, no-holds-barred arena are raised, Charlie and Max, against all odds, get one last shot at a comeback.[2]

Cast

- Hugh Jackman as Charlie Kenton
- Dakota Goyo as Max
- Evangeline Lilly
- Kevin Durand as Ricky
- Anthony Mackie
- James Rebhorn
- Rima Fakih
- Karl Yune as Tak Mashido

Production

Filming

Filming began in June 2010 in Detroit, Michigan, Mason, Michigan, Leslie, Michigan and Grosse Ile, Michigan. The robot boxing action is being filmed with motion capture technology. Former world welterweight champion Sugar Ray Leonard is serving as an adviser for the boxing sequences. 19 animatronic robots have been constructed for the non-boxing scenes.[3]

References

[1] Real Steel (2011) (http://www.imdb.com/title/tt0433035/)
[2] "A First Look at Hugh Jackman's *Real Steel*" (http://io9.com/5563598/a-first-look-at-hugh-jackmans-real-steel), Marc Bernadin. io9, June 15, 2010.
[3] "In Hugh Jackman's 'Real Steel,' the robot titans go pugilistic" (http://www.usatoday.com/life/movies/news/2010-06-15-realsteel15_ST_N.htm), Anthony Breznican. *USA Today*, June 15, 2010.

External links

- *Real Steel* (http://www.imdb.com/title/tt0433035/) at the Internet Movie Database

Article Sources and Contributors

Hugh Jackman *Source*: http://en.wikipedia.org/w/index.php?oldid=400444851 *Contributors*: 05ahmedaf, 13melek, 212district, 23skidoo, 6afraidof7, 777sms, A8UDI, AHRtbA==, AMK1211, Acroterion, AdamFact, AdjustShift, Aguilarp, Ahoerstemeier, Aidan Dravencole, Ajphctp46, Aka042, Alan Liefting, Alansohn, Alaric Deschain, AlexDotta, Alfredosolis, Alientraveller, Alison, AlistairMcMillan, All Hallow's Wraith, Alpichino x, American Eagle, Amoammo, Amystoner, Anal-leakages, Andy Marchbanks, Anita bonner, Antandrus, Antipastor, Antiuser, Arch dude, Arnuld, Ataboy23, Attaboy39, Ayaztr2, Ayrton Prost, Aznkid120, Azucar, Badalia, BallsUpYourArticles, BananaFiend, Baristarim, BarretBonden, Bart133, Bbb23, Bearcat, Beardo, BelzerBall, Bencey, Bender235, Bhumiya, BigBrightStars, Bignole, Binadot, Blackeagle, Bloosyboy, Bonecrusher, Bongwarrior, Bookcat, BoomerAB, Bornaz Sebastian, BostonRed, BoundaryRider, Bovineboy2008, Brian1979, Buemer, Burntsauce, C45207, CJMylentz, CTerry, CambridgeBayWeather, Canley, Capt. James T. Kirk, Cartoon Boy, Catgut, Cbl62, Cessemi, Chairman S., Chaosdruid, Charlie blue, Chastain3, Cheeseblock, Chicheley, Chinchy, Chocolate tweety, ChokeSlamFromHell, Chowbok, Christieag, Christoffph, Chuckisback53, Cjassebi, Clangfarter, Clemwang, Clockingoo, Closedmouth, CmdrClow, Cnwb, Colonies Chris, Commander Shepard, CommonsDelinker, Conscious, Coop41, Courcelles, Cpl Syx, Craigofva, Crash Underride, Crumbsucker, Crumpton, D0n0t.p4n1c, D6, Da monster under your bed, Danausi, DarkMissy, DavisxBloome, Daydreamer198, Dean 2 da o, Deathangel1312, Deb, Deckiller, Decltype, Deltaquadboi, DemonBarberTodd, Deor, Derbeth, Dgies, Digata200, Digestible, Dirtyterdy, Discospinster, Djbj16, Doczilla, Doktor Waterhouse, Donmike10, Dou Gweler, Doulos Christos, Dowew, DoxTxob, Dr who1975, Dr. Blofeld, Dr. McGrew, Dragon2eden, Dragonmaster88, Drkarthi, Drumchief, DubbleM, Dugwiki, Dusti, Dustyfog, Dybryd, Dylankidwell, Dysepsion, Dysprosia, ESkog, Ealgian, Ed g2s, EddieBernard, Elockid, Elsonlau, Ely1, Emerson7, Enviroboy, Epbr123, Erik, Erynne Lasgalen, Escape Orbit, Fallout boy, Fandraltastic, Fartclanger, Fartclanger2, Fetchcomms, Fieldday-sunday, Figaro, Finalnight, Finduilas 09, Fishhook, Fistful of Questions, Flowerpotman, ForkScratcher, Foxlair, Francs2000, Fratrep, Funkymotherfreaker, Furik, Fvw, Gaius Cornelius, Garion96, Gaudio, Gdavidp, Gene Nygaard, Geniac, Gentzkowmp, Georgeboy, Getupkid245, Geweiner, Gifford924, Giggy, Gilliam, Gimboid, Gimmetrow, Godjirra, Goldx55, Gondry, Grafen, Graham87 GrahamHardy, GregorB, Gryffindor, Guat6, Hall Monitor, HamburgerRadio, Hammersfan, Hannahcrazy, Harley Quinn hyenaholic, Hatgreg, Havardj, Headstrong neiva, Hephaestos, Her3tie, Homagetocatalonia, HorsePunchKid, Hotdogfarmer, Hotwiki, HouAstros1989, Hound25, Hu12, Hugh Jackman, Hullaballoo Wolfowitz, IW.HG, Ian.thomson, Ianblair23, Icseaturtles, InShaneee, Inhighspeed, Invincible Ninja, Irishguy, Ixfd64, J.delanoy, JBond5, JBsupreme, JDC808, JForget, JMS Old Al, JNW, Jack Cox, Jack O'Lantern, JackofOz, Jagfan71, Jakerunnnnnn, Jakezing, JamesB3, Jaranda, Javert, Jchudson, JeanColumbia, Jeff G., Jeff79, Joeyconnick, John Smythe, JohnInDC, Joliboy, Jordancelticsfan, Josiah Rowe, Jsokko, Jsr20081, Just James, Justaduckyguy, Justme89, Jwilliamb24, Jéské Couriano, K1Bond007, Kaisersanders, Kakofonous, Kal-El, Kanonkas, Katalaveno, Katieh5584, Kchishol1970, Kd3569, Keithh, Kevin, Khunglongcon, Kikadell, Kingpin13, KirosValyntine, Kjd, Kmccoy, Kmmontandon, Kostisl, Kross, Kukini, Kyros, LaVidaLoca, Lady Aleena, Lahiru k, Lanford, Larrybob, Leader Vladimir, LeaveSleaves, LedgendGamer, Lence, Leroivonstandish, Levineps, Lifeiscrazy, Lightmouse, Lilac Soul, Lilhits, Lilibit2, Lilmizbway, LiteraryMaven, Little Mountain 5, LittleOldMe, Loca pixie, Locke Cole, Loganrogue24, Longhair, Lost4eva, LovesMacs, Lowellian, Luckz, Lugnuts, Luke4545, Luna Santin, MER-C, Maciste, Mad Hatter, Madchester, Malfourmed, Marbehtorah-marbehchaim, Marcg106, Marcus patrick, Marcuspatrick2, Martarius, Marthix, Marx01, Mary Bongiovi, Mattbr, Mattkyu, Mauls, Mav, Maxis ftw, Mayumashu, Mcblush714, Mccawley75, Meaghan, MelodicMarmoset, Mentaka, Mentifisto, Michellecrisp, Microcruzer, Mikeblas, Mirken21, Mlaffs, Mm40, Monn Jackman, Moonraker0022, Mperezrosas, MrSkaloon, Mrtenquestions, Mtbaker2000, Muscle31, Mykalman02, Nasos95360, Natalie Erin, Nehrams2020, Newt, Nickj, Njriley55, Nlu, Nnfolz, Noah Salzman, Noisyoyster, Nowordneeded, NuclearWarfare, Nv8200p, ONEder Boy, OSFockewolf, Obi-WanKenobi-2005, Ohnoitsjamie, Okki, Oli Filth, OllieFury, Olly150, Onebravemonkey, Oneiros, Opcakeover, Oxymoron83, PTSE, Padawane, Pag293, PakiboyCDN, Papa November, Paul A, Persian Poet Gal, Phaeton23, Pharaoh of the Wizards, Piano non troppo, Pikahomie, Pinkadelica, Playvert, Polypipe Wrangler, Potterharrymorion, Prolog, Pseudonym001, Puckly, Pyfan, Pyjeon, Pyrohackphreak, QmunkE, Quaidy, Quantumobserver, Quentonamos, Qwfp, RC-0722, RadicalBender, Rafaelrosa, RainbowOfLight, Rakkar, Razorflame, Rbb1181, Realist2, RedWolf, Redranger241, Redwolf75, Reem Butt, Reezy, Remygreen, Reneecurrie, Riaanvn, Rich Farmbrough, Rick Block, Ritto Revolto, Rjwilmsi, Rk99, RoadieRik, Robin Chen, RockMFR, Rodhullandemu, Roisterer, Rokcorbust, Romarth, Romdoll, RossF18, Rossrs, Rtyq2, RyanGerbil10, SGGH, SKS2K6, Saeglopurguff, Salamurai, Salsb, Sarah, Scharfie, SchnitzelMannGreek, Scientizzle, ScottDavis, Scythre, Sergay, Sesshomaru, SethCohn111, Shannon W, Shawnhath, ShelfSkewed, Silversurfer06, Sintonak.X, Sjakkalle, Sketchee, Smartse, SniperLegend8, Softlavender, Sohan.s, Soliantu, Somno, Son of Kong, SpNeo, Spartaz, Spiderfoot, SpikeJones, Splateagle, Squarehippies, Squishy Vic, Sry85, Starcross, Stephen, SteveLamacq43, Stewggrifin, Stlhd89, Stormedelf, Stu, Stutley007, Sunali, Sweetguy12, SxcGal24, TAnthony, TFOWR, THEN WHO WAS PHONE?, TJive, TMC1982, Tabercil, TakuyaMurata, Tassedethe, TastyPoutine, TeaDrinker, Ted87, Tedder, Teelaofbrisingr, Tell-Tale Ghost, The Filmaker, The Iceman2288, The JPS, The Kreator, The Kreator 11, The Kreator 9, The Red, The Thing That Should Not Be, The wub, TheReaderOfOz, TheRedPenOfDoom, Thehomerunkid, Thiseye, Thivierr, Thomadactyl, Thornstrom, Timclare, Tinton5, Tomenes, Tonkurts, TommyP, Toughpigs, Tpbradbury, TravisAF, Treybien, Troycrazy8, Tubesurfer, Turian, TutterMouse, Tyw7, Ulric1313, Uncle Dick, UpstateNYer, UrMommaWhor, Uru19777, Utcursch, UtherSRG, Uziblaster Vii, Vegaswikian, Vera26, Vicer, Victory93, Visor, Vitaedigest, Viyyer, Vulturell, WadeSimMiser, Wafulz, Waggers, Walter Breitzke, Ward3001, Weapon X, Welsh, Werewolf0001, Whiteobama, Who, Who then was a gentleman?, Wiki-troller, WikiLaurent, Wildhartlivie, Willking1979, Wj32, Wll6568, Wmahan, Wolverine1990, Woohookitty, Wor0001, Wtmitchell, X-MenGirl22, Xaleksandra, Xezbeth, Xn4, Xp54321, Xxxsacheinxxx, Yamamoto Ichiro, Yamla, Yesgokul, Yisraelee, Yosef.Raziel, Yourownplaces, Zacgoodall, Zartanis, Zengar Zombolt, Zombie433, ZooFari, 1377 anonymous edits

Law of the Land *Source*: http://en.wikipedia.org/w/index.php?oldid=355891320 *Contributors*: After Midnight, Anythingyouwant, Bearian, DragonflySixtyseven, Ianblair23, IndulgentReader, J Bar, Longhair

Correlli *Source*: http://en.wikipedia.org/w/index.php?oldid=333252011 *Contributors*: Misterkillboy, Shouldbaggypantsbebanned

Blue Heelers *Source*: http://en.wikipedia.org/w/index.php?oldid=400802880 *Contributors*: *drew, 97198, AJDLib56, AceMyth, After Midnight, Asa01, Atomicelectric, BKBTE, Ben King, Blitzwurst, Bobblewik, Bookandcoffee, Bovineboy2008, Breno, Cameron Scott, Canis Lupus, Canley, Carbonite, Chris Keating, Christopherelliott, Chuq, Clerks, Coz 11, Crusoe8181, DXRAW, DaGizza, Daniel99091, David Gerard, Daydream believer2, Dazza, Diabeticgirl, Dieselgav, Discospinster, Dmbon, Duster97, Dylan93, DynaBlast, ElSaxo, Estel, FMAFan1990, Fabbalus, Feraudyh, Figaro, Florrie, Floss880, Freakofnurture, Freikorp, FreplySpang, Fuhghettaboutit, Gaius Cornelius, Geo Swan, Giraffedata, Grutness, Hugo999, Ian Page, Ianblair23, Iridescent, J Bar, JKMelb, JaGa, JackofOz, Jay Firestorm, Jeffq, Jherschel, Joshstephen, Joymcc2000, KatCassidy, Keith D, Kkbhe, Lelalie, Leostar20, LilHelpa, Livitup, Longhair, MMuzammils, Martarius, Maxdillon, Maxim, MegX, Megan1967, Meisterkoch, Michaelbeckham, Mild Bill Hiccup, Nancyallen, Nath85, Nickyo c 10, NielsenGW, Nufy8, Ohconfucius, Cng elvin, Paul A, Paul foord, Pcenere, Peachey88, Peter McGinley, Pichpich, PigFlu Oink, Pinethicket, Precinct13, Preisler, Pucki, Pumpmeup, Quale, R'n'B, Radiostarelle, Rebecca, RedWolf Rjwilmsi, ST47, Saber girl08, ScottMHoward, ShelfSkewed, Shell Kinney, Slj, Squash, Steven J. Anderson, Stickeylabel, Stingers fan, Strum that guitar, Stuartfost, Syrthiss, Tabletop, Tassedethe, TheAllSeeingEye, TheTito, Theslider09, Tim1357, Tony Sidaway, Ulric1313, UnitedStatesian, UpdArch, Violetriga, Welsh, Wernher, Wesell4u, WikHead, Wilberforcehumphries, Wmurph, Wongm, Woohookitty, Zamias, ZayZayEM, 388 anonymous edits

The Man from Snowy River (TV series) *Source*: http://en.wikipedia.org/w/index.php?oldid=387964612 *Contributors*: Batman tas, Cander0000, Crystallina, Dorftrottel, Figaro, Gz260, Longhair, Mrdungx, Philip Trueman, Reflex Reaction, SidP, UpdArch, 20 anonymous edits

Erskineville Kings *Source*: http://en.wikipedia.org/w/index.php?oldid=395619708 *Contributors*: Adolphus79, Ansell, Bunny Mischief, Canley, Cashie, David Gerard, Dl2000, Donmike10, Gurch, Khatru2, Kwah-LeBaire, Longhair, Lugnuts, Pearle, Pegship, Quaidy, Sare99, Skier Dude, The consultant, WA Burdett, 3 anonymous edits

Paperback Hero (1999 film) *Source*: http://en.wikipedia.org/w/index.php?oldid=398336269 *Contributors*: Blessedsboom, Chris the speller, Debresser, Dl2000, Freakofnurture, Kathleen.wright5, Kwah-LeBaire, Longhair, Lord Cornwallis, Lugnuts, Skier Dude, Sreejithk2000, StAnselm, Stephen Bain, Tabletop, Tamariki, The Wild West guy, Зейнал, 6 anonymous edits

X-Men (film) *Source*: http://en.wikipedia.org/w/index.php?oldid=399914728 *Contributors*: -5-, 152.163.197.xxx, 1magneto45, 2D, 64.105.112.xxx, 97198, A gx7, Actryan, Addshore, Adraeus, Agustinaldo, Ajo0894, Alakazam, Alansohn, Alataristarion, Ali'i, Alientraveller, AlistairMcMillan, Amchow78, Ameliorate!, Anakinjmt, Andrzejbanas, Andymarczak, Anna Lincoln, Apostrophe, ArmadilloFromHell, Arniep, Art1991, Avitya, Azucar, BOP tk, Balder19, Balls Mahoney, Bando26, Basel15, Bensin, Bignole, Binx, Blainster, BookhouseBoy, Bounty hunter 72, Bovineboy2008, Boyar, Bryan Derksen, Bryansinger, Bryce32, Bsadowski1, Buchanan-Hermit, Byu14, CapDac, CharlotteWebb, Ched Davis, Chris9086, ChrisGriswold, Christiem, Cimon Avaro, Codiak723, ContiAWB, Conversion script, Cooldude3240, Cuenca, Curps, Cyberstrike3000X, Cypherpunk, Cyprus2k1, DMC30, Dalton Imperial, Darkness2005, Darth Mike, Darth Panda, DarthSidious, Depressed Marvin, Dicgeman, DoctorWho42, DoubleCross, Dr. Blofeld, Drunkmule, DuaneThomas, Dylankidwell, EJBanks, EVula, Editor2008, Egan Loo, Emersoni, Emperor, Empty2005, Emvee, EnglishEfternamn, Erik, Esradekan, Evanherk, Everything counts, Evilgidgit, Favonian, Fayenatic london, Felisse, Flewis, Fortebiast, Freak in the bunnysuit, Fritz Saalfeld, Fritzpoll, Gabbe, Gabriel Duvall, Gary King, Gay Cdn, Ghidorah5464, Girolamo Savonarola, Graham87, Granpuff, Griefenhate, Grimey, Gtrmp, Gz33, Happy-melon, Havok, Hawaiian717, Haya shiloh, HoneyBee, Horkana, Hornean, Hotwiki, Hpfan1, Hulamoth, Iainuki, Iamjosh, Ianblair23, Iconoclast09, Idiot american, Ike-bana, IllaZilla, ImperatorExercitus, InShaneee, Init, Invincible Ninja, Irishguy, Isinbill, Island, Ithinkhelikesit, J Greb, J.delanoy, J218cnw8, JDspeeder1, Jal11497, Jason One, Jasonglchu, Jb-adder, Jck5000, Jebnaut, Jeff G., JethroElfman, Jniech, Joeyconnick, Jogers, Jordancelticsfan, Joshwim8, Josiah Rowe, Jpgordon, Jump Guru, Jumping cheese, KK24, Kanjilearner55, Kara Zor-El, KazSmurf, Kchishol1970, Keeper Garrett, Kidlittle, Kieranthompson, Kitch, Koavf, Kollision, Koyaanis Qatsi, Kryptonian250, Lailat al quadar, Lamrock, LarryTheGreat, Leader Vladimir, Lee Daniel Crocker, Levineps, Liftarn, Lightmouse, Lil Flip246, Loganck, Lord Hammu, Lordphillock, Lowellian, Lundse, MJD86, Maciste, Madchester, Mallanox, Mani1, MaoZhengfu, Marcus Brute, MarkSutton, Martarius, Martinsizon, Master Yugin, Master of Puppets, Masterpiece2000, Maxamegalon2000, Mclay19, Mesaana, Mesm277, Mike Selinker, Millahnna, Mimroro, Minh91, Morbeen4444, Morriswa, Mr-susans, Mrblondnyc, Mumblingmynah, Naddy, Nathaniel26, Nathen, Nerrolken, Newsjunkie, Nhl4hamilton, Nick R, Nightscream, Nightscreamnovi, Noahkai, NormanEinstein, NorrYtt, Ocatecir, OldRightist, Olessi, Olivier, Onomatopoeia, Ophois, Osubuckeyeguy, Ottawa4ever, Ozzzy-21, Passive, Patrick, Paul A, Paul730, Pauley2483, Pax:Vobiscum, Pd THOR, Pdonahue, Peanut4, Pedro cunha, Pegship, Pentasyllabic, Petadeo, Pieboyjr, Popsracer, Postdlf, PowerMutant, Prem555, Prof. MagneStormix, Qrsdogg, Radoslaw10, Recyclopedia, Red, RedWolf, Reddi, Redl@nds597198, Remember, Renesis, Rgbng, Rich Farmbrough, Rjwilmsi, RobJ1981, Robertayee, Robertotr, Rompechompo, Rorschach567, Rossdawg, Rparle, S0ulreaper, SJP, Seven2, Shadow Android, Sharp962, Shawnc, Shimmin, Shinji nishizono, Singularity, Sinjinsmyth, Sintonak.X, Skoojal, SkyWalker, Slysplace, Solomy, Spiderguy, Spidey104, Spinerod, StaticGull, Steel, Stemonitis, Stormie, Stratege, Stroppolo, Sturm55, Sugar Bear, SunCreator, SuperSonicTH, Surgo, SweetP112, T-borg, TMC1982, Template namespace initialisation script, Thadius856, Thai guy 01, The Divine Comedy, The Filmaker, The Rogue Penguin, The Thing That Should Not Be, The wub, TheGreenFaerae, Thehuntero, Thewinekone, ThisIsMyUsername, Thiseye,

Thom32, ThuranX, Timeineurope, Timwi, Tommyt, Tony1, Trans4mers, Treecko 09, Trusilver, Tsum, Tuxedo junction, TylerXKJ, Typhoon966, USN1977, Uighdfghdefj, UltimatePyro, Unforgiven486, UtherSRG, Utilizer, Uziblaster Vii, Valfontis, VolatileChemical, WBardwin, WLU, Ward3001, Warreed, WesleyDodds, Weyes, WhisperToMe, Who, Wikinick, Wildroot, Will-B, Wimp Deep Heesh, Wizkid357, Wylr, X-Man2007, Xezbeth, Xtra3847, Yincrash, Zafiroblue05, Zink98, Zoey Kemp, Zoicon5, Zotel, ^demon, 817 anonymous edits

Kate & Leopold *Source*: http://en.wikipedia.org/w/index.php?oldid=398498949 *Contributors*: All Hallow's Wraith, Alleborgo, Andromeda, Andycjp, Arteitle, Atrian, Balmung0731, Bender235, Big Bird, Bovineboy2008, Branddobbe, Brian Mulholland, Brittle heaven, CelticJobber, Danbarnesdavies, David Gerard, Deror avi, Diamantina, Doczilla, Doniago, Drat, Drbreznjev, Elisabeth100, Figaro, Gabbe, Geschichte, Grandpafootsoldier, GuanoLad, InfamousPrince, Jeff Muscato, Jokes Free4Me, Karenjc, Kate, Kintetsubuffalo, Kiwidude, Kuralyov, Lady Aleena, Levineps, Lilac Soul, Lugnuts, Mallanox, Mamathomas, Mr Smokey, Nabokov, Naominovik, Nomad0404, Notbyworks, Oagersnap, Okki, PBP, PHDrillSergeant, Paulburnett, Peng, Plop, Pnkrockr, Profx89, Queenmomcat, RicJac, Richard Arthur Norton (1958-), Ricky81682, Rivazza, Rooh23, Ryan524, Savolya, TakuyaMurata, The Transhumanist, TheTwoRoads, Thefourdotelipsis, Timrem, Tonks78, Treybien, Varlaam, Vchao, WOSlinker, Wendell, Wikanon1, Wsw16, Yashveer r, ZZ3, 111 anonymous edits

Someone Like You (film) *Source*: http://en.wikipedia.org/w/index.php?oldid=398007164 *Contributors*: *drew, 97198, AN(Ger), Andycjp, Bovineboy2008, Caiuscamargarus, CerberuS, Cypherpunk, David Gerard, DeWaine, Debresser, Donmike10, Dugwiki, Eddie Nixon, Emurphy42, Erianna, FlieGerFaUstMe262, Garion96, Illnab1024, InfamousPrince, Jacobko, Jayjg, Kerowyn, Luiza1202, Mattbrundage, Oddibe, Pegship, Plumcouch, Plumpurple, Pshent, Rich Farmbrough, SFTVLGUY2, Santryl, Suckstobeabum, The Transhumanist, TheMovieBuff, TomCat4680, Treybien, Xezbeth, 62 anonymous edits

Swordfish (film) *Source*: http://en.wikipedia.org/w/index.php?oldid=399797153 *Contributors*: *drew, Aasi007onfire, AdamDeanHall, Ahruman, Ajshm, AlanFord, All Hallow's Wraith, Andonic, Andrzejbanas, Arthur Rubin, Arvindn, Ashmodai, AspiringEntrepreneur, Bakilas, Berserkerz Crit, BilCat, Bill, Blink182av, Bovineboy2008, BowChickaNeowNeow, Canderra, CanisRufus, Cburnett, CelticJobber, Chegis, Chidoll, Chrysrobyn, Commander Shepard, ConradKilroy, ContiAWB, Daedalus969, Dammit, DarkseidX, Davidbod, Deltabeignet, Dethme0w, Donreed, DoubleCross, DurotarLord, Dyl, EagleOne, Editor37, Edward, Elonka, EncMstr, EncyclopediaUpdaticus, Erianna, Ericgandhi, Error, Fan-1967, Filmafficianado, Fireaxe888, Firsfron, Florian Adler, FrankRizzo2006, Frecklefoot, Funeral, Gabbe, Ghirlandajo, Ghosts&empties, GregorB, Gurch, Gwaur, J.D., Jackregan, Jaranda, Jdobbin, Jmg38, Kalaong, Kbdank71, Kevin23, Kraxler, Kurt Shaped Box, Kusma, Levent, Liftarn, LilHelpa, Lilpatriot, M3taphysical, Mahjong705, MarcK, Mipadi, Monkeyhousetim, Monujohnson007, Muad, Niteshift36, NitroOverdriveX, Ntsimp, OS2Warp, Omegium, Omicronpersei8, Oscarthecat, PKT, Paintman, Paulmallon, Phydend, Pissant, Pizza1512, Polylerus, Ppapadeas, Pschroeter, RFerreira, Ravuya, Rfernand, Robrtprch22, Rorschach567, RossF18, Samuel Blanning, Sannie, Schwenkstar, ScottyV89, Shyamkavi, Solarius, Surten, T mang, Tedtheothee, The Transhumanist, TheMovieBuff, Tim!, Treybien, Typhoon966, Uberdude85, Ubiquity, VZakharov, Verdatum, Verne Equinox, Wadems, Werdna, Werideatdusk33, WikiBahal, Wool Mintons, Xezbeth, Y2kcrazyjoker4, Zombie433, 218 anonymous edits

X2 (film) *Source*: http://en.wikipedia.org/w/index.php?oldid=400617685 *Contributors*: -5-, 1magneto45, 5 octaves, A, AJHalliwell, Ace Class Shadow, Agustinaldo, Ajshm, Alakazam, Alexander Miseler, Alientraveller, Ameliorate!, Analoguedragon, Andrewm1986, Andrzejbanas, Andycjp, Angr, Antmusic, Anupamsr, Apostrophe, Archnihil, Aumakua, Auric, AuronSam, Awakeandalive1, Azucar, BD2412, Baaleos, Bacteria, Baystatethrasher, Bignole, Biocyte, BladeRyder, Bovineboy2008, Brad M., Brokenyin, Buchanan-Hermit, Bud0011, Caltas, CapDac, Cbrown1023, Cdc, Cerealkiller13, Chiller1800, Chris1219, ChrisGriswold, Christiem, Christopher Parham, Claregoslant, Clawson, CmdrClow, ContiAWB, Csbodine, CyclopsAngelGambit, Cyprus2k1, DMC30, Da Joe, Daniel Case, Dann-Fonda, Darkness2005, Dave420, David Gerard, DavidDouthitt, Dawkeye, Depressed Marvin, Doc cadence, DoctorWho42, Doo Doo, Dopalanko13, DoubleCross, Dr. Blofeld, Dr. McGrew, Dstorres, Dto, EEMIV, EVula, Easchiff, Edokter, Eggebrecht.jack, Ehdee, Elipongo, Emperor, Emperor001, Empty2005, Epbr123, Erik, Esaborio, Everyoneandeveryone, Everything counts, Evilgidgit, F J, Fayenatic london, Freak in the bunnysuit, FrenchIsAwesome, Fritz Saalfeld, Gabbe, Gabriel Duvall, GhostFace1234, Girolamo Savonarola, Gods Refuse, GoingBatty, Gonzalo84, Gran2, Granpuff, Gravidef, Gray Spot, Gtrmp, Gurch, GusF, Gwdr500, HalfShadow, Happy-melon, HarleyHyde2386, Havok, Hbdragon88, Higher Ruin, Hotwiki, Howcheng, Hydrargyrum, Iainuki, Ikrichter, Imladros, Indigenius, Infrangible, Intractable, Invincible Ninja, Irishguy, Ishako, Island, Ithinkhelikesit, J Greb, J.delanoy, JIP, JPG-GR, Jamielynn cena, Jason One, Jasonbraaten, Jay32183, Jb-adder, JesseRafe, Jj137, Joelee.org, Joeyconnick, John-1107, Johnnyauau2000, Jordancelticsfan, JosephJames6, Josephjames21, JoshuaZ, Josiah Rowe, Jp.bc, Jrockley, Jupiter1984, Jwad, Jwolfe, Jynx980, KNHaw, Kakashi-sensei, Karl-Henner, Karrmann, Kchishol1970, Kdau, Kdbwest, Kentaru z, Kieranthompson, Koavf, Kross, Kukini, L33th4x0rguy, Lamentation, LeonWhite, Leonidas23, Lexi Silverstone, Lord Hammu, Lord Phillock, Lordphillock, Lowellian, MSchmahl, Madchester, Mahjongg, Mallanox, Marcus Brute, Marionleenor, Martarius, Martinsizon, Martpol, Master Deusoma, Master Yugin, Mboverload, Mclay19, Meph1986, Mice, Michael C Price, Michael Devore, Mike Selinker, Millahnna, Minesweeper, MinnesotanConfederacy, Miv246, Mjrmtg, Momomo555, Morriswa, Morwen, Moshe Constantine Hassan Al-Silverburg, Mr-susans, Mrblondnyc, Mrmannyman2, Mrs benoit, Msa1701, Mule Man, Muéro, MysteryDog, Nalvage, NawlinWiki, Nehrams2020, Neil.ferns, NickBarlow, Nickdude9110, Nightstallion, Nikki311, Noclevername, NormanEinstein, Notmicro, Nv8200p, Ocatecir, Olessi, Ommnomnomgulp, Onomatopoeia, Osubuckeyeguy, Otheus, PRRfan, Paloma Walker, PantheraLeo, Passive, Paul A, Pax:Vobiscum, Pedro cunha, Pegship, PepsiMax181, Petadeo, Phoenix-forgotten, Pikawil, Pinkfloydfan, Poulsen, Prem555, Prof. MagneStormix, Quentin X, RVDDP2501, Radosław10, Randysem, Razer64, Rbb l181, RedWolf, Reddi, Reflex Reaction, Remember, Repmax, ResidentialPenguin, Rjwilmsi, RobJ1981, RoryS89, Rtkat3, S onson, Sambangs, Sandstein, Sango Kirara, ScudLee, Seanmilloy, Sehsuan, Shadowolf, Sharp962, Shoeofdeath, Shredder 187, SidP, Sintonak.X, SkyWalker, Slysplace, Songmaster2005, Soxrbest, Spathic!!, Spinerod, Stanley Ipkiss, Stelio, Stormscape, Stroppolo, Supersaiyanplough, TJ Spyke, TMC1982, TRBP, Tech007, Template namespace initialisation script, Tenebrae, Tertiary7, Thai guy 01, That Guy, From That Show!, The Filmaker, The Iconoclast, The Rogue Penguin, The wub, TheOnlyOne12, Theweirdalien, Thomas Blomberg, Thue, ThuranX, Tim from Leeds, Timwi, Tommy2010, Tommyt, Tony1, Toocoolrahul, Toquinha, Trampikey, Treecko 09, Tregoweth, Trevor MacInnis, Treybien, Tullyman, Tuxedo junction, Txomin, TylerXKJ, Typhoon966, Ulric1313, UltimatePyro, UtherSRG, Vader200591, Vanje, Vantey, Velho, Viperpulse, Vocaro, WLU, Wames, WesleyDodds, Wetman, Who, Whodhu, Whomp, Wildroot, Willbyr, Wingsandsword, WolfRisingSun, WookMuff, X-Man2007, Xezbeth, Xinoph, Yachtsman1, Yashman21, Zepp900, Zippanova, Zoicon5, 751 anonymous edits

Van Helsing (film) *Source*: http://en.wikipedia.org/w/index.php?oldid=396047575 *Contributors*: ...---...SOS, 03jkeeley, 23skidoo, A reader 01, A3 nm, AGToth, Aatami, Adonis Albattross, Aebliss, Agustinaldo, Alai, Alientraveller, Allissonn, Alucard 16, Am088, Amonet, Andonic, Andrzejbanas, André Koehne, Angelcaballero, AquaRichy, Aradek, Ardavu, Arpingstone, Avatarfan2345, Azes13, BD2412, BertieBasset, Blackmetalbaz, Bobo192, Book maniac, Bovineboy2008, Bradybang, BrckoGOS, Bryan Derksen, Canis Lupus, Capricorn42, Carson.C.M, Catpedantic, Cclarke, Charly0731, Chris 42, Ckatz, Clashfrankcastle, Coallen, Codenamecuckoo, Colin4C, ContiAWB, Cool blade, Cordless Larry, Cparmar, Croctotheface, Crzycheetah, CyberSkull, D4, DJsunkid, Daedalus969, DanMonkey, Darrenhusted, Dave-ros, David Gerard, Davidhorman, Davodd, DeWaine, DeadEyeArrow, Deftonesderrick, Denstat, Design, Deville, Discospinster, Doniago, DrOxacropheles, Drat, Drrock, Dual Freq, Duvin, EVula, Eddygarfield19, Editor182, Eekerz, EliasAlucard, Ellenbp, Elockid, Emersoni, Emperor001, Eugene van der Pijll, EvenEternity, Evilgidgit, Ewlyahoocom, ExpressingYourself, FaithLehaneTheVampireSlayer, Farlstendoiro, Finite, Fitch, FlieGerFaUstMe262, Fortdj33, Freikorp, GORIZARD, GRuban, Gabbe, Gaius Cornelius, Galactic war, Gavia immer, Gero, Geshpenst, Giant89, Gimboid, Gimmetrow, Gnrlotto, Graham87, Grant the Wise, Gtrmp, Halmstad, HannuMakinen, Happy Feet Guy, HappyInGeneral, Hawaiian717, Holothurion, Hughlover1968, Hydrargyrum, Iamstillhiro1112, Indisciplined, Indu Singh, Infaracrity, Infrogmation, Inyrface, Irishguy, Ixfd64, Izalithium, JB 16, Jackfork, JamesAM, Jason One, Jason Palpatine, Jaybling, Jayunderscorezero, Jmrowland, JodyB, Joe Wallace, John K, John Smythe, Johnny Vega, Josh Parris, Journalist, Judgesurreal777, Juliancolton, Karasuhebi, Kidlittle, KieranO653, Kingpin13, Kinu, Kirill Lokshin, Kjp993, Kman618, Koavf, Konczewski, Kukini, Kuralyov, LadyGodivaMarian, Legedevin, Lievfan666, Lord loss210, Louis Do Nothing, Lozza dearnley, Luiza1202, MK, Mad Hatter, Mahjong705, Mani1, Mark Sheridan, Marktreut, MarnetteD, Martarius, Master Deusoma, Master of Puppets, Mathel, Matthew Auger, Maxis ftw, Mbinebri, Mboverload, McLar eng, Meelar, MegX, Moviefan2k4, Mr Psi, Mriya, MythCreator, NeonWolf, NightWolf214, Noirish, ONEder Boy, Octane, Optakeover, OwenBlacker, PIrish, Padishar, Palnatoke, Parable1991, Paul A, Paulburnett, Pazu13, Peanutdude, Pegship, Phil Boswell, Phil1984, Pic Editor960, Pictureuploader, Piecraft, PigFlu Oink, Pinikas, PollyNim, Possecomitatus, Power level (Dragon Ball), Prem555, Prep101jl, Professor Ninja, Puckly, Purple Paint, R'n'B, RCanine, RMajouji, Radiant chains, RadicalBender, Raviaka Ruslan, Rcwc, Rebelstrike, RedWolf, Relly Komaruzaman, Rexpatel2006, Richfife, Ritto Revolto, RobertG, Rpresser, Rursus, Rustdrake, SD6-Agent, SDC, Sailorsaurus, Schmiteye, ScudLee, Seaphoto, Sesshomaru, SilentC, Sinistro, Sjones23, Skew-t, SkinnyZan, Skorpio-88, Softlavender, Son of Kong, Str1977, Stylinhawaiian7, Sushidroid, TAnthony, TMC1982, TTN, Tabletop, TaggedJC, Tagger9980, Tai112, Tekkenboygriffiths, Template namespace initialisation script, The Rogue Penguin, The wub, TheMovieBuff, TheSuave, Tignarius, Tim1965, TinyMark, ToxicAllure, TransUtopian, TravellerDMT-07, Trialsanderrors, Typer 525, UberMan5000, Ukexpat, Underneath-it-All, Unknows Username, Uthanc, Vague Rant, Vampirehunter007, Vegaswikian, Veledan, Vincent de Ruijter, Vkil, Vlad, Volker89, Wasabi fandango, Websurfer246, Wendy clear, Wernher, Wesley, Whispering, Who, WikiXan, Wikipe-tan, Wolfmind, Woohookitty, Wootoftheday, Xezbeth, Xinoph, Y2kcrazyjoker4, YUL89YYZ, Yankees10, Yayaya114660446, Zachorious, Zoe, Zombie433, Zwetelina, Zythe, Шизомби, 595 anonymous edits

Van Helsing: The London Assignment *Source*: http://en.wikipedia.org/w/index.php?oldid=397521589 *Contributors*: Andrzejbanas, David Gerard, Emini4, FilmFemme, GoingBatty, Grandpafootsoldier, Hqb, Ironmonger117, Kuralyov, Lenin and McCarthy, MarnetteD, Martarius, Masaruemoto, Master Deusoma, Melaen, Saurabh 10ben, Sesshomaru, Shsh, Tawny26, Yakiv Gluck, 24 anonymous edits

Stories of Lost Souls *Source*: http://en.wikipedia.org/w/index.php?oldid=371701229 *Contributors*: AN(Ger), Beardo, Dl2000, Gurch, Rholton, Tassedethe, Tbannister, TechLight, TubularWorld, Vchao, Verkhovensky, 5 anonymous edits

Happy Feet *Source*: http://en.wikipedia.org/w/index.php?oldid=399284670 *Contributors*: 041744, 1samwyz3, 99DBSIMLR, AAA!, ACBest, AEMoreira042281, AKGhetto, ALadinN, AN(Ger), AUG, Aang-kai, Aaron Schulz, Aaronaeb, Abce2, Abdurahman49, AddDeWitt, Ailley, AirLiner, Ajmint, Akcarver, Alandavidson, Alansohn, Albino Bebop, Albrozdude, Ale jrb, Alejo123, Alexforcefive, Alfirin, Alhoon, Alrightypewriter, Alxeedo, Amarkov, Ameliorate!, Ancientanubis, And1987, Andrewpmk, Andrzejbanas, AndySimpson, Andycjp, Angam, Angr, AnmaFinotera, Ann Stouter, Antandrus, Apple1013, Aralvarez, Archerchef, Archie325, ArchonMagnus, Arrkhal, Art1991, Aseelmunzirbarghouti, Ashmoo, Aspects, Athaenara, AuburnPilot, Aunatrea, Auntof6, Autocratique, Avs5221, BA 744, Bac2futurfan, Baltimorehare, Bazzargh, Bedford, Bencey, Benjaminlobato, Benzy19, Berserkerz Crit, Bettia, Bgunsberger, Big Bird, Bigmoviezone, Bill, Blue Dingo, BlueMario1016, Bob the Rabbid, Bobdylanfan, Bored461, Bovineboy2008, Brandon, Breno, BrotherFlounder, Bryan H Bell, Bt8257, Bumm13, C.Fred, CBM, CTVampSlayer, Canglesea, Casper2k3, Cat's Tuxedo, Catgut, Cbrown1023, Cbuckley, Ccacsmss, Chanlyn, Chaoticfluffy, Chard513, CharlotteWebb, Checkerfly, Chibibibi, Chowbok, Chrislk02, Church of emacs, Cigammagicwizard, Cinephobia, Classicfilms, Closenplay, CloudNine, Cloudbound, Clyde Miller, Cncxbox, Codetiger, ColdFusion650, Colonies Chris, Conti, ContiAWB, Cooldani95, Countmall, Crystallina, CrystallinetheHedgidna, Ctbolt, Cunard, Cxz111, CyberSkull, Cyrus XIII, Cyster, DH85868993, Dakane, Dale Arnett, Dancey2, Dancter, DanielEng, Darth Panda, David in DC, Deb, Debresser, Declan Clam, Deej30, Delldot, Denisgomes, DennyColt, DerHexer, Design, Destron Commander, DevastatorIIC, Dfrg.msc, Directormtb, Discospinster,

Diti, DivineAlpha, Dkp, Dogface, Dominicrusho, Dpenguinman, Dpm12, Dreadstar, Duschinono, Dwmr, EJBanks, Ebyabe, Edwpat, Elcairo, Elendil's Heir, Elil, Emerson7, Enpitsu, Eqdoktor, Eric82oslo, Erik, Erik9, Esanchez7587, Esn, Esrever, Evanerss, Everyguy, Ex nihil, Exozero, Extraordinary Machine, F, FF2010, FMAFan1990, FMAN, Fagstein, Falconfly, Falconleaf, Famer, Faradayplank, Fastily, Favonian, Fayenatic london, FeldBum, Figure-Headed Guy, Firelordazulon, Firetrap9254, Flair Girls, Flubeca, Forsteri, Franck Drake, Free-encyclopedia, Freshh, FriscoKnight, FuriousFreddy, Fusek71, Fuzzy510, GDonato, Gadfium, Gail, Gdavidp, Gdo01, GerardKennedy, Gilliam, Glen, Got118115147, Goth67, Gothmog26, GracieLizzie, Gurch, Guybrush, Gwernol, Gyrferret, Happyfeetluvr22, Happyft, Hdt83, HeartofaDog, HenkvD, Henry W. Schmitt, HenryJthefilmist, Hensleyb, Herbm, Hewie7, Hgkamath, Hiddekel, Hinatagal101, Hjfhksdjf, Holdaway, Hooperbloob, Horseagle, IKR1, Iamwisesun, Ian T, Ianjones50, Ianthegecko, Icseaturtles, ImSpidey2, InfamousPrince, Inter16, Irishguy, Irk, IronGargoyle, J Bar, JAF1970, JLaTondre, Jabbathenut, JackSparrow Ninja, Jane-21, JarakMaldon, Jason.cinema, JeanColumbia, Jedi94, Jeff3000, Jeltag-the-Ferret, Jemstone66, Jerry, Jimeree, Jinjoo, Jitterro, Jmanigold, JoeSmack, JohnI, Johndburger, Jon513, Jonathan.s.kt, Josh Parris, Joshfriel, Jp.bc, Jrhoadley, Jt spratt, Jtryan, Juliaholcomb, Jusdafax, Jwy, KConWiki, Kaneshirojj, Karin127, KathrynLybarger, Kchishol1970, Keilana, Kelisi, Kenicks, Keyser Söze, Kirill Lokshin, Kjhstuph, Klosk12, Knute, Kollision, Konczewski, Kotsu, Krisster, Kuralyov, Kwah-LeBaire, Las Vegas JD, Leafyplant, Leflyman, Legedevin, LegioXIII-SPQR, Leonard^Bloom, Leslie kawakami, LibLord, Little Mountain 5, Lo2u, Longhair, Lordmuffin, Loren.wilton, Lradrama, Lubrio, Luigi-ish, Luis1972, LukeSurl, Luna Santin, MADMAX1998, MER-C, MPD01605, MackSalmon, Mackeriv, Macunuva, Madman, Maideniron, Malerin, Manderiko, Marcg106, MarkSutton, MartinDK, Maxim, McNoddy, Mecko192, MeegsC, MegX, Melanie Jordan, Meno25, Midnight Comet, Midnightcomm, MikeLondon, Mikecraig, Mikeymoo333, Milerz91, Millahnna, Mimzy1990, Minochige, Miranda, Miskwito, MistaTee, Mj khazali, Monkeys 9711, Monz, Movingimage, Mr Stephen, MrClegg, MrMacMan, Mschel, Mushroom, Myanw, N. Harmonik, Natureguy1980, NavarroJ, Nehrams2020, Neutrality, New Jack Swing, Nhrenton, Nickksnow, Nina phunsta, Nintendofan88, Nitrosuperspeed, No Guru, Nocarsgo, Norsehorse89, Notfound, Nr1moviefan, NrDg, Nssdfdsfds, Nuggetchild, Ocatecir, Octane, Optigan13, Orderinchaos, Oscarthecat, Otingocni, Overcasts, Oxymoron83, Ozone77, PHXsuns3434, PJ Pete, PMDrive1061, Paddyslacker, Paradoxian, ParalysedBeaver, Peecee1978, Pejorative.majeure, Penciltapper, Pendo 4, Pengo, PennsylvaniaPatriot, Persnickety, PeruAlonso, Peteb16, Peter Ellis, PhattyFatt, Phbasketball6, Philip Trueman, Phone beeps, Pigeonarmy, Pigman, Pineapplex, Pingveno, Pixelface, Pnevares, Pnkrockr, PokeFan2006, Ppk01, PrinceRegentLuitpold, PrisonMan, Procrastinatrix, Prolog, Pronoiac, Ptikobj, Quentin X, Quesar, QuintanaDS, RB972, RFBailey, Radosław10, Raghuvansh r, Rangerkom, Rapomon, RattleMan, Raymond arritt, Raymondwinn, RealityTelevisionFan, Reinoe, Rescue Guy, Revrant, Rhindle The Red, Rholton, Riana, Ric168, Richard Barrett, Richfife, Rje, Rjwilmsi, Rklawton, Rmallins, Robin Chen, Rockysmile11, Ronhjones, Rougeblossom, Royboy193456, Rtkat3, Ruby (Land Before Time) Lover, Rwlinda, RyanGerbil10, Ryulong, SISLEY, SKS2K6, SabineLaGrande, Sad mouse, Sander123, Sardanaphalus, Scalytail, Schissel, Scout of truth, Scratte Lover, Sd31415, Seattlenow, Secret Saturdays, Semchin, Sergeant.cross, Sesshomaru, Shaolin128, ShawnVW, ShelfSkewed, Shoito, Shortmalay, Shotwell, Shuffdog, SidP, Siddharth Mehrotra, Silent Tom, Simonus, Singster90, SixteenBitJorge, Sjones23, Skudrafan1, Skypurevis, Smalljim, Smash, Smurffluvr, Snowman Guy, Snowolf, Solumeiras, Sotakeit, Sp3000, Spazure, Spitacular, Squallhart, Staecker, StarSpangledKiwi, Statarius, Sterry2607, Steven Weston, Steven Zhang, Steverapaport, Strom, SyntaxError55, Synthe, Szyslak, TDC99, TKD, TPIRFanSteve, Tad Lincoln, Tamariki, Tarra emerald51394, Tastes like lead, Tayljon, Tbboy13, TeaDrinker, Teak the Kiwi, TerrenceandPhillip, The 80s chick, The Gilly, The Merciful, The Rogue Penguin, The Thing That Should Not Be, The Wild West guy, The wub, TheAnimal117, TheCoffee, TheST, Theworldstinks, Thirteen squared, Tiago nicastro, Tiddly Tom, Tide rolls, TinFoil, Titoxd, Tmlpalmsurfer, Tntnnbltn, Tomithicus, Tpal3, TrapStilton, Tregoweth, Trivialist, TwilightMan, Underneath-it-All, Uthabiti, UtherSRG, Uzume, VG Cats Tipe 2, Veinor, VernoWhitney, Viroxor, WWGB, Wafulz, Ward3001, Warpozio, Websurfer246, Weiko676, WestKateLobsterMan14, Wheels0132, WhisperToMe, Wikieizor, Wikipe-tan, Williamnilly, WillyofToxteth, Wimt, Xnuala, XxTrillvilleXX9, Y2kcrazyjoker4, Yamaguchi先生, Yardserror, Yllosubmarine, Zak Hammat, Zanimum, Zoe, Zzuuzz, Ζεύς, Basil, 1643 anonymous edits

Flushed Away *Source*: http://en.wikipedia.org/w/index.php?oldid=394732377 *Contributors*: A ness, Abdurahman49, Acolyte of Discord, Adamshappy, Adpete, Ahmad123987, Ajsh, Alaric Deschain, Alistair Stevenson, Allan64, Altermann, Andromedabluesphere440, Andrzejbanas, AnmaFinotera, AnthonyA99, Apartmento, Arch dude, ArchStanton69, Art LaPella, AtreemFromVenus, Avelinforl32, Badgernet, Beardo, Beemer69, Bejnar, Belovedfreak, Bencey, Bill, Billbl, Black Kat, BlueStarz, Bluecatcinema, Blues-harp, BoyoJonesJr, Bozoid, Bradeos Graphon, Brittany Ka, Btdurant, Bumblebee Bay, Butseriouslyfolks, CBDunkerson, CLW, CNash, Cab88, Calicore, Can't sleep, clown will eat me, Captain Günsche, Carl.bunderson, Cartoon Boy, Cartooner32, Cat's Tuxedo, Chaosfan99, CharlotteWebb, Chem-awb, ChesterG, Cholten99, Clarityfiend, Clerks, Cnota, Colonies Chris, Cooksey, CoolKatt number 99999, Correctonator, Count de Ville, Coz2112, Crazysane, Crotchety Old Man, DJ Spider Pig, DTVEST, Dan500, Dancingcyberman, Darkness2005, David Gerard, DavidHolden, DavidJohns, Davie4264, Dbiel, Dcs315, Dddstone, Deltasim, Destron Commander, Dhodges, Djdannyp, Dobrevano, Doctor joshi, DoxTxob, Dpm12, Dreaded Walrus, Duncancumming, EALacey, Eddie Kennedy, Eekerz, Einstein runner, Ekaterina tony, Elliot.kw, EngineerScotty, Esn, Evice, Exhausted Auk, FMAFan1990, Farmerjesse, Flair Girls, Flowerparty, Fordmadoxfraud, Furrykef, Gaius Cornelius, Gheorghe Zamfir, GhostFace1234, Glorious Amphibian Dawn, Glow-in-the-Dark Guy, GracieLizzie, Gran2, Granpuff, Gwaka Lumpa, Histrion, Hofnerbassman, HoneyBee, Hut 8.5, Hybrid Guy, Hyperizer, Ian Rubin, Ie007, Iheartkarate461, Imax80, Indianabrick, InfamousPrince, Iowaseven, Iridescent, Isecore, JAF1970, JQF, JYi, Jack Stark, Jarry1250, JerzeyBadboi1217, Jienum, Jmac3568, John254, Jumbo Juice, Kaboomski123, Kalaong, Kasparov, Kchishol1970, Kimmymarie24, Kimwells, Kjhstuph, Kjlewis, Klaus Kratchet, Kollision, Kooshmeister, Korenyuk, Kylegordon, Lawsonrob, LeonUser, LtPowers, Luvinchicken45692, MPerel, Madchester, Malkmut, Mangojuice, Manson08, Marikun, MarkBarl, Markcambrone, MarnetteD, Marquis De Carabas, Masaruemoto, MaxieLogoFan, McAusten, Mcepitome, MegX, MegaHL90, Ment al, Merkurix, Metasyntactic D, Mike Selinker, MikeyChalupa, Millahnna, MindyTan, Misza13, Mjmoves, Mng777, Moneasha, Movingimage, Mrtgrady2, Mushroom, Mysdaao, NBbeauty, NapoliRoma, Naturalist765, Nausikaa, NawlinWiki, Nedlum, Nezickson, Nixeagle, Nowordneeded, NrDg, Ntsimp, Ocatecir, Oobug, Oscarthecat, PJ Pete, PMDrive1061, Palfrey, Penrithguy, People Week Guy, Phil Boswell, Pjoef, Playhouse Disney, RC-0722, RdCrestdBreegull, Redranger241, Redrats, Relly Komaruzaman, Reza mirhosseini, Rhino131, Rjwilmsi, RobJ1981, Rodimus Rhyme, Rogerborg, Rossin, Royboy193456, Runner5k, Rusty5, Salamurai, Salavat, Sarah, ShakingSpirit, Shoejar, Shoeofdeath, Sigma 7, Simhedges, Skypurevis, Skywalker 007, Smash, StephenBuxton, Stuntbaby, Swatopluk, TKD, Tailsfanj99, TehDogfather, Tehw1k1, Tekken101, The 80s chick, The JPS, TheEvilBlueberryCouncil, Theworldiscruel, Thorn969, Thriceplus, Tiria, Tometheus, Tony1, Topsy kretts3330, Tregoweth, Tresaqwe, Trogga, Typhoon966, USA 5000, Uniformation, VerasGunn, Vertigozooropa, Vl'hurg, Wack'd, WatermelonPotion, Wavy G, Wtooher, Wyatt915, Wylr, Wynnara, Ye Olde de la Man, Yorozu, Yourecrazy, Zenohockey, ZeroJanvier, Zippanova, Zodiac Guy, Zumester, Калий, 693 anonymous edits

The Prestige (film) *Source*: http://en.wikipedia.org/w/index.php?oldid=399559130 *Contributors*: 91nacho, Abubakr aries, Adhityagan, Adithyachinky, Aguillory, Ajd, Alantex, Alaric Deschain, Alientraveller, Alii h, Amoammo, Anarchia, Andrzejbanas, Anticipation of a New Lover's Arrival, The, Arbero, ArielGold, Asyndeton, Atropos, Bart133, Billhenderson, Bjones, Bluebulb, Bluedustmite, Bobcheezy, Borgx, Bovineboy2008, Brainscar, Bryan H Bell, CBM, CDA, Calliopejen1, Captain Crawdad, Cbastian, CeruleanFilms, Chad44, Chris 42, Chris the speller, Chris1219, Chupon, CoasterKev2000, Cognita, ConradKilroy, Cop 663, Cornucopia, Countess Nessa, Cphillips26, Cwang13, CyberSkull, Daniel5127, Darrenhusted, Darth Nata, DaveTheJackal, David Gerard, Davidbspalding, DeansFA, DelMone, Deon Steyn, DerHexer, Diza, Djarnum1, Dkkicks, Dmanning, Dmytro, Doczilla, Dominictimms, Donald McKinney, Dongdongwiki, Dr Archeville, DropDeadGorgias, DropShadow, DtTall, Dubkiller, Dumpster cakes, Dysepsion, Dzhim, EHOLLIDAY, ERcheck, Easchiff, Elf, Eloipfeiffer, Emb021, Emperor, Emurphy42, Eric Shalov, Erik, Evans1982, ExtraDry, FMAFan1990, Fang Aili, Feeeshboy, Fences and windows, Finduilas 09, Flatbread2003, Flowerkiller1692, Floydgeo, FrankRizzo2006, FrenchIsAwesome, Fusek71, GKR, Garyjostone, Geoff B, Get It, Ghostwords, GlassCobra, Gnixon, Gonzalo84, Grenavitar, GrimGrinningGuest, Gunslinger, Gwernol, HaroldPGuy, Hazelfo, Hegria66, Heliomance, Hellagood, Henrikjadda, Henryodell, Hiphats, Hongooi, Hoof Hearted, IIILeafGreenIII, IIIthe 13thIII, IPSOS, Iamthedeus, Ian Pitchford, Ibanez RYM, Invincible Ninja, Inzy, Irishguy, JAD51287, JDEDIT, JForget, JYi, Jack Stark, Jack Upland, JamesAM, Janejellyroll, JanessaVR, Jason.cinema, JavOs, Javsav, Jboice35, Jclemens, Jdamron, Jess0501, JimDunning, JnB987, JodyB, JonathanFreed, Jondennis, Jordancelticsfan, Ju66l3r, Juansmith, Jumpcut, Kadin2048, Kalle234513142251, Keegan, Khaighle, Kieff, Kingnixon, Kintetsubuffalo, KittyFantastico, Kpillai, Kribbeh, LOL, La Pianista, Ladida, Lee lid, Leithp, Lew19, Linkracer, Litalex, Lord Cornwallis, LostLikeTearsInRain, LtMuldoon, MPerel, Maberizk, Maciste, Magnum17x, Mar bells87, Mark Rizo, Markthemac, Marquis De Carabas, Master Deusoma, MaxVeers, Mazin07, Mboverload, Mcdanielpj, Mclay19, Mcsee, Meegs, Mhanagan, Michael Essmeyer, Mojosam, Moozipan Cheese, More than diamonds, Mosca, Moshe Constantine Hassan Al-Silverburg, Mr.Z-man, Mrgez, Muteknee, Mwltruffaut, MysticalGenesis, Naterchico, Nathanjones15, Nehrams2020, NekoFever, NickHodges, Nihil novi, Niknafs, Noah04, Ohpilot, Oscarthecat, Osubuckeyeguy, Otnemem naf, Otolemur crassicaudatus, Pablo Alto, Para82, Pennyjw, Phil Sandifer, Phildogg82, Platypus222, Popageorgio, Powerpiper, Ppntori, President Rhapsody, Prestige814, Qst, Qutezuce, Qwerty Binary, R'n'B, RB972, Radaar, RattleandHum, Rayato, Red stucco, RepublicanJacobite, RevanX, Reverend Loki, Rich Farmbrough, Richfife, Rje, Rjwilmsi, Rodney Boyd, Roscelese, Rutherfordjigsaw, Ryanyomomma, S Luke, Schweiwikist, SeanNovack, Sesu Prime, Seventy-one, ShadowX81, Shaunthered, Shibidee, Shsilver, Siddhant, Simon12, SimonD, Sjyglm, Smetanahue, Smikel, Smokingintherain56, Smokizzy, SpOnGeFaN818, Speedoflight, Spookyadler, Steve, SuedeHead, Sugaki, Sumple, Svetovid, Sweens112, TK421, Tbonnie, Techman224, The Anome, The Filmaker, The Great Honker, The Professor (Matt), The.charma.bum, Thiseye, Tilman, Timberlax, TommyStardust, Tony1, Treybien, Trusilver, Tt 225, Tynedanu, Typhoon966, UberMan5000, Unrescued, Upholder, VJDocherty, Viriditas, VlovesPRESTIGE, Voracious reader, Vovikb50, WLNB, Walkiped, White Devil, Whitoflawen, Wibbler, WikiWalsh, Wikiteur, Wildhartlivie, William Graham, Wilson2007, Wolfer68, Woohookitty, Wowaconia, XWidMoRex, Xizer, Yamakiri, Yllosubmarine, Yoursvivek, Yvwv, Yworo, Yzzug, ZZ9pluralZalpha, Zippanova, Zirnevis, Zombie433, Zondor, 689 anonymous edits

The Fountain *Source*: http://en.wikipedia.org/w/index.php?oldid=399242521 *Contributors*: Aaron Bowen, Adamrice, Alaric Deschain, Aldenrw, Alientraveller, Allen4names, Andrzejbanas, Angiet17, AniRaptor2001, Arbero, Arcayne, Argantael, Ary29, Axem Titanium, Azabith, B9 hummingbird hovering, BD2412, Babajobu, Babystar69, Barros, Benbest, Bencey, Bignole, Black Kite, Blogbourri, BlueMint, Bobo192, Boggie, Bovineboy2008, Brz7, Buddhipriya, BurgerKingFanatic, CJLL Wright, CalvinL2, Can't sleep, clown will eat me, Canoro, Causa sui, Clemwang, Closedmouth, Codemonkey, Colonies Chris, ConfuciusOrnis, Contributor777, Count Ringworm, Cyrus XIII, Danjacobrubin, Decrease789, Deepblackwater, Dinflux, Doc Velocity, Donald McKinney, Doncram, Dreamcast88, Dsturnme, Dunne409, Dylan Lake, ERcheck, Eep², Elambeth, Eloipfeiffer, Enfestid, Ericherren, Erik, Esn, Espresso PUMP, Euryalus, Evanreyes, FMAFan1990, Famousdog, Fanglekai, FlashSheridan, FrankRizzo2006, Freemarket, FreplySpang, GENtLe, Gaius Cornelius, Gargaj, Gaunt, Geoff B, Giraffedata, Gishgilbadon, Goethean, Granpuff, Gsham, Guat6, HDCase, Hr2, Huntster, Iansmcl, Icarus of old, Ie007, Ike-bana, Impeal, Indigae, Invisiblelemur, Irishguy, Itatton, J. Fanning, J04n, JaffaCakeLover, JayKeaton, Jef pearlman, Jeff Saxton, Jeffness, Jeph0112, Jerome Charles Potts, Jesuswasajew, JimVC3, Jlajesus, Joanberenguer, JoeSmack, Joffeloff, JohnnyGerms, Judson, Kamaki, Kerowyn, Kethinov, Kezia Taxt, King kong92, Kintetsubuffalo, Knile, Koavf, Kre-Ko-Ach, Kubigula, Kune171, Laboris Dulcedo, Lightmouse, Lights, LilDice, Littledude835, Liveopiate, Loengard, Logofan97, Lord Bodak, Loremaster, LostLikeTearsInRain, M3taphysical, Mach Seventy, MadManAmeica, Madchester, Magioladitis, Marylandwizard, Mbutts, MemeGeneScene, Mentaka, Mike239, Mlle thenardier, Mouse2k, Muchness, Mustang dvs, N Norder, Nabil2199, Ndufour, Nehrams2020, Neil Clancy, Nekospecial, NickW557, Nino.shoshia, Nips, Noelicsage, Nowordneeded, Omgoleus, Oneoverzero, Ospinad, P4p5, Pacific PanDeist, Parkerpunk, Pd THOR, Pegship, Perohanych, Petesmiles, Pigsonthewing, Pldms, Plumbago, Pomte, Prot D, Psym, Qwerty Binary, RJHall, Radosław10, Redbaron1969, Remyvhw, Rich Farmbrough, Rickdawg00, Rje, Rjwilmsi, Rufusmuse, Ryanmcdaniel, Sephiroth2.0, Shinmawa, Shirik, Shoffstall, Sidewinder468, Silver Dirt, Smetanahue, Softlavender, Spudstud, Squant, Sskoog, Steve, Steven Walling, Sugar Bear, Swikid, TCorp, TMC1982, TakuyaMurata, Thalter, The Filmaker, The Yeti, The undertow, TheDuff, Thedarkestclear, Themindset, Tiger Trek, Tony1, Transity, Treybien, Typhoon966, V3rt1g0, Vanished User 0001, Viriditas, Visor, Walterk29, Warrenpe, Westurtle0, Witan, ZacBowlingAlt, Zachorious, Zippanova, 473 anonymous edits

Scoop (2006 film) *Source*: http://en.wikipedia.org/w/index.php?oldid=390278250 *Contributors*: Achle, AgentPeppermint, AmericanLinden, Amir Rahat, Amoammo, Andrzejbanas, Angrynight, Apascover, ArtAsLife, Attilios, BaconLover, Balthazarduju, Bigbadbyte, Boggie, CJMylentz, Carmela Soprano, Cartoon Boy, Chad44, Chocolateboy, Crumbsucker, Darkieboy236, Darrenhusted, David Gerard, Donald McKinney, Ehmjay, Emc2, Enpitsu, Erik, FMAFan1990, Fallout boy, Films addicted, Fitgolfpro, Freshh, Gabbe, Gampe, Garion96, Geomapboy2, Giorgio, Gordond, GrahameS, Gunslinger, Hpfan1, Icarus of old, Jack O'Lantern, Jmathias1216, Jordancelticsfan, Jordi G, Kanamekun, Kisssule4ka, Klaustus, Lquilter, Marxist88, Nehrams2020, Ohnoitsjamie, Okki, Oscarthecat, Osubuckeyeguy, Patrick, Per Olofsson, Perceive, RattleandHum, Spamguy, Supernumerary, THB, The JPS, The Wrong Man, The undertow, Topebrown7, Treybien, Ume, Upholder, Uucp, Wool Mintons, 98 anonymous edits

X-Men: The Last Stand *Source*: http://en.wikipedia.org/w/index.php?oldid=398512789 *Contributors*: *drew, -5-, 1magneto45, 5 octaves, 7, 97198, A, A Clown in the Dark, AAFL, ABVS1936, AJfif0907, ANSWER 12, APACOlypse27, AUburnTiger, Aaron Bruce, Abhijay, Acegikmo1, Achle, AdamDeanHall, Adamtierney, Addict 2006, Agustinaldo, Ahmad123987, Ahoerstemeier, Ajo0894, Ajshm, Alakazam, Alexanderj, Alexkasper, Alfiboy, Ali K, Alientraveller, AlistairMcMillan, All True Warriors Strive for Dinner, Allemannster, Alphachimp, Anakin1138, Anakinjmt, And1987, Andrei G Kustov, Andrzejbanas, Animedude360, AnmaFinotera, Antandrus, Anticipation of a New Lover's Arrival, The, Anton-2492, Antrophica, Apostrophe, Argor251, Ariasne, Arkham316, Armbrust, Arpitt, Art1991, Arthur Rubin, Aspects, AssistantX, AussieLegend, Axem Titanium, Ayrton Prost, Aznphu4u, BDrischBDemented, BTTNext, Bachrach44, Balls Mahoney, Bananabum96, Banazir, Basel15, Bastique, Batzarro, Bbatsell, Bdevoe, Beano, Beeglebug, Ben-Bopper, Bender235, BetsyBraddock, Bignole, Biocyte, Blackstar7129, Blahaccountblah, Blindman shady, Bobblewik, Bocker, Borisblue, Bovineboy2008, Breadocide, Brentredinger, Brian Kendig, Brian0918, Brittflick 1994, Broco03, Bryan H Bell, BryanG, Bsod2, BuBZ, Buchanan-Hermit, Buckeyes1186, ButchRocket, CRON, CallidoraBlack, Can't sleep, clown will eat me, CapDac, Cappio, CardinalDan, Carlroller, Carmanf, Casbboy, Cat-five, Cbrown1023, Cerchak, Charles Matthews, Charley28, Chcknwnm, Ched Davis, Cholmes75, Chris McFeely, Chris Z, Chris1219, ChrisGriswold, ChrisTheDude, Christianster45, Chrysalis, Chzz, Cigammagicwizard, Cirt, Ckatz, Claritas, Clashfrankcastle, Clivedanderly, Closedmouth, Clq, Cmcginnis, CmdrClow, Codemastercb, Cohesion, ColDickPeters, Cole Leader, CollisionCourse, Cooksey, Cooldude3240, CovenantD, Cowman109, Creepy Crawler, Cremepuff222, Crisu, Croat Canuck, Crumbsucker, CyclopsAngelGambit, CyclopsScott, Cytang, D climacus, DJ Mike TJG, DMC30, DOHC Holiday, DP07, DSatz, Da 1, Dalf, Dallas rocks, Dallas t. lawrence, DallasEpperson, Dan121887, Dann-Fonda, Dannyboybaby1234, Darev, DarkLord013, Darkman117, Darrenhusted, Darth Panda, Das Baz, DaveR, Davecrosby uk, David Gerard, Dead man's hand, Deathphoenix, Deathregis, Debuskjt, Defilak321, Depressed Marvin, Digitalme, DiogenesNY, Dionasalis, Directormtb, Discospinster, Dismas, Djej1, Dkurohige, Doc W, Doc cadence, Doczilla, Dodgerleigh, DoubleCross, Download, Dr Blix, Dr. Blofeld, Dr. McGrew, Dr. R.K.Z, Dr.Dude, DrBat, Draky, DropDeadGorgias, Drpryr, Drwarpmind, Dstorres, DuaneThomas, Dude 93, Dyanega, Dylankidwell, Dynesclan, E. Sn0 =31337=, EEMIV, EVula, Ebyabe, Editor2008, Edokter, Efrafra, ElCharismo, Elatanatari, Eleos, Eljudio23, Emperor, Emperor001, Empty2005, Emurphy42, Endurer, Erebus555, Erik, Eshaeffer, Evaunit511, Everyguy, Everyoneandeveryone, Ex Pluribus Unum, Extransit, Extraordinary Machine, Fabricationary, Facto, FallenWings47, Fayenatic london, Fhb3, Fieldday-sunday, Figma, Finduilas 09, Firebug, Fish1941, Fitch, Flameninja311, Flibbert, Foofighter22, Forteblast, Franz xavier, Fratrep, Freak in the bunnysuit, Frecklefoot, Frecklegirl, FredMSloniker, Freemarket, Frosty0814snowman, FrozenPurpleCube, Fschoenm, Funquotes, Gabby jay, Gabriel Duvall, Gaff, Gail, Gaius Cornelius, Galahaut, Gangsta4Life, Gareth Owen, Garhdo, Gdo01, GeneralDuke, Ghilz, Ghostchild23, Girolamo Savonarola, Gjeremy, Gogo Dodo, Gonzalo84, Granpuff, GreatGatsby, Grim56, Gurch, Habib101, HalfShadow, Hallandnash, Harej, HasBeenCorrected, Hatramroany, Havardj, Havok, HawkMcCain, HellCat86, Help plz, Hetar, HiDrNick, Hippi ippi, Holek, HoodedMan, Horkana, Hotwiki, Howcheng, Hpfan1, Hrab0001, Hu Phan, Hudd, IFsANDsBUTs, IKR1, Iamjosh, Iceman219, Iconoclast09, Igordebraga, InShaneee, Inahsed, Inaxdaze, InfamousPrince, Inflames88, InnerCityBlues, InsaneZeroG, Invincible Ninja, Iridescent, Irishguy, Isinbill, Ixfd64, Ixistant, J Greb, J.A.R.U.L.E, J.delanoy, JQF, JYi, Jaderaid, Jaganath, Jal11497, Jamdav86, James Emtage, James26, Jamesb1, Jamesmassola, Jamesxtreme, Jamielynn cena, Jason.cinema, Jaybenad, Jb-adder, Jdot01, Jean grey, Jebbo, Jedcred, Jedd the Jedi, Jennifer B, Jersey emt, Jgp, Jienum, Jivlain, Jmlk17, Jmorphman, Jobe457, Joelvanatta, Joeyconnick, John O'C, John Smythe, JohnRussell, Jordan Brown, Jordancelticsfan, Joseph Q Publique, Josh Gentry, Josiah Rowe, Jp.bc, Ju66l3r, Juliancolton, Jump Guru, Jupiter1984, Justoverthebay, K1Bond007, KL, Kamikaze, Karumn, Kashami, Kbdank71, Kchishol1970, Kdbwest, KeezerBoo, Kenneth Vergil, Khalid alkhajah, Kherith, Khernitz, Kidlittle, Kieranthompson, Killdevil, Killerman2, Kilo-Lima, Kimpire, Kintetsubuffalo, Kittynboi, Kontar, Korean turtle87, Kozmik Pariah, Krabs502, Krabs504, Krabs514, Kx1186, Lanford, LaurC, Lauredhel, LeaveSleaves, Lenonn, LeonMcNichol, LeonWhite, Leonidas23, Lid, Lil Flip246, Logan 2006, Lord Akkarin, Lord Hammu, Lostheroesmath, LucklessLamb, Luigi-ish, Luk, Lwieise, MWB1138, Ma3nocum, Mad Hatter, Madchester, Maestro25, MagicBez, Mallanox, Malo, Manning Bartlett, Manwithbrisk, Mar bells87, Marcsin, Marcus Brute, Mareino, Martarius, Master Deusoma, Master Yugin, Master son, Matt Heard, Matteh, Mattman00000, Mattwegrzyn, Max3197, Mbcvkdsbvfjkess, Mclay19, Meatwod, Mediafollower, Menthys, Metamagician3000, Metron4, Mets501, Mhanagan, Mhking, Mike R, Mike Rosoft, Mike Selinker, MikeAllen, Millahnna, Mineralè, Mishy dishy, Misterstark, Mixedboyzero9, Mjrmtg, Morningblur, Morriswa, Mr-susans, MrMoonMoon, Mrblondnyc, Msa1701, Musha, Mushroom, Myscrnnm, Myspirit, N. Harmonik, Nalvage, Napalm06170312, Narimans, NawlinWiki, Ncanca, Necrothesp, Netkinetic, Nicoshock, Niqua230, Nixeagle, Noah044, Noclevername, NorthernThunder, Novacatz, Nrcavsbaseball12, Nutiketaiel, Obi-WanKenobi-2005, Ocatecir, Ocee, Ohnoitsjamie, OjeB, Olessi, Omglazers, Onomatopoeia, Ophois, Orca1 9904, Osaghae88, Oscarthecat, Osubuckeyeguy, Ou tis, Owen, Oxymoron83, P-Chan, Padillah, PantheraLeo, Passive, Patrick, Paul730, PeeJay2K3, Peekgeek, Pegship, Pennyforth, Pentasyllabic, Penwhale, Percy Meza, Percy Snoodle, Persianprince, Pharaoh of the Wizards, Pho3nix-, Pho3nixflame69, Phoenix V, Pichote, Pictureuploader, Pikawil, Pinkfloydfan, Pioneeer21, Plactus, PleaseStand, Plorimer, PokeFan2006, PowerMutant, Powerbomb1411, Powzer19, Prem555, Prof. MagneStormix, Professor London, PrometheusX303, Proofing, Psuedonym, Psyphics, Punkwitch44, PurpleKoopa, Qst, RHaworth, RVDDP2501, RaCha'ar, Radolph, Raider Duck, Rajakhr, Rajrajmarley, Random James, RandomStringOfCharacters, RazielZero, RealityTelevisionFan, Rebecca, Rekiwi, Renesis, Repulsion, Rerngrit, Reverse Gear, Rglong, Rich Farmbrough, Richfife, Rick Block, Ricky540, Ritchy, Rjwilmsi, Rldivaofrl, Robertvan1, Robwingfield, Rodimus558, Roguemaster83, Ronhjones, Ross bender7, RossF18, Rossignol-X, Rst20xx, Rtkat3, Runnermonkey, S onson, S3000, SG, SPUI, SaintHammett, SaliereTheFish, Sandoz, Sanfranman59, Sauceyboy, Scarlet buckeye, Schmendrick, Schmirius, Sean Whitton, Searcher007, Sega381, Sentinelcs22, Serein (renamed because of SUL), Serpent-A, Sha-Sanio, Shadow Android, Shadow007, ShadowHntr, Shadowolf, Shan246, Sharp962, Shawn81, ShelfSkewed, Shiirow, Siddharth Mehrotra, Sigma 7, Silent Tom, Silverdragonn, Silverk212, Sin-man, Sintonak.X, Sirana, Skinjob, Skullord, SkyWalker, Skyler13, Skypurevis, Smee, Soapergem, SodiumHydroxide, Songmaster2005, Sonic Shadow, Spaced1999 AKA, Spebudmak, Speedeamongt, Spinerod, Spinoff, Spinolio, Spmcdill, Srikeit, StarNeptune, Steel, Steve1138, Steveking 89, Stevenj, Stroppolo, StuffOfInterest, Super own, Supernumerary, Susurrus, T-1000, T-borg, TKD, TMC1982, Tassedethe, Tathunen, Tenebrae, Tertiary7, TestPilot, Tgunn2, Thai guy 01, Thanos6, The Filmaker, The Giant Puffin, The Invisible Hand, The JumpStation, The Legendary Ranger, The Placebo Effect, The Rogue Penguin, The josh17, The wub, TheArmadillo, TheKoG, TheOnlyOne12, TheTarmanCometh, TheWindshield, Theman55, Theshibboleth, Thingg, Thricecube, Thue, Thunderbrand, ThuranX, ThylekShran, Tide rolls, Tntnnbltn, Tombseye, Tomkurts, TommyStardust, Tommyt, Tony1, Torourkeus, TotalTommyTerror, Totallyprocrastinating, Toxin1000, Tregoweth, Tromatic, Truth in Comedy, Turf93, Tve4, Twintone, TylerXKJ, Typhoon966, Typhoonchaser, UKER, USN1977, UltimatePyro, Undermedveten, Unholymidjet, UnitedStatesian, Urutapu, Varlaam, Vedantm, Vendetta411, Vishnava, WBardwin, WStewart07, WagByName, Warlaw, Warpfactor, WarriorGoddess, Wavy G, Wayward, Werideatdusk33, Wes!, WesleyDodds, Whimper, Whodhu, Wiki alf, Wikiguy85, Wildbudda, Wildroot, Will-B, Windowstothesoul, Wipeout 13, Wjhonson, WkpdTed, Wrad, Wtstoffs, X-man1963, Xfpisher, Xhienne, Xodus900, Yahnatan, Yamaguchi先生, Yanadi, Yiuxa, YoshiroShin, Yung Dice, Zacattakk22, ZachPruckowski, Zandperl, Zanimum, Zephyran, Zepp900, Zeppocity, Zooba, Zosobaggins, Zsxxszzsaasz, Zythe, 3242 anonymous edits

Viva Laughlin *Source*: http://en.wikipedia.org/w/index.php?oldid=399795718 *Contributors*: Ackatsis, AdamDeanHall, Antmusic, Anynom75, ArkansasTraveler, Azumanga1, Bearcat, Bevo, Bobblehead, CRiyl, CanisRufus, CoolKid1993, Cyril Washbrook, DanielTAR, Danigro89, Deliriousandlost, FMAFan1990, Fnlanzr, Jeffrey O. Gustafson, Jelmo, Jim856796, Johndburger, Josh Parris, Kbdank71, Kedarus, Koavf, KringleK, Lakeyboy, Lifeiscrazy, Mbrstooge, Milchjon, Mrschimpf, Mukkakukaku, Pinkadelica, ShawnVW, Shikinluv, Shouldbaggypantsbebanned, Slakr, Softlavender, Stephen, Storm05, TMC1982, TashTish, TerraHikaru, Tomm3, UnitedStatesian, Voldemore, Waterrob, Wine with Dinner, Woohookitty, Yukichigai, 79 anonymous edits

Deception (2008 film) *Source*: http://en.wikipedia.org/w/index.php?oldid=397611126 *Contributors*: AN(Ger), Ace1701713, Andrzejbanas, Arbero, Atheuz, Badalia, Beardo, Chantessy, Chillroy, Commander Shepard, David Rush, Djbj16, Donmike10, DoubleCross, Elsonlam1, Eric Yurken, Gipgopgoop, Grandpafootsoldier, Greenrd, Iridescent, K72ndst, Kalleman, LeaveSleaves, LinkToddMcLovinMontana, Lugnuts, Mister BV, NawlinWiki, Obi-WanKenobi-2005, Onesius, P. Buasuwan, Peeeeeeeeta Zimunz, Pixelface, Pmod, Pop goes the weasel, Portia327, Re non verbis, Rl10452, Schmiteye, Sharkface217, Skier Dude, SkyWalker, Steve, Stevepoland, Strongy820, Tohd8BohaithuGh1, Trogga, TubularWorld, Varlaam, Wnick99, YUL89YYZ, 61 anonymous edits

Australia (2008 film) *Source*: http://en.wikipedia.org/w/index.php?oldid=399910243 *Contributors*: 97198, AKR619, After Midnight, Afterwriting, Akim RU, Alanmurphy1994, Alansohn, Alientraveller, And1987, Andreclos, Andrew Powell, AndrewHowse, Andrwsc, Andrzejbanas, Andycjp, Angela26, Anoderate1, Anonymous Dissident, Ansett, Aridd, Ashleybfly, AskFranz, Aussiepete, Backslash Forwardslash, Badwolftv, Balthazarduju, Bam pop tickle, Basketball110, Bazthegreat, Bender235, Bidgee, Bigforrap, Binks, Bisbis, BlazerKnight, Bluez bekztra, Bneidror, Boomtish, Bovineboy2008, Bradley583, Branddobbe, Brentonay, Brideshead, Brudder Andrusha, Bullzeye, Caiaffa, Camw, Carmela Soprano, Cashie, Changhao, Chasingsol, Christianster45, Closedmouth, Cop 663, Cperrott2, CunningWizard, Dale Arnett, Danausi, DanielDeibler, Darkfrog24, Deltabeignet, DomEgan1, Doniago, Donmike10, Dr Shiggy, Drewerd, Duffbeerforme, Dungodung, EKindig, Editbringer, Edward321, El monty, Elonka, Enter Movie, Erik, Erik9, Esperant, ExpressingYourself, Ganturaviana1, GeorgeLouis, Goodtimber, GorgeCustersSabre, Grandpafootsoldier, Granpuff, Grant65, Greglocock, Gunbound02, Happypatatoes, Harrigan, Hckd, HeatherReMix, Heirx, Heliotrope5, Iamajpeg, InfamousPrince, IronGargoyle, J.D., JackofOz, Jarrod76, Jazzandbebop66, Jeff G., Jemiller226, Jeremy Butler, Jondennis, Jslasher, Jules90, Kintetsubuffalo, Kostisl, Krakatoa, Kungcho, Kwah-LeBaire, LeaveSleaves, LeeNapier, Lilac Soul, Longhair, Lotje, LtNOWIS, Lttljvd, Lugnuts, MJisnotmylover, Majorclanger, Malkinann, Mark, Massimo Macconi, Mentifisto, Michael Bednarek, Million Moments, Mister BV, Misterkillboy, Moncrief, Moror, MovieMadness, Mr Stephen, Mygerardromance, NaliniL, Nathankamal, Nick carson, Nightcrawlerislurking, Nmnbc, Normchimpy25, NorthernThunder, Ohconfucius, Ondewelle, Opera hat, Outback photographer, Patrick, Persian Poet Gal, Pickers123, Pinkadelica, Prodego, Professor carlos, Promking, Radosław10, Ralphy512, Ramsatya, RandomStringOfCharacters, Rebecca, Reinthal, Rich Farmbrough, Rjwilmsi, Rmky87, Roaring Siren, Ron whisky, Rougevelvet, SISLEY, Saberwyn, Saros136, ScottDavis, ScottJ, ScottMHoward, Seki rs, Shadowjams, Shaliron, Shariravi30, Sheila by the Shore, Sirgreene, Smash, Soetermans, Softlavender, Srushe, Steve, Sus scrofa, Swizzleglitter, TRBP, Tabletop, Teatreez, Th1rt3en, The Fern Outside, The MARVEL, The Thing That Should Not Be, TheJosh, TheLastAmigo, TheLeopard, TheMovieBuff, Theda, Thingg, Toeffifee, Tony1, Truthanado, Ttfreck, TutterMouse, Vampvan, Vanished User 0001, Varlaam, Victory93, Wikimania21, Woftam, Woohookitty, Xaviateur, Yvwv, Ὁ οἶστρος, 康非字典, 梅酒, 417 anonymous edits

The Burning Season (2008 film) *Source*: http://en.wikipedia.org/w/index.php?oldid=391193793 *Contributors*: Alan Liefting, Annielogue, Bovineboy2008, KConWiki, Lugnuts, Mark Lungo, 4 anonymous edits

X-Men Origins: Wolverine *Source*: http://en.wikipedia.org/w/index.php?oldid=400812243 *Contributors*: -5-, 3615fun, 5150pacer, A, A Nobody, AGAGALADY, Aaaxlp, Aawaravineet, Acebloo, Acebulf, Acid2base, AdamDeanHall, After Midnight, Aherbert2289, Aktsu, Alansohn, Aleenf1, AlexDotta, Alexei Mac, Alexius08, AlienX2009, Alientraveller, All Hallow's Wraith, AlphaFactor, AnmaFinotera, Annericelover, Antuan10, Apostrophe, Arakunem, Areaseven, Arielleoftherel, Aristophanes68, Arrell, Artemisboy, Artichoker, Asfarer, Atheologic, Attackoftheham,

Avalik, AzureCitizen, Backslash Forwardslash, Bakilas, Balloonman, Barger94, BasementSkits, Bazzel, Behellmorph, Bencey, Bensin, Benstiller22222, Bfuente1, BigBrightStars, Bignole, Bihco, BillieJean2K, Blackmetalbaz, Bleemsz, BlueJaeger, Blum41, Bobby Stiles, Bodominjarvi, Bovineboy2008, Boyton, Brandon, Briaboru, Bryceia, Buck Mulligan, Buddy13, BugInWax, Bulbakuki, Caconrad0825, CambridgeBayWeather, Cameron Scott, Capedia, CardinalDan, Cargoking, Carl Francis, Carlp1994, Cedric diggory, Chasingsol, Ched Davis, Chigawiga, Chiranjeev009, Chocolateboy, Chowbok, Chris Capoccia, Chris G, Chris McFeely, Chris the speller, Chris1709, Chrisigjbhudh, Chrismyree123, ChubbyMarvin, Cirt, Coder Dan, Coin945, CollisionCourse, Cometstyles, Control-alt-delete, Cooksey, Corey.7.11.1992, Cougars2012, CovenantD, Crazy4metallica, Creepy Crawler, CunningWizard, DARQ MX, DCincarnate, DMC30, DaL33T, Damaband, Dann-Fonda, DarkPhoenix2.0, Darkhelios, Darkness2005, Darkspartan4121, Darrenhusted, Das Ansehnlisch, Datn, Dautermann, Daydreamer198, DeWaine, December21st2012Freak, Dekisugi, Depressed Marvin, DepressedPer, Dezaras Prime, Diabound, DigitalC, Discospinster, Dismas, DivineAlpha, Doberman Pharaoh, Doczilla, Don B, Doniago, Dopalanko13, Doreo, Dou Gweler, Download, Dr. McGrew, Dragon1027, Dragonmaster88, Duffmovies, Dusk83, DylanWirta, Dynesclan, EVula, Eaglestorm, Elmopedia89, Emperor, Emperor001, Empty2005, Enter Movie, Enviroboy, Epbr123, Erik, Erik9, Evans1982, FF7SquallStrife7, Fab-me, Faethon Ghost, Faithlessthewonderboy, FallenWings47, Fierce Beaver, Filmcritik, Fishsticks64, Florencelau, Fordmadoxfraud, Forrestdfuller, Forsavious, Foxwarrior140, Freak in the bunnysuit, Fribble34, Friginator, FriscoKnight, Frosted14, Frultbat, GPanesarJatt, GWST11, Gaara the Fifth Kazekage, Gabriel Duvall, Gadget850, Gail, Gayuh, GentlemanGhost, Geppenguin, Giantdevilfish, Girolamo Savonarola, GiygasFlake, Gman124, Gmfreak, Godcthulha, Gogo Dodo, Goku1st, Gpsov, Graapuff, Gtcipher1080, Gubarenko, Gwarm, Gwen Gale, H1nkles, HBK1961, HDCase, Habanero-tan, Haleth, Harish, Havok, Healy6991, Hibernian, Hiroe, HoppingRabbit34, Horkana, Hotwiki, Humanman651, IAmTheCoinMan, Iceknight90, Igordebraga, IllaZilla, Imnotoneofyou, Invincible Ninja, Isinbill, Iustinus, Ixfd64, J Greb, J.delanoy, JDspeeder1, JHeroes, Jagfan71, Jairdavid, Jall_497, Jamdav86, Jaros428, Jaydec, Jedd the Jedi, Jeffrey O. Gustafson, Jerem43, Jerky Chid, JesseGarrett, Jezhotwells, Jfry3, Jhsounds, Jienum, Jimbo online, Jimmy2823, Jm222, Jmendez, JœLoeb, John Biancato, Journeyman, JoyaOscura, JuhoV, Justin Mauger, Kascnef82, Katamari38, Kikkokalabud, KiLa Koz, Killy mcgee, Kingpin13, Kintetsubuffalo, Klow, KnavishClcut, Knee427, Koavf, Kollision, Konczewski, Konictszikillasz, Kraftlos, Kubigula, Kujoe7474, Kvn8907, LUUSAP, Largoss, Latics, Lenno0x22, LeoStarDragon1, Leonidas23, Levibep92, Lg1tispears, LifeStroke420, LiquidOcelot24, Lizzyc3, LonerXL, Loqutisss, Lord Crayak, LovesMacs, Lshutfupe, Lugnuts, Luiza1202, Luminum, Lyserg16, M.arunprasad, Mad Hatter, Madchester, Maester Seymour, Magnius, Man The Face Stealer, Maple Leaf, Mappase, Marc-Olivier Pagé, Marcus Brute, Marthix, McSly, Meaghan, Medleystudios72, Meme3234, Mentifisto, Metropolitan90, Mike Selinker, Mikemoral, Mikeywarrior, Millahnna, Miq, Mister BV, Misterdan, Misterkillboy, Moeron, Morriswa, Moviefan2k4, Movieman72, Mr pand, Ms1992, Msa1701, Mwhite148, Mysdaao, N. Harmonik, Natalie Erin, Nehrams2020, Nellynel7619, Nimajneb965, Noclevername, Noyka, OBloodyHell, ONEder Boy, Obi-WanKenobi-2005, ObiWan353, Odie5533, Odin's Beard, Oknazevad, Ominae, Oniongas, Onlybyu, Ont, Ooikh, Ophois, OrangeDog, Orangejuicesimpson, Osubuckeyeguy, Ottre, OverlordQ, Paisleyd, Passive, Pennyforth, Pennywisdom2099, Peregrine Fisher, Persian Poet Gal, Phil Boswell, Philip Trueman, Phoenixrcd, Pinkgothic, Pinoyboy, Planewalker Dave, Plasticspork, Platypus222, Playstaffan, Portia327, Possum, Powerbomb1411, Prakharprabhakar, Prashanthns, Prem555, Qqlovesyou, QuasiAbstract, Raiku Samiyaza, Ramceo, Razorflame, Red08, Redranger241, Reevnar, Rehevkor, Retodon8, Rhino131, Rich Farmbrough, Richard Myers, RichyBlack, Ricky81682, Ripper404, Ritchy, Rizalninoynapoleon, Rjwilmsi, RobJ1981, RobNS, Robocoder, Ronark, Rovastar, Rrawpower, Rsreston, Rtkat3, Rundinj, Rurik16, Ruyter, Ryan-McCulloch, Rypcord, Ryulong, Saint Guy, Sambangs, Saminassar10, Samuelcole, Samus949, Sb1990, SchftftyThree, ScoobyFan14, Scottrb, Semajdraehs, Sesshomaru, Sha-Sanio, ShadowRatchet92, Shan96, Sharp962, Shikexue2, Shlomke, Shoodofmon, ShowToddSomeLove, Showtime2009, Sigma 7, SilentmanX, Skarebo, Skarl the Drummer, SkyWalker, Snowman Guy, Soul phire, Spider-manfan7, SpikeJones, Spinerod, Squishy Vic, Squishydog2, Stalney81, Statostatostato, Stats2009, Steam5, Stephen Day, Steve, Stevenrasnick, Stewartbe, Stewggrifin, Stonedsurd, Stunt Airman Amaha, Styles369, Super Steve, SuperFlash101, Supervehicle, T-1000, T3chl0=3r, TMC1982, Tabletop, TaerkastUA, Tailkinker, Tatsh, Teancum, Teh roflmaoer, Tekkenzone, Tellyaddict, Tenebrae, The Haunted Angel, The Iceman2288, The Thing That Should Not Be, TheRealFennShysa, TheStarter, Themeparkfanatic, Thingg, Thomas Blomberg, ThuranX, Tide rolls, Tidybowlboy182, Time keeper 10, TitanOne, Tmaes, Tomas e, Tomkurts, Tony1, Transformers24, Travissimo, TroyeSivan, TrueLicense909, Truman86, Ttc817, Twinsday, Typhoon966, UKER, UltimatePyro, Uncle Dick, Unionhawk, Vash 15, VatoFirme, VerasGunn, VijayKPillai, Wascow, Waygugin, Weirdvision, Werideatdusk33, WhisperToMe, WhoIsWillo, WikiFew, Wildroot, Willp4139, Wolffie44, Woody182, Woohookitty, World Cinema Writer, Wwehurricane1, Xiaoyaozi, Xpi6, Y2J RKO, Youfor456, Yung Slasher, Zenlax, Zerabp, Zidane tribal, Zmikey1996z, Zombie433, Zondor, Zstar930, Zythe, 1900 anonymous edits

Real Steel *Source*: http://en.wikipedia.org/w/index.php?oldid=399009770 *Contributors*: Betty Logan, Bovineboy2008, Delicious carbuncle, InfamousPrince, Johnlongbond, Jtgi, MMetro, Martarius, MikeAllen, Ndboy, Nehrams2020, TigerByTheTail, Treybien, Trumpetrep, Woohookitty, 18 anonymous edits

Image Sources, Licenses and Contributors

License

CPSIA information can be obtained at www.ICGtesting.com

232823LV00004B/7/P